THE LATE MEDIEVAL
RELIGIOUS PLAYS
OF
BODLEIAN
MSS DIGBY 133
AND E MUSEO 160

EARLY ENGLISH TEXT SOCIETY
No. 283
1982

here to ent a dyvil w . . . .
to avance . . . . ab folowyth . . . . . .
spech spokyn to sytt down in a chayr

belyall | Ho ho be holde me þ mygty prince of þe partys infernall

Next vnto lucyfer I am in magestye
by name I am nominat þe god belyall
no of more myght nor of more excellence
my power yt pryncypall & now of most soferaynt
In þe tempyll & senogogys . . . denyeth me to honour
my busshopys therto my moton þei wyll þe sone devours
I have moryd my platfray . . . . . ana
to pserw & put downe by powyrs royall
therto þe sectys of damaske . . libra
all sectys as do worshyp in hym god spyrnall
therdeth yt rospyryd w owt any fanour at all
my busshopys hath thosyn way most wyschorut
them to pserw howse name yt saulus
go thus as a god most hye in magestye
I rayne . . zul on creaturs humayns
w soueraigne seuote sorys to yt my deyte
mans mynd yt applicant as I wysse to ordeyne
my laws shall encreaseth wherof I am fayne
yet of late I have hard of no nenys truly
wherfor I long tyll I speke w my messeg mercury

THE LATE MEDIEVAL RELIGIOUS PLAYS

OF

BODLEIAN MSS DIGBY 133 AND E MUSEO 160

EDITED BY

DONALD C. BAKER
JOHN L. MURPHY
AND
LOUIS B. HALL Jr.

Published for
THE EARLY ENGLISH TEXT SOCIETY
by the
OXFORD UNIVERSITY PRESS
1982

Oxford University Press, Walton Street, Oxford OX2 6DP

London Glasgow New York Toronto
Delhi Bombay Calcutta Madras Karachi
Kuala Lumpur Singapore Hong Kong Tokyo
Nairobi Dar es Salaam Cape Town
Melbourne Auckland
and associate companies in
Beirut Berlin Ibadan Mexico City

British Library Cataloguing in Publication Data

The late medieval religious plays of Bodleian MSS
Digby 133 and E Mus. 160. – (Early English Text
Society. Original series; 283)
1. English drama – To 1500
I. Baker, Donald C II. Murphy, J L
III. Hall, Louis B IV. Bodleian Library
MS (Digby 133) V. Bodleian Library MS
(e Museo 160) VI. Digby plays VII. Series
822'. 2'08   PR1262
ISBN 0-19-722285-4

Printed in Great Britain
at the University Press, Oxford
by Eric Buckley
Printer to the University

PREFACE

THE original edition of the Digby plays and the plays of Bodleian MS e Museo by F. J. Furnivall, on which all subsequent editions and commentary have been based, is now a century old. Furnivall's text is generally quite good, but his commentary and presentation of the text are frequently inaccurate and misleading. In view of the great increase of interest in the late medieval English religious drama, and the peculiar importance of all the plays in these groups, there is no need to apologize for an edition to replace Furnivall's. Although there is no relationship between the plays of the Digby MS 133 and those of MS e Museo, we have printed them again together for bibliographical convenience because of their long association.

We wish to thank Dr R. W. Hunt and the staff of the Bodleian Library for their kind help, and the curators for permission to print the plays and plates. Among many who have aided us over twelve years in one way or another we wish particularly to thank Dr Frederick Emmison, formerly archivist of Essex, who was helpful in his search for records of Myles Blomefylde; Professor Angus McIntosh, Professor Glynne Wickham, Dr A. I. Doyle, and Mr M. B. Parkes responded promptly and helpfully to our queries. We wish to thank Professor Norman Davis for many criticisms and suggestions with respect to linguistic matters, and Dr Pamela Gradon, whose assistance went far beyond that required of the Society's Secretary. Former students, Dr Michael J. Preston, Dr Robert Schuler, and Dr John Coldewey, all assisted in a variety of ways. Elizabeth Baker's uncomplaining proof-reading saved us from many more errors than remain.

We wish to thank the staff of the Norlin Library of the University of Colorado for their help, and the Council for Research and Creative Work of the University of Colorado for generous assistance.

CONTENTS

INTRODUCTION

1. DIGBY 133

BODLEIAN MS Digby 133 (No. 1734 in *A Summary Catalogue of Western Manuscripts in the Bodleian Library*) is a quarto paper volume, iii+169+ii. It contains these items: Galileo's *Discorso del Flusso e Reflusso del Mare* (in two italic hands, dated 1616), ff. 1ʳ–21ʳ; Roger Bacon's *Radix Mundi* (a tract on the philosopher's stone, dated 1550), ff. 22ʳ–36ʳ; the play *The Conversion of St. Paul*, ff. 37ʳ–50ᵛ; the tracts *De Theorica Trium Superiorum (Planetarum)*, ff. 51ʳ–52ʳ, *De Epiciclo Lunae*, ff. 53ʳ–57ʳ, and *De Capite et Cauda Draconis*, ff. 57ʳ–58ʳ, one leaf of tables, f. 59ʳ, following these treatises, and a blank leaf, f. 60ʳ (some notes on f. 60ᵛ)[1]—all the tracts and notes, ff. 51ʳ–59ʳ, are in the one, mid-sixteenth-century hand; a tract, *Trattato dell'Arte Geomantica* (early seventeenth century, in two italic hands, incomplete), ff. 61ʳ–94ᵛ; the play *Mary Magdalen*, ff. 95ʳ–145ʳ; the play *Candelmes Day and the Kyllyng of the Children of Israelle* (hereafter called *The Killing of the Children*), ff. 146ʳ–157ᵛ; and the morality play, *Wisdom* (also known as *Mind, Will, and Understanding*), incomplete, ff.158ʳ–169ᵛ. There are two unnumbered nineteenth-century blank leaves at the front and two at the end of the volume; a third unnumbered blank, of the seventeenth century, begins the Galileo tract. The other leaves of the book are numbered in early pencil in the upper right corners.

The volume does not have the Digby binding (tooled brown calf with the Digby arms stamped in gold upon the covers). The present binding is a nineteenth-century Bodleian replacement in a seventeenth-century style—brown calf, with simple lined tooling around the edges, and the partial titles and press mark stamped in gold on the spine.

The various pieces in the book are physically distinct. The paper is of varying sizes, and the gatherings and foldings are

---

[1] Though the catalogue (W. D. Macray, ed., *Catalogi Codicum Manuscriptorum Bibliothecae Bodleianae*, Oxford, 1883, *pars nona*, pp.138–9) lists the treatise *De capite et cauda draconis*, it does not number it separately, and thus lists nine items instead of the ten given here.

different (most are quarto, though *Mary Magdalen* is octavo). The name or initials of Myles Blomefylde on three of the Digby plays (*The Conversion of St. Paul*, *Mary Magdalen*, and *Wisdom*), and the fact that the main scribe of *The Killing of the Children* was also the scribe of *Wisdom* provide the only continuity of hands among the manuscripts in the volume. Another link is that the author of *Mary Magdalen* apparently borrowed a passage from *The Killing of the Children* (*MM*, ll. 217–24, *KC*, ll. 97–104).

We know little of the early history of MS Digby 133.[1] Much of Sir Kenelm Digby's library had been given him in 1632 by Thomas Allen, his tutor at Oxford, and, like Digby, an enthusiastic collector of scientific and alchemical works. The present manuscript is a typical Allen–Digby book, a collection of alchemical, magical, astrological, religio-literary works. However, none of the works in this volume is named in Bryan Twynne's catalogue of the Allen library (Bodleian MS Wood F. 26). Though this does not prove that none of the contents of MS Digby 133 was in Allen's library, it is improbable that any would have been. Three only of the items were listed as the contents of the book when the presentation catalogue (MS Digby 234a) was compiled for the gift of Digby's library to the Bodleian in 1634. The catalogue was not exhaustive, but it is odd that the cataloguer chose the first, second, and fifth items in the book (Galileo, Bacon, and the geomancy tract), ignoring *The Conversion of St. Paul*, which has much larger paper than the first two, and omitting *Mary Magdalen*, the longest book in the volume. Three of the plays appear for the first time in the notebooks of Gerard Langbaine. In two books, Bodleian MSS Langbaine 4 and 19, the plays *The Conversion of St. Paul*, *Mary Magdalen*, and *The Killing of the Children*, are noted. Langbaine's notebooks date from the 1640s. The incomplete *Wisdom* text appears for the first time as 'A play' in the 1697 catalogue (Vol. I, p. 83) of the Bodleian Library. Traces of Langbaine's examination of MS Digby 133 may be seen on the third blank at the beginning of the volume, and on the title page of the Galileo tract, where Langbaine has written 'K.D. 133.'

---

[1] We have previously discussed a number of these matters: D. C. Baker and J. L. Murphy, 'The Late Medieval Plays of MS Digby 133: Scribes, Dates and Early History', *Research Opportunities in Renaissance Drama*, x (1967), 153–66. On two matters of importance, as will be noted, we have changed our opinions.

Some clue as to the relation of the plays to the rest of the book may be found in the numbering of certain gatherings. This numbering is in brown ink, and in the same hand throughout. The number '1' has been written on the bottom of the second blank recto of the Galileo tract, marking a gathering of ten leaves; '2' is at the foot of f. 10r, marking a gathering of six; '3' appears on f. 16r, marking another six; '4' on f. 22r (first page of *Radix Mundi*), marks a gathering of four, as do '5' on f. 26r, '6' on f. 30r, and '7' on f. 34r. The last leaf of *Radix*, f. 36r, has a gathering number '8', indicating that *Radix* had once been a part of a longer manuscript. There are no further numbers until '12' on f. 61r; *The Conversion of St. Paul*, ff. 37r–50v, and the astrological tracts, ff. 51r–60v, are thus unnumbered. There can be no question of the gathering numbers' having been trimmed by a bookbinder, because the paper of these gatherings is slightly larger than that of the preceding manuscripts. On f. 61r the numbers resume with '12', marking a gathering of four leaves. Numbers '13' on f. 66r (c), '14' on f. 65r (b), '15' on f. 69r, '16' on f. 71r, '17' on f. 73r, '18' on f. 75r, '19' on f. 77r, '20' on f. 79r, '21' on f. 81r, '22' on f. 83r, '23' on f. 85r, '24' on f. 87r, '25' on f. 89r, '26' on f. 91r, and '27' on f. 93r all mark 'gatherings' of only two leaves (each pair is separately sewn). The tract on geomancy is incomplete after f. 94, and obviously had originally continued for another leaf, which would have carried the number '28'. The leaves of the tract are independently numbered in ink in the upper right corner, ff. 1–34, upon which the later pencil numbering of MS Digby 133 has been superimposed. The original numbering of the tract had been confused by an early misbinding, and as a result f. 5 of the tract (f. 65 of MS Digby 133) comes after f. 7 (f. 67). The person who numbered the Digby leaves in pencil clarified the matter by marking the affected leaves thus: f. 64 (a), f. 66 (c), f. 67 (d), f. 65 (b).

On the first leaf of *Mary Magdalen*, f. 95r, appears the gathering number '29' in the same hand as the other gathering numbers. This gathering is of sixteen leaves; the number '30' on f. 111r marks another sixteen; '31' marks one of eight on f. 127r, '32' marks one of four on f. 135r, and '33' marks one of eight on f. 139r (seven actually, for the last leaf was removed early). The plays *The Killing of the Children* and *Wisdom*, the last two books of MS Digby 133, have no gathering numbers, though a '66' appears on the bottom right corner of f. 152r, and the first four leaves of *Wisdom* are numbered at the bottom in small Roman. These are in different hands and are unrelated to the gathering numbers.

It would seem that originally the volume which is now MS Digby 133 consisted of only those books whose gatherings were consecutively numbered, i.e., the Galileo treatise, the *Radix Mundi* (plus one or more books following, comprising gatherings 8 to 11), the treatise on geomancy (before the last two leaves were lost), and *Mary Magdalen*. Perhaps this original form of MS Digby 133 is what is implied in a copy of Digby's presentation catalogue which the Bodleian Library caused to be made (MS Digby 234b) in which the note '*olim* 158' occurs over the description of MS Digby 133.[1] Whether this is the case or not, clearly at one point MS Digby 133 was broken, a number of leaves (gatherings 8 to 11 and 28) lost or removed, the plays *The Conversion of St. Paul*, ff. 37–50, *The Killing of the Children*, ff. 146–57, *Wisdom*, ff. 158–69, and the astrological tracts, ff. 51–60, being added. We do not know whether ff. 37–60 and ff. 146–69 were added all at the same time or not, but probably they were. Of the plays, it would seem that only one, *Mary Magdalen*, could have been in the book at the time the gatherings were numbered, which would have been some time between 1616 (the Galileo tract bears this date) and 1634, the date of the Digby bequest.

It is possible that the keeper of Digby's library had an existing volume (*olim* 158?) broken up and the new, enlarged, volume created because he had acquired the other three plays, two of them with the same 'Myles Blomefylde' or 'MB' signatures of *Mary Magdalen*, and perceived some relationship among them.

The Myles Blomefylde who wrote his name or initials on three of the plays—*The Conversion of St. Paul*, *Mary Magdalen*, and *Wisdom*—was born in Bury St. Edmunds, Suffolk, in 1525, studied at Cambridge, was licensed by the university to practise physic in 1552, and lived in Chelmsford, Essex, from the 1560s to his death in 1603. He was not only a doctor but an alchemist and practitioner of white magic.[2] Blomefylde was an avid collector of books, and

---

[1] The Bodleian had two copies made of the Digby presentation catalogue (MS Digby 234a): these are MSS Digby 234b and c. In MS Digby 234b Langbaine describes the Digby manuscripts by their present numbers, and on the flyleaf table of their original numbers MS Digby 133 is listed as '*olim* 158'.

[2] See 'Miles Blomefield', *Dictionary of National Biography*, ed. L. Stephen, v (London, 1886), 288, and later editions. Other sources are C. H. Cooper and T. Cooper, *Athenae Cantabrigienses*, i (Cambridge, 1858), 327; J. Venn and

possessed a library ranging over the fields of mathematics, history, geography, alchemy, and religious apologetics, which included, in addition to the plays in MS Digby 133, the unique copy of *Fulgens and Lucres*.[1] Unfortunately, we have only an imperfect idea of the fate of Blomefylde's books after his death, or how these plays came to be associated with the Digby bequest to the Bodleian. There seem to be no other Blomefylde associations in the rest of Digby's books, and, considering Blomefylde's habit of writing on his books, it must be presumed doubtful that any of the other items in MS. Digby 133 had ever belonged to him, for they bear none of his writing; however, his ownership of some of the items, particularly the play *The Killing of the Children*, cannot be ruled out. If Blomefylde had owned this play, it is possible that a link between Blomefylde's books after his death in 1603 and Digby's library was John Stow. The note 'the vij booke' on the first leaf of *The Killing of the Children* was stated by Furnivall[2] to be in Stow's hand, and it does appear to be. That Stow may have known Blomefylde is suggested by a note to a short poem, 'The Battle of the Psalms', in one of Stow's manuscripts (BL MS Add. 29729, f. 2r), that it was copied 'Out of Master Blomfelds boke . . .'. But, of course, the Blomfeld referred to may not have been Myles.

We know somewhat more about the earlier history of the plays in MS Digby 133. Although the dialects of the plays indicate that they originated in Norfolk or Suffolk, Myles Blomefylde's signatures on the three give clear evidence that for a part of their history they were in Chelmsford, Essex. One of them, *Wisdom*, very probably had at one time been at the monastery at Bury St. Edmunds.

J. A. Venn, eds., *Alumni Cantabrigienses* (Cambridge, 1922), Pt. 1, p. 168; and I. Gray, 'Footnote to an Alchemist', *Cambridge Review* (30 November 1946), pp. 172–3. The latter gives for the first time details of Blomefylde's life in Chelmsford. All, however, confused Myles Blomefylde with William Blomfild, probably a relative, author of *Blomefild's Blossoms*, an alchemical poem. The error is corrected for the first time by R. Schuler in 'William Blomfild, Elizabethan Alchemist', *Ambix*, xxx (1973), 75–87, and 'An Alchemical Poem: Authorship and Manuscripts', *The Library*, V, xxviii (1973), 240–2. We and Schuler use the spelling of the surname which was preferred by each man.

[1] In addition to *The Conversion of St. Paul*, *Mary Magdalen*, and *Wisdom*, and Medwall's *Fulgens and Lucres*, Myles owned at least eighteen other books, which are described in D. C. Baker and J. L. Murphy, 'The Books of Myles Blomefylde', *The Library*, V, xxxi (1976), 377–85. John Coldewey kindly called our attention to another book, STC 3180 in the British Library, too late to be included in our article.

[2] *The Digby Mysteries*, p. 1.

The Digby MS contains about two-thirds of the play, the whole text of which is preserved in the Macro Manuscript now in the Folger Shakespeare Library. The Macro *Wisdom* has always had Bury St. Edmunds associations, for it carries an ownership inscription of a monk Hyngham, who probably was Richard Hyngham, an abbot of Bury 1474–9.[1] The manuscript was later owned by the Revd Cox Macro of Bury. The texts of the two copies of *Wisdom* are, as we shall see, very close, and might well have originated from a common exemplar. Although one could not argue from text that the two copies must have been together at Bury, there is an interesting Blomefield association. A William Blomfild, later an alchemist and dissenting preacher, was a monk at Bury before the Dissolution.[2] The relation between William and Myles is unknown, but they were both Bury men, and Myles owned the unique copy of William's work 'The Regiment of Life'. From Myles's notes on this book we have almost all we know of William's career. It is, in short, possible that the Digby *Wisdom* passed from Bury to Myles by way of William. Indeed, it is possible, as we have elsewhere suggested,[3] that all the Digby plays were transmitted in this way. The fact that *The Killing of the Children* is largely in the hand of the scribe who wrote the Digby half of *Widsom* would argue that, if the Digby *Wisdom* had its origin at Bury, then so probably had *The Killing of the Children*. Some strength is provided for this slender hypothesis by the nature of the Macro manuscript itself. At least two and probably three of the late fifteenth-century plays in it, very similar in language and style to the Digby plays, were at Bury—*Wisdom*, *Mankind*, and probably *The Castle of Perseverance*. Bury may well have been a centre of dramatic activity with which all the Digby plays could have been associated.

It is very probable, however, that one or more of the Digby plays were acquired by Myles from the Chelmsford play book, which we know was in the keeping of the Chelmsford church-wardens, of whom Myles was a prominent member.[4] Plays were performed at Chelmsford, particularly in the 1560s and 1570s, and the play book was highly valued by the churchwardens, who took

[1] See M. Eccles, ed., *The Macro Plays*, EETS 262 (1969), pp. xxvii–xxix.
[2] For William Blomfild's life, see Schuler's two articles.
[3] 'The Late Medieval Plays of MS Digby 133', pp. 165–6.
[4] Myles kept the churchwardens' accounts between 1582 and 1590; his records are found from f. 58^r to f. 99^v, MS ERO D/P 94/5/.

care to keep it safe during one year when performances were halted.¹ Though Myles was not given the play in charge on this occasion, he may well have been on others. There is no record in the account book of what happened to the play book, but there are occasional records of other trafficking with books, and the church-wardens on one occasion bought a book from Myles.² Considering the rather extensive collection of books for a man of his time and means that Myles possessed, there appears the strong possibility that he would have been at least a keen bidder for the play book. Perhaps the unique copy of *Fulgens and Lucres* came from the same source. Recent research has produced substantial evidence that at least two of the Digby plays were acted at Chelmsford in the early 1560s.³ If they were performed at Chelmsford at this date, this would clearly have been a second career for the plays, which, as we shall see, must have had their origins as travelling plays in Norfolk, Suffolk, and Cambridgeshire much earlier. The theory of transmission to Myles by way of the Chelmsford play book does not, of course, rule out the possibility that the Digby plays, or some of them, had been at one time at Bury St. Edmunds.

2. THE CONVERSION OF ST. PAUL

The Manuscript

The quarto leaves measure approximately $8\frac{1}{2}'' \times 6\frac{1}{8}''$, and occupy ff. 37–50 of the volume. The manuscript of the play is a basic single gathering of ten leaves, ff. 38–44 and 48–50. These ten leaves are sewn between ff. 42 and 43. The first leaf of the manuscript, f. 37, is pasted on to the left inner margin of f. 38ʳ, Apparently f. 37 is alone because its other half, which would have been f. 51, was removed at an early date. The original manuscript of the play would, then, have been a gathering of twelve quarto leaves, the twelfth, f. 51, being a blank. This would be congruent with the present group of three complete watermarks. Added to the original manuscript is a gathering of four leaves (the fourth leaf

¹ The playbook, which was valued at £4, was given by the churchwardens into the keeping of George Martindale in 1574 (f. 41ʳ, MS ERO D/P 94/5/1). There is no record of its final disposition. Myles became a warden in 1582.
² MS ERO D/P 94/5/1, f. 34ʳ.
³ See the materials published by John Coldewey, 'The Digby Plays and the Chelmsford Records', *Research Opportunities in Renaissance Drama*, xviii (1975), 103–21. See also the study by Robert Wright, 'Community Theatre in Late Medieval East Anglia', *Theatre Notebook*, xxix (1974), 24–39.

is cut to a stub), ff. 45, 46, and 47, which contain a supplementary scene (the Belyall episode).

The watermark of the basic manuscript is one of the most commonly encountered types in late fifteenth- and early sixteenth-century paper, a gloved hand surmounted by a five-pointed star; the fingers are together, with thumb apart. The glove is tied at the wrist, and there is below the wrist an Arabic '3'. This mark does not correspond exactly to anything in Briquet or Heawood, but it is very close to Briquet 11369[1] and Heawood's 137.[2] All these styles are attributed by Briquet and Heawood to the first three decades of the sixteenth century, and all are of French origin. The marks are found on f. 38 (bottom of mark), f. 39 (bottom), f. 40 (top), f. 48 (bottom), f. 49 (top), and f. 50 (top). The mark of the inserted gathering, ff. 45–7 is also a hand, but with fingers spread apart. Because one of the original leaves was cut to a stub, the entire mark cannot be discovered.

The manuscript is, on the whole, in quite good condition, although f. 37 is very dirty, and the outer margin of the verso has been mended with no damage to the text. Apparently the manuscript had been folded twice for some time before being included in the present volume, for the fold creases are still quite clear.

The principal scribe of *The Conversion of St. Paul* wrote the whole play with the exception of ff. 45–7 and certain directions. He wrote in an unidiosyncratic Anglicana hand with a few secretary features. He employed the characteristic Anglicana *g*, final 'sigma' *s*, looped *d* and *e*. He preferred the secretary *r* to the Anglicana long *r*, but used both. The secretary *a* is used generally in preference to the Anglicana form. The minims are splayed. The scribe experimented with a more formal style for the first nine lines of f. 37ᵛ (ll. 27–35) which looks like the work of another scribe, but we are now convinced that it is not, for occasional beginnings of lines occur later in the manuscript that resemble the forms of this passage.[3] This scribe wrote in brown ink throughout and averaged thirty lines to a page.

The inserted scene of Belyall and Mercury (ff. 45–7, ll. 412–515 of the text) is in quite a different and later style of hand, predomin-

[1] C. M. Briquet, *Les Filigranes* (Geneva, 1902, reprinted 1968).

[2] E. Heawood, 'Sources of Early English Paper Supply II: The Sixteenth Century', *The Library*, x (1930), 437.

[3] Our earlier argument is in 'The Late Medieval Plays of MS. Digby 133', p. 154.

antly secretary. This scribe used the secretary *g* with crossed top, the two-stroke secretary *e*, the secretary *a* and short *r*, and the late style of secretary final *s*. The scribe employed both the secretary *d* and the Anglicana looped form. The style of the writing would suggest a date of twenty to thirty years after that of the rest of the manuscript. The second scribe cancelled the beginning of Saul's sermon on f. 44^v, wrote the inserted Belyall episode, then re-copied the beginning of Saul's sermon on f. 47^v. This scribe used brown ink throughout and averaged only about twenty lines to a page.

A third hand appears three times in the manuscript to write the instruction 'Daunce' (the right margin of f. 37^r, and the left margins of ff. 39^v and 43^v); this hand probably also wrote '*Diabolus*' in the left margin of f. 44^r, indicating the insertion of the Belyall episode which, as we have seen, is in a different hand. These words are in black ink, and seem to have been added at about the same time as the Belyall episode, and seem to be closely connected with it.

Myles Blomefylde's full name appears in his hand at the top of f. 37^r.

The scribes used the common abbreviations of the period. A line or arc drawn above a word usually means a dropped nasal but can indicate a number of missing letters, particularly the vowel *y*, which both scribes prefer to *i*. The usual *-er*, *-ri*, *-ra*, and *-ro* symbols are used consistently. The superscript *r* usually means *-ur*, but may be simply *r*. The occasional bar on final *ll* seems superfluous, as do the flourishes of final consonants. The looped abbreviation for final plural and genitive we have expanded as *-ys* rather than *-es* in view of the spelling practices of the scribes. Neither scribe distinguished between *y* and *þ*. The normal abbreviations *y^t* (*þat*), *y^u* (*you*, *þou*), *w^t* (*wyth*) occur in both scribes.

The scribes normally separated speeches by lines, and frequently marked new stanzas by paragraph symbols. The main scribe wrote the speakers' names in the right margins above the speeches, but occasionally wrote them in the centre of a page. The 'Belyall' scribe put the speakers' names in the left margins. The directions are normally in the middle of a page and set off by lines and brackets from the verse. The main scribe rarely bracketed rhymes, the 'Belyall' scribe never. There is little punctuation in the manuscript, and that is confined to an occasional raised point to mark a caesura. There are no catchwords, though occasionally the name of the next speaker appears at the foot of a page. The manuscript has no ornamentation or rubrication.

The date of the basic manuscript is clearly the first quarter of the sixteenth century, as indicated by watermarking and the style of the principal scribe. The episode of Belyall and Mercury would appear, from the style of its hand, to date from the 1550s.

The text seems a fairly competent copy; there are a number of errors, but many are corrected. A few words appear to have been dropped, and perhaps a line or two, but the loose, ranting nature of many of the speeches makes it difficult to ascertain original wording.

There is no formal title given to the play in the MS, but the principal scribe has written on f. 50ᵛ '*finis co[n]uercionis Sancti Pauli*'.

Versification

The lines of *The Conversion of St. Paul* are the usual four-stress verses found in most East Anglian drama of this period.[1] They occasionally contract to three-stress or expand to five or even six according to the rhetorical demand. The number of syllables varies greatly, but the lines seem to have a base of eight syllables which may, in the 'tumbling metre' lines of the ranting speeches of Saul, Caiphas, and Anna, reach sixteen syllables. But most of these longer verses seem to require only four stresses.

Rhyme royal is the consistent stanzaic pattern of the play. There are ninety-four stanzas in all (not counting the two repeated stanzas at the beginning of Saul's sermon). An apparently missing line (which Furnivall, Manly, and Adams number, but we do not) between ll. 496 and 501 reduces one of the stanzas to six. An isolated couplet is found at ll. 211–12, and lines 395–7, a speech of Primus Miles, may be the *abb* remainder of a rhyme royal stanza but no sense seems to be missing. Probably a speech of the Secundus Miles originally made up the stanza. Otherwise, the play, including the Belyall addition, is uniform.

Except for occasional passages, particularly in the ranting speeches of the added Belyall scene, alliteration is not a prominent feature of the verse. It is highly improbable that the lines have lost any alliteration during the years of the play's performance prior to

---

[1] K. Schmidt, *Die Digby-Spiele* (Berlin, 1884), p. 29, erroneously described the verse as '5 mal gehobene heroïsche vers . . .'.

the writing of the surviving copy, for, if anything, alliteration tended to increase rather than diminish during a play's active life. The rhyming is of a piece with the run-of-the-mill quality of the verse, being heavily dependent upon multisyllabic rhymes, particularly with the *-yon* and *-able* suffixes, and is characterized by a willingness of the poet to make do with imperfect rhymes (e.g. *curse-rectus*, ll. 213, 215; *flyte-lett*, ll. 332, 334).

Language

The language of both scribes is East Midland with a number of features found in East Anglia.

Some characteristics of East Anglia: the reflex of OE *-ht* shows a very unsettled condition which is also found in the Paston letters,[1] the *Ludus Coventriae*, and in the *Mary Magdalen* of Digby 133. In the hand of the main scribe may be found *flyte* 332, *knytys* 62, 82, *ly3t* 255, 371, *lythtys* 250, *myght* 360, 403, *my3t(e)* 173, 285; we also find *3* spellings with no historical *-ht* basis: *perfy3t* 348 and *abou3te* 27. In the hand of the 'Belyall' scribe are *thow3te* 455, 470, *wrow3te* 436, and *ow3te* (out) 466.[2] The spellings indicate the loss of the fricative before *-t* characteristic of East Anglia in the fifteenth century.

Two spellings, the reflex of OE *sc*, are well known in Norfolk texts: *xal* 193, *schall* 29, 31, 33, 233. The *x*- spelling is much more frequent in *Mary Magdalen* and other distinctly Norfolk texts. With both scribes of *The Conversion of St. Paul, shal(l)* is preferred. The reflex of OE *hw* is generally *wh* as in *whych(e)* 23, 186, and *whoo* 11, but there are single examples of *wyche* 4 and *wo* 158, common in East Anglia.

The main scribe uses two instances of *mych(e)* 225, 311, a spelling frequently found in an area around Cambridge, Bury St. Edmunds, and Thetford; both scribes use *moch* 262, 465, 490, a spelling found in Essex as well as in the south and west.[3] A few instances of the reflex of OE *i* or *y* as *e*, a characteristic spelling of East Anglia (though not confined to that area) found especially in *Mary Magdalen*, appear, e.g. *thether* 196. The main scribe uses

[1] N. Davis, 'The Language of the Pastons', *Proceedings of the British Academy* (London, 1954), pp. 122–3, 126.

[2] In *Ludus Coventriae* the scribes sometimes use *-ght* to represent *-th* in the inflexion of pres. indic. 3 sg.

[3] M. L. Samuels, 'Some Applications of Middle English Dialectology', *English Studies*, xliv (1963), 86, map 4.

ony 47, 392; the 'Belyall' scribe uses *any* 423, 436. Samuels indicates that the spelling *ony* appeared in East Anglia (and North Midlands as a secondary spelling) and that the spelling *any*, though found widely, was dominant in the Midlands.[1] The preterite of *see* is *sey* 104 and *syest* 106, dominant spellings in the south and west but secondary in East Anglia.[2]

Other points of interest are the following:

> Final unstressed *e* of ME is used with and without etymological basis and shown to have been lost in pronunciation in the spellings of both scribes, as one would expect at this date: *breth* is rhymed on *dethe* 267, 268 (the latter is spelled in the text both with and without -*e*); *name* and *blame* are rhymed on *am* 270, 272, 273, etc.
>
> The reflexes of OE $\bar{æ}^1$ and $\bar{æ}^2$ are written primarily as *e* and are rhymed with themselves and vowels derived from OE *ĕ*, *ēo*, *ēa*: *were, ere, bare, gere* 92, 94, 97, 98; *breth, dethe* 267, 268; *mete, strete* 281, 282; *lede* (conduct), *nede* 551, 553; *stede, indede* 622, 623.
>
> The reflex of OE *ā* is regularly written *o* and rhymed on the reflexes of OE *ō* or *o* as *goo* with *doo* 195, 196; *more* with *perfore* 351, 352.
>
> The reflex of OE *a* before the lengthening group -*nd* is represented principally as *o*: *stond(e)* 286, 504, 597 (the latter rhyming on *sonnd* and *bonde* 594, 596); *vnderstond* 363 (though *vnderstande* 158), and, in the Belyall episode 521; *hond* 295 but *hand(e)* 51, 57, 146, and the latter is rhymed on *lande* 147 and on *londe* 57, 59.
>
> The reflexes of OE *ĭ* and *ȳ* are consistently *y*, except for *thether* noted earlier and *besynes* 166: *lytyll* 191, 363, *mykyll* 109, *pryke* 184; sustained in rhymes: *fynd, mynd* 221, 224; *betyde, slyd*, 99, 101; *lyst, thryste, myste*, 284, 286, 287.

The main points of verbal inflexion:

> The pres. indic. 2 sg. (and past tense of weak verbs) is -*st*: *dost* 90, *hast* 300 (but *doyst* 468 and *hadyst* 484 by the 'Belyall' scribe), *mayst* 283; and the special forms such as *art* 211, *shalt* 195, 221.

---

[1] M. L. Samuels, 'Some Applications of Middle English Dialectology', *English Studies*, xliv (1963), 86, maps 5, 6. It must be remembered that Samuels's conclusions are based on material dated prior to 1450.　　　　[2] Ibid. 92.

Pres. indic. 3 sg. is predominantly *-yth*, or *-eth* if the morpheme is preceded by *y* or *i*: *dystroyeth* canc. 14, *defendyth*
149, *sayth* 538; by the 'Belyall' scribe: *dystroyth* 515,
deneyth 417, *encreasyth* 430. Twice the *-ys* form is used,
once by each scribe: *foysonnys* 512, *confoundys* 547. The
3 pl. normally has no ending, but a few *-th* forms occur
with auxiliaries: *doth* 391, 446, *hathe* 424. The past
plural has no ending.

There is no imperative inflexion.

The infinitive is written without *-n*: *make* 29, *aske* 31, etc.,
and confirmed in rhyme *foo* on *doo*, 53–4.

The past participle of weak verbs is *-yd*: *bepayntyd* 103,
commaundyd 277, *blynyde* 223, etc., but there are some examples adopted from Latin without addition of an ending:
infecte 321, *nominate* 414. The strong verb past participle
is usually with *-n*: *fallyn* 453, *takyn* 141, *chosen* 310, etc.,
but there are examples without ending: *forsake* 201, and
OE strong verbs of Class III are without ending: *founde* 81.

The present participle is usually *-yng*, but *-eng* is found after
y at the end of the stem: *prayeng* 221, *sayeng* s.d. after 411.

The inflexion of nouns for plural and genitive is *-ys* unless
the morpheme is preceded by *y*, in which case it is *-es*:
dyscypulys 170, *chyrchys* 171, *lythtys* 250, *dayes* 265, *sytyes*
(cities) 421. There is a single exception, *chylder*, 236.

The inflexion of pronouns: the 2 pl. is consistent with both
scribes: *ye* in nominative 22, 275, 662, and *yow* oblique 8, 53,
353, etc. There is one example of *yow* in the nominative,
96. The 3 pl. is consistently the *th-* or *þ-* forms: *they* 21, 27,
307, etc., *þei* 142, 178; *them* 25, 26, 574; *ther* 25, 306, *þer* 446.

The vocabulary illustrates the typical aureate language of the
Digby plays and of all East Anglian drama. One word,
applicant (docile) 429, appears only once in *OED*, this
example; two words are in *OED* as only from Digby 133:
redarguacyon 47, *potestacyon* 177; *nominate* (named) 414,
conctypotent 595, *postulacyon* 44, *supernall* 422, are the first
OED entries for these words. *OED* cites this play for the
last entry under *supplexion* 359, the first being 1325.
Voluptuosyte 446 has entries from 1325 to 1450 but not the
later Digby appearance.

There is nothing about the language that would suggest that *The Conversion of St. Paul* is appreciably older than the basic manuscript, i.e. the first quarter of the sixteenth century. Nor is there anything about the language of the second scribe (of the Belyall episode) which would contradict the evidence of the inserted gathering which points to the mid-sixteenth century. Schmidt declared[1] that the language of the poet was East Midland, but that the language of the scribe was southern. But there seems to be no conflict of dialect between authors and scribes, but rather the generally mixed dialect expected in texts of this date.

Sources of the Play

The chief source of *The Conversion of St. Paul* is, as Poeta tells us (l. 11), the Acts of the Apostles (chapter 9: 1–27). In addition, passages are derived from the office for the feast of the conversion of St. Paul (25 January) and the feast in commemoration of St. Paul the Apostle (30 June), and, indirectly, one of St. Augustine's sermons (No. 189, *Sermo 14 de Sanctis*). The particular passages are discussed in the notes. A more general and pervasive influence on the play is the treatment of St. Paul's conversion as it appeared in Jacobus de Voragine's *Golden Legend*. There is no evidence for any direct influence (in the sense of translation) from the Latin liturgical plays, of which one survives in the thirteenth-century Fleury play book (printed by Young, ii, pp. 219–24). Nor is there any evidence of influence upon our play of the fifteenth-century *Jeux de Martire S. Estienne et de la convercion S. Pol* (printed by E. Fournier in his *Le Théâtre français avant la Renaissance*, Paris, 1872, pp. 2–11). The only similarity in this case, other than the general one of plot, is that in both Saul has companions. The concerns of the plays are, however, quite different, and Saul's sermons are on different subjects, the virgin birth in the French play and the Seven Deadly Sins in the English. That our play and the surviving European plays are all descended, as Craig says,[2] from the same liturgical seed, is clear, but Craig's language implies a much closer relationship among them than appears to be the case.

The present play, though short, is much developed beyond its liturgical and Biblical sources. The direct quotations from the

---

[1] Schmidt, *Die Digby-Spiele*, p. 28. He does not take into consideration that there are two scribes.

[2] *English Religious Drama* (Oxford, 1955), p. 312.

Acts, though many, are only a small portion of the play. The *Stabularius* scene (similar in origin to the *Ungentarius* scenes in some German plays?) and the ranting speeches had stretched the play beyond the bare outline of the New Testament story long before a second author inserted the Belyall episode between ff. 44 and 48. This latter, like the ranting speeches and the *Stabularius* scene, is of a type common in the late religious drama, and is quite similar to the scene of diabolic disappointment in *Mary Magdalen* (ll. 722–47).

The Biblical sources themselves have also been expanded and/or misread by our poet. Caiphas and Anna, of course, do not appear in the account of Saul's conversion in the Acts; they are drawn instead from John 18: 13. The Acts speak only of a principal priest both in Jerusalem and Damascus. Our author is apparently confused, and has Caiphas and Anna in both Jerusalem and Damascus. This seems to have originated in the author's shaky Latin, for he appears to have misread Acts 9: 21: 'Nonne hic est, qui expugnabat in Jerusalem eos, qui invocabant nomen istud; et huc ad hoc venit, ut vinctos illos duceret ad principes sacerdotum?' This he translated, as the speech of 'seruus sacerdotum', ll. 572–5: 'Whate, ys not thys Saule that toke hys vyage / Into Jerusalem, the dyscyplys to oppresse? / Bounde he wold bryng them, yf ony dyd rage / Vpon Cryst . . .' This naturally puzzled Furnivall, who suggested that the line should have read 'Damascus' (p. 49). The error leaves one in some doubt as to just where the writer thought the last scene was taking place, but Poeta concludes correctly enough: 'As the Bybull sayeth *dim[i]serunt eum summitten[te]s in sporta* / And Saule after that, in Jerusalem *vera* / Joyned hymself and ther accompenyed / With the dyscyplus, wher thei were vnfayned' (ll. 652–5).

The author has also introduced a new destination for Saul— 'Liba' (l. 32), which Schmidt[1] thought resulted from the poet's fantasy. The author may have vaguely thought of 'Libya' as a near eastern location not far from Damascus, but more probably it is a misreading of 'Lydda' which appears in the same chapter of Acts (9: 38), or a confusion of the name of that city with Libya, which is cited in Acts 2: 10 as the homeland of some who listened to Peter preaching at Pentecost.

The influence of *The Golden Legend*, as we observed, is more to be

[1] *Die Digby-Spiele*, p. 24.

seen in the emphases of the play than in specific features of language. In its interpretation of the significance of Saul's conversion, derived from Augustine, *The Golden Legend* probably is responsible for some of Paul's characteristics in the play. In Caxton's translation:

Poule had in hym thre vyces. The fyrst was hardynes whiche is noted whan it is sayd þat he went to the prynce of preestes. And as the glose sayth not called but by his owne wyll and enuy that enticed hym. The seconde was pryde and that is signyfyed by that he desyred and syghed the menaces and thretenynges. The thyrde was the entent carnall and the vnderstandyng that he had in the lawe.[1]

The 'hardynes' and 'pryde' account for the ranting character of Saul, and 'pryde' for his appearing like an 'aunterous knyth'. But, of course, one must admit that Saul's character would probably have been drawn in this way in any case to indicate the depth of the conversion when it came. The emphasis of *The Golden Legend* upon Saul's vices, on the other hand, may well account for the emphasis upon the Seven Deadly Sins in the play, specifically in St. Paul's long sermon. The Belyall passage, of course, was a later addition, but its emphasis upon the Seven Deadly Sins was pretty clearly drawn from St. Paul's sermon. More specifically, one is tempted to suggest that the phrase 'menaces and thretenynges' of Caxton's translation might have been responsible for the play's 'Which conspyreth the dyscyplys with thretes and menaces' (l. 23) rather than the author's own translation of Acts 9: 1: 'Saulus autem adhuc spirans minarum et caedis in discipulos Domini . . .'

Poeta's concluding exhortation 'To whoys lawd ye syng—*Exultet celum laudibus!*' follows the familiar custom of ending the play with a hymn, or a reference to one. The *Exultet coelum laudibus* was a popular hymn which existed in many forms in praise of specific saints and the Virgin, and in its form exalting the Apostles given below was one of those hymns *de communi Apostolorum* called for by the breviary for the vespers of the feast of the conversion of St. Paul:

> Exsultet coelum laudibus,
> Resultet terra gaudiis
> Apostolorum gloriam
> Sacra canunt solemnia.[2]

---

[1] The Caxton translation is quoted from the edition of Wynkyn de Worde (London, 1527), f. 82ᵛ.

[2] G. M. Dreves, ed., *Analecta Hymnica Medii Aevi*, ii (Leipzig, 1888), 74.

The Play—Its Nature and Staging

The original play—before the Belyall episode was added—
consisted of three sections, each prefaced and followed by a short
address to the audience from Poeta, who was the introducer of the
play. We cannot dismiss the possibility that, originally, as his title
could imply, he was the writer as well. In the first, Saul appears,
'lyke an aunterous knyth', and makes his boast that he will
exterminate all those who follow the Disciples. He goes to Caiphas
and Anna, priests of the temple in Jerusalem, to ask for letters of
authority for his persecutions. The priests gladly grant them, and
Saul gathers two knights as his travelling companions, and makes
ready. Saul's servant goes to the stablegroom to order Saul's horse,
and there follows the sort of buffoonery so familiar in late medieval
drama. Saul then mounts, and with his knights rides 'abowt þe
place, owt of þe place'. Caiphas and Anna congratulate themselves
on their good fortune in having such a stout champion, and the
first section of the play closes. Poeta says 'Fynally, of þis stacyon
thus we mak a conclusyon, / Besechyng thys audyens to folow
and succede / Wyth all your delygens, þis generall processyon'.
The scribe has, however, headed this speech '*Poeta—si placet*',
indicating that there might be some circumstances in which the
speech might not be given. The scribe has written '*Finis istius
stacionis et altera sequitur*' after this optional speech.

The second section begins with a short address by Poeta, and
Saul enters with his knights, announcing his purpose to ride to
Damascus, and swearing to bring the Disciples bound to Jerusalem.
This is interrupted by 'a feruent, wyth gret tempest, and Saule
faulyth down of hys horse'. God speaks to Saul, and strikes him
lame and blind, while the knights offer their help: 'Here the
knyghtys lede forth Sale into a place . . .' God then appears as
Christ to Ananias and directs him to Saul in Damascus. The
knights meanwhile discuss the fearsome event, and Saul is praying.
Ananias very reluctantly goes to Damascus, to the Street Called
Straight, and baptizes the grateful Saul, who announces his
willingness to follow the Disciples. This section ends with another,
summarizing speech by Poeta, who announces the conclusion of
the second station and the beginning of a third, 'thys pagent at
thys lytyll stacyon'.

The knights report (in Jerusalem, presumably) to the priests, who are unwilling to believe the turn of events. Meanwhile, Saul is pursuing his new calling in Damascus, preaching a longish sermon on the Seven Deadly Sins. At this point the later writer introduces the Belyall scene, cancelling the beginning of Saul's sermon. The added scene is a simple one, with Belyall boasting of his sway over mankind, and longing for news of the world. Mercury enters spectacularly and reports that their champion, on whom they had so much depended, has gone over to the other side. After the usual fury of disappointment, Belyall decides to inspire his 'busshopys' (presumably Caiphas and Anna) to cause his death. They vanish in a fiery flame, and Saul, in Disciple's clothing, is allowed to preach his sermon. A servant of the priests of Jerusalem discovers him and brings him before the priests (who are now apparently in Damascus: in Acts there are no priests mentioned in Damascus, only the 'Judaeos, qui habitabant Damasci . . .'). After announcing that he has, in fact, converted, Saul '*recedit paulisper*'. Amazed by his treachery, Caiphas and Anna determine to kill him. To this end, the gates of Damascus are shut. But an angel appears to Saul and warns him of his danger; Saul determines to escape over the wall 'In a beryng baskett or a lepe, anon' and the play ends. Poeta summarizes and begs the indulgence of his audience in the usual manner, urging them to sing *Exultet celum laudibus*.

Scholars have paid considerable attention to the staging of *The Conversion of St. Paul* because it seems to be unique among surviving English plays. From the stage directions of the manuscript, and from the remarks of Poeta, it has been concluded that the play had a series of three stages and that the audience followed the actors from one stage to another.[1] Recently, however, Professor Mary del Villar[2] has argued that this assumption is wrong and that we have misunderstood Poeta's remarks. She argues that the words 'folow and succede' (l. 155) are to be taken in the sense of 'to pay attention to, and understand', and the phrase 'this general processyon' (l. 157) is to be taken as meaning 'this story'. However, 'folow' in the sense of 'understand' would not have been a normal meaning in late Middle English (and is not recorded in *MED*), nor

---

[1] Furnivall, *The Digby Mysteries*, p. ix, thought that the 'wagons' moved with the audience. For the traditional view, see Craig, p. 313.

[2] 'The Staging of The Conversion of Saint Paul', *Theatre Notebook*, xxv (1970–1), 64–8. R. Hosley, 'Three Kinds of Outdoor Theatre before Shakespeare', *Theatre Survey*, xii (1971), 33, is inclined to agree with del Villar.

would 'succede', which is used in l. 344 of the play in the usual sense of 'to follow after'. Also, 'proces', which the playwright uses on several occasions (ll. 9, 163), is the word for 'story', and 'processyon' in late Middle English meant generally what it means today. Professor del Villar in any case observes that these key words are in a speech designated '*si placet*' in the manuscript, and thus might have been spoken or not as Poeta chose. Professor del Villar suggests that *The Conversion of St. Paul* was produced in a place-and-scaffolds theatre, in the round, rather in the manner of the *Castle of Perseverance* according to Southern's reconstruction.

Another interpretation has been proposed by Professor Glynne Wickham,[1] who suggests that the play was probably presented in a market square, near an inn yard, and that it utilized two pageant wagons (a Jerusalem and a Heaven cart). He thinks that the audience surrounded the playing area and did not 'succede' from station to station, but that the stages or pageant wagons moved into the playing area one after another as the scenes changed, and that this activity is what is meant by the MS note after l. 161, '*Finis istius secunde stacionis et sequitur tercia*'. Professor Wickham emphasizes the singularity of '*sequitur*' and argues that the pageant rather than an audience must be intended. He points out that the audience, if it is actually being invited to move (following l. 154), is invited to do so only once, for there is no repetition. This interpretation is not altogether convincing. Professor Wickham seems to strain the meaning of '*sequitur*', which does not necessarily refer to physical movement at all; it is the normal word used in books to indicate that another matter follows. It *may* mean that another wagon follows, but it does not seem likely. In any case, the stations do not correspond with fixed sets; the second station, for example, is clearly an open area, the road to Damascus, though it is probably in the area of the Heaven stage, as Wickham suggests. As for the audience's not being invited to move a second time, there would have been no need since the last two scenes essentially take place in Damascus.

A third interpretation of the staging has essentially reaffirmed the traditional view.[2] Professor Raymond Pentzell, however,

---

[1] 'The Staging of Saint Plays in England', *The Medieval Drama*, ed. S. Sticca (Albany, N.Y., 1972), pp. 99–119.
[2] R. Pentzell, 'The Medieval Theatre in the Streets', *Theatre Survey*, xiv (1973), 1–21.

insists upon three separate locations in town streets, and thus fails
to deal satisfactorily with the fact that the audience is not asked to
move a second time. His over-all discussion, despite misinformation
on the nature of the manuscript, is more persuasive than those of
Wickham and del Villar and he points out an interesting analogy
with the stations of the cross.

It is important to keep an open mind about the staging of a play
like *The Conversion of St. Paul* for it clearly went through at least
two important phases in its life (as the much later Belyall episode
testifies), one probably as a travelling play in Cambridgeshire and
East Anglia, and a second probably as a town play in Chelmsford,
Essex. Although many of the plays of East Anglia were apparently
designed for production in the round, we must not assume that all
were.

The language of the stage directions and of Poeta is fairly
specific. There were three stations. Whether they were separate
playing locations (or carts) is not entirely clear. It would seem,
however, that at an early part of the play's history there was an
occasion for the players' wanting the audience to move from one
station to a second. At this point only two 'sets'—carts or platforms
—would have been absolutely necessary: Jerusalem (with its stable)
and Heaven. Though the latter is not a station, some elevated place
must have been required as a platform for God, and as a source of
the lightning that stuns Saul. A third set involving the temple in
Damascus and the house in the Street Called Straight seems almost
as necessary. Clearly the Heaven stage or cart would have been
near the Damascus stage, so that together they would have been
one playing area for the conversation of God with Saul after the
'feruent', God's instructions to Ananias, and Ananias' visit to Saul
in Damascus, and the almost simultaneous marvelling of the
knights at the wonder they have seen. The 'place', or clear playing
area between Jerusalem and the Heaven–Damascus stages would
have been the area in which the horses were ridden, and in which
the light was seen. The distance between Jerusalem and the
Heaven–Damascus centre could not have been great, because, if it
had been, surely the audience would have been asked to move a
second time, beyond the 'place' in which Saul and his knights ride.

The directions which are preserved in our manuscript suggest,
in short, that the play was at one time performed in relatively
narrow confines, e.g. a broad street. Such a location might have

required the stations to be arranged in a row, rather than grouped in a circular area. If this were so, then the need for the audience to move from the Jerusalem stage beyond an open space to the Heaven–Damascus area becomes understandable. If the playing area had been originally a circle, then the audience by surrounding the action would have had no need to move from one place to another.

Both the size of the play and the optional nature of Poeta's remarks after l. 154 would suggest, however, that, whatever had been the original practice in the staging of *The Conversion of St. Paul*, this was a play which was readily adaptable to whatever playing conditions might prevail, and whatever size of audience might appear.

Some time, perhaps twenty or so years after our manuscript was written, some alterations were made to the play, and three 'Daunce' notations were inserted, as we have seen. Perhaps the addition of this entertainment was made as an option in case it was decided to limit Poeta's remarks to the third part of the play. A little earlier, the Belyall scene had been added (that it *was* earlier is suggested by the word '*Diabolus*' introducing the scene, a word apparently in the same hand as the third hand 'Daunce' notations). The writer of the added scene was probably inspired by the pagan Saul's swearing (l. 29) by 'the god Bellyall'. The scene, though largely buffoonery, is not entirely an excrescence, for it adds to the theme that the 'busshopys' Caiphas and Anna are agents of false gods in their persecution of the Christians. The scene also, in its emphasis upon the Seven Deadly Sins, serves as an appropriate introduction to Saul's sermon. All in all, it seems an effective addition to the play.

But the insertion of the Belyall scene may have altered the nature of the play somewhat. At least three distinct locations or stages were now required, in addition to the 'place'; the play is about one-fifth longer, and perhaps it had now (in the 1540s–1550s) become a place-and-scaffold type of play. But it is curious that there is no addition to the speech of Poeta at the beginning of the third section which takes into account the very spectacular new scene. And, of course, the optional speech of Poeta which asks the audience to follow is not cancelled, as one might expect it to be.

The equipment needed for the performance of the play was probably not elaborate. Besides the carts (or whatever) representing

Jerusalem, Heaven and Damascus, the horses and costumes (Saul as an 'aunterous knyth'), there would have been simple devices of gunpowder for the divine light as well as (later) for making the devils' spectacular exit and Mercury's entrance. With the addition of the later scene, a throne-cart or stage is clearly required for Belyall who, after his boast, sits '. . . downe in a chayre' (s.d. f. l. 410).

3. MARY MAGDALEN

The Manuscript

The manuscript of *Mary Magdalen* occupies ff. 95ʳ–145ʳ of MS. Digby 133, and the average size of the leaves is approximately $8\frac{1}{4}'' \times 5\frac{3}{4}''$ The octavo gatherings are: two of sixteen leaves, ff. 95–110 and ff. 111–26, one of eight, ff. 127–34, one of four, ff. 135–8, and one of seven (formerly eight), ff. 139–45. Early in the manuscript's history the leaf which would have been f. 146 was torn out.

The paper is uniform, having the same watermark throughout, an elaborate pot containing flowers. The pot has an ornamented base, a large handle, and a design of fluting that twists up and around the pot's sides. The mark is not very close to any in Briquet, but resembles his 12593 and 12594 more than most. Its design is in keeping with the elaborateness of these late pots, which Briquet dates *c*.1515–25. The seven gatherings have seven whole marks (half marks appear on ff. 96, 97, 100, 101, 116, 117, 122, 126, 127, 130, 135, 136, 139, 142), and so we assume that originally there were fifty-six leaves altogether. The gathering of four (which contains both halves of the watermark) had clearly lost its second four leaves before the manuscript was compiled. The loss of the final leaf, then, accounts for the present number of leaves, fifty-one.

The date of *c*.1515–25 suggested by Briquet for this type of watermark is quite compatible with the date suggested by the writing of the single scribe who wrote the whole play in a rough *cursiva currens* which combines late Anglicana forms with secretary features. Furnivall stated (p. xv) that both the *Mary Magdalen* and the Belyall episode of *The Conversion of St. Paul* were written by the same scribe, but this is not so.[1] The *Mary Magdalen* scribe uses both the Anglicana and the secretary *r*, the Anglicana looped

---

[1] See our comparison in 'The Late Medieval Plays', p. 155.

d, and the secretary *a*. The Anglicana looped *g*, the looped *e* and the final sigma *s* are employed throughout. The writer does not distinguish þ and *y*, and sometimes uses ȝ for both *y* and þ, and frequently for intervocalic *s* (/z/) as well, e.g. ȝe may be *ye* or þe, and *these* is sometimes spelled theȝe or ȝese (see 'The Presentation of the Texts'). The scribe seems not to have had a very firm grip on the significance of some of the traditional abbreviation symbols. Superscript *r* frequently means only *r*; the -*ra* mark is used as a nasal and vocalic abbreviation as well. Final flourishes are, as is normal in the period, very inconsistent in their significance. The flourished final *r* seems, however, to mean -*re* as reflected in rhyme patterns, and we have expanded. The occasional bar on final *ll* seems meaningless. A dotted arc above a word indicates omission of either vowel or nasal, sometimes both, but is frequently superfluous. The other common marks are used normally: the superscript vowel after þ or *g* indicating -*ra*, -*ri*; the crossed descender of þ for *per* and the looping cross for *pro*; the superscript -*er* mark; and the usual abbreviations for *wyth*, *and*, *that* and *thou*. All abbreviations which seem significant have been expanded in accordance with the scribe's spelling habits, e.g. -*ion* is -*yon*, -*es* is -*ys*, and -*er* in many words is rendered -*yr*.

The scribe uses both brown and black ink, brown to f. 115ᵛ, and black for the remainder. Paragraph symbols marking stanzas are in red through f. 100ʳ and thereafter are in brown or black. He separates speeches by lines in red as well as black. Names of speakers are in brown until f. 100ʳ, and thereafter are in red. The directions, both English and Latin, are in red. Names of speakers are normally in the right margins, but sometimes appear in the middle of the page, and, for the first few pages, in the left margins. Stage directions are normally in the middle of the page. Margins are lined in brown ink through f. 104ᵛ, and thereafter are lined with a light knife cut, but with no damage. Punctuation is sparse, limited to an occasional virgule. Rhymes are occasionally bracketed. The scribe averages twenty-four lines to the page, though his writing becomes less cramped about the middle of the manuscript. There are no catch words, though on occasion a speaker's name concludes a page.

Our manuscript is a poor copy. One can only speculate on the number of missing lines but the number is probably over thirty. Some are obvious, particularly the short tail-rhyming lines which were commonly bracketed and written in the right margins of late medieval poetic texts. The inconsistency of our scribe (and perhaps of his exemplar as well) in bracketing rhymes may have led him to miss several. On occasion, he bracketed the wrong lines (see the textual notes). But not only has the scribe omitted many lines, he has also confused speeches and speakers on occasion (e.g. ll. 131, 727, 1015), got lines out of order (e.g. ll. 1243–4, 1437–8), and copied directions out of place (e.g. after l. 1796). He repeated a two-line speech (ll. 426–7 as 436–7), skipped a leaf (ff. 141ᵛ–142ʳ), made many errors, and on rare occasions corrected some. Far from being a text written at leisure in a shop or a monastic scriptorium, or copied carefully for an important purpose, this is a very hurried copy, probably made under conditions of some stress. At the bottom of f. 129ʳ the scribe, after having finished two pages in succession with the speakers' names at the bottom but with no room left to begin the speeches, has written 'Jhesu mercy', which Furnivall printed as a line (his l. 1481) but which we take to be an exclamation, probably of frustration and dismay.

The Latin inscription in red at the end of the play (f. 145ʳ) '*Explycit oreginale de sancta Maria Magdalena*' is usually taken to mean that the manuscript was a playing text. It certainly, however, is not to be understood to mean that ours is the original text of the play, for it is a copy, and, as we have observed, a very bad one. Very probably the scribe simply copied the inscription which he found at the end of his exemplar. One can only speculate on exactly what the following quatrain, which desires the 'redars' to 'Blame connyng and nat me' should 'ony thyng amysse be', should be taken to mean. Because of the plural address, it would seem that the copy was not made for an individual. The 'redars' could, of course, have been players as well as readers in the usual sense. But it is not likely that a company of players would have found this text very useful because of the many confusions and errors.

At the top of the manuscript's first leaf (f. 95ʳ) appears 'MB' in the hand of Myles Blomefylde. On the verso of the final leaf (f. 145) there are written vertically, from the top to the bottom, two staves of plainsong with this inscription below: 'Sollf thes ij playnsonges and ye xall soollff ony of þe viijᵗʰ tewnys.' This is in another hand and apparently has no relation to the play or to the manuscript. On the same page, in the opposite direction, is written 'And and Aue' in yet another hand.

Physically, the manuscript is in good condition; there is the usual fraying, but without damage to text. The first and last leaves are rather dirty, and the outer margins have been reinforced, as has the outer margin of f. 119. There is some staining in the first few leaves, but no damage to text.

Versification

Our play has the usual four-stress verse (running to five or more in expanded or 'tumbling' lines) to be found in the late medieval drama of East Anglia. In the tail-rhyming and bob-and-wheel stanzas the shorter lines have three stresses and sometimes two. The scribe's confused copying (and his exemplar may have been corrupt as well) has left the stanzaic structure of the play chaotic. Previous editors have made no effort to sort out the play's lines into their stanzaic units. The only analysis that we know is that of Schmidt,[1] which Ramsay dismissed[2] as a failure because of '. . . the necessity of re-writing the whole play that it would involve'. But Schmidt's thesis, that the confusion of stanzaic forms is largely owing to imperfect copying, seems to us quite sound, and we have undertaken the task of sorting out the stanzas. It is true, however, that we have been led to much greater emendation than have previous editors in trying to deal with verse and stanzaic form as well as with sense.

Taking into account some twenty imperfect stanzas, and some forty individual lines that have no clear association, there remain 110 double quatrains (*ababbcbc*), 92 *abab* quatrains, 20 eight-line tail-rhyming stanzas (*aaabcccb*), 1 twelve-line tail-rhyming stanza, 3 nine-line tail-rhyming stanzas, 1 fifteen-line, 3 fourteen-line, 2 thirteen-line, 2 twelve-line, and 3 ten-line bob-and-wheel stanzas, 8 irregular ten-line stanzas, 6 rhyme royal stanzas, 14 other seven-liners of various patterns, 7 six-line tail-rhyming stanzas, 10 other six-liners of various arrangements, 16 five-line stanzas of some variety, 8 couplets (two Latin), and the twelve-line single-rhymed '*Leccyo Mahowndys*'. In addition, there are twenty-nine unrhymed lines (six Latin) which seem to have been written as single lines.

As we have observed, over thirty lines appear to have been lost; these are the most obvious instances, involving loss of sense and

---

[1] 'Die Digby-Spiele', *Anglia*, viii (1885), 387–90.
[2] R. L. Ramsay, ed., *Magnyfycence*, EETS, ES 98 (1908), pp. cxxxix–cxl.

rhyme within well-defined syntactic and stanzaic units. We postulate (but do not number in our text) the following missing lines: after l. 228 four lines, the second half of an eight-line *aaabcccb* tail-rhyming stanza; after l. 237, the first *b* line of a double quatrain *ababbcbc*; the *a* rhyme line following l. 328; at least two tail-rhyming lines missing in the passage ll. 498–536; a tail-rhyming line after l. 542 (missing rhyme-word is probably 'take' rhyming with 'sake' of l. 546); after l. 670, the ultimate or penultimate line of a rhyme-royal stanza; almost certainly one line in the passage after l. 726 (the speech of the Tercius Diabolus who is introduced in the preceding stage directions, but whose name is omitted as a speaker); probably three lines after ll. 737–9, the second half of a six-line tail-rhyming stanza *aabccb* (though no sense seems lost); probably the last *c* line of a double quatrain ll. 846–52; after l. 920 the second *b* line of an *abab* quatrain; at l. 944 the following line of the opening quatrain of a nine-line bob-and-wheel stanza; probably a *c* rhyme-line of an *aaabcccb* tail-rhyming stanza after l. 1175; in ll. 1241–8 a line from a tail-rhyming stanza, the problem further complicated by a misplaced line; probably a *c* rhyme-line after l. 1310; after l. 1333 a *c* rhyme-line from a six-line *aabccb* tail-rhyming stanza; one line after l. 1353 in a double quatrain; in ll. 1349–55 either one line of a rhyme royal or two lines of a double quatrain; between ll. 1439 and 1445 one line from an eight, leaving an unrhymed line (l. 1443); after l. 1495 the last line of a double quatrain; in ll. 1520–5, at least one line of a rhyme royal stanza or two lines of a double quatrain; after l. 1529 probably the last four lines of an eight-line tail-rhyming stanza; a line of a quatrain after l. 1701; and after l. 1893 the last *c* rhyme-line of a double quatrain.

We are reasonably sure that the above lines are missing, although the question of textual loss is a vexed one. It is probable that our scribe, careless as he was, should not be blamed for all the loss. It may be that, particularly in the cases of the truncated tail-rhyming stanzas, the play's author or a reviser may have cut the speeches and not bothered to cast the remainder in another form. Part of the roughness may be put down to natural loss, for *Mary Magdalen* seems to have been a play that had an active life over some years; and part can perhaps be blamed on additions, particularly in the ranting speeches, which may have arisen as a result of ad-libbing. It can surely be no accident that the most formless speeches in all the late medieval drama are those of the bombastic characters.

The poet of *Mary Magdalen* uses alliteration to a great extent, and it is most pronounced, as one would expect, in the boasting and ranting speeches, such as the Imperator's opening speech, and the boasts of Cyrus (ll. 49–84) and the King of Marcylle (ll. 925–49), Herod's bombast (ll. 140–56) and Pilate's vaunt (ll. 229–49). The devils generally speak in alliterative verse, and so do generally the characters of power and/or evil. The minor characters generally do not (excepting in some burlesque scenes). The speeches of Mary Magdalen, Jesus, and the rest of the 'good' characters are sometimes alliterative, but not emphatically so. In this play as in the other East Anglian drama, alliteration is frequently indicative of arrogance and impertinence.[1] An exception apparently is the speech of Cyrus (ll. 49–92 and 265–77) who, though a 'good' character, must introduce his part of the play, and his speech is therefore cast likewise in the same mould. In addition to the reflection of character, then, alliteration has the function of emphasizing themes and of underlining new directions in the action, particularly in opening speeches.

A somewhat similar purpose seems to be served by variation in the stanzaic forms. The main sections of the play are in double quatrains. The first bob-and-wheel stanza occurs in the Devil's first speech (ll. 366–80). The World (ll. 385–93) speaks in another, and the bulk of the scene involving the World, the Flesh, Satan, and Lechery (ll. 409–39) is in tail-rhyming stanzas. The other devil scenes (e.g. ll. 722–47) have predominantly a tail-rhyming pattern. The King of Marcylle's opening speech (ll. 925–49) concludes with a bob-and-wheel; the Devil's speech (ll. 963–92) closes with a long bob-and-wheel; the burlesque scene of the priest and the boy (ll. 1143–209) is marked by tail-rhyming stanzas and irregular patterns; the pagan priest's last speech in the scene (ll. 1228–49) is composed of a long bob-and-wheel and a tail-rhyming stanza. The scenes of the shipmaster and the boy (ll. 1395–445, 1716–922) are marked by bob-and-wheel and tail-rhyming stanzas. Mary Magdalen, on the other hand, speaks only once in the bob-and-wheel stanza (ll. 1947–60) in a scene with the King and Queen of Marcylle, and the last speech of the priest which

---

[1] In *Mary Magdalen*, for instance, the King of Marcylle drops most of his alliteration after he is converted.

closes the play is in a bob-and-wheel. Otherwise, the good characters eschew tail-rhyming stanzas and the bob-and-wheel as they do alliteration.

This division of purpose for stanzaic form and rhetoric is characteristic of *Mankind*, *The Play of the Sacrament*, *Wisdom*, and other plays of the area as well.[1] For instance, the proportions of verse divided into double quatrains, quatrains, and tail-rhyming stanzas in *The Play of the Sacrament* and *Mary Magdalen* are very much the same. Similar rhetorical patterns are found in these two plays, such as the catalogues of spices, wines, diseases, etc. (*PS* ll. 150–88, 608–21; *MM* ll. 344–51, 470–80), and occasionally identical phrases such as 'be clyffys cold' (*PS* 100, *MM* 55). But such similarities exist, too, between the rhetoric of *Mary Magdalen* and *The Castle of Perseverance* (see notes), *The Conversion of St. Paul*, *The Killing of the Children*, as well as that of some later plays, such as *Mundus et Infans* and the *Four PPs* (and all have in this regard probably some relation to the folk plays).

Language

About the language of *Mary Magdalen* we can be somewhat more definite than about that of any other of the plays: it is distinctly East Anglian, with obvious Norfolk features. E. J. Dobson pronounced *Mary Magdalen* and the *Ludus Coventriae* both Norfolk texts.[2] Among these Norfolk features, found to some degree in *The Castle of Perseverance*, *Mankind*, and *Wisdom* (Macro), as well are:

The reflex of OE *hw* is frequently *qw* (or *qu*) and *w*, e.g. *qwat* 240, 523, etc. for *what* (*what* is also used); *woo* for *who* 311; *wos* for *whose* 6, 9, etc.; *woso* for *whoso* 57, 150, etc. (*wh*-forms predominate, however). As in the texts of this area, the reverse of this feature occurs, and *wh*- frequently appears for *w*-, e.g. *whorshep* 384 for *worship*, *wher(e)* for *were* 405, 971, etc.

The reflex of OE *sc* initially in 'shall' and 'should': there are 150 instances of *xal(l)* to four of *shall*; but practice is less consistent elsewhere, with *xulddys* (2 sg.) and *xuld* appearing in eight instances against nine of *shol(l)d* and *shvld*.

---

[1] See the discussion by Eccles, *The Macro Plays*, pp. xxxii–iii, xl.
[2] 'The Etymology and Meaning of *Boy*', *MÆ*, ix (1940), 146.

Spelling of words containing earlier *-ht* shows the unsettled condition typical of the area and the period: *knyth* and *brygth* rhyme in 1230, 1232; the usual spelling in the play of *-ht* is *-th*, but frequently it is *-gth*, and on occasion a simple *-t* as in *browt* 208 and *myty* 12. There is an interesting set of variations on 'daughter': *dowtter* 99, *dowctor* 416, *docctor* 877, and *about* is *abowgth* 154.

The reflex of OE *i* and also of *y* is normally written *e*: *berdys* 51, *betternesse* 604; *cleffys* 55; *fefty* 654; *hellys* (hills) 1198; *kendnesse* 1342; *kesse* 1073; *lef(f)e* (1sg. live) 506, 766; *therd* 1322; *whech* 79, 183, 1975; *ded* (aux. *did*) 652, 920, 1074, 1325. Occasionally it is written *y*: *kynd, onbynd, fynd* 94, 96, 97; *blysse, kysse* 345, 347; *wynne, synne, begynne* 377, 378, 379. Words of foreign origin are spelled in the predominating way: *cete* (city) 473, 1358; *merrorys* 73; *mesteryys* 2040; *speryt* 602, 733, 2100; *vesyte* 1128; *trenite, trenyte* 718, 1394, etc.; and Latin words *felium* s.d. 2030; *sene* (*sine*) s.d. 1971, *sperytus* 717.

Other spellings found in the East Anglian area: *ony* 36, 122, 969, etc., twenty-five instances; *swych(e)* 28, 457, etc., twenty-two instances; *mych(e)* 504, 631, etc., nine instances. *Therknesse* (darkness) 689, 769, 773 is a spelling recorded by *OED* only for East Anglia, and usually considered characteristic of Norfolk.[1] The scribe uses *w* for *v* in several instances: *weryauns* 92; *awansse* (advance) 385; *wayn* (vain) 595; *awant(t)* 925; *wycys* (vices) 1083; *wexyd* (vexed) 1576; *wergynnys* 2022; *wytory* (victory) 2094. The loss of *l* in 'world' is seen in East Anglian texts, notably *The Castle of Perseverance*; the *Mary Magdalen* scribe consistently spells 'world' as *word* (the scribe of *The Castle of Perseverance* spells it *werd* and also *werld*).

The spelling of this scribe is quite variable. He uses ʒ not only as the usual equivalent of *y* but in many cases to represent þ and *th* (which are more frequently used by the scribe): *ʒe* (the) 425, 584, 664, 1251; *ʒe* (thee) 593, 601, 641; *ʒese* (these) 555; *ʒether* (thither) 1881. Norman Davis observed these oddities in the spelling of scribe B of *The Pride of Life* (this scribe used ʒ for initial *h*, a practice not found in *Mary Magdalen*).[2] Our scribe also uses ʒ

---

[1] Ibid.

[2] *Non-Cycle Plays and Fragments*, EETS, Supplementary Series 1 (1970), p. xci.

for /z/ (e.g. *La3arus, ple3auns*) and once for /g/ (*ile3ant,* 505). To avoid confusion we have printed *3* as *þ* or as *z* where so used, and as *s* where the scribe's spelling habits justify it (i.e. *plesauns*).

Other points of linguistic interest are the following:

Final unstressed -*e* of ME is used with and without etymological basis and shown to be lost in pronunciation: *com* (imp.) 1269 rhymes on *Rome* 1271; *rede* (OE *rǣd*) rhymes on *brede,* 540, 541.

OE *a* before *nd* is not consistent, though generally it is written *o*: *bond* 1838 rhymed on *stond* 1842; *hand* 1445, 1906, both rhymed on *lond* 1444, 1904; *hond* 1799 rhymed on *lond, ondyrstond* 1797, 1798; *land* 1371 and *lond* 205, 1379, etc., twenty-two instances rhymed on *sond* and *lond* as above.

The reflex of OE *ā* is normally written *o*: *othe* rhymes on *bothe* 1949, 1947; *foo, fro,* and *so* rhyme in 15, 17, 18; *non* and *everychon* in 984, 986; *soo* and *doo* 830, 832. Reflex of OE. *aw* is written *ow* as *knowe* in 619 rhymed with *grow* 621.

OE *ǣ*[1], *ǣ*[2], and diphthongs *ēa, ēo* are all represented as *e* and rhymed, regardless of origin. *Deth*(*e*) 802, 841; *ded* 1319 rhymed on *Godhed* 1321, on *adred* 1768; *bere* (carry) 1779 rhymed on *ere* (ear) 1778, and 2074 rhymed on *fere, ther* 2076, 2077; *dere* (beloved) 530 rhymed on *lere, pere, maner* and *nere,* 527, 528, 531, 532; *mede* 267 rhymed on *drede, bede* (bed), *led* (the metal) 265, 270, 272; *rede* rhymed on *brede, stede* 541, 542; *hart*(*t*) is spelled thus 47, 639, 640, and rhymed on *stertt* 221, 224.

The main points of verbal inflexion:

Pres. indic. 2 sg. (and pa. 2 sg. of weak verbs) ends in -*yst* or -*t*: *knowyst* 639, *hast* 662, 701, etc.; *dedyst* 672, *owttyst* 674, *knewyst* 696; but *thynkys* (*þou*) 591.

Pres. indic. 3 sg. generally ends in -*yt*(*t*) or -*it* and rarely -*ett*: *stondyt* 6, *growyt* 20, *obeyit* 31, *makyt* 505, *makett* 1000, *beryt* 533, *comit* 1662. There are a few instances with -*is* or -*ys*: *bringis* 18, *davnnys* 35, and a rhyming series *tellys, rebellys, dwellys* 123–5; and a few with -*eth*: *wassheth* 667, *wypeth* 670. The auxiliaries are *doth* 122, 172, etc., *hath*(*e*) 183, 769, etc. Normally the present plural has no ending, but there are a few in -*n*: *abydyn* 16, *don* 283, 537, *byn*, 160, 1116, etc., *desyern* 721, *arn* 811. The past plural has no ending.

Normally the imperative has no ending, but there is an occasional *-th* plural: *seyth* 647, *goth* 847.

The infinitive is usually written without inflexion: *drede* 207, *se* 728, etc.; but many examples of the ending occur, usually written *-yn* when the word is not monosyllabic: *restyn* 568, *sekyn* 613, *rewlyn* 1689, *abydyn* 301, *synkyn* 746, etc.

The past participle of weak verbs is commonly *-yd*: *blessyd*, *obscuryd* 714, *temptyd* 734, *delayyd*, *begylyd*, *diffylyd* rhymed 1030, 1031, 1033; but there are a few in *-t*: *promtyt* 602, *dempte* 662. Past participles of strong verbs normally end in *-yn*: *wondyyn* 23, *forsakyn* 767, *beholddyn* 658, *shavyn* 503; but some have no ending: *com* 494, *smet* 519. The prefix is not used. Both *ʒede* 975 and *went* 376, 388, 820 appear as past participles. The present participle is consistently *-yng*, *ynge*.

The plural and genitive ending of nouns is generally *-ys*: *lawys* 33, *cleffys* 55, *cay[tyfys]* 58, *spycys* 112, *wedys* 1083, *spynys* 2023. A few examples of other spellings are found: *riches* 102, *watyris* 1498, *vertuus* 1085, *dectours* 650. One *-n* plural is found: *fon* 1288.

Of the personal pronouns, *ye (ʒe)* is employed in the nominative and *yow* in the oblique, though there are a few instances in which *yow* is used in the nominative: 422, 423, 424, 835. For the 3 pl. the regular form is *pey* in the nominative, *hem* in the dative-accusative (though there occurs a single instance of *them* 1518); and *per (ther)* for the genitive, with a single instance of *hyr* 1523.

The vocabulary has considerable interest, principally in the many 'aureate' or learned words and terms; two are perhaps unique: *advertacyounys* 921, and *enabyte* 683 cited by *OED* only from this play. Four other words have their first entry in *OED* from *Mary Magdalen*: *asemlaunvs* 387 (the last entry in Spenser 1596), *ileʒant* 505, *pacyfycal* 1592, and *santificatt* 1554, past participle of *sanctify*. *Cardyakyllys* 1363 (heart pains) has its first entry in Langland, its last in this play; *comfortacyo(w)n* 338, 750, 792 has entries from 1400 to 1552, *comfortatywys* 338 (comforting drugs) has

entries from Langland to the eighteenth century; *tormentry*
1002 (torture) has *OED* entries from 1375 to 1534. Another
interesting word is *cure* 294, 2127, which, although it can
in context have the usual meaning of the ecclesiastical
word, probably here is a variant of *cover*, and as such would
seem to be localizable in the East Anglian area where it
appears in several texts—the *Ludus Coventriae* and the
works of Lydgate and Capgrave.

Because of the very rough nature of the scribe's work, one
cannot pronounce with any confidence on such a matter as scribal
interference, but the variety of forms, such as *kynd* and *kend*,
would suggest that it was considerable. The probability that the
play had been copied more than once, and the presence of such
indicators as the *hem* form of the pronoun, not yet replaced by
them, would lead us to conclude that the text was somewhat older
than our present copy; the language would suggest the end of the
fifteenth century rather than *c.*1520–30 indicated by the manuscript. Against this should be placed the apparent copying by the
writer of *Mary Magdalen* of a passage from *The Killing of the
Children*, a play which is probably not much older than the date of
1512 on the manuscript. But since it is at least possible that both
playwrights copied this passage from another play, such evidence
cannot be conclusive.

Sources of the Play

The sources of the play are clearly two: the New Testament
accounts of the central events of the first part (the dinner at the
house of Simon and Mary's washing of Christ's feet, the aftermath
of the crucifixion and Christ's appearances to Mary and the other
weepers), and *The Golden Legend*'s outline of Mary's life, but
particularly her subsequent career as a missionary, her desert
hermitage, and her death. The author seems to have been very
familiar with both sources, for he has selected episodes from each
and woven them together. For instance, although most of the
non-allegorical material of the first part of the play is drawn from
the New Testament, the author has selected *The Golden Legend*'s
account of Mary's immoral life (after the death of her father) to
serve as the centrepiece of this section. At times the author has
followed his source very closely—the story of the dinner at Simon's

house is a studied paraphrase of Luke. But frequently the writer
has elaborated or trimmed his material. In the story of Mary's
weakness after the death of her father, the author has taken the
three sentences of Jacobus de Voragine and from this created the
allegorical structure of the temptation of Mary, the tavern scene,
the assault upon Magdalen Castle, and her capitulation. The
playwright has accepted the conflation of the various New Testament women into the Magdalen of medieval legend (the prostitute,
the woman from whom Christ cast out seven devils, the sister
of Martha and Lazarus, the woman who washed and anointed
Christ's feet, the woman who stood vigil at the crucifixion, who
brought ointment for the body, who discovered that Christ had
risen, and to whom Christ appeared),[1] brought the whole story
to bear on the brief account in *The Golden Legend*, and translated Mary into Everyman, representing as she did to medieval
man the victory of grace, contrition, and penance over human
frailty.[2]

In addition to elaborating his sources, the playwright was also
given to altering them considerably. For instance, to have followed
The Golden Legend in the treatment of Mary's exile and journey
to Marseilles would have involved many other characters (she is
accompanied by Lazarus and Martha, St. Maximian, St. Cedony,
Marcelle her chambermaid, and others) and thus would have
created difficulties; in the play she goes alone. In *The Golden
Legend* Mary is exiled by vengeful Jews, and her arrival in Marseilles is providential. In the play she is ordered by Christ to go
to Marseilles. The embarkation in *The Golden Legend* is sad; in
the play, it is voluntary and comic. Again, the poet has altered the
account in *The Golden Legend* by greatly shortening the episode
of the king and queen of Marseilles' conversion. He has also
drastically changed the episode of the death and revival of the
queen of Marseilles. In *The Golden Legend*, Saint Peter assures
the king that his wife is only sleeping, and that his son is safe. In the

---

[1] See M. Malvern, *The Magdalen*, Ph.D. thesis, Michigan State University,
1969, and V. Saxer, *Le Culte de Marie Madeleine en occident* (Paris, 1959), and
H. Garth, 'Saint Mary Magdalene in Medieval Literature', *Johns Hopkins
University Studies in Historical and Political Science*, lxvii (1950), 347–452.
[2] C. Davidson, 'The Digby *Mary Magdalene* and the Magdalene Cult of the
Middle Ages', *Annuale Medievale*, xiii (1972), 70–87, and D. L. Jeffrey, 'English
Saints' Plays', *Medieval Drama*, ed. N. Denny, Stratford-upon-Avon Studies
16 (1973), pp. 69–89, give analyses of the thematic structure of the play.

play there is no such assurance, and the ensuing miracle has a dramatic effect it would not otherwise have had. And, finally, the poet has used a single priest to 'hossell' Mary before her death rather than the stageful of characters that *The Golden Legend* requires. Throughout, the playwright has adapted a story that he knew well, and which perhaps he had before him, to the needs of his play. The pertinent passages from *The Golden Legend* are cited in our notes.

The playwright has also, of course, used or paraphrased passages from the Bible and various hymns, and these are discussed in our notes to these passages.

We have already referred to the passage in *Mary Magdalen* (ll. 217-24) which seems to have been borrowed from *The Killing of the Children* (ll. 97-104). In the latter, it is a speech divided among the four knights who are replying to Herod's command that they should slaughter the children:

PRIMUS MILES.   My lord, ye may be sure that I shalle not spare,
          For to fulfille your noble commaundement,
        With sharpe sword to perse them alle bare,
          In all contrees that be to you adiacent!
SECUNDUS MILES.   And for your sake, to obserue your commaunde-
                                  ment!
TERTIUS MILES.   Not on of them alle oure handes shalle astert!
QUARTUS MILES.   For we wole cruelly execute youre judgement,
        With swerde and spere to perse them thurgh the
                                  hert!

In *Mary Magdalen* a version of these lines is spoken by Herod in reply to Tiberius' command:

    Be her sekyr I woll natt spare
        For [to] complyshe hys cummavnddment,
    Wyth sharp swerddys to perce þe[m] bare,
        In all covntres wythin thys regent,
        For hys love to fulfyll hys intentt.
    Non swych xall from ower handys stertt,
        For we woll fulfyll hys ryall juggement
    Wyth swerd and spere to perce [þem] thorow þe hartt!

There can be little doubt that, if one of these passages was borrowed from the other, the author of *Mary Magdalen* was the borrower. Not only is the speech somewhat awkward in the mouth of proud Herod, but the *Mary Magdalen* version is shortened at the expense of some intelligibility; each line is a bit shorter, and two important words are missing. The over-all pattern would suggest that it is the author of *Mary Magdalen*, not our scribe's hurried copying, that is responsible for the awkwardness of the passage.

The implications of this relationship are not at all clear. It seems that, on linguistic and other grounds, the two plays are by different authors, in spite of a general similarity of rhetoric and style. A possibility is that the author of *Mary Magdalen* was a member of a group of players who possessed a copy of *The Killing of the Children* among others, and when he came to write his extravaganza, he borrowed from the available texts. Or perhaps the writer of *Mary Magdalen* borrowed sections of another play, from which the author of *The Killing of the Children* had independently and more accurately borrowed. Professor Wickham has suggested that the writer of *Mary Magdalen* compiled the play from a number of available popular scenes.[1] There are, however, no parallels anywhere to the bulk of the materials in our play. The author may well have borrowed and adapted several of the set ranting scenes which change little from play to play, but clearly the basic structure of *Mary Magdalen* must be attributed to its author.

The Nature and Staging of the Play

Mary Magdalen has a multitude of scenes and characters; it has over forty speaking parts, but we cannot be exact because we do not know the numbers of some groups. The play begins in Rome with Tiberius Caesar making his boast, and ordering his provost to discover those in his empire who disobey the Roman gods. The scene shifts to the Holy Land where Cyrus, father of Mary, Martha, and Lazarus, boasts of his wealth, praises his children, and gives his property to them. Back in Rome, Tiberius orders a messenger to Jerusalem to make sure that Herod kills all 'harlottys' who rebel against the laws. Herod is seen making his boast, but his 'phylyssoverys' prophesy that one shall come greater than Herod; Herod rages, and his anger is given focus by the arrival of Caesar's messenger. Herod orders his soldiers to kill all troublemakers. Pilate boasts, and Caesar's messenger comes to him. At the Castle

[1] 'The Staging of Saint Plays in England', p. 112.

of Magdalen Cyrus dies, leaving Martha and Mary in the care of Lazarus.

The World, accompanied by Pride and Covetousness, enters and boasts, as does Flesh, accompanied by Sloth, Gluttony, and Lechery. The Prince of Devils, accompanied by Wrath and Envy, follows. During Satan's boast it becomes apparent that Hell's chief target is Mary. She is not initially mentioned by name, though Wrath refers to the enemy as 'hyrre'. Satan enlists the World and the Flesh to aid him. The Seven Deadly Sins then, under the leadership of Lechery and the Bad Angel, besiege the Castle of Magdalen, anticipating by dumb-show Mary's subsequent yielding; Lechery enters and persuades Mary to accompany her to a tavern in Jerusalem. There Curiosity, disguised as a gallant, seduces Mary, and she and her lover depart.

The Bad Angel reports their success to the World, Flesh, and Devil. The Devil returns to Hell stage (they have been meeting at the tent of the World), and Mary enters the 'place', rejoices in her lover, and goes to sleep in an arbor. Simon the Leper comes forth from his house and announces the supper that he has planned for the famous prophet in the land. Meanwhile, a Good Angel approaches the sleeping Mary and moves her to remorse. The Prophet (Jesus) and his Disciples pass near Mary and encounter Simon, who invites them to his house. Mary follows after them, enters Simon's house, and anoints the feet of Jesus. Simon's scornful thoughts about Mary are perceived by Christ, who upbraids Simon and forgives Mary her sin. Upon this, the seven devils 'dewoyde' from her (actually from the house, where they have been 'kept closse'). Mary expresses her thanks, Jesus and the Disciples leave, and the Good Angel rejoices.

At Hell stage Satan, Belzabub, and Belfagour whip the Bad Angel and the devils who have failed. Satan then orders the other devils to set Simon's house afire. Mary returns to her castle, and Lazarus suddenly becomes ill. Mary and Martha seek Jesus, who promises to send his grace. When the sisters return to the castle, Lazarus dies and is buried. Mary and Martha conduct Jesus to the tomb, and Jesus calls Lazarus forth, to the rejoicing of all.

In Marseilles the king makes his boast and with his queen sits down to a royal banquet. At Hell stage a devil enters crying, telling of Christ's harrowing of hell (the playwright has chosen to omit the crucifixion). Back in Jerusalem, the three Marys enter weeping;

they address the Holy Cross, then go to the tomb. The *quem quaeritis* is much abbreviated, there being only the announcement by the angels that Christ has risen. The Marys then tell the news to Peter and John who in turn go to the tomb. Mary Magdalen goes apart from the other Marys and Jesus appears to her in the *hortulanus* scene. Jesus then 'avoydyt', and Mary tells the others what she has seen. Shortly, Jesus appears again to all the Marys.

In Marseilles the king and queen are preparing a heathen service. The priest and his boy engage in broad farce including the '*Leccyo Mahowndys*'. The scene moves to Jerusalem where Pilate learns that Christ has risen. He sends word to Herod who in turn informs Rome. Tiberius is told Pilate's and Herod's story that the disciples have stolen the body of Jesus. In the place again (near Jerusalem) Mary enters, with a disciple of her own. The heavens open and Jesus praises his mother; he directs an angel to tell Mary Magdalen to go to Marseilles. In the place, a ship enters, the mariner and his boy singing and engaging in farce similar to that of the priest and his boy. Mary hails the ship and is taken to Marseilles.

Mary comes before the king and queen of Marseilles and speaks to them of Christ. Ignoring the king's bluster, Mary tells them of Creation and salvation. The king challenges her to a test of gods, but the king's idols fail to perform. Mary prays for a sign and a cloud descends from heaven and sets the temple afire. The priest and his boy 'sink', and the king 'gothe hom'. He takes to his bed and rages against Mary, and she goes into a lodge nearby and prays for aid. In Heaven Jesus directs his angels to assist in converting the king; they descend to Mary and dress her in white. Mary and the angels, bearing lights, go to the king's bed, and a warning is delivered to the king while he sleeps. When he awakes he tells his queen of the troubled dream. The king orders Mary brought before him; he tells her that he will convert, provided that his wife is enabled to bear a child (this request is not in the text but Mary grants his boon as if he had asked it). Immediately the queen feels the child stir in her womb, and the king and queen convert. Mary tells them of Peter, and the king decides to visit the Holy Land, investing Mary with his power in his absence. The queen demands to go too, and after some argument she accompanies the king to the shore where they encounter the ship that had brought Mary. They sail, but before long there is a great storm, during which the queen gives birth and dies. The crew, fearful of bad luck from the dead body, demand that the queen be cast out; the king pleads instead that she be placed on a nearby rock. The mother and child are put on the rock and the ship sails to the Holy Land. The king goes ashore and encounters Peter, who baptizes him. They are to go to the Stations of the Cross together and visit the holy places. The king re-embarks and the ship sails for Marseilles, passing the rock where the queen and her child were left, and to the king's joy they are alive. The queen tells him that, thanks to the Virgin and to Mary Magdalen, she has been with him in spirit, been baptized, and visited the holy places as well.

They return to Marseilles and praise Mary, who blesses them and returns the kingdom to them. They beg her to stay with them, but Mary determines to go into the wilderness. In Heaven Jesus directs his angels to raise Mary into the skies and feed her with manna. A priest in the wilderness witnesses this phenomenon and seeks Mary out, begging her to reveal to him the secret of her grace. She describes her life, and the priest returns to his cell. In Heaven Jesus announces that Mary's earthly life is to end. Two angels instruct the priest to take the sacrament to Mary, who then dies peacefully, and her soul is received in Heaven to the rejoicing of the angels. The priest prepares for the burial of Mary and then speaks an epilogue, blessing the audience and asking them to join in *Te Deum laudamus*.

Mary Magdalen is physically the most elaborate single play in the English religious drama. Much attention has been devoted to the proper classification of the play.[1] It is both a miracle play and a morality play, a composite of saint play and morality technique, together with a number of traditional scenes of the cyclic drama. The morality devices give flesh to the story when tradition is silent, and make explicit the application of the legend of Mary to the instruction of Everyman.

Although lacking the subtlety of *The Castle of Perseverance*, our play surpasses that great morality as theatrical spectacle. *Mary*

---

[1] G. R. Coffman describes it as the best surviving example of a miracle play, 'The Miracle Play in England', *SP*, xvi (1919), 60, and Craig, pp. 87, 324, argues that it is a mystery play. Pollard's description seems most sound: 'It is miracle . . . as treating the life and death of St. Mary Magdalene. It is a mystery play, by virtue of the introduction of scenes from the life of Christ. It is a morality play, as exhibiting the contest between good and evil', *English Miracle Plays, Moralities and Interludes* (Oxford, 1890), p. 193.

Magdalen is, in many ways, the culmination of the late medieval
East Anglian popular drama. Its scenes are more elaborate, its
language more polysyllabic, than those of any other play. If one
ranting speech was good theatre, why not more? The playwright
begins with Tiberius Caesar himself, whose ranting is effective in
that he is first and greatest on stage(such tongue-and-mind-twisting
language was undoubtedly useful in quieting an unruly audience).
Each subsequent boast is less effective. With our poet(and generally
in the drama of the period) the boast is synonymous with introduction; in succession, Tiberius, Cyrus, Herod, Pilate, the World, the
Flesh, and the Devil, have at least thirteen lines of rant, so that
we are not surprised that alliterative line-fillers appear in speech
after speech. Nor is there any wonder that these ranting speeches
tend more than others to lose their form, to add or drop lines or
words, and frequently to degenerate into alliterative nonsense. But
to be fair, most of the rant is confined to the first 1,000 lines, leaving
the King of Marcylle to provide, before his conversion, the bombast in the latter part of the play (even after his conversion he
announces in the manner of Herod his determination to persecute
all nonconformers!).

The sheer mechanical daring of the play matches its rhetoric.
The author provides lightning from Heaven striking the 'maw-
mentys' of the King of Marcylle; there are angels ascending and
descending (and Mary, too); a house is burned, seven devils are
'voyded' from a house, and there is the famous ship.

The very repleteness of the play has caused scholars to assume
that it was the result of accretion. Craig[1] suggested that the seed
of the play was the New Testament material, and that the other
materials had gathered around it, being added over the years by
various writers. He adduced as evidence for this theory the simple
double quatrains of the 'seminal' parts, as opposed to the 'decadent'
verse of the additions. This argument does not stand examination
because, as we have seen, the entire play is basically in double or
single quatrains, with the tail-rhyming and bob-and-wheel stanzas
restricted for the most part to the devils' scenes and the comic
scenes, as was usual in the late drama. In fact, though the rhetoric
and verse alter somewhat according to the scene, the language
itself—the inkhorn words, loose syntax, and polysyllabic rhymes—
is quite constant throughout the play. We conclude that, though

[1] *English Religious Drama*, pp. 315–16.

the play may not all have been composed at one time, and though some scenes were probably drawn from other plays, there appears to have been a single author of the play as it stands.

In our emphasis upon the sheer theatricality of the play, we should not overlook the fact that *Mary Magdalen* is essentially serious, and was written by one who knew his New Testament, knew his *Golden Legend*, and was capable of writing numerous stage directions in Latin. We cannot assume that he was a cleric, but that he was seems probable. The play, performed in a rural and unsophisticated area or even in a town like Norwich, must have been very effective. The spectacular elements enforce a consistent moral and theological message: penance. A secondary theme, that of the active and contemplative life, is inherent in the materials.

The method of the play's production and the identity of the players are unknown. As with most East Anglian religious drama, we do not know where or under what circumstances *Mary Magdalen* was performed; we do not know whether it was a local play or a travelling play. Unlike *The Play of the Sacrament* or *The Castle of Perseverance*, it offers us no clues in references to places or people. Lincoln has been suggested as a site, but the language would seem to rule this out.[1] Professor Wickham recently proposed Ipswich as a possibility,[2] and Professor Bennett, Bishop's Lynn.[3] Our opinion is that, in spite of the elaborateness of the equipment required for the play, *Mary Magdalen* was very probably, like *The Castle of Perseverance*, *Mankind*, and *The Play of the Sacrament*, a travelling production.[4] It shares, as we have pointed out, very many of the features of these plays.

One is tempted to speculate that a group of players who might have performed *Mary Magdalen* was a religious company, perhaps one of the groups of friars who, we know, did perform plays on occasion.[5] The great similarity of language and rhetoric among

---

[1] H. Ritchie, 'A Suggested Location of the Digby "Mary Magdalene" ', *Theatre Survey*, iv (1963), 51–8.

[2] 'The Staging of Saint Plays in England', p. 115.

[3] Jacob Bennett, in his essay 'The *Mary Magdalene* of Bishop's Lynn' (*SP* lxxv (1978), 1–9), argues on linguistic and other grounds for Bishop's Lynn.

[4] Pentzell argues, p. 23, that, because of its elaborateness, *The Castle of Perseverance* was not a travelling play, but this seems to underrate the capabilities of the medieval players and to ignore the clear implication of the banns.

[5] The evidence for friars' participation in plays is well established, most notably by the famous Wycliffite *A Treatise of Miraclis Pleyinge*, T. Wright and

these plays suggests, not that one 'company' did them all, but that the groups were loosely associated, knew one another, and certainly knew the various plays. A monastery such as the great house at Bury St. Edmunds might well have been a centre of such dramatic activity. The association of the Macro plays with Bury has been discussed, and the possible association of the Digby *Wisdom* with the same house has been suggested. As we have seen, there is some evidence that *Mary Magdalen*, together with one or two other Digby plays, was subsequently performed in the 1560s at Chelmsford, but this is surely a second career for such plays.

Furnivall divided *Mary Magdalen* into two parts, the first ending at l. 924, and Adams printed the text only to this point. Such a scheme breaks the play after the raising of Lazarus, and before the King of Marcylle makes his boast. As Craig remarks,[1] there is no good reason for such a division, and certainly the manuscript offers no suggestion. We have not attempted any divisions in our text, and have indicated in brackets the locality of the action only when it is not made clear at once by the stage directions of the manuscript. Although scene or act division has the advantage of making reference easier, such division gives quite a misleading impression of the play. The action was largely continuous, switching back and forth from one area and set of characters to another, occasionally overlapping.

The staging of *Mary Magdalen* presents complex problems; we have no plan to guide us, and must deduce what we can from the stage directions and the juxtaposition of the actions. Adams proposed[2] an elaborate 'in-the-round' arrangement in the manner of the drawing in the Macro manuscript. He provides for eight 'sedes', and assumes that they will serve doubled functions in the two halves of the play. Pollard[3] suggested that only two pageants

J. O. Halliwell, eds., *Reliquiae Antiquae*, ii (London, 1843), 42–57. See Lawrence Craddock, 'Franciscan Influences on Early English Drama', *Franciscan Studies*, x (1950), 383–417, and D. L. Jeffrey, 'Franciscan Spirituality and Early English Drama', *Mosaic*, viii (1975), 17–46. Jeffrey thinks that the Digby plays have a Franciscan provenance. They may have, but there is no evidence for this in the manuscript other than the presence of Bacon's *Radix Mundi*, a well-known treatise which might have been found anywhere, and which carries the date 1550, which would seem to put it well after the period of any Franciscan participation in popular religious drama.

[1] Op. cit., p. 316.
[2] *Chief Pre-Shakespearean Drama* (Boston, 1924), p. 225.
[3] *English Miracle Plays, Moralities, and Interludes*, p. 193.

might have been needed, and Furnivall[1] had assumed that a single pageant with two or three stages might have sufficed. Both the latter scholars apparently thought of the play as a processional performance. In the introduction to his edition of *Mary Magdalen*, Lewis[2] surveys the theories proposed for the arrangement of the playing area and stage, most of which assume the arena-and-scaffolds ('in-the-round') method. Lewis himself prefers a semi-circular staging (p. xxi), as does Wickham.[3]

Nineteen distinct locations are mentioned in the stage directions or text. The central playing area or 'place' must have served for many of these (the place or 'placea' is mentioned five times in the stage directions). But certain locations clearly required structures. Rome had at least a throne for Tiberius (l. 19). The stage of Hell is specifically called a stage (s.d. following l. 357) and has a top area and a Hell-mouth beneath. There must have been a stage for Heaven, though it is nowhere referred to as such. It must have been of some height, for a cloud descends from it and burns the King of Marcylle's pagan temple (after l. 1561). Angels descend from it, and Mary is raised 'in nubibus' (after l. 2030). The top was probably closed by a curtain or 'clouds', for a stage direction following l. 1348 states 'Her xall Hevyne opyn and Jesus xall shew'. The 'house' of Simon the Leper was the scene of the dinner, of the 'voydyng' of the devils, and the house is set on fire by the devils. The Castle of Magdalen is likewise one of the principal stages, and it may well have looked like the famous castle in the Macro manuscript plan, a frame structure with castellated top perched upon wooden legs.

We must assume that some sort of stage or tent was used for Jerusalem, perhaps shared by Herod and Pilate, with a table outside for the tavern, and a bench near by for Mary to lie down upon. Less elaborate arrangements may have existed for the World and the Flesh, though a tent was certainly used (l. 386: the World says 'I pray þe, cum vp onto my tent'). The palace of the King of

[1] Op. cit., p. xi.
[2] *The Play of Mary Magdalene*, Ph.D. thesis, University of Wisconsin, 1963, pp. xvii–xxii.
[3] 'The Staging of Saint Plays in England', p. 112. R. Hosley, 'Three Kinds of Outdoor Theatre before Shakespeare', p. 31, regards *Mary Magdalen* as an 'in-the-round' play, and apparently so does R. Pentzell, p. 10. Pentzell's discussion is weakened by his assumption that the Digby plays were a kind of cycle, and used the same playing area; there is certainly no evidence for this.

Marcylle was probably a stage which could accommodate the king's table and bed as well as his temple, and was probably of two levels, with the temple and idols above, and the table, at which the banquet was held, on the lower level. We remember that the temple was set afire by a cloud from heaven, and 'þe pryst and þe clerk xall synke' (s.d. following l. 1561), presumably into a lower level. Such an arrangement would have been within a short distance of the Heaven stage, for the convenience of the cloud descending upon the temple. There would also have been an arrangement of some sort attached to the king's stage representing the 'old logge wythowt þe gate' (s.d. following l. 1577) where Mary retires. Another setting of some importance is the rock on which the king's wife and child are laid; this could possibly have been used for both Lazarus' and Christ's sepulchres. The playing area probably had another tent or screen for the sudden appearances and disappearances of Christ (see his appearance to Mary, following ll. 1095 and 1124).

Finally, we must consider the ship. We need not envisage a ship as elaborate as one shown in D. van Alsloot's *Isabella's Triumph* (1615), but it was probably impressive.[1] A large frame with a ship painted on either side and masts protruding from it might have been built so that the mariner and his boy could walk inside it, holding the frame with straps across their shoulders. A canvas skirt painted with waves attached to the frame could conceal the feet of the crew and passengers.

What evidence we have in the text for the arrangement of the locations is not very satisfactory. If the circular arena-and-scaffolds method was used, it would likely have been complex. The constant movement in the play must have been very troublesome if the audience had been placed as Southern speculates for *The Castle*. The semi-circular disposition argued by Lewis and Wickham, in which the stages are located close together around one side of the place, and the audience around the other, would seem much

---

[1] Wickham, in his 'The Staging of Saint Plays in England', p. 115, seems to entertain the idea that the ship might have been a real one. A more probable possibility may be found in his *Early English Stages*, i (London, 1959), 223-4, in which he quotes from the description of a 1501 tournament: ' ". . . anoon cam owte . . . for the defendeours, Guyllam de la Ryvers . . . in a goodly shippe borne up with men, within himself ryding in the myddes; . . . and the sides of the ship covered with cloth peynted after the colour or lykeness of water." '

more suitable for *Mary Magdalen*. But dogmatism is unprofitable, for *Mary Magdalen* may well have been played in a variety of circumstances, sometimes in an open field, or in a large square, on occasion as an arena-with-scaffolds play, at other times as a play with stages gathered in a semi-circle and separated by the platea from the audience.

4. THE KILLING OF THE CHILDREN

The Manuscript

The manuscript of *Candelmes day and the kyllyng of þe children of Israelle* is found at ff. 146ʳ–157ᵛ of MS Digby 133. The quarto leaves average $8\frac{1}{2}''\times 6\frac{1}{8}''$, and are divided into a single gathering of ten leaves, ff. 148–57 (sewn between ff. 152 and 153) and a pair of leaves, ff. 146 and 147, which are separately sewn and pasted on to the inside margin of f. 148ʳ. The reinforcement of the inner margins of most leaves obscures the relationship of this outer pair to the rest of the manuscript. It is difficult to identify the watermark owing to this repair, but it is a hand surmounted by a five-pointed star, found on ff. 146 (top of mark), 147 (bottom), 150 (bottom), 151 (top), 154 (bottom), and 155 (top). This mark could be any of several in Briquet, for the wrist is too obscured for identification. It is unlike the mark in the paper of *The Conversion of St. Paul* in that the fingers and thumb are all well apart. The paper of the book would seem to have been three folio sheets, for there are three complete watermarks.

One-third of a leaf is tipped in at the bottom between ff. 152 and 153; this contains an added speech. There is no watermark on this partial leaf.

The manuscript is, on the whole, in poor condition. All the leaves have been repaired, some many times. All outer margins have been reinforced, with the result that occasionally paragraph or stanza markers are obscured. Inner margins of the first half-dozen leaves are also reinforced. A little staining and much browning are found throughout.

The main scribe wrote all of the manuscript except for ff. 155ᵛ–156ᵛ, and the first two lines of f. 157ʳ. The full title of the play, *Candelmes day and the kyllyng of þe children of Israelle*, is in the principal scribe's hand at the top of f. 146ʳ, as are the two dates of 1512 on either side of that page, one in Arabic and one in Roman numerals. The main scribe is also responsible for the list of players and the third date of 1512 which are found on f. 157ᵛ.

The writing of the principal scribe is superficially similar to that of the principal scribe of *The Conversion of St. Paul*. Furnivall (p. xv) stated that they were the same, but they are really quite different. The main scribe of *The Killing of the Children* writes an unidiosyncratic style of an even more pronounced Anglicana character than that of *The Conversion*. He eschews the secretary *a*, which the scribes of *The Conversion* use consistently, and employs both varieties of the Anglicana *r* (and the secretary *r* occasionally), whereas the scribes of *The Conversion* use the figure-2 secretary *r* much more frequently than the long Anglicana *r*. The main scribe of *The Killing of the Children* consistently bars final *ll*, apparently to indicate a final *e*, but the main scribe of *The Conversion* does not. The main scribe of *The Killing of the Children* distinguishes between *þ* and *y*, but the scribes of *The Conversion* do not.

The second hand of *The Killing of the Children*, which wrote ff. 155ᵛ–156ᵛ and the first two lines of f. 157ʳ, is very different from that of the main scribe, though the general style is similar. Its strokes are thicker, and the letters are crudely formed. This second hand does not distinguish between *þ* and *y*. The second hand varies between the Anglicana looped *e* and the secretary two-stroke *e*, whereas the principal hand uses the former. Both scribes of *The Killing of the Children* have the habit of suspending a final consonant plus -*e* by means of a dotted arc over the last letter, e.g. *worshiþ̂* = *worshippe* and *Joseþ̂* = *Josephe*. This dotted arc also serves as a nasal suspension. Both scribes employ the usual abbreviations for -*er*, -*re*, -*ro*, -*ra*, -*ri*, -*ur*, *with*, *and*, *the*, *that*, *you*, and *thou*. As we have noted, the bar on final *ll* seems significant, and we expand to -*lle*; likewise, the flourish after final -*r* seems to indicate -*re*, judging from the scribes' spelling and rhyming practice. We have expanded all plural and genitive abbreviations to -*es* as the dominant spelling, though the scribes use both -*ys* and -*is* as well. We ignore the flourishes after final *d*, *g*, and *t*, as well as the barring of *h*.

The main scribe brackets the rhymes, the second does not; the first scribe marks stanzas by a paragraph symbol, the second scribe does so only infrequently. Both scribes usually place the speakers' names in the right margins, though occasionally the first scribe puts them in the middle of the page. Stage directions are in the

middle of the page. Speeches and stage directions are set off by
lines. The principal scribe uses a raised dot to mark caesuras and
the second scribe the virgule. The principal scribe uses a dark
brown ink throughout, the second, a black. The main scribe
averages about twenty-eight lines per page, the second scribe
about thirty. There are no catchwords or ornamentation in the
manuscript.

Although we have elsewhere expressed a contrary opinion, we
now believe that the principal scribe of *The Killing of the Children*
is also the man who wrote the Digby copy of *Wisdom*.[1]

Some errors of anticipation and the presence of the second scribe
should prove conclusively that our text is not the original of the
play. However, the copy is an authoritative, if not authorial, one.
The principal scribe frequently alters what makes good sense to
what, apparently, made better sense to him. He seems to have
been responsible for the reorganization of the first scene and the
elimination of the business (f. 147^v) in which Watkyn the messenger
reports to Herod that the three kings have gone home by another
way. These alterations took two forms. The messenger's speech
(ll. 8–13 of the cancelled speech) was found to be confusing with
its 'I shalle fulfille'—in view of the fact that Watkyn goes on to
report without having left Herod's presence—and so was altered
to 'I haue fulfilled'. This was only an apparent improvement, for
after all, Watkyn has only just received the order. It would appear
that some more radical change was then made, and an additional
speech added on a tipped-in partial sheet like that found between
ff. 152 and 153. This is suggested by the presence of a circled cross
against the seventh line of Herod's speech; this symbol elsewhere
(opposite l. 357, f. 153^r) indicates the point at which additional
lines are to be inserted. There is no indication that a partial leaf
had been tipped in between ff. 147 and 148, but such a supplement
could have been easily removed, leaving no trace.

Subsequently, it was decided to cancel the material on f. 147^v
altogether. Herod's speech at the bottom of f. 147^r and his speech
at the top of f. 148^r were then joined. This required only a slight
alteration (the change of 'A, now I perceyue . . .', which implies
that Herod has just received information, to 'I do perceyue',
which has no such implication). This much is fairly clear, but we
have no good idea of what larger revision may have taken place.

[1] See our earlier discussion in 'The Late Medieval Plays', p. 156.

The main scribe may have been in the last stage of cutting down and adapting a somewhat longer play to more modest requirements. Some indication that this may have been the case is found in the fact that the stanzaic form of the present play is consistently double quatrain except for three rhyme royals. There are three rhyme royal stanzas in the cancelled scene alone. One may speculate that an earlier form of the play may have been marked by a more even balance of double quatrains and rhyme royals. Perhaps such a play might have included the business of Watkyn's leaving at Herod's request and his subsequent return. In spite of the apparent integrity of the manuscript, one cannot, because of the peculiar state of ff. 146 and 147, rule out the possibility that a pair of leaves might have been removed when a revision was made (the last two speeches of f. 147^v form a quatrain which might have been part of a rhyme royal stanza or double quatrain, for no other quatrain is found in the play). Another indication of revision is the fact that for his first several speeches Watkyn is called simply 'Messanger', and as an afterthought 'Watkyn' is twice written in before 'Messanger'. Subsequently the scribe has consistently written 'Watkyn'.

In addition to undertaking this extensive revision, the main scribe has cancelled the second scribe's *finis* on f. 157^r, added a couplet to what had been the final speech, then added two stanzas to Poeta's speech. He also wrote the list of players and the date on f. 157^v. One would guess that a scribe who would take such liberties with his text was more than merely a scribe, but that he had something to do with the actual presentation of the play. It is just possible that the scribe was the author of the play, making another copy and revising it with the help of an assistant.

The statement on f. 157^v that 'Jhon Parfre ded wryte this booke' is the most curious puzzle provided by the manuscript. This assertion is in a different hand from those of the scribes, and is apparently somewhat later. At the foot of the preceding page the same hand had written 'Jhon Parfe ded wryte', but then crossed out the abortive sentence and wrote the complete version on f. 157^v. The writer may have meant to convey that a John Parfrey was the author of the play, for a manuscript of twelve leaves would have been called a 'booke'. It is unlikely that John Parfrey was the name of the scribe who literally 'wrote' the book, for, although many scribes signed their work, it would be unusual for a scribe to be named by another. It may be, however, that the sentence means simply that a John Parfrey compiled (or caused to be compiled) the book of which this manuscript was a part (originally, that is, not MS Digby 133). That this was often the sense in which such a phrase would be meant is supported by notes in many of Stow's manuscripts which make a similar claim in cases where we know that Stow himself was neither the author nor the scribe of the works. We have been unable to discover which John Parfrey is referred to. The family was widespread in Norfolk and Suffolk, and several contemporary John Parfreys are found in the records of those counties.[1]

In the general introduction to MS Digby 133 we have already discussed the significance of 'the vijth booke' which appears at the top of f. 146^r in a hand not found elsewhere in the manuscript. There are a few other marks in the margins of leaves, but these seem to have no bearing on the history of the manuscript.

Versification

The stanzas are double quatrains *ababbcbc*. There are three rhyme royal stanzas in the play (ll. 315–21, 322–8, 358–64) and three in the cancelled leaf f. 147^v. At the end of this cancelled leaf there is a quatrain which may or may not have been intended as such. A five-line stanza *abbba* is at ll. 345–9, and there are two couplets, ll. 313–14 and 549–50.

The lines are frequently of the 'tumbling' variety, highly extra-metrical, varying between seven and sixteen syllables. In the ranting speeches the lines tend to be longer, but this is not a consistent pattern. In spite of the length of many lines, the verses seem to be basically the four-stress variety found throughout the East Anglian drama of the period.

Alliteration, though present in Herod's early speeches, is not a feature of the play.

Language

The language is East Midland with some East Anglian characteristics, but rather fewer than that of *Mary Magdalen*. The reflex

---

[1] See the town meeting book preserved in the Clerk's Office, Thetford, for the reference to the Parfreys: *Ancient Deeds, Evidences, and Memorials relating to the Borough of Thetford, Collected and Arranged* by George Bird Burrell, *Thetfordiensis*, 1800 (Thetford Borough Offices). Also see the archdiaconal and consistorial wills in the Norwich Record Office for the years 1509–29.

of OE *i* and *y* is frequently *y*, but more commonly *e*: *heder(e)* 19, canc. 1; *hedyr* 308, *wheder* 255, *besy* 56, *mende* (mind) 520, 533, the former rhyming on *wende, sende, mankende*, the latter on *menkende*; *mynde* appears twice 47, 561, the latter rhyming on *ende*. The normal spelling of *any* is *ony* canc. 4, 5, and 160, 213, 265.[1] The reflex of OE *hw* is usually *wh*, but is frequently *w*, as in *wiche*, eighteen instances (12, 112, 236, etc.) compared to four of *whiche* (480, 484, 487, 514). The word *sharme* 142 (scream, OE *cirman*) is described by H. T. Cozens-Hardy as characteristically Norfolk.[2]

The principal features of spelling and pronunciation:

The reflex of OE *-ht* is generally written *-ght*: *bright, myght, right, sight* rhyme in 106, 108, 109, 111; *wrought, brought, nought, thought* rhyme in 351, 353, 354, 356. As in *The Conversion of St. Paul* and *Mary Magdalen* the spelling is extended to words without etymological basis: *parfight* 446, *despight* 247, etc. These spellings show the loss of the fricative before *-t*.

The reflex of OE *sc* is *sh*.

The loss of final unstressed *-e* is confirmed by many rhymes: *seen, bene* 86, 88; *region, euerychone* 93, 95; *beforn, borne*, 126, 128, etc.

The reflex of OE *ǣ*[1] and *ǣ*[2] is written *e* and rhymed on reflexes of OE *ēa, ēo, ē*: *slepe, crepe* 185, 187; *hethe, dethe* 70, 72; not rhyming, *fere* 141, *drede* 159.

The reflex of OE *ā* is normally written *o*: *bonys* canc. 20, *gon* 48, *goo* 349, 380, *hoolle* 29, *more* 159, 212, etc.

The reflex of OE *a* before lengthening groups is usually *o*: *bonde* 43, *bronde* 64, *long* 163, *hond* rhyming on *lond* 246, 248; but *hande* rhymes on *stande* 386, 388, and is found unrhyming 102, 214, 417, etc.

Main features of verbal inflexion are the following:

Pres. indic. 2 sg. ends in *-st*: *comyst* 195, 200; *knowist* canc. 15, and auxiliaries *woldest* 145, *hast* 451, *haddist* 164, *art* 409, *shalt* 228.

Pres. indic. 3 sg. is *-th*: *betoknyth* 489, *bryngeth* 377, *longith* 118, *longyth* 511, *seith* 127.

[1] See 'Some Applications of Middle English Dialectology', p. 90, map 6.
[2] *Broad Norfolk* (London, 1893), p. 23.

Pres. indic. pl. is normally without inflexion: *sharme and crye* 142, *fight* 224, *spille* 175; there are a few examples in -*n*: *ben(e)* 88, 112, *joyen* 501, and in the auxiliary *han* 474, 519.

The imperative plural has no ending except in *syngyth* 484 and *doth* 53, 56, etc.

Infinitives are generally without inflexion: *chaunge* 456, *yeve* 516, *sle* 302, *slake* 494; however, *fleen* appears in a rhyming series with *seen, ben, tene* 162, 164, 165, 167, and *don* rhymes on *anon* 218, 221.

The present participle is normally -*yng*, but -*eng* and -*ing* are found: *tarieng* 86, *praying* 254.

Past participles of weak verbs are consistently -*id*, *ed*, and -*yd*. Strong verb past participles normally end in -*n*, but there are a few without ending, e.g. *take* 347.

Spelling of the genitive and plurals of nouns is distributed among -*es*, -*ys*, -*is*, with -*es* predominating: *Goddes* 6, *kinges* 3, *dowes* s.d. after 432; *dowys* 416, *wyffys* 281, *virgynes* 54, *virgynis* 483, *lawis* 396.

Of the pronouns *ye* is regularly nominative and *you* oblique. The social distinction of the plurals and *thu, the* is rigorously maintained. For 3 pl. *thei* (*they, þei*) 38, 80, etc.; *ther* 35, 94, etc.; *them* 44, 66, etc., *hem* 516, 544.

Polysyllables abound in the play's vocabulary, but there is only one word, *letification* (rejoicing) 26 that could be classed as an inkhornism, and *OED* cites only this instance.

There is nothing in the features of the language which would suggest an appreciably earlier date than the 1512 written on the manuscript.

Sources of the Play

The sources of *The Killing of the Children* are simply the brief accounts of the two principal episodes, the slaughter of the Innocents and the presentation of the infant Christ in the temple, found in Matthew and Luke, respectively. It is possible that *The Golden Legend* may be the source for some of the symbolic explanation in the Purification scene, but certainly the *Legend* has not been drawn upon for any part of the Herod play. Nor does it seem that any other popular compilation of devotional materials lies behind the scenes. Probably the most important sources in addition to the

New Testament were other plays, sermons, and such offices as
those for matins for the Feast of the Purification. We have noted
probable ultimate sources for various passages.

The Nature and Staging of the Play

The Poeta who speaks the prologue and the epilogue is similar
in name and function to that in *The Conversion of St. Paul.* The
prologue proclaims the entertainment to be for the feast of the
blessed Saint Anne (26 July), and recounts the lineage of the Virgin
and the nature of her marriage to Joseph. Last year, he tells us,
his group showed the play of the Shepherds and the Three Kings;
this year the play is to be of Our Lady's Purification and, subsequently, of Herod and the slaughter of the Innocents. He then
encourages the minstrels to play and the 'virgynes' to dance before
the play begins. But the first play is that of Herod and the
children.

Herod boasts of his good fortune and threatens all who rebel
against his laws. In a scene subsequently cancelled by the scribe,
Watkyn, his messenger, tells Herod that the three kings have
deceived him and gone home another way. In a rage, Herod orders
his four knights to go throughout the land, killing all children
below the age of two years, 'to kepe my liberte'. The knights
promise their obedience and depart; Watkyn, the comic figure,
offers himself to aid in this task, and asks to be made a knight.
After some buffoonery, Herod promises to make Watkyn a knight
if he acquits himself well against the mothers of the children.
Watkyn goes with the knights and they all '*walke abought the place
tylle Mary and Joseph be conveid into Egipt*'. An angel appears and
warns Mary and Joseph; Joseph gathers his tools and escorts Mary
and the infant Jesus into Egypt. As they go out of the place '*þe
goddes shalle falle*' (presumably in the temple of Herod in Jerusalem), and the women of Israel enter. The knights and Watkyn,
who have been walking around the place, attack them. There is an
exchange of threats between the wives and the knights, and the
knights kill the children. The mothers then turn upon Watkyn,
who is fearful of women armed with distaffs, and they beat him.
The knights rescue Watkyn, and report to Herod. When Herod
hears from Watkyn the curse the women have pronounced upon
him, he is overcome with fever and chills, and, after a brief rant,
dies.

The second play or action begins when Simeon enters at the temple in Jerusalem and speaks of the prophecy of the Messiah, the fulfilment of which he has prayed to see. Mary and Joseph enter the temple, bringing their child and two doves. Simeon greets them, pronouncing the *Nunc dimittis*, and expresses his joy that the prophecy has been fulfilled and that he has lived to see the child. Anna the Prophetess (who is apparently on the scene, for she is not described as entering) directs the attendant virgins, '*as many as a man wille*', to hold the candles. They all go in procession about the temple, Simeon explaining the mystical significance of the three parts of the candle, the wax, the wick, and the flame. Simeon gives the baby back to Mary and prophesies the crucifixion. Anna the Prophetess then directs the virgins in a dance. Poeta returns and apologizes for the imperfections of the play, and promises next year to show Christ among the Doctors in the Temple. Poeta calls for another dance, and the play ends.

It is not entirely certain that in their present form the two parts of the play were always to be acted together, despite the prologue's summary. It is clear from Poeta's prologue that one action followed the other as complete entities, the only connection being the presence of Joseph and Mary in the first, in the brief scene of their flight to Egypt. The fact that Poeta's prologue gets the order of the two plays wrong would seem to indicate not loss of memory, but that there were occasions on which the two parts or two plays might have been presented in the Purification–Massacre order, and that the prologue has preserved one such occasion. There is nothing in the text of the two parts to prevent such a reversal, though the manuscript presents the events in a more appropriate chronological order, and certainly in the proper festal order, the feast of the Holy Innocents being 28 December and the Feast of the Purification 2 February. On at least one occasion *The Killing of the Children* was presented without the Candlemas Day play, for the manuscript at f. 153ᵛ, after l. 388, has the note, in a hand not that of the scribe, '*Vacat ab hinc*', indicating that all that followed, i.e. the Candlemas play, was to be omitted.

Poeta's prologue may have been written for a special occasion. It is interesting that Poeta emphasizes the Candlemas part of the play in keeping with the presentation to be made on the day of the Feast of St. Anne. The play, although appropriate enough for the occasion, is not peculiarly suitable for the Feast of St. Anne;

other subjects would have been more suitable. The prologue, and especially the short epilogue, might have been written for a specific performance, emphasizing the appropriateness of the play for the occasion, and reversing the order of the parts of the play for that particular performance.

But the plain statement in the prologue that 'The last yeere we shewid you in this place / How the shepherdes of Cristes birth made letification, / And thre kynges . . .' joined with the statement in the epilogue that '. . . the next yeer, as we be purposid in oure mynde, / The disputacion of the doctours to shew in your presens' would seem to indicate that this composite play was part of a cycle presented one part at a time annually on St. Anne's Day. Even though Craig's arguments about the St. Anne's Day plays are inferential and debatable,[1] such a possibility must be granted.

However, the peculiar nature of the prologue and epilogue, the reversed order of the episodes, and the '*Vacat ab hinc*' note, cause us to entertain another possibility: that the play belonged to a group that had a regular tour schedule of towns, presenting different plays at different towns. Such a group might have a varied play book. It might do a series of plays upon St. Anne's Day over the years for a particular town, and yet the plays themselves would be available for playing under other conditions elsewhere, and, in the case of a composite play like the present one, the two parts would be available for playing separately. *The Killing of the Children* does not seem to be a local play, and it bears the marks of the professional drama of the period and area. Such an explanation, while entirely hypothetical, fits the peculiar nature of the text better than the theory that the play is simply part of a St. Anne's Day cycle.

The argument of H. R. Patch[2] that *The Killing of the Children* was once a part of the *Ludus Coventriae*, occupying the place now filled by two plays, the 'Purification' and the 'Massacre of the Innocents', is provocative but not very convincing. Patch speculates that our composite play was originally a part of one of the cycles (characterized by double quatrain stanzas) from which the present text of the *Ludus Coventriae* was created. The 'Purification' and 'Massacre' plays then supplanted our text, which was cast adrift. The evidence Patch adduces is, first, the order of the episodes,

[1] *English Religious Drama*, pp. 265–80.
[2] 'The *Ludus Coventriae* and the Digby *Massacre*', *PMLA* xxx (1920), 324–43.

Purification–Massacre, which is in the *Ludus Coventriae* and the Prologue to the Digby *Killing of the Children* and nowhere else; second, the fact that the Digby prologue refers to the play of the shepherds having been played the previous year and the epilogue promises the disputation with the doctors for next year tallies with the preceding and following plays found in the *Ludus Coventriae*; and, last, the fact that the double quatrain of the Digby play is matched in the play immediately following in the *Ludus Coventriae* —the play of Christ in the Temple. In this connection Patch also makes much of the 'tumbling' metre found both in *Ludus Coventriae* and the Digby play. However, the very similarity of versification among the East Anglian plays which Patch notes detracts from the force of his argument. He seems to ignore the fact that, in spite of the prologue, the order of the episodes in the play is not that of the *Ludus Coventriae*. He further ignores the three rhyme royal stanzas in the Digby play (to say nothing of the three that were cancelled) in his discussion of dissimilar forms in the plays. And, finally, the date of 1512 on the manuscript of *The Killing of the Children* is over forty years after the *Ludus Coventriae* date of 1468 which is found at the end of the Purification play, which, according to Patch, was substituted for the Digby version.

The staging of *The Killing of the Children*, considered either as one play or as two, must have been quite simple. The stage directions call for a place, and there is no indication that any stages or carts were called for other than two, one for Herod's palace at Jerusalem with its temple and gods which must fall down, and the temple at which Simeon receives the Christ child. Much of the play's effect depends upon simplicity and juxtaposition, as when, following l. 232, the knights and Watkyn walk about the playing-area until Mary and Joseph escape into Egypt. The play could have been performed under almost any circumstances, in a market square, or a broad street, or green. It would appear to have been, like so many of the East Anglian plays, the text of a travelling company.

One problem confronting this interpretation, however, is the list of players on f. 157ᵛ, for the scribe uses 'pleyers' rather than parts or roles. Altogether seventeen are called for, and this number accounts for only one virgin, whereas we know that they were at least plural, and in the directions (following l. 464) we are told that they are '*as many as a man wylle*'. Presumably then, seventeen is a conservative estimate. There is not much room for doubling, for Joseph and Mary appear in both parts, and it does not seem likely that the battling mothers of the first part should become the virgins of the second. The virgins would perhaps have been village girls collected for the occasion. The large number of players for so small a play does give some support to Craig's theory that it was part of a local annual religious drama.

5. WISDOM

The Manuscript

The manuscript of MS Digby 133's part of the morality play *Wisdom* (also called *Mind, Will, and Understanding*) occupies the final twelve leaves, ff. 158ʳ–169ᵛ. The leaves are a single gathering, quarto, sewn between ff. 163 and 164, and measure $8\frac{1}{2}'' \times 6\frac{1}{8}''$. Our manuscript is probably half its original length (the Macro full-text manuscript of *Wisdom* is two twelve-leaf gatherings). It is clear that a second gathering of up to twelve leaves was lost from the manuscript at some time before MS Digby 133 was put together in its present form. The last page and first page of the Digby *Wisdom* are quite dirty, and this condition would suggest that the manuscript had been in its fragmentary state for some time before being included in MS Digby 133. This inference is supported by the fact that the pattern of insect damage in the left margins of the first three leaves is not matched by any corresponding damage in the later leaves of *The Killing of the Children* manuscript, which immediately precedes it.

Again the watermark is a hand, but with laced wrist, a cross on the palm, fingers together and thumb apart. It is surmounted by a five-pointed star. The mark is No. 46 in Heawood, who suggests a date before 1506.[1] It is found widely in the second half of the fifteenth century, and is encountered among the Paston papers. The mark is on ff. 162 (bottom of mark), 165 (top), and 167 and 169 (almost all the mark is present on each of the last two). It would seem, therefore, that three homogeneous folio sheets made up the gathering of twelve.

The manuscript is in quite good condition. There is some staining and a few leaves have been repaired, and there is the usual

---

[1] 'Sources of Early English Paper Supply', *The Library*, ix (1929), 294.

fraying of the outer margins, but there is little loss of text. A few insect holes are in the first three leaves, affecting, but not causing the loss of, some words. Some spots of green ink are on ff. 160–1, but again there is no loss of text.

Our scribe was a careful workman who made relatively few errors. In spite of Collier's assertion that he was the same man who wrote the Macro full-text manuscript[1] the two scribes are very different in style. The Digby scribe is, however, apparently the same man who wrote the manuscript of *The Killing of the Children*. The style of the scribe in *Wisdom* is in general more formal than his style in *The Killing of the Children*, and the minims are less splayed. The manuscript of *Wisdom* gives throughout the impression of being somewhat older than that of *The Killing of the Children*, an impression which is supported by what evidence the paper can provide. As one studies the hands, however, and observes that as the *Wisdom* scribe warms to his task and his writing becomes less formal, the writing more and more resembles that of *The Killing of the Children*. Though there remain some slight differences, such as the tops of the *g*, all the basic letter formations seem identical. The description of the main hand of *The Killing of the Children* therefore applies to the hand of *Wisdom* as well. The *Wisdom* scribe distinguishes *þ* and *y*, and uses the normal abbreviations. His spelling practice suggests that barred final *ll* should be expanded to *-lle*, flourished final *r* to *-re*, a dotted arc above a final consonant to *-e* or double final consonant and *-e* (e.g. *thanne*, *worshippe*), as in *The Killing of the Children*. Abbreviations of the genitive and the plural of nouns are expanded to the scribe's favoured *-es* spelling, though he also used *-ys* and *-is*.

The scribe has written throughout in brown ink, averaging 30–32 lines per page. The directions are in red ink, and normally are in the centre of the page; the names of speakers are in the right margins. Speeches are divided by lines and the rhymes are bracketed. There is little punctuation, but a raised dot is occasionally used to mark the caesura, and virgules occur in the directions. At the top of the first page, f. 158ʳ, is 'MB' in Myles Blomefylde's hand. At the bottom recto of the first four leaves are the numerals i–iv in a later hand. There are no catchwords or decorations.

---

[1] J. P. Collier, *The History of Dramatic Poetry to the Time of Shakespeare*, ii (London, 1831), 235, 287.

We would judge that the Digby half-text of *Wisdom* is a some-what earlier product of our scribe than *The Killing of the Children*, which carries the date 1512. We would, on the basis of style of writing and the watermark of the paper, suggest a date of 1490–1500 for the Digby *Wisdom*. This dating, if valid, would put the Digby copy a little later than the full Macro text which seems older on grounds of style, and, if its previous owner was Abbot Richard Hyngham, who was abbot of Bury 1474–9, is very probably fifteen or twenty years older than the Digby manuscript.

Our text is clearly a copy rather than an original, as is made obvious by some errors of anticipation. But in general it is a sound copy, a much more careful one than the Macro text. The relation between these texts is of some importance. Professor Eccles says little on this point, remarking only that the Digby is independent of the Macro text because the Digby has five lines and a direction not found in the Macro.[1] However, the extra direction in the Digby was added by a later hand. Four of the five lines missing in Macro were lost for obvious reasons. Lines 448, 496, 600, and 720 were lost because the scribe of Macro's exemplar must have been inconsistent—as indeed those of both the Macro and the Digby are —in placing the tail-rhyming lines to the right of the page. All four of these are tail-rhyming lines that the Macro scribe failed to pick up. The fifth, l. 66, was lost when the Macro scribe was moving from the bottom of one page to the top of the next. Textually, it might almost be maintained that the Macro could have been copied from the Digby. And indeed, Bevington in his introduction to the Folger Facsimile edition of the Macro plays[2] argues that this would have been possible. However, not only does the Macro manuscript appear to be older than the Digby, but there are also at least three instances in the texts which make it very difficult to believe that either scribe could have acquired his individual reading from the other: l. 296 Macro 'That þe sensualyte þey brynge not yow behynde' and Digby 'That the sensualite thei bryng not to mynde'; l. 421 Macro 'I kan not belewe thys ys trew' and Digby 'I can beleve that ye say is trewe'; l. 548 Macro 'Many a soule to hell I wyn' and Digby 'Many a soule from hevyn I wynne' (MS originally 'to hevyn', corrected by later hand). Both versions of the

---

[1] *The Macro Plays*, p. xxx.

[2] *The Macro Plays*, The Folger Facsimiles Manuscript Series I (Washington, D.C., 1972), p. xix.

C

three lines make sense in context. The differences could have resulted from a common corrected original in which the direction of the alteration was not entirely clear. This is, we think, what happened. The Macro and Digby texts are very close. The differences between them are almost all simple, hurried copying lapses, mostly on the part of the Macro scribe. The closeness of the texts, and the possible Bury St. Edmunds association of most of the plays in both manuscripts, leads us to conclude that the most probable explanation of the relationship between them is that both were copied from a common exemplar. We cannot assume for such plays the existence of whole families of manuscripts; it is quite unlikely that more than a handful of copies of any of these plays was ever made.[1]

Some peculiarities shared by Macro and Digby which point to a common exemplar are: l. 58, in which both have *specially* when the rhyme demands *speciall* (the Digby scribe later corrected to *specialle*); l. 175, in which both Macro and Digby have *euer* when the correct reading must have been *neuer*; l. 338, where both have *whan* for *whom*; l. 378, where both Macro and Digby read *proyut* for *proue*; l. 395, where both omit the *er* abbreviation in *perissh*; l. 679, where both read *ther* for correct *thei*; l. 716, in which both read *hestys* when the rhyme demands *hettys* (to which Eccles emends the Macro text). Another probable instance is in l. 543, where *in* appears to be omitted in both texts.

An interesting curiosity is in l. 511, which in Macro as Eccles prints it is 'hanip la plu joly!' and in Digby as we print it is '. . . and it happe la plu joly!'. Furnivall printed the Macro reading as *hamp*, which we believe correct, because what must have happened was that the exemplar of both manuscripts used an abbreviation which the Digby scribe also used and the Macro did not, an arc over a dot placed above the last letter of a word to indicate a doubled (or additional) final consonant plus a final -*e* (the Macro scribe occasionally draws a straight line over a dot, but this is always a simple nasal abbreviation). The exemplar probably

---

[1] The case of the Chester cycle, because it survives wholly or partially in eight texts, would seem to be an exception. But all except two of the texts postdate the active life of the plays, and would appear to be copies in response to an antiquarian interest. See R. M. Lumiansky and David Mills, eds., *The Chester Mystery Cycle, A Facsimile of MS Bodley 175*, Leeds Texts and Monographs, Medieval Drama Facsimiles I, gen. ed. A. C. Cawley (University of Leeds School of English, 1973), pp. vii–xi.

had a dotted arc over the *p* of *hap*, and the Macro scribe took it for
the usual nasal abbreviation, and so expanded the word to *hamp*,
having by oversight omitted the previous *and it*. The Digby scribe
kept the mark, for it accorded with his own practice, and he saw
no need to expand and make 'sense' of it (Furnivall printed *hape*
in his Digby edition). The Digby reading, properly expanded,
therefore retains the correct reading of the line, 'We wille be
fressh, and it hap*pe* (if it should happen) la plu joly!'. Eccles tries
to make sense of the Macro *hamp* and reads the third minim as an
i; the result is a rare Old French word *hanip*, meaning wine cup,
which makes no good sense in context. Differences in practice
between the Macro and Digby scribes account for other variations;
the Digby scribe distinguishes between *þ* and *y*, and the Macro
does not, for instance, and we have the reason for Digby's getting
the correct *yougthe* in l. 18 against Macro's *thowte*, and *fayre* in
l. 69 against Macro's *father*.[1]

As to the textual quality of the two copies, Eccles says only that
the readings of the Digby must be taken into account. This he does
extensively, adopting Digby readings in over sixty cases, and
maintaining Macro readings in several other instances in which
Digby readings seem clearly better, e.g. Macro *Thys* (l. 289) vs.
Digby *Thus*; Macro *tempte* (l. 345) vs. Digby *tempte hym*; Macro's
For, for . . . vs. Digby's *But for* . . . (l. 373); Macro's *I ma vowe* vs.
Digby's *I avowe* (l. 625). There are, of course, instances of superior
Macro readings (e.g. in ll. 240, 260, 369, 403, 455, 497, 652, 663,
and 679) where the Digby scribe has dropped a word or miscopied.
But the Digby is on the whole very much superior, and this is not
surprising given the appearances of the two; Digby is neatly laid
out, formally written, whereas the Macro seems to have been a
hurried job.

And, finally, both texts have five-line tail-rhyming stanzas where
one would expect the normal six-line stanzas; we postulate, but
do not number, missing lines after ll. 552 and 578.

The chief value of the Digby text is as a corrective of the Macro full
text, and therefore we do not emend in the interest of improving
the Digby text, but only in such instances as are obviously the result
of scribal slips (such as missing abbreviations) or in a few instances
in which words or parts of words have been lost in the margins.

[1] The latter point was previously noted by N. Davis, in his review of the
Folger facsimile of the Macro Plays, *N. & Q.* ccxx (1975), 78–9.

Versification

The stanzaic form is, of course, the same as that of the Macro text. The double quatrains and the tail-rhyming *aaabcccb* stanzas dominate. All but ten of the 145 stanzas in the whole play, as Eccles points out, have eight lines. Eccles observes as well that the tail-rhyming stanzas are introduced in the Lucifer or Lucifer-dominated scenes. We have also noted this pattern in the *Mary Magdalen* and other East Anglian drama. The basic four-stress pattern of the lines also changes as the scenes of the temptations begin, with Lucifer's speeches having a much less regular stress pattern, sometimes dropping to two and rising to five or six. Alliteration, not a feature of the verse generally, likewise occurs in the Lucifer-dominated scenes.

Language

As one would expect, the language of the *Wisdom* fragment is the same as that of *The Killing of the Children*, written mostly by the same scribe. The language of the Digby text is also close to that of the Macro, the chief difference being that the Digby scribe does not represent OE. *sc* in *shall* and *should* by *x* as does the Macro. The dialect is East Midland with East Anglian features.

Characteristics suggestive of East Anglia:

The reflex of OE *i* and also of *y*, though normally spelled *i* or *y*, does appear as *e* in a few words: *wete* (know) 1; *mende* 55, 183; *hedyr*, *thedyr* 199; *knett(e)* rhymed on *dette* 194, 196, rhymed on *sett* 229, 231; *levith* 495; *besy* 406. Words from OF illustrate the same tendency, e.g. *meroure* 31.

The reflex of OE *-ht* is spelled so as to indicate loss of the fricative: the normal spelling *-ght* is extended to words without historical *-ht*, e.g. *perfight* 56, *whight* (white), s.d. following 16, and *abought* rhymed on *dowte* 464, 467.

The reflex of OE *hw-* appears as *w-* in *wiche* 5, 136, 269, etc., twelve instances, against *whiche* 178 only. Two other spellings found in East Anglia are: *moch(e)* 414, 482, 600, etc., and *ony* 351, 618.

Other points of interest in pronunciation:

The final unstressed *-e* is written erratically and was undoubtedly lost; this is confirmed in rhymes: *lete* with *grett* 49, 51, *blisse* with *is* 70, 72, *cam, blame, dame* 112, 113, 115.

The reflexes of OE *ǣ¹*, *ǣ²*, *ēa*, *ēo*, *e* are all represented by *e* and rhymed together: *sprede, wede, dede* (*deed*), *hed*, (*heed*), *nede, fede* rhymed 453–5, 457–9; *mede, hede* 672, 676, *nede, spede* 504, 508.

The reflex of OE *ā* is normally *o*: *go* 319, 371, etc.; *more* 97, 415, etc. (but *mare* rhyming on *welefare, spare, care, spare, hare* 735–7, 739–41); *lore* 418 rhyming on *thore, more, euermore, before, bore*, 413–15, 417–19.

The reflex of OE *a* before lengthening groups is generally *o*: *brondes* 114, *longe* 242, *lombe* 490, *londe* 732; but *hand* in the first s.d. and s.d. after 692, and *lande, stand, hande* rhyming on *wynnand, reynand, vsande* 677, 678, 681, 682, 683.

The main points of verbal inflexion are:

Pres. indic. 2 sg. is *-est* or *-ist*. 3 sg. is generally *-eth, -yth, -ith*: *accordith* 5, *strengtheth* 55, *enduryth* 532, etc. The ending *-s* appears only in one rhyme series: *telles, dwelles, compelles, spelles*, 270, 272, 273, 275; *hase* is rhymed on *deface, place, face*, 174, 176, 177, 179, and on *grace, lace, mase* 575, 576, 578, 579. These last indicate that the *-s* of *has* was not voiced. The 3 pl. is usually without ending, but a few examples with *-n* occur: *ben(e)*, 56, 364.

The imperative has no ending.

The past participles of weak verbs have *-ed, -yd* endings, but there is one *-eth* (*applyeth* 178). About half the strong verb past participles end in *-n*; examples without ending are *take* 240, *spoke* 64. The present participle ending is normally *-yng*, but there is a rhyme series *wynnand, reynand, vsande*, 681–3.

The infinitive is normally without ending, the *-n* occurring only in *sene* (see) 59.

The genitive and plural morpheme of nouns is *-es, -ys, -is*, and *-s*, but *bren* (brows) 196, and *children* 406.

Of personal pronouns, the 2 pl. nominative *ye* is distinguished from the dative-accusative *you* (*yow, yowe*) consistently. The 3 pl. *thei* is the nominative, *ther(e)* the genitive, and *hem* the dative-accusative; a single instance of *them*, 68, is found.

Of interest in the vocabulary, a few 'aureate' terms occur (in

addition to those remarked by Eccles): *pawsacion* (pause)
463 is recorded in *OED* only from Lydgate to Digby;
reporture 265 recorded by *OED* in Digby and Medwall;
retenaunce (retinue) 686 is recorded from Langland to
Digby.

Sources of the Play

We have nothing to add to the thorough treatment by W. K.
Smart and Eccles.[1]

The Nature and Staging of the Play

Wisdom is an elaborate moral and psychological play in which
the contest between Christ and Lucifer for the possession of man's
soul is dramatized. Wisdom is Christ, and begins the play by
addressing the audience upon his nature, and then speaks to the
character *Anima*, the human soul, upon the significance of Wisdom
for him, and the nature of his salvation. The parts played by the
three powers of the Soul, the Mind, the Will, and the Understanding, are explained to *Anima*. But the happy co-operation of
these 'mights' is interrupted by the appearance of Lucifer, who
offers a convincing analysis of the *vita mixta* as opposed to the *vita
contemplativa*. The Mind, the Will, and the Understanding are
unable to combat this, or to comprehend a *vita mixta* which is
not wholly given over to the pleasures of the world. The incapacity
of man for true moderation is well perceived and demonstrated by
the playwright. The Mind is given over to the abuses of Maintenance, or personal power in defiance of the law; Understanding is
given over to achieving power by abusing the law (manipulation of
the courts); and Will to the satisfaction of the desires of the flesh.
These three activities are mimed in an elaborate masque or dumb-
show in the middle of the play, and at the beginning of the mime
of the gallants and prostitutes, the Digby text ends. In the Macro
text the powers of the Soul are recalled to their allegiance by the
intervention of Wisdom, and the play ends happily for all but
Lucifer.

Wisdom is a play in which pageantry clearly has a large role.
The description of costumes is elaborate in the extreme. But we
must not be misled by the lack of physical action into dismissing

[1] W. K. Smart, *Some English and Latin Sources and Parallels for the Morality
of Wisdom* (Menasha, Wisconsin, 1912), and *The Macro Plays*, pp. xxxii–xxxiv.

Wisdom as a dull play. The dialogue between Lucifer and the three mights of the Soul is clever and frequently witty; the eternal themes are expressed as issues of the day and must have found a receptive audience. Some attempt to achieve an audience participation as well is indicated by the Devil's taking a '*shrewd boy*' with him (s.d. after l. 550) as he goes his way '*cryeng*'.

W. K. Smart long ago made a strong case for *Wisdom*'s having been a monastic play designed for performance before an audience of monks.[1] His evidence was drawn from the strongly theological nature of the play, the first part of which is derived from the kind of mystical and devotional treatises (the *Orologium Sapientiae* and the *Scale of Perfection*) which would have been the ordinary reading of the monks. He also thought that the opposed ways of life, the *vita contemplativa* and the *vita mixta* as presented in the play, argued monkish interests, and that Lucifer's suggestion that they 'Leve your nyse chastyte, and take a wyff!' smack strongly of monastic problems. Molloy argued against this interpretation, pointing out the weakness of assuming a monastic background in view of the apparent employment of women in the play, the lack of Latin in the stage directions, etc., and suggested that *Wisdom* may have been acted by students at an Inn of Court.[2] Merle Fifield has written of it as a professional play which could have been part of the repertory of a travelling company.[3] Against this, Eccles points out that it would probably have had banns if it had been a travelling play.[4] Chambers' suggestion[5] that it was a school play has no evidence to support it.

We do know that in all probability it was acted; the presence of 'cutting' indications in the play (the '*va . . . cat*', also in the Macro manuscript) strongly suggests this. The existence of two copies of the play also lends strength to the probability of *Wisdom*'s having been a live play, not a closet drama for meditation. Its association with the monastery at Bury need not argue that it was ever acted by the monks, but it is at least possible. Eccles' suggestion that it might have been presented by men and women of a town is a good

[1] Op. cit., p. 86.

[2] J. J. Molloy, *A Theological Interpretation of the Moral Play Wisdom, Who is Christ* (Washington, D.C., 1952), p. 84.

[3] 'The Use of Doubling and Extras in *Wisdom*', *Ball State University Forum*, vi (1965), 65–8.

[4] Op. cit, pp. xxxiv–xxxv.

[5] *The Medieval Stage*, ii (Oxford, 1903), 438.

one,[1] but it need not rule out a monastic association as well. Such a play might have been a co-operative venture in a town like Bury. This would be consonant with the sparseness of Latin directions, the monkish themes, the presence of women (the parts could have been acted by boys, but the directions describe them as 'matrons'), and the large number of parts, thirty-eight in all, as Fifield counted them.[2] But the matter must remain quite indefinite. As Fifield pointed out, doubling could well have reduced the number of players actually required to six professionals, a musician, and a number of townspeople for the non-speaking roles, and so we cannot rule out the possibility that *Wisdom* was a professional play, not too unlike *Mankind*, performed by a touring group (the non-survival of banns would not be surprising; *Mankind* has none either). The fact that the scribe of the Digby *Wisdom* wrote most of *The Killing of the Children* would make this possibility a little stronger.

As to the actual staging, we are little better off in our knowledge. There is no clear indication in the directions that there were stages, mansion-houses, tents, or whatever. We cannot rule out any method of performance, but it would seem that, originally at least, the play was designed for a minimum of scenery and staging. The characters simply walk on and off a single playing area. The sort of spectacular setting which would have been provided by a hell stage or Lucifer's throne seems to be provided instead by costume. What little we can adduce from the directions would seem to suggest that the play was originally performed in a bare area, like a hall or the nave of a church.

6. PREVIOUS EDITIONS OF THE DIGBY PLAYS

The first appearance in print of any of these plays was that of Thomas Hawkins' edition of *The Killing of the Children* in his *The Origins of the English Drama* (Oxford, 1773). The text was poorly transcribed, and there is little commentary or glossing. The edition of all four plays by Thomas Sharp for the Abbotsford Club in *Ancient Mysteries from the Digby Manuscripts* (Edinburgh, 1835) was an ambitious undertaking which attempted to provide a diplomatic text with an extended introduction and glossary. However, the text contains many errors and silent emendations. Sharp also began the practice of printing the plays in the order *The*

---

[1] Op. cit., p. xxxv.   [2] Op. cit., p. 66.

Killing of the Children, The Conversion of St. Paul, Mary Magdalen,
and *Wisdom*. W. Marriott included *The Killing of the Children* in
A Collection of English Miracle Plays or Mysteries (Basel, 1838),
basing his text upon Hawkins. *The Killing of the Children* in
Hawkins' text made another appearance in *The Journal of Sacred
Literature and Biblical Record*, NS x (1867), 413–29, together with
a few notes on Biblical allusions and some interesting observations
on the Norfolk–Suffolk dialect. F. J. Furnivall's New Shakspere
Society edition of 1882, which was reprinted by the Early English
Text Society as No. 70 in its Extra Series (1896, reprinted 1930,
1967), gave for the first time a reliable text, but little glossary or
commentary. Furnivall followed the Sharp order of the plays, argu-
ing that the massacre of the Innocents would precede the other
celebrations in the ecclesiastical calendar, as if they were all part
of a cycle. But the plays seem to have no clear relation to one
another, and we present them as they occur in the manuscript.
Furnivall's text of *The Conversion of St. Paul* has one more line
than ours; his text of *Mary Magdalen* has one more line; and his
text of *Wisdom* has two more lines than ours. These discrepancies
are discussed in the notes.

A. W. Pollard's *English Miracle Plays, Moralities, and Interludes*
(Oxford, 1890) printed 375 lines of *Mary Magdalen* from Furnivall's
text, but corrected several errors in Furnivall and added some very
useful notes. Though J. M. Manly's text of *The Conversion of St.
Paul* in his *Specimens of the Pre-Shakspearean Drama*, i (Boston,
1897) was that of Furnivall, he considerably improved it with a
number of plausible emendations, some at the suggestion of G. L.
Kittredge. J. Q. Adams used Manly's version of Furnivall's text
of *The Conversion of St. Paul* in his *Chief Pre-Shakespearean
Drama* (Boston, 1924), but made a number of emendations of a
questionable nature, so that his text is not so good as Manly's. He
also printed the first 992 lines of *Mary Magdalen* from Furnivall,
making a number of useful suggestions. The Manly–Adams text
of *The Conversion of St. Paul* was printed in a normalized version
by F. J. Ticknor in *Earlier English Drama from Robin Hood to
Everyman* (New York, 1929), and he also printed most of Furnivall's text of the Digby *Wisdom* fragment. L. E. Lewis's University
of Wisconsin Ph.D. thesis of 1963 presented a new and considerable
edition of *Mary Magdalen* with very useful notes. *The Killing of
the Children, The Conversion of St. Paul,* and *Mary Magdalen*

were edited by Fr. V. M. Devlin as a Ph.D. thesis for University College, London, in 1966. We have examined this work, but have been unable to make use of it. In 1975 David Bevington produced a new anthology, *Medieval Drama* (Boston), designed to replace the Adams text. He has used the Manly–Adams text of *The Conversion of St. Paul* with some emendation, and has printed the whole of *Mary Magdalen*, basing the first half on Adams. Though he has improved punctuation, he has unfortunately introduced many new errors so that Furnivall's text is much to be preferred. Glynne Wickham produced a modernized text of *The Conversion of St. Paul* for students' use in his *English Moral Interludes* (London, 1976).

A rotograph of the manuscript of *Mary Magdalen* was published by the Modern Language Society of America in 1929.

As far as we know the only one of the Digby plays to have been translated into another language is *The Killing of the Children*, published as *Lichtmess oder der Bethlehemitische Kindermord: Heiligenschauspiel von John Parfre*, translated and introduced by Dr Fricke (Berlin, 1911).

7. CHRIST'S BURIAL AND CHRIST'S RESURRECTION FROM MS E MUSEO 160

Manuscript

The manuscript in which the plays that we call *Christ's Burial* and *Christ's Resurrection* are found is No. 3692 in the *Summary Catalogue of Western Manuscripts in the Bodleian Library*. Its shelf mark is e Museo 160 (*olim* 226), and it was acquired by the Bodleian 'before 1680'.[1] It is a quarto manuscript bound in seventeenth-century calf, since re-backed; the leaves are numbered in modern pencil, iv + 176. The four leaves at the beginning numbered in roman are blank; they were originally a gathering of eight, but the first four have been clipped to stubs. What would have been f. 173 was also cut close, and a blank gathering of four added at the end; these were numbered ff. 173–6 as a continuation of the book. Both gatherings of blanks were apparently added to the original manuscript book when it was re-bound in the seventeenth century. Another leaf, which would have been f. 61, was also cut to a stub, and left unnumbered, resulting in gathering F's having only eleven

[1] ii, Pt. 2, p. 732.

leaves. The collation, considering only the 172 (of 174) leaves of the original manuscript *as rebound*, is: A^8 B^{12} C^{12} D^{14} E^{12} F^{11} (of 12) G^{12} H^{12} I^{12} J^{10} K^{12} L^{12} M^{12} N^{12} $O^{9(of\ 10)}$. A special case is J, an artificial and disorganized gathering of ten, formed when the book was re-bound; this will be discussed in its proper place. The size of the leaves is roughly $8\frac{7}{10}'' \times 6\frac{1}{10}''$. The plays occupy the last three gatherings, ff. 140–72.

We will refer to the plays separately, though they are two parts of one religious drama, or acted meditation. Scholars have referred to them both as two plays and as one, but because there are some interesting differences between the two parts, we have decided to treat them separately and number the lines independently. To be absolutely consistent, we perhaps should treat the prologue individually as well, but we have, for convenience, numbered its lines with those of the first play.

The plays in MS e Museo 160 have been edited twice, by Thomas Wright and J. C. Halliwell, *Reliquiae Antiquae*, ii (London, 1843), pp. 124–61, and by F. J. Furnivall, *The Digby Mysteries*, New Shakspere Society (London, 1882), pp. 169–228. The latter was republished for the Early English Text Society, Extra Series 70, in 1896 as *The Digby Plays*, and reprinted in 1930 and 1967. The first edition by Wright and Halliwell was extremely inaccurate but printed the text so as to make clear the stanzaic structure. Furnivall's edition was accurate, but printed the verse without generally making the stanzaic pattern clear. Furnivall asserted that the plays 'evidently once belonged in the Digby MS 133',[1] i.e. that containing *The Conversion of St. Paul, Mary Magdalen, The Killing of the Children*, and half of *Wisdom*. This statement, as will be seen in our discussion of MS e Museo 160, is clearly not correct.[2] Our text contains 1,628 lines (including the prologue), or three fewer than Furnivall's. He numbered the four lines announcing the end of the first and the beginning of the second play, which are not bracketed and do not rhyme; we have not numbered them. Furnivall omitted one line of the second play, l. 364, numbered one line twice (his 971–2), and failed to number one Latin line in *CR*, l. 691, which is bracketed by the writer as a verse.

---

[1] p. vii.

[2] We have previously discussed this matter: D. C. Baker and J. L. Murphy, 'The Bodleian MS *e Mus*. 160 *Burial* and *Resurrection* and the Digby Plays', *RES*, NS xix (1968), 290–3.

Our discussion of the manuscript will be much more extensive than normally would be required, but in view of the important relationship between the plays and the other contents of the book, which have received little attention, we think that this is justified. Approximate provenance and date of the plays will emerge from this examination.

The bulk of the book, ff. 1ʳ–108ʳ, contains an interesting work, half meditative prayer and half chronicle.[1] It is apparently the composition of the scribe, who has based it, he tells us on f. 92ʳ, on Rolewinck's *Fasciculus Temporum*:

> It is to be knowene that this last hundreth ȝere,
> which I call the xv hundrethe, is not complete after
> the boke callit *Fasciculus Temporum*, for that endes
> in the ȝere of our lord mcccc threscor and fourteyne.

The writer's original idea was to provide a series of images of piety from the Old Testament, beginning with Adam and Eve. He intended to provide a drawing of each patriarch and prophet, and beneath, a brief verse summary of his life, and a meditative prayer.[2] The plan was clearly to follow and elaborate the condensed, almost outline form of the *Fasciculus*. The writer begins by citing Jerome (f. 1ʳ) as authority for the belief that the Old Testament patriarchs should be regarded as saints. His plan is plain:

> Now in this present treyte ar made into ynglishe
> meter a prayere to ychon of the said holy faders
> patriarkes and prophetes, with a pictor of þe sam.

The result will be a combination of prayer and chronicle:

> Therfor this trete is made in maner of prayere
> that the reder lese no tym, for yf he dispose

---

[1] In C. Brown and R. H. Robbins, *The Index of Middle English Verse* (New York, 1943), p. 21, this is listed as No. 119 and described as 'a series of ten prayers to the Patriarchs—92 lines'. For the *Supplement*, eds. Robbins and J. Cutler (Lexington, Ky., 1965), the entry has been accurately expanded, though no mention is made of the drawings.

[2] It is not exactly an emblem work, but bears some resemblance to the sort of meditation-help described by T. W. Ross, 'Five Fifteenth-Century "Emblem" Verses from Brit. Mus. Addit. MS. 37049', *Speculum*, xxxii (1957), 274–82. Ross's manuscript is, like ours, Carthusian and northern. It also contains a history of the Charterhouses, a *Horologium*, and an epitome of Sir John Mandeville's travels. This manuscript is discussed by Woolf in *The English Religious Lyric in the Middle Ages* (Oxford, 1968), *passim*.

hym þerto in the redinge, he shalle praye devowtly
and lern gud vertues and haue a knawlege of the
cowrse of holy scripture which God graunt at his pleasure.

The prayers are in the form of poems, in four-stress lines of an
abab bcbc cdcd pattern of rhyme which, in the longer prayers,
extends to a great and ingenious length. There are occasional
prose passages to interrupt the flow of the verse.

The first prayer is to Adam, and the first man and his consort
are represented in a rough line drawing in a box which takes up
half the page. The second is to Abel. Only two drawings were in
fact executed, on ff. 1ᵛ and 2ʳ, though boxes were provided on each
page through f. 26ʳ, after which this part of the plan was abandoned.
Some of the empty boxes are filled by a later hand with those crude
cartoons which inhabit so many manuscripts and early books.
The prayers and historical accounts of the patriarchs continue
through the Old Testament and are extended through the saints
of the New Testament. The idea of the book is then broadened to
become a chronicle of the saints in the centuries after Christ. As
this progresses, more of the writer's attention is given to the details
and legends of history, the saints being frequently relegated to
brief summaries and prayers at the end of each century. By the
time that the Middle Ages are reached, the prayers have been
subordinated to the chronicle, which is filled with complaint about
the times. The fourteenth and fifteenth centuries in particular are
interesting. The writer's remarks on the plagues of the fourteenth
century give something of the flavour of the work:

> So grete a pestilence felle by chaunce,
> That to the whik it was fulle hard
> To bery the dede; so felle it farde
> That in many townes was non wonnynge.
> O Jhesu, to chasty this warlde
> With thy rod oft thus thou dos it dinge!
> In hevyn was seyn a marvolus thinge,
> Which callit is the candille rownd.
> Anone after com foloynge
> þe cruciflagellatores vnsownde.
> Opon tham-selfe made thei many wound,
> Betinge with sharp whippes sore.   (f. 89ᵛ)

At f. 102ʳ the writer ceases his meditative chronicle and begins
a list of the priors of the 'hed howse of Carthusia'. The terms in

which he discusses these priors and their deeds make it perfectly clear that the writer himself was a member of the order. He refers to 'our customes and our statutes clene' (f. 103ʳ), and smugly contemplates Christ's clear preference for the Carthusians:

> Lovid be þou Jhesu for this store.
> It semys thou lufes Charthusia more
> Than certen othere places he[r]e,
> That so gud preletes ordeyns þerfore.   (f. 103ᵛ)

Our poet concludes his chronicle with a Jeremiad against the abuses of his own day and against the infidels, and cries out to Christ for help. He ends, a little sadly, on f. 108ʳ; 'This endit the viiiᵗʰ day afor Christmemes[se] . . . ȝer of our Lord Jhesu MD and xviii wher the . . . matere failes.' (Some loss of words caused by damage to the leaf.) Although the *Fasciculus Temporum*, as we have seen, provided the framework for this remarkable prayer and chronicle, and in many prose passages scattered throughout the chronicle Rolewinck is simply translated, nevertheless our writer has achieved the not inconsiderable feat of composing over 6,000 lines of verse elaborating the material gleaned from Rolewinck. He has frequently added material from other sources, particularly in the last three centuries. Though he occasionally gets a stanza pattern wrong, he makes remarkably few mistakes. These he usually corrects at the bottom of the page. That this was largely original composition is not only clear from what the writer tells us, but also from the fact that he occasionally leaves part of a page blank, making a note to himself to fill it in when he comes across other saints or events.

The chronicle is throughout in one hand, though the colour of the ink varies from brown to black, and the size of the hand varies.

On f. 108ᵛ is found a part of a poem on the events of the year 1520; it deals with the Field of Cloth of Gold, and the various natural disasters and bits of gossip of the year, and this is continued on f. 114ʳ after intervening romance fragments, concluding with the story of a rich London merchant who hanged himself, a 'deth vnsound', as the writer puts it. Most of this 'poem' was published by Wright and Halliwell in the same volume with the *Burial* and *Resurrection* (pp. 117–18), but its leaves, like those around them, have been badly mouse-nibbled with loss of several lines. It is in the handwriting of the previous 108 folios, and does not seem to be a separate poem, but rather a belated continuation of the earlier work.

Part of a romance of Sir John Mandeville and Sir Marc of Venice occupies the intervening leaves between ff. 108 and 114, and a piece of the romance follows, on f. 115ʳ. These leaves are disarranged, the proper order, as demonstrated by M. C. Seymour,[1] being as follows: ff. 113ᵛ, 109ʳ, 109ᵛ, 110ʳ, 110ᵛ, 111ʳ, 111ᵛ, 112ʳ, 112ᵛ, 115ʳ. Blank or pasted over with a supporting leaf are ff. 113ʳ, 114ᵛ, and 115ᵛ. This portion of the manuscript may be in a different hand from that of the chronicle, but there are many points of similarity between them, and there is a strong possibility that they are the same. Seymour states that these leaves are certainly not a part of the original MS e Museo 160,[2] and they may not be, for they have clearly been organized in their present state at a date later than the composition of the whole manuscript, probably when the book was re-bound in the seventeenth century. However, the romance is in the same continuing quatrains as found in the chronicle, the capitals are rubricated and the rhymes bracketed in the same way, and the subjects of the romance are such as would have interested the writer of the chronicle, who mentions Sir John on f. 88, and has several references to the 'Gret Sowdan' who figures in the romance.

The story of the romance is thoroughly Christian in tone, and is in keeping with a dominant theme of the later chronicle, which is fear of the infidel. It would seem possible that, if the romance folios had not been previously associated with what is now MS e Museo 160, the later bookbinder, working with materials from the same sources and noting the similarity of writing, assumed that the romance materials belonged to the same book, and so included them. Our opinion is that the hands of the two works are the same, and that very likely they were both originally in the same book. Subsequently, the book was broken, the leaves containing the romance, the last three leaves of the chronicle, and the leaves of the 'poem' of 1520, were badly nibbled by mice (in rather similar damage-patterns), and some leaves were lost. The seventeenth-century bookbinder pieced together what loose leaves

---

[1] 'Mandeville and Marco Polo: a Stanzaic Fragment', *AUMLA* xx (1964), 39–52. Part of the fragment had previously been printed by W. C. Hazlitt as 'The Commonyng of Ser John Mandevelle and the gret Souden', in *Remains of the Early Popular Poetry of England*, i (London, 1864), 153–8.

[2] Ibid., p. 39.

from the middle of the book he could find, and bound them, unfortunately in the wrong order, back into the book. These loose leaves, ff. 106ʳ–15, are the 'J' gathering of the collation.

On f. 116ʳ, in the same writing as the chronicle, begins an English translation of the hundred meditations appended to '. . . that buke callit the Cloke of Eternalle Wisdom . . .'. These were a popular supplement to Suso's *Horologium Sapientiae*. The present translation is clearly not by the writer of the chronicle, for he ascribes to previous translators two of the prefaces. This work continues to f. 136ʳ.

At f. 136ᵛ is found, in a different hand, the *Fifteen Articles of the Passion*, beginning 'It is rede in þe miracles of our Lady . . .'. This item is not listed in the *Summary Catalogue* description of MS e Museo 160. It is the only piece in the book which is clearly not in the main hand, but it is continuous with the rest of the manuscript, sharing f. 136 with the preceding work. The *Fifteen Articles* ends on f. 139ʳ, and f. 139ᵛ is a blank.

Our plays begin on f. 140ʳ and conclude on f. 172ʳ. They are clearly in the same hand as that of the bulk of the manuscript. It is a rough *cursiva currens* with characteristic secretary features such as the crossed *g*, the 'figure-2' *r*, and kidney-shaped final *s*. The writer uses the common symbols for *-er, -re, -ur, -ra, -ro, -re, with, that, thou*, etc. An *i* above a word is normally expanded to *-ri*; the superscript *a* is expanded usually to *au*, but occasionally to *an*. The horizontal stroke above a word is expanded to whatever the writer's practice would seem to require, normally minims, but frequently vowels as well. The flourished final *r* seems significant, and we expand to *-re*; the barring of final *ll* is consistent, and we expand to *-lle*. The writer's final loop for plurals and genitives of nouns is expanded to *-es*. There are frequent superfluous abbreviation marks, such as horizontal strokes, barred final *h*, flourished final *d*, *t*, and *g*, which we ignore. The writer does not differentiate between þ and *y*. Capitals are marked with vertical red strokes and rhymes are bracketed in red. Paragraph marks in red are used in the first half of *CB* and its *planctus*, and in the speeches of Peter, Andrew, and John in *CR*. Virgules mark caesuras and colons serve for question marks. Directions and speakers' names in *CB* are written in red, as are additions and corrections, all of which seem to be in the same hand. We say 'seem' because some additions are in very small letters. Speakers' names and directions in *CR* are

normally in the same black ink as the text; an exception is the red
ink of directions on ff. 170ʳ–172ʳ. Until f. 147ᵛ of *CB* speakers'
names and the directions are crowded into the margins; after
this they are neatly spaced in the middle of the pages. For the
same first fourteen pages the speeches are separated by red lines.
The text averages 27–30 lines a page. There are no catchwords.

Just as the bulk of the manuscript is in the same hand, so is
the paper of the book largely homogeneous. Over two-thirds of the
paper in the original manuscript bears the same water-mark: a
hand with fingers together and thumb apart, with an alpha on the
palm, and surmounted by a five-pointed star. This is similar to
Heawood's 134[1] (but Heawood's example has a six-pointed star).
The leaves having this mark are the first thirty-six and the last
thirty-three, and ff. 55–108. A similar mark is found on ff. 37–50
and 116–39, but this mark does not contain the alpha on the palm.
Folios 51–4 are smaller paper, and are marked with a fleur-de-lis
similar to several in Briquet.

Date and Provenance of the Plays

The chronicle is dated at its conclusion 1518, and its continuation concerns the events of 1520. This material and the plays are
in the same hand, and the manuscript is generally homogeneous
both in its subject matter and in its paper. Clearly, a date of not
far off 1520 is probable for the plays as well. Because the chronicle
was evidently written by a Carthusian, a Carthusian house is the
probable origin of the plays. The dialect of the manuscript, as
will be seen, is north-eastern, probably southern Yorkshire.

There were three Charterhouses in the north-eastern area,
Mount Grace and Kingston-upon-Hull in Yorkshire, and Axeholme in Lincolnshire. Although a Carthusian from the north
could easily have been in one of the southern houses, there are, as
we shall see, certain local references in the chronicle which seem
to fix Yorkshire as the area in which the chronicle and plays were
written.

Both the houses of Mount Grace and Kingston-on-Hull enjoy
some evidence suggesting them as places of composition. Mount
Grace, in the parish of East Harsley in the Cleveland Hills of the
North Riding, is suggested by references to King Henry VI, in a

[1] E. Heawood, 'Sources of Early English Paper Supply II: The Sixteenth
Century', p. 440.

sense the second founder of the house. These references are highly
laudatory, e.g.:

> So holy King Herrey the vi[th] of Yngland
> ȝit not canoniset ne set vp in shryn
> With ij° deuout prestes, os I vnderstand.   (f. 96[v])

This passage occurs in a series of prayers to popes and saints of
the fifteenth century. King Henry was regarded with varying
degrees of veneration in the period, but the deep reverence of this
passage, together with several others in the chronicle, suggests
a particular veneration. Mount Grace was founded shortly after
8 February, 1397/8, by a licence granted by Richard II to Thomas
de Holland, Duke of Surrey, and Earl of Kent.[1] Thomas gave over
to it his own manor of Bordelby as a seat, and endowed it with
various properties all over England. The Duke, however, became
involved in conspiracy against Henry IV, and was murdered by
men of Cirencester on 7 January, 1399/1400. The condition of
his foundation was then precarious, but the house managed to
continue. On 19 November 1440, Henry VI confirmed the monks'
title to the majority of their lands, and subsequently showed other
signs of favour. This excellent reason for Henry's being held in
high regard at Mount Grace would argue that house to be a
plausible home of MS e Museo 160. Another piece of evidence is
non-committal, except for the general proposition that the manuscript is a Yorkshire product. On f. 99[v] of the chronicle the writer
cites, as testifying to a miracle, 'þe vicar of Mownt Grace, ȝit
on lif'.

It is somewhat more likely, however, that MS e Museo 160 was
written at Kingston-on-Hull. There are two local references that
make this probable. On f. 96[v] of the chronicle there occurs a prayer
to 'the holy vicar of Brantingham . . . / With þe vicare sister þe
damselle welle doand'. Brantingham was a village about five miles
west of the site of the priory at Hull. The invocation occurs again
on f. 99[v]. A repeated reference to such little-known figures of piety
whose popularity was most probably local would suggest the nearby priory at Hull. Further, there is a reference in the 'historical
poem' on f. 114[r] to the falling of the church steeple in Beverley,

[1] W. Dugdale, *Monasticon Anglicanum*, vi, Pt. 1 (London, 1830), pp. 22–3.
See also E. M. Thompson, *The Carthusian Order in England* (London, 1930),
pp. 229–35.

just a few miles north of Hull. Even the remark about the vicar of
Mount Grace sounds rather like a reference to another house than
the writer's own.

Perhaps we should not totally dismiss the house at Axeholme in
Lincolnshire, but we have found no local references that would
fit. We have examined a number of the surviving books from the
medieval libraries of Mount Grace, Kingston-on-Hull, and Axeholme, with a view to checking writing and allusions against those
in MS e Museo 160, but have met with no success.

MS e Museo 160 offers little else as a clue to its provenance. On
f. 171^v a hand different from that of the bulk of the manuscript has
scribbled at the bottom 'written by me W..........lns' (leaf
torn). This is apparently the same hand which has written on the
leaf stub between ff. 60 and 61 'William Benson Dewllyns'. We
have been unable to trace this name. On the bottom half of f. 172^r,
another hand has copied out the first two lines of f. 171^v, and this
has been smeared and blotted. Below this appears the name
'Thomas' twice in still another hand, and below that, a scrap of
plainsong. The lower part of the leaf is torn away. On f. 172^v
appears some scribbling, what appear to be bars drawn for more
musical notation, and below, in a box, what might be an astrological
table. Furnivall remarks (p. 171) that 'The MS. is lettered on the
back: "Cronol. Papish Play"'. If this existed once it exists no
longer. We have been unable to trace the manuscript prior to its
appearance in the Bodleian 'before 1680'.

Versification

The two plays have considerable metrical variety, but the basic
stanza is the six-line *rime couée*, *aabccb*, the *b* lines having three
stresses generally, and the others four. This was a very popular
stanza, the vehicle for many romances and some plays. *CB*
contains 81 of these stanzas, or 486 lines of 862, and *CR* 66, or
396 lines of 766. This basic stanza is varied from time to time,
either deliberately or confusedly, some examples having seven and
some five lines, scattered throughout both plays. *CB* opens with
eight-line stanzas, *aaabcccb*, of the sort used in the Chester plays.
There are ten of these in the first 138 lines of the play, and they
are not encountered again. The longer *a* lines generally contain
four stresses and the shorter *b* lines three, but extra syllables
frequently obscure the pattern. The writer's consciousness of his

stanzaic structure throughout is made clear by his bracketing his rhymes. The prologue of *CB* is a single long stanza, *ababbcbcdeeed*, of the 'bob-and-wheel' variety, the first *d* containing only three syllables.

In one part of each play the basic stanzaic pattern is broken at considerable length. In *CB* the *planctus Mariae*, consisting of three distinct poems, occupies ll. 622–787. The first lament, 'Who cannot wepe, com lerne at me', is in eights, basically four-stress, *ababbcbc*. This is a common stanza, found in the *Ludus Coventriae*, the York Cycle, and in at least one *planctus*.[1] There are thirteen of these stanzas. At l. 726 begins a five-stress rhyme royal lament with the occasional refrain 'Which sumtym gafe yow mylk of my pape'. This lasts for five stanzas; a five-stress seven-liner (one stanza of six) with occasional refrain 'Remembere myn awn son, þat ʒe sowket my breste', continues for five more stanzas to l. 794. Nine couplets follow, and the rest of the play ends in a chaos of *rime couée*, couplets, and single lines.

In *CR* a steady flow of *rime couée* is interrupted at l. 267, where a lament by Peter begins, and takes the form of alternating sevens and sixes, the sevens being five-stress rhyme royal (though frequently with six and even seven stresses), and the sixes being *aabccb*, but with roughly three stresses in all lines, rather than the four and three of the *rime couée*. This lasts until l. 398. The *rime couée* makes a brief appearance until l. 416, where a new series of rhyme royal stanzas begins, and dominates until l. 514. There follow two Chester-type eights, the only two in the second play, and the stanzaic pattern from there to the end of the play is very irregular, with rhyme royal, *rime couée*, quatrains, couplets, single lines, and ending with a long 'bob-and-wheel' stanza, somewhat like that of the prologue to the plays.

Some alliteration is found here and there, especially in *CB*, but alliteration is not a feature of these plays.

Our plays' verse is rough, but not totally incompetent. The poet is nearly always fluent, and normally a respectable rhyme dominates, though, of course, he does rely upon *-ion* and *-lye* identical rhymes to some extent. The writer uses a virgule with consistency to mark caesuras in the longer lines of the eights and rhyme royal

---

[1] The *planctus* is found in Camb. Univ. Lib. MS Ff. 5. 48, and printed as No. 7 in C. Brown's *Religious Lyrics of the Fifteenth Century* (Oxford, 1939), pp. 13–16.

stanzas, placing it normally after the fourth or sixth syllable, but sometimes marking two caesuras in the same line.

Nature of the Plays: Sources and Relationships

We have gone into aspects of the manuscript and versification to such an extent because we believe they provide nearly conclusive evidence as to the general nature of these plays, and considerable evidence as to their origins. It is evident, considering the homogeneous nature of the manuscript, that the writer is also the writer of the vast meditative chronicle which fills two-thirds of the manuscript. We think that the evidence supports our conclusion that the plays were written by a Carthusian, near the year 1520, in a house in Yorkshire, probably Kingston-on-Hull.

It is fairly clear that the writer of the manuscript was also in a real sense the author of the plays, that is, he shaped his materials to his purpose in much the same way as he had elaborated Rolewinck into his meditation-chronicle. Further, an examination of the excision of certain lines in the manuscript by the writer, using the same red ink which he employed for corrections and rubrication of capitals, reveals that his original purpose, that of composing a verse meditation on the burial and resurrection, had changed to that of writing the meditational dramas.

The work had been prefaced on f. 140^r by 'The prologe of this treyte or meditation off the buryalle of Criste and mowrnyng þerat'. On f. 140^v occurs in red ink, in the same hand, the note 'This is a play to be played, on part on Gud Friday afternone, and þe other part opon Ester Day after the resurrection in the morowe, but at ⟨the⟩ begynnynge ar certen lynes which ⟨shuld⟩ not be said if it be plaied, which . . .' (damage to the bottom of the leaf). The announcement that the work was a play has been rather crowded in at the bottom of the leaf. Although the writer still leaves the option of reading the work as a treatise, his revisions make the dramatic purpose paramount. Some two dozen lines in *CB* are crossed out in the first half of the play; all contain narrative material, such as 'Then saide Iosephe right peteoslee'. Some pieces of narrative are overlooked and remain in the text, e.g. l. 80.[1] It is important to

---

[1] Furnivall's note 'The poetaster has again forgotten that he's writing a play' (p. 174), is crude, but perhaps nearer the mark than Woolf's speculations in *The English Religious Lyric* that a corrector has turned the work into a play (p. 263), or her revised opinion in *English Mystery Plays* (London, 1972), p. 422,

note that when the writer has crossed out such extraneous material, he is still usually left with the six-line stanzas which are the basic vehicle of the play. This would indicate that he is revising himself in the process of turning narrative, perhaps prose, sources into drama. (That he is to some extent relying upon verse material, however, is revealed by his occasional corrections of errors made as a result of anticipation of rhyme words, as in *CB* 297, where he has written, then crossed out 'content' after 'welle', and following with 'assent' in the first *b* of an *aabccb* stanza; he has anticipated the rhyme 'content' in the last *b*, thus suggesting that he is using at least some material in the same stanza form as that of the plays.)

Other evidence of the changing purpose of the writer may be found in the fact that the names of the speakers, together with paragraph markers, are crowded into the margins until a point about half-way through *CB* (coinciding with the disappearance of narrative devices in the verse), after which point the names of speakers and directions become carefully spaced, and the indentation symbols are abandoned except for the *planctus*. It is clear that after f. 147ᵛ our writer is no longer of two minds about what he is doing.

The first play begins on Good Friday evening with a meditation by Joseph of Arimathea, who opens the drama by calling attention to the weeping of the Marys ('Methink I here lamentation', l. 55). The three Marys then exchange laments with Joseph, and the Magdalen describes the crucifixion, which Joseph has not seen, though he has heard the distant shouting. Joseph inquires about the Virgin, and the Magdalen describes her reaction. The last words on the cross are discussed, and the implication of Christ's sacrifice. Mary Magdalen then launches into a brief lament which is stopped short when Joseph announces that he sees Nicodemus coming. They then all go to Calvary and begin to take down the body from the cross. John and the Virgin appear (return?), and the Virgin's lamentation begins. She takes Christ's body in her arms in the traditional *pietà* fashion.¹ The three *planctūs* of her long speech end with John, Joseph, Nicodemus, and Mary

that a corrector was restoring the text to its original, dramatic form. In both opinions Woolf overlooks the evidence of the stanzaic structure, the fact that there are no narrative elements to be removed after the first half of *CB*, and the conclusive fact that all the writing and correcting are in the one hand.

¹ See Woolf's *The English Religious Lyric*, *passim*, for a discussion of the *pietà* tradition.

Magdalen consoling her and attempting to persuade her to leave. This they finally do, and *CB* ends with the Magdalen planning to go to buy the ointments, and Joseph and Nicodemus recalling the prediction that Christ will rise on the third day.

The second play opens on Easter morning with a lament by Mary Magdalen on her way to meet the other Marys and anoint Christ's body. When they arrive at the tomb, an angel appears and tells them that He has arisen, and will appear to the disciples in Galilee. The Magdalen is overcome with remorse because she has not stayed by the tomb; if she had, she would have seen the rising. The three Marys then go their ways, looking for Christ. Peter enters, weeping bitterly. His lament parallels that of Mary Magdalen, for he, too, has not remained faithful. At the end of a prolonged *planctus*, he falls to the ground, weeping. John and Andrew enter and try to comfort him, reminding him that Christ had foreseen all their weaknesses, and that He has given Peter the Keys. Peter is consoled, and leaves. Mary Magdalen returns, in her search for Christ, and He appears to her as a gardener. She recognizes him after he speaks her name, and, after the *Noli me tangere*, has a brief and moving speech of thanksgiving. The other Marys return and learn the good news; Christ then appears to all three. The Marys sing the *Victime Paschali*, and John, Andrew, and Peter run in and join the singing. After this, Peter asks Mary for news, and is told of the Resurrection. The Apostles run to the tomb and find that He has indeed gone. They rejoice, and join again with the Marys, singing *Scimus Christum*, and John concludes with what sounds very much like a normal conclusion of late medieval drama:

> Joyfully depart we now owt of this place,
> Mekly abidinge the inspiration of grace,
> > Which we belefe
> Schalle com to vs this nyght!
> Now, farwelle, euery wighte!
> We commend yow alle to his myght
> > which for vs suffert grefe.   (ll. 760–6)

The first play seems deliberately lacking action. The events of the crucifixion are seen, as it were, off-stage; the lamentation is heard from a distance. The spectacle of taking down the body from the cross is very spare, and no business at all is actually seen, though we hear Joseph giving brief instruction to Nicodemus. The *pietà* scene dominates the rest of the play. The action of the second play is more extensive, but involves no 'business', just coming, going, and speaking. Although the plays may have originated, and probably did originate, as a second thought, the writer has selected his materials in such a way as to combine the features of meditation and drama in a very practical way.

The two dramas could easily have been played in a priory. The long, analytical laments in both plays are meditation for the speakers and hearers as well, in much the same way as the writer describes the purpose of his meditative chronicle earlier in the manuscript. The audience, if there was one, was intended to be brought into the 'action' in a way quite without parallel in other religious drama. The lamentation goes on far too long for modern taste, but the experiment of mixing meditation with drama is a most interesting one, and seems to be unique. There is, as we have indicated, no evidence that the plays were ever acted; as far as we know, the only performance took place on Easter Friday and Sunday of 1974 in Southwark Cathedral, London.

All the materials in MS e Museo 160, excepting the romance, are strongly meditational in nature, in the tradition of Carthusian emphasis upon affective piety.[1] It seems clear that the plays began as an extended meditation. What gave the writer the idea of turning them into plays is an interesting subject for speculation. He might have seen the plays of York, or perhaps a presentation of the slightly shorter cycle at Beverley, which would be a more likely contemporary influence, and was, apparently like the Wakefield plays, derived from those of York. At any rate, even if the contemporary drama had impressed our writer, there is little of the bustle of the cycles in these two plays. Rather, as we have suggested, the plays seem to be meditation enacted, though the forms from which liturgical drama had sprung are, of course, apparent, particularly in the *quem quaeritis* and the *hortulanus* scenes of *CR*. A tradition of liturgical drama may have survived in the northern houses so late, though there is little evidence on the question. An analogy with liturgical drama seems to have been in the author's mind, in the idea of dividing the play and using the traditional Easter sequences as the climax of the *CR*; but there is no sugges-

---

[1] For a brief treatment of the Carthusian fondness for the *imago pietatis*, see Woolf, *The English Religious Lyric*, pp. 377–8; her discussion of Brit. Lib. Add. MS 37049 sheds considerable light on this topic.

tion of his having designed it to form a part of the liturgy, either in his own description of f. 140ᵛ, or in any of the directions of the text. Nor is there any evidence from Carthusian liturgy to indicate whether special circumstances might have helped create the plays. In any case they are clearly not a throw-back to the origins of drama in the liturgy, or in any sense a development from them, but rather, the dramatization, on an ancient analogy, of contemporary meditational materials.[1]

The meditational materials of which we have spoken can be described both as quite specific and as irritatingly intangible. We can be reasonably sure that parts of the *Cursor Mundi* and various devotional treatises lay behind the plays, and that certain *planctūs*, of which related separate poems survive,[2] were worked into the plays, but the question of what exactly were the forms of the materials used is not likely to be answered.

[1] Grace Frank's summary of the relation of *planctus* to drama should be noted: '. . . the various *Planctus*, though potentially dramatic, remained lyrical and static, so far as we know, and though adapted ready-made into the later plays, seem in no instance to have been the starting point of any surviving text', *Medieval French Drama* (Oxford, 1954), p. 21. Perhaps our plays are an exception to this generalization, but it is doubtful. Craig's theory that the plays are a 'late rewriting of a play that had been developed within a church', *English Religious Drama*, p. 319, is mistaken; the materials here were never a play, or there would have been no need to turn them into one. V. A. Kolve, in *The Play Called Corpus Christi* (London, 1966), p. 35, suggests that 'It is to such plays that the Latin drama of the Church led, not to the plays called Corpus Christi'. In the sense that development is implied, the first part of the statement is clearly incorrect; the second part is true enough.

[2] G. C. Taylor, 'The English "Planctus Mariae" ', *MP* iv (1907), 24–9, discusses the relationship of the *Cursor Mundi* to *CB*. Two *planctūs* with the 'Who can not wepe com lern at me' refrain survive; one is a four-stanza, nine-line *aaaabbbcc* version in Trinity College Cambridge MS 1450, printed by E. K. Chambers and F. Sidgwick, *Early English Lyrics* (London, 1921), pp. 144–5, and in the John Rylands Library MS 395, printed by C. Brown, *Religious Lyrics of the Fifteenth Century*, No. 9, pp. 17–18, and by R. L. Greene, *Early English Carols* (Oxford, 1935), p. 121. A fragment of this *planctus* is also found in Trinity College Cambridge MS O. 9. 38 and is printed as No. 21 by A. G. Rigg in *A Glastonbury Miscellany of the Fifteenth Century* (Oxford, 1968), p. 86. The other is a poem in twelve-line stanzas, of which these texts are known: Bodleian MS 423, Trinity College Dublin MS 160, and Brit. Lib. Harley MS 2274, the last printed by R. Garrett, '*De Arte Lacrimandi*', *Anglia*, xxxii (1909), 269–94; and a highly condensed version published by D. C. Baker, ' "Therfor to Wepe, Cum Lerne Off Me", a *Planctus* fragment in MS Corpus Christi College Oxford F. 261', *MÆ* xxxviii (1969), 291–4. A *planctus* with a refrain similar to another in *CB* is found in Camb. Univ. Lib. MS Ff. 4. 48: it has an eight-line stanza, with the refrain 'The childe is ded þat soke my brest', and is printed by C. Brown, *Religious Lyrics of the Fifteenth Century*, No. 10, pp. 18–22.

The primary treatises which created the *planctus* tradition, the 'ymage of pitee' literature of the late Middle Ages, were the pseudo-Anselm *Dialogus Beatae Mariae et Anselmi de Passione Domini*,[1] the *De lamentatione virginis Mariae* (or *Liber de Passione Christi*) attributed to St. Bernard,[2] and the pseudo-Bonaventure *Meditationes vitae Christi* and the lament in the *Stimulus Amoris*.[3] Another treatise, attributed to Origen, was the *De Maria Magdalena*,[4] which dealt with the weeping of the Magdalen in much the same way as the others described the lamentation of the Virgin. There is a certain sameness among all these works, and one can easily see why. The New Testament does not provide much by way of description of the lamentation for Christ. The authors of these treatises were forced back to the Old Testament for models of lamentation; the chief themes and formulas of the complaints are therefore expressed in the language of Isaiah, Jeremiah, David's lament for Absalom, and above all, in the language of the Song of Songs. The pseudo-Bernard treatise, which Miss Woolf elects to name simply the *Quis dabit*[5]—from its opening words taken from Jeremiah ix: 1, *Quis dabit capiti meo*—shares a good deal of language in particular with the pseudo-Anselm work, including this famous question, though in the Anselm tract it has not so prominent a role. The famous plea *Quis mihi det ut ego moriar pro te, fili mi* (2 Kings 18: 33) appears also in the two works, and much of the phrasing is similar. But the two have different patterns; the *Quis dabit* is a direct lament, whereas the *Dialogus* employs Anselm to question the Virgin. There are also two other important differences for our concerns. In the Anselm tract the Virgin's responses, though emotional, nevertheless contain a fairly systematic account of the crucifixion. In the Bernardine the Virgin's responses deal to a far greater extent with her feeling; the details are out of chronological order, and in her speeches the erotic language of the Song of Songs plays a large role; the latter is missing in the *Dialogus*.

[1] J.-P. Migne, ed., *Patrologia Latina*, clix (Paris, 1854), cols. 271–90.
[2] An inadequate edition is that of the *Patrologia Latina*, clxxxii, cols. 1133–42. This lacks the famous opening, the five hundred or so words of the conclusion, and is altogether nearly two thousand words shorter than the normal text, which can be found in any *Opera Omnia* through the seventeenth century. Our citations are from the *Opera Omnia*, ii (Venice, 1616), pp. 302^v–305^v.
[3] *Sancti Bonaventurae Opera*, xii (Venice, 1756).
[4] *Homilia X, Origenis Adamantii Opera*, ii (Paris, 1619), 291–4.
[5] *The English Religious Lyric*, p. 247.

The Bonaventura pieces are of two kinds. The long *Meditationes* is a narrative of the whole range of Christ's life, and the set pieces involving lament by the Virgin are much shorter than the Bernardine or the Anselm tracts. The short lament in the *Stimulus Amoris* seems to have no bearing on our plays. We will discuss the possible influence of the Bonaventuran tradition upon our plays in connection with the *CR* lament of Peter. The pseudo-Origen *De Maria Magdalena* uses a form similar to that of the Anselm tract, and, like the Bernardine *Quis dabit*, significantly employs the language of the Song of Songs. There is considerable overlapping between the Origen homily and the *Quis dabit* in the use of language from the Song of Songs.

These two works, the *Quis dabit* and the *De Maria Magdalena*, have clearly contributed most to the background of the e Museo 160 plays. As H. Thien pointed out long ago, much of the language of *CB* has its ulimate origin in the *Quis dabit*,[1] and, as Rosemary Woolf has recently argued, some incident and language from the Origen treatise are to be found in *CR*.[2] How did this material find its way into the plays? The answer is probably, but not certainly, that the influence was indirect. These famous *planctūs* affected all aspects of the meditative tradition, and their key phrases, found in our plays, were frequently brought together in circumstances quite different from those in the *planctūs*. For instance, in just two pages of the *Chartre of the Abbeye of the Holy Gost* the phrases '. . . queram quem diligit anima mea', 'Quaesivi et non inveni', 'Revertere, revertere, sunamitis, revertere', 'Adjuro vos filie Ierusalem, si inveneritis dilectum meum, annuncietis quia amore langueo', and 'Quis dabit capiti meo aquam et oculis meis fontem lacrimarum . . .' are to be found.[3] Particularly, the *Quis dabit* affected the *Cursor Mundi*, which in turn seems to have influenced our plays, though indirectly. Not only is the basic stanza of the plays that of the relevant section of the *Cursor*, but similarities of language occur, including a suggestion of the phrase 'who can not wepe, com lern at mee' in the first *planctus* of CB.[4] There are not many parallels, however, and it would seem that if the playwright

[1] *Über die englischen Marienklagen* (Kiel, 1906), pp. 57–66.
[2] *English Mystery Plays*, pp. 333–5.
[3] C. Horstman, ed., *Yorkshire Writers*, i (London, 1895), 346–7.
[4] G. C. Taylor, 'The English "Planctus Mariae" ', pp. 24–9, compares the rhetorical patterns in passages of the *Cursor Mundi* and *CB*, and discusses similarities of language.

had been working directly from the *Cursor Mundi*, much more of the language would have been similar.

The argument against our writer's employing the *Quis dabit* and the *De Maria Magdalena* directly, that is, versifying from them as he had done in the chronicle from the *Fasciculus Temporum*, is, chiefly, that the order in which the echoes and episodes appear does not correspond. It is also difficult to understand why the writer was content with the conventional phrases and incidents popular in derivative tracts and poems instead of using some of the even more colourful language and episodes from the treatises themselves. Further, most of the Bernardine language in *CB* is found only in the *planctus*. It would appear that our writer was using, from whatever sources, material containing the stock stuff of the *planctus* convention rather than working directly from any of the seminal treatises.

In certain cases this material was the already-written *planctus*. We have seen how, in *CB*, the writer inserted three distinct *planctūs* with individual refrains and stanzaic forms into his play, even varying his punctuation practice to indicate the stanzas by paragraph marks (which he probably had copied directly from the manuscript he was using). In *CR* it would appear that the long *planctus* of Peter, and the consolation by John and Andrew, which breaks the lamentation of Mary Magdalen into two parts, was originally an independent poem, since its stanzaic patterns— alternating stanzas of seven-line, five-stress, with six-line, three-stress—differ markedly from anything else in the plays. Several stanzas of this, too, are marked by paragraph indentation symbols which might have been taken over from the writer's original. The *planctus* of Peter presents an interesting problem, for though the tears of Peter are an ancient theme, and there is some treatment in the French drama, we have been unable to find elsewhere anything remotely parallel to this extensively developed episode.[1]

It is in connection with the consolation of Peter that the greatest likelihood of some influence from the pseudo-Bonaventure *Meditationes* must be seen. Though not nearly so extensive as the

---

[1] The theme of Peter's elaborate penitence was particularly developed by Peter Comestor's *Historia Scholastica* (*PL* cxcviii, cols 1619–24), and is commonly found, as in Arnoul Greban's *Le Mystère de la Passion*, eds. G. Paris and G. Raynaud (Paris, 1878). See J. Szövérffy, 'The Legends of St. Peter in Medieval Latin Hymns' *Traditio*, x (1954), 275–322, for a general discussion of the background.

scene in *CR*, there is in Chapter 84 of the *Meditationes* quite an elaborate treatment of Peter's remorse, and he is consoled by John and the Virgin (but not by Andrew, who appears in *CR*; and, of course, the Virgin is not in this scene in *CR*). Further, there is the possibility that, in a very general way, the *Meditationes* served as a framework for the materials of the plays. In it all the scenes of the plays occur, though frequently in quite different form, and the *Meditationes* is likewise heavily indebted to both the *Quis dabit* and the *De Maria Magdalena* in the lament scenes. The author of the *Meditationes* cites both Bernard and Origen in these passages, and uses some of the same language. It would be rather surprising if the writer of our plays were unacquainted with the *Meditationes*, for it was not only extremely well known in its Latin form, but also in the English prose translation of parts made by the playwright's fellow Carthusian, Nicholas Love, probably the prior of Mount Grace in the early part of the preceding century. But there is no evidence that it was before our author as he wrote, and his restriction of the plays to the themes that he treats strongly suggests that it was not. However, the meditation-structure of the Bonaventuran narrative, and the meditational nature of the plays, together with the possible link of the Peter episode, might indicate the *Meditationes* in the far background of the plays. We indicate in our notes some possible echoes of the *Meditationes*, and one possibly derived from an English verse translation of part of the treatise.

It is fairly certain that the basic immediate source materials for the two plays were different. The directions of *CB* are mostly in English, those of *CR* in Latin. Additional evidence is that we seem to have different sets of Marys. In *CB*, three Marys are mentioned, apparently in addition to the Magdalen (cf. speakers' names, ll. 61-6, 'prima Maria', 'secunda Maria', 'Thrid Mary', followed by 'Mavdleyn'): the two Marys beside Magdalen named in *CB* are Jacobi and Salome (ll. 139-43), but later the two are Jacobi and Cleophe (*CB*, l. 612). In *CR* the other two Marys are Jacobi and Cleophe, and Salome does not appear. The tradition was confused from the New Testament onwards, but normally a writer would adopt one or another of the traditions, and it is unusual to find different patterns used in so short a space. This would seem to suggest different sources for the two plays.

Various images and phrases might have been brought to the plays from quite a number of sources, of course. For instance, some of the other material in the e Museo 160 may have contributed. A common figure, strikingly expressed in *CB*, is the comparison of the crucified Christ to a book:[1]

> 'Cum hither, Joseph, beholde and looke
> How many bludy letters beyn writen in þis buke,
> Smalle margente her is'.   (ll. 271–3)

In the versified *Hundred Meditations* we find (f. 131ʳ):

> Thow beheld thy son a bludy buke
> Dedly hinginge on a tree . . .

There are other parallels to language of the plays to be found in the *Hundred Meditations*, but none so specific as this one.

One interesting aspect of the two plays is the way in which the figure of Mary Magdalen so completely dominates them, even allowing for the long *planctus* of the Virgin in *CB*. The subtitle might well be 'Off the wepinge of the Mawdleyn' rather than 'Off the wepinge of the iij Maries' which the writer has crowded in red ink toward the bottom of f. 140ᵛ. In *CB* when she describes the crucifixion to Joseph of Arimathea Magdalen uses much of the language usually assigned to the Virgin. In *CR* her character is much influenced by the tradition of Origen, and again has language usually attributed to the Virgin. The assignment to the Magdalen by Origen of the '[Filie Ierusalem] . . . Nunciate dilecto meo / Quia amore langueo' (*CR*, ll. 594–7) is somewhat more 'dramatically' appropriate for the Magdalen than for the Virgin, who speaks these words of the wound of love in the *Quis dabit*.[2] The character of the Magdalen sustains *CB* through the long static *pietà*; and her role in the *hortulanus* of *CR*, her *planctus*, paralleled by that of Peter, conveys even something of excitement. The remorse felt by the great penitents, Mary and Peter, contrasted with the surprise and joy at their release, and the triumphant singing of the sequences

---

[1] For a discussion of this figure, see Woolf, *The English Religious Lyric*, pp. 212–14, and D. Gray, *Themes and Images in the Medieval English Religious Lyric* (London, 1972), pp. 129–30.

[2] Awareness of the appropriateness to the Magdalen of this love language is seen early (e.g. St. Gregory's *Homilia in Evangelia*, No. 25); verses 1–4 of Chapter 3 of the Song of Songs compose the first *lectio* of the first nocturne of Matins for St. Mary Magdalen's feast day, 22 July. In the poetry of the passion, the 'Quia amore langueo' is also spoken by Christ, as in the poem 'In the vaile of restles mynde' of MS Camb. Univ. Lib. Hh. 4. 12, printed by Furnivall in *Political, Religious, and Love Poems*, EETS, os 15 (1866), 150–9.

of Easter, are rather moving as our writer has put them together. The significance of the Magdalen, as a symbol and witness of salvation,[1] is more clearly evident here than in any of the cycle plays, and this clarity is in its simple way dramatically effective.

One other relationship of the plays remains to be considered, in our opinion a non-existent one. In 1955 Hardin Craig in his *English Religious Drama* stated (p. 375) 'It now appears . . . that the main body of [Nicholas Grimald's] *Christus Redivivus* was translated into Latin from the play of the Burial and Resurrection in Bodleian MS *e Museo* 160 . . .'. Craig is referring to the work of Patricia Abel on Nicholas Grimald; she published an article in 1955 in which she set forth the evidence for this claim.[2] The only similarity which appears to us between the works is in the presence of Mary Cleophe in both as the third Mary. This is interesting, but does not support such an assertion. The other vague similarities of language are those which are common to the literature of the passion, and the bulk of the episodes of Grimald's play, as Miss Abel admits, has no counterpart in the MS e Museo 160 plays. Ruth Blackburn has also recently rejected this suggested link.[3]

Language

The language is a mixture of forms from the North Midlands and southern Yorkshire which can be characterized as a highly contaminated Yorkshire dialect.

Two strata of spellings are discernible in the manuscript, the first and most distinct a northern stratum as was described by Schmidt[4] and the second a conglomerate of forms localized in the North Midlands and East Anglia. These same mixed characteristics are discernible in the *planctūs* of the Virgin in *CB* and of Peter in *CR*, though these laments, as we have seen, were incorporated whole from other sources.

[1] The background of the symbolism of Mary Magdalen is discussed by V. Saxer, *La Culte de Marie Madeleine en occident*, and other works mentioned on p. xl n. 1 of our Introduction. Particularly useful is J. Szövérffy's '*Peccatrix Quondam Femina*: A Survey of the Mary Magdalen Hymns', *Traditio*, xix (1963), 79–146. An interesting treatment of the pseudo-Origen homily is J. P. McCall's 'Chaucer and the Pseudo-Origen *De Maria Magdalena*: A Preliminary Study', *Speculum*, xlvi (1971), 135–41.

[2] 'Grimald's *Christus Redivivus* and the Digby Resurrection Play', *MLN* lxx (1955), 328–30.

[3] 'Nicholas Grimald's *Christus Redivivus*: A Protestant Resurrection Play', *ELN* v (1968), 247–50.

[4] K. Schmidt, 'Die Digby-Spiele', *Anglia*, viii (1885), 393–404.

The reflex of OE *ō* is predominantly *u*: *blud(e)*, *bludy* CB 129, 286, 628, *CR* 174, 340, etc.; *gud(e)*, *gudly*, *gudnes(e)* CB 6, 148, 182, etc., *CR* 68, 145, 461, etc.; *luk(e)*, *lukyd* CB 89, 189, 696 (one instance of *looke* CB 271); *rud(e)* CB 604, 677, *CR* 163 but *rood(e)* CB 128, *CR* 658. Words of this development rhyme without regard to spelling.

Other spellings suggesting northern provenance are *hinge* (hang) infin. CB 397, 398, 762, *hinges*, *hingeth* pres. 3 sg. CB 71, 116, 337, *hynge* past sg. CB 176 (the *i*- spelling found in northern homilies); *wald* (OE *wolde*) CB 88, 200, *CR* 53, 362, etc., but *wold(e)* CB 401, 489, *CR* 227, 507, 527 (*wald* is found in *Cursor Mundi*, Rolle, Minot); the 3 pl. personal pronoun is customarily spelled with *a*: *thay*, *þay* CB 165, 308, etc., *CR* 25, 139, etc., *tham*, *thaime*, *þam* CB 268, 407, *CR* 44, 626, 661, but genitive *their(e)* CB 164, 166, 405, *CR* 23, 35 (only one instance of *thair* CB 13). The reflex of OE *sc*- is twice *sch*: *schal(le)* *CR* 435, 763, three times *sal(le)* CB 513, *CR* 571, 747. The spelling *shall(e)*, however, dominates.

Words of northern provenance are: *tille* (prep.) eighteen instances, as sign of infinitive CB 428, 608, 846, *CR* 125, 386, 479; *garre* *CR* 35, *haylsinge* CB 744, *kirke* *CR* 384, *mekille* *CR* 273.[1]

Evidence of the second stratum, the North Midlands and East Anglia, is not as strong. The fem. pron. *scho*, *sho* is found: CB 151, 159, 180, 448; *CR* 105, 522, 542. Ian Scott located this spelling north of a line extending through Cheshire, northern Staffordshire, and Derbyshire, with pockets occurring in western Leicestershire, Warwickshire, and Gloucestershire.[2] The use of *e* where *i* is normally found is characteristic of East Anglia, as we have seen in the Digby plays.[3] In our plays we find *peteose*, *peteosly*, *petyfully* CB 158, 167, 188, 258, *CR* 12 (with twenty-eight instances of *pité* and derivatives in the *i* spelling), *resen(e)*, *resyn(e)* *CR* 193, 217, 699; *besely(e)*, *besines(s)* *CR* 147, 293, 576. The writer's practice is about equally divided between *sich*—CB 34, 299, *CR* 749—and *such* (eight instances). M. L. Samuels[4] locates *sich* in a strip extending from Cambridgeshire through Northampton-

---

[1] R. Kaiser, 'Zur Geographie des mittelenglischen Wortschatzes', *Palaestra*, ccv (1937), 178–278.
[2] M. W. Bloomfield and L. Newmark, *A Linguistic Introduction to the History of English* (New York, 1963), p. 221.
[3] N. Davis, 'The Language of the Pastons', pp. 120–44.
[4] 'Some Applications of Middle English Dialectology', p. 86, map 4.

shire, Leicestershire, into Cheshire. There are four instances of
ony (*CB* 132, 261, 184, *CR* 617) compared with three of *any*.
Samuels indicates that *ony* extended across the North Midlands
from Norfolk to Leicestershire.[1] Our writer prefers *os(e)* in thirty-
eight instances (*CB* 187, 225, *CR* 20, 205, etc.) to *as* ten instances).
MED records *os* in the Harleian MS of *Speculum Christiani*, the
dialect of which its editor identifies as East Midland with numerous
northern forms.[2] The spelling occurs in various lyrics of the late
fifteenth and early sixteenth centuries, at least one of which was
written in Yorkshire; others of the lyrics have characteristics of
northern, North Midlands, and East Anglian regions.[3]
Other features of pronunciation are:

Final unstressed -*e* is written with no consistency as would be
expected in a manuscript as late as this.

The reflex of OE *ā*, including words in which it developed
from *a* before a lengthening group, is normally written *o*:
bold CB 542, *cold CB* 86, 98, *hold(e) CB* 265, 443 (ten instances); *gost(ly) CB* 278, *CR* 744; *holi, holy(e) CB* 49, *CR*
213, 384; *mor(e) CB* 143, 227, *CR* 144, 222; *non(e)* rhymes
on *son, ton*, and *alone CB* 781, 783, 786, 787, and is found
consistently with this spelling; *stone* rhymes on *done CR*
176, 179, and *sor(e)* is consistently so spelled; *longe, longer
CB* 16, 157, *CR* 2, 507; *lond CB* 408 (but *land CB* 407, *CR*
31); *stonde, stondes CB* 442, 452 (but *stand CB* 54, 128, *CR*
68, 405); *wronge CB* 17 (but *wrangfully CR* 487); and
knoo, knowest CR 285, 269 (but *knaw, knawes, knawen, knav
CB* 5, 496, 515, *CR* 71, 274, 648).

The reflex of OE. *æ* regardless of origin is generally written
e, though spellings *ei, ey, ai, ay* can be found: *let(t) CB*
298, *CR* 116; *ther(e) CB* 170, *CR* 99; *clennesse CB* 589
(but *cleyne CB* 32, *CR* 124). There are two instances of *war
CB* 718, *CR* 704, but the rest are *were*. Words of this
development rhyme widely regardless of origin: *brede, rede,*

---

[1] Ibid., p. 90, map 6.
[2] G. Holmstedt, ed., *Speculum Christiani*, EETS, os 182 (1929), p. xciv. The
spelling *os* is also found in such East Anglian texts as the Paston letters.
[3] *Religious Lyrics of the Fifteenth Century*, Nos. 33, 52, 89, 99; R. H. Robbins,
ed., *Historical Poems of the XIVth and XVth Centuries* (Oxford, 1959), Nos.
145B, 232 A.1, 439; H. A. Person, ed., *Cambridge Middle English Lyrics* (Seattle,
Washington, 1962), No. 38.

dede CB 28–30; *dere, here, chere, bere, nere, spere, pere, heare* (hair) *CB* 70–1, 73–5, 77–8, 96, 100; *wepe, kepe, depe, slepe CB* 147, 150, 719, 721–2.

The ME usual *e* before *r* is written *a* in a few instances: *warkes CB* 34 (though *werke* also appears *CR* 230); *hart, harte(s) CB* 125, 225, *CR* 4, 48, fifty-seven instances in all, but *hert(e), hertes CB* 542, 578, *CR* 168, 182, eight instances in all. Only *hart(e)* is rhymed, with other words in *a: starte CB* 125–6, *parte CR* 753–4, *smarte CB* 191–2.

The reflex of OE *u* is usually *o: com(e) CB* 669, 693, etc. (but *cum CB* 271); *loue, love CB* 1, 292, *CR* 598, etc.; *son(n)(e) CB* 183, 476, *CR* 81, 150, etc.; *bot CB* 48, 269, *CR* 110, eight instances compared with *but*, fifty instances.

The main points of verbal inflexion:

Pres. indic. 2 sg. (and past 2 sg. of weak verbs) is normally -*st: seest CR* 268, *knowest CR* 269, *didist CB* 526, *hast CB* 291, *CR* 304, etc., but *haves CB* 403. The normal form of *to be* is *art(e) CR* 61, 587, etc., but *is CB* 393. The earlier northern inflexion -*s* is found also: *wepis CR* 140, 603 and *sekes CR* 603.

Pres. indic. 3 sg. in -*es* predominates over -*is* or -*ys*. There are a few endings in -*th: hingeth CB* 337, *doth(e) CB* 613, 811, *CR* 24, etc. (though there are six instances of *dos(e) CB* 730, *CR* 524, etc.), *drawethe CB* 859, *lyeth CR* 113. The writer prefers *has(e)* for the auxiliary in fourteen instances, but also uses *haues* eight times. The form *hath* does not appear in either play.

The present plural is normally without ending, but *ben, beyn CB* 193, 272, *CR* 462, 682, etc., and *spekes CB* 163.

The imperative plural is without ending, and the infinitive is likewise uninflected.

Our writer uses the -*inge*, -*ynge* ending for the present participle, though in the chronicle section of the manuscript a number of -*and* forms appear. In the past participle of weak verbs the writer prefers *i* or *y* over *e* as the vowel of the inflexion, and varies the consonant between *d* and *t*. The writer uses only one example of -*n* past participle for the strong verb that has not survived into modern usage: *commen CR* 497.

The plural and genitive morphemes of nouns are predominantly -*es*, but there are many examples of -*is*. Exceptions are *childer* CB 166 (and *childeren* CB 198), *brether* CR 507. The 2 pl. pronoun *ye* nominative and *you* dative-accusative are frequently found used in singular address: *ye* sg. CB 87, 109, (*was ye*), 331, 571, etc., *you* sg. CB 72, 118, 479, CR 391, etc. The singular forms *thou* and *thee* are used for address to God and for intimate address, but we also find *yee* CR 319, *your* CR 320, 321 so employed. The 3 pl. pronouns we have already seen: *thay*, *tham*, *their*.

SELECT BIBLIOGRAPHY

BIBLIOGRAPHIES

BROWN, C. and ROBBINS, R. H., *The Index of Middle English Verse*. New York, 1945.

ROBBINS, R. H. and CUTLER, J. L., *Supplement to the Index of Middle English Verse*. Lexington, Ky., 1965.

STRATMAN, C. J., *Bibliography of Medieval Drama*. Berkeley and Los Angeles, 1954. New edn., 2 vols., New York, 1972.

WELLS, J. E., *A Manual of the Writings in Middle English 1050–1400*. New Haven, 1916, and *First to Ninth Supplements*, 1919–51. (New edn. in progress.)

CONCORDANCE

PRESTON, M., *A Concordance to the Middle English Shorter Poems*. Compendia 6, Leeds, 1975.

—— *A Concordance to the Digby Plays and the e Mus. 160 Christ's Burial and Resurrection*. Ann Arbor, 1977.

TEXTS OF THE PLAYS

DIGBY PLAYS

Ancient Mysteries from the Digby Manuscripts, ed. T. Sharp. Abbbotsford Club, 1835.

The Digby Mysteries, ed. F. J. Furnivall. New Shakspere Society, 1882. Reprinted as *The Digby Plays*, EETS, ES 70 (1896, reprinted 1930, 1967). Also contains *Christ's Burial* and *Resurrection*.

The Digby Plays, rendered into Modern English by A. J. Brock and D.G. Byrd. Dallas, Texas, 1973. A prose version.

An Edition of the Digby Plays (Bodleian Digby 133), with Introduction, Notes and Glossary, ed. V. M. Devlin. Ph.D. thesis, University College, London, 1965–6. Omits the *Wisdom* fragment.

The Digby Plays: Facsimiles of the Plays in Bodley MSS Digby 133 and e Museo 160, intro. D. C. Baker and J. L. Murphy. Leeds Texts and Monographs. Medieval Drama Facsimiles, iii, gen. eds. A. C. Cawley and S. Ellis. Leeds, 1976.

EDITIONS OF INDIVIDUAL DIGBY PLAYS

Chief Pre-Shakespearean Dramas, ed. J. Q. Adams. Boston, 1924. Contains *The Conversion of St. Paul* and the first 992 lines of *Mary Magdalen*.

Earlier English Drama from Robin Hood to Everyman, ed. F. J. Ticknor. New York, 1929. Prints a normalized version of *The Conversion of*

St. Paul and a shortened, normalized version of the Digby *Wisdom* fragment.

English Miracle Plays, Moralities, and Interludes, ed. A. W. Pollard. Oxford, 1890; 8th edn., 1927. Prints 375 lines of *Mary Magdalen*.

English Moral Interludes, ed. G. Wickham. London, 1976. Prints *The Conversion of St. Paul*.

Lichtmess oder der Bethlehemitische Kindermord: Heiligenschauspiel von John Parfre, ed. Dr Fricke. Berlin, 1911.

Medieval Drama, ed. D. Bevington. Boston, 1975. Contains the complete, normalized, texts of *The Conversion of St. Paul* and *Mary Magdalen*.

The Origins of the English Drama, ed. T. Hawkins. 3 vols., Oxford, 1773. Vol. I contains *The Killing of the Children*, subsequently reprinted by W. Marriott in his *A Collection of English Miracle Plays or Mysteries*, Basel, 1838, and by an anonymous editor in *The Journal of Sacred Literature and Biblical Record*, NS x [1867], 413–29.

The Play of Mary Magdalene, ed. L. Lewis. Ph.D. thesis, University of Wisconsin, Madison, 1963. Published on demand by University Microfilms, Ann Arbor, Michigan.

Sancta Maria Magdalena. Reproduced from MS Digby 133, fols. 95–145 (recto), in the Bodleian Library, Oxford. The Modern Language Society of America, 1929. Collection of Photographic Facsimiles, No. 116.

Specimens of the Pre-Shaksperean Drama, ed. J. M. Manly. 2 vols., Boston, 1897–8; 2nd edn. 1900. Contains *The Conversion of St. Paul*.

EDITIONS OF THE PLAYS FROM BODLEY MS e MUSEO 160

Reliquiae Antiquae, eds. T. Wright and J. O. Halliwell, ii. London, 1843.
The Digby Mysteries, ed. F. J. Furnivall. See above.

EDITIONS OF RELATED TEXTS

The Chester Plays, ed. H. Deimling and Dr Matthews. EETS, ES 62 (1892, reprinted 1926, 1959), 115 (1916, reprinted 1935, 1959).

Cursor Mundi, ed. R. Morris, v. EETS 68 (1878, reprinted 1966).

'De arte lacrimandi', ed. R. M. Garrett. *Anglia*, xxxii (1909), 269–94.

Early English Carols, ed. R. L. Greene. Oxford, 1935, 2nd edn. 1977.

'Five Fifteenth-Century "Emblem" Verses of Brit. Mus. Addit. MS. 37049', ed. T. Ross. *Speculum*, xxxii (1957), 274–82.

A Glastonbury Miscellany of the Fifteenth Century, ed. A. G. Rigg. Oxford English Monographs, Oxford, 1968.

Hymns to the Virgin and Christ, ed. F. J. Furnivall. EETS, OS 24 (1867, reprinted 1973).

Ludus Coventriae, or The Plaie called Corpus Christi, ed. K. S. Block. EETS, ES 120 (1922, reprinted 1960).

The Macro Plays, ed. D. Bevington. Manuscript Series I, the Folger

Facsimiles. Washington, D.C., 1972. See the review by N. Davis, *N. & Q.* ccxx (1975), 78–9.

The Macro Plays, ed. M. Eccles. EETS 262 (1969).

The Macro Plays, eds. F. J. Furnivall and A. W. Pollard. EETS, ES 91 (1904, reprinted 1924).

'Mandeville and Marco Polo: a Stanzaic Fragment', ed. M. C. Seymour. *AUMLA* xx (1964), 39–52.

Meditations on the Life of Christ, ed. and trans. I. Ragusa and R. Green. Princeton, 1961.

Meditations on the Supper of Our Lord and the Hours of the Passion, ed. J. M. Cowper. EETS, OS 60 (1875).

Mind, Will and Understanding: A Morality, ed. W. B. D. D. Turnbull. Abbotsford Club, 1835. (The Macro *Wisdom*.)

The Mirrour of the Blessed Lyf of Jesus Christ/A Translation of the Latin Work Entitled Meditationes Vitae Christi/Attributed to Cardinal Bonaventura Made Before the Year 1410 by Nicholas Love/Prior of the Carthusian Monastery of Mount Grace, ed. L. F. Powell. Oxford, 1908.

Non-Cycle Plays and Fragments, ed. N. Davis. EETS, Supplementary Series 1 (1970).

The Non-Cycle Mystery Plays, together with the Croxton Play of the Sacrament and the Pride of Life, ed. O. Waterhouse. EETS, ES 104 (1909).

Origenis Adamantii Opera, ii. Paris, 1619. *Homilia X*, the *De Maria Magdalena*, pp. 291–4.

Political, Religious, and Love Poems, ed. F. J. Furnivall. EETS, OS 15 (1866, reprinted 1962).

Religious Lyrics of the Fifteenth Century, ed. C. Brown. Oxford, 1939.

Religious Lyrics of the Fourteenth Century, ed. C. Brown. 2nd edn. revd. G. V. Smithers. Oxford, 1952.

Remains of the Early Popular Poetry of England, ed. W. C. Hazlitt, i. London, 1864.

Sancti Bernardi Opera Omnia, i. Venice, 1616. The *Quis dabit* is found on ff. 302^v–305^v.

Sancti Bonaventurae Opera Omnia, xii. Venice, 1756. The *Meditationes* is found on pp. 379–526.

' " Therfor to Wepe, Cum Lerne Off Me": A *Planctus* Fragment in MS Corpus Christi College Oxford F. 261', ed. D. C. Baker. *MÆ* xxxviii (1969), 291–4.

The Towneley Plays, eds. G. England and A. W. Pollard. EETS, ES 71 (1897, reprinted 1952).

Two Coventry Corpus Christi Plays, ed. H. Craig. EETS, ES 87 (1902; 2nd edn. 1957, reprinted 1967).

The Wakefield Pageants in the Towneley Cycle, ed. A. C. Cawley. Manchester, 1956.

Wisdom, ed. J. S. Farmer. The Tudor Facsimile Texts. London and Edinburgh, 1907. (The Macro *Wisdom*).

The York Plays, ed. Lucy Toulmin Smith. Oxford, 1885 (reprinted 1963).

Yorkshire Writers, ed. C. Horstman, ii. London, 1896.

STUDIES AND ARTICLES RELATIVE TO THE DIGBY PLAYS

BAKER, D. C. and MURPHY, J. L., 'The Late Medieval Plays of MS Digby 133: Scribes, Dates, and Early History', *Research Opportunities in Renaissance Drama*, x (1967), 153–66.

—— —— 'The Books of Myles Blomefylde', *The Library*, V, xxxi (1976), 377–85.

BENNETT, J., 'The *Mary Magdalene* of Bishop's Lynn', *SP* lxxv (1978), 1–9.

BEVINGTON, D., 'Political Satire in the Morality *Wisdom Who is Christ*', *Renaissance Papers 1963*. Durham, North Carolina, 1964, pp. 41–51.

BOWERS, R. H., 'The Tavern Scene in the Middle English Digby Play of *Mary Magdalene*', . . . *All These to teach: Essays in Honor of C. A. Robertson*, eds. R. A. Bryan, C. M. Alton, and A. A. Murphree. Gainesville, Fla., 1965, pp. 15–32.

'BURIENSIS', 'Myles Blomefylde and William Blomefield's Metrical Writings on Alchemy', *N. & Q.* i (November 1849), 60.

CHAUVIN, SISTER MARY JOHN OF CARMEL, *The Role of Mary Magdalene in Medieval Drama*. Washington, D.C., 1951.

COLDEWEY, J. *Early Essex Drama: A History of its Rise and Fall, and a Theory Concerning the Digby Plays*. Ph.D. thesis, University of Colorado, Boulder, Colorado, 1972.

—— 'The Digby Plays and the Chelmsford Records', *Research Opportunities in Renaissance Drama*, xviii (1975), 103–21.

DAVIDSON, C., 'The Digby *Mary Magdalen* and the Magdalen Cult of the Middle Ages', *Annuale Medievale*, xiii (1972), 70–87.

DOBSON, E. J., 'The Etymology and Meaning of *Boy*', *MÆ* ix (1940), 121–54.

FIFIELD, M., *The Castle in the Circle*, Ball State Monographs, vi (Muncie, Indiana, 1967).

—— 'The Use of Doubling and Extras in *Wisdom*,' *Ball State University Forum*, vi (Autumn 1965), 65–8.

Fulgens and Lucres, eds. F. S. Boas and A. W. Reed. Tudor and Stuart Library. Oxford, 1926.

GRAY, I., 'Footnote to an Alchemist', *Cambridge Review* (30 November 1946), pp. 172–4.

GREEN, J. C., *The Medieval Morality of Wisdom Who is Christ*. Nashville, Tenn., 1938.

GREEN-ARMYTAGE, R. N., 'Myles Blomefylde', *TLS* (5 November 1925), 739.

JEFFREY, D. L., 'English Saints' Plays', *Medieval Drama*, ed. N. Denny, Stratford-upon Avon Studies 16 (London, 1973), pp. 69–89.

—— 'Franciscan Spirituality and Early English Drama', *Mosaic*, viii (1975), 17–46.

JONES, M. L., *Pilgrimage from Text to Stage: A Study of the Staging of Mary Magdalen*. Ph.D. thesis, University of Colorado, Boulder, Colorado, 1977.

MALVERN, M., *The Magdalen*. Ph.D. thesis, Michigan State University, East Lansing, Michigan, 1969.

MEPHAM, W. A., 'A General Survey of Medieval Drama in Essex: the Fifteenth Century', *Essex Review*, liv (April 1945), 52–8.

—— 'A General Survey of Medieval Drama in Essex: the Sixteenth Century', ibid., liv (July 1945), 107–12; continued in the October issue, 139–42.

—— 'Medieval Plays in the Sixteenth Century at Heybridge and Braintree', ibid., lv (January 1946), 8–18.

—— 'Medieval Drama in Essex: Dunmow', ibid., lv (April 1946), 57–65; continued in July issue, 129–36.

—— 'Municipal Drama at Maldon in the Sixteenth Century', ibid., lv (October 1946), 169–75; continued in January 1947, 34–41.

—— 'The Chelmsford Plays in the Sixteenth Century', ibid., lvi (July 1947), 148–52; continued in the October issue, 171–8.

MOLLOY, J. J., *A Theological Interpretation of the Moral Play Wisdom Who is Christ*. Washington, D.C., 1952.

The Old English Versions of the Gesta Romanorum, ed. F. Madden. Roxburgh Club. London, 1838.

PATCH, H. R., 'The *Ludus Coventriae* and the Digby *Massacre*', *PMLA* xxx (1920), 324–43.

PENTZELL, R., 'The Medieval Theatre in the Streets', *Theatre Survey*, xiv (1973), 1–21.

RITCHIE, H., 'A Suggested Location for the Digby "Mary Magdalene" ', ibid., iv (1963), 51–8.

SCHMIDT, K., *Die Digby-Spiele*. Berlin, 1884. (Treats *The Conversion of St. Paul* and *The Killing of the Children*.) This is erroneously listed in Stratman's Bibliography (1954), p. 149, as an edition of the plays; the error is corrected in Stratman's second edition.

—— 'Die Digby-Spiele', *Anglia*, viii (1885), 371–404. (Treats *Mary Magdalen* and *Wisdom*, 371–93.)

SCHULER, R. M., 'An Alchemical Poem: Authorship and Manuscripts', *The Library*, V, xxviii (1973), 240–2.

—— 'William Blomfild, Elizabethan Alchemist', *Ambix*, xx (1973), 75–87.

SMART, W. K., *Some English and Latin Sources and Parallels for the Morality of Wisdom*. Menasha, Wisconsin, 1912.

SMITH, SISTER M. FRANCES, *Wisdom and Personification of Wisdom occurring in Middle English Literature before 1500*. Washington, D.C., 1935.

VELZ, J. W., 'Sovereignty in the Digby *Mary Magdalene*', *Comparative Drama*, ii (1968), 32–43.

VILLAR, MARY DEL, 'The Staging of *The Conversion of St. Paul*', *Theatre Notebook*, xxv (1970–1), 64–8.

WICKHAM, GLYNNE, 'The Staging of Saint Plays in England', *The Medieval Drama*, ed. S. Sticca (Albany, N.Y., 1972), pp. 99–119.

WRIGHT, R., 'Community Theatre in Late Medieval East Anglia', *Theatre Notebook*, xxiv (1974), 24–39.

ZUPITZA, J., 'The Digby Mysteries', *The Academy*, xii (1882), 281. (Furnivall's reply is in the same issue, p. 297.)

STUDIES RELATING TO THE PLAYS OF BODLEY MS E MUSEO 160

ABEL, P., 'Grimald's *Christus Redivivus* and the Digby Resurrection Play', *MLN* lxx (1955), 328–30.

BAKER, D. C. and MURPHY, J. L., 'The Bodleian MS *e Mus*. 160 *Burial* and *Resurrection* and the Digby Plays', *RES*, NS xix (1968), 290–3.

BLACKBURN, R., 'Nicholas Grimald's *Christus Redivivus*: a Protestant Resurrection Play', *ELN* v (1968), 247–50.

LINDER, A., *Plainte de la Vierge*. Uppsala, 1898.

McCALL, J. P., 'Chaucer and the Pseudo-Origen *De Maria Magdalena*: A Preliminary Study', *Speculum*, xlvi (1971), 135–41.

SCHMIDT, K., 'Die Digby-Spiele', *Anglia*, viii (1885), 371–404. (Treats the *Burial* and *Resurrection*, pp. 393–404.)

SZÖVÉRFFY, J., ' "Peccatrix Quondam Femina": A Survey of the Mary Magdalen Hymns', *Traditio*, xix (1963), 79–146.

—— 'The Legends of St. Peter in Medieval Latin Hymns', *Traditio*, x (1954), 275–322.

TAYLOR, G. C., 'The English "Planctus Mariae" ', *MP* iv (1907), 1–33.

THIEN, H., *Über die englischen Marienklagen*. Kiel, 1906.

THOMPSON, E. M., *The Carthusian Order in England*. London, 1930.

WECHSSLER, E., *Die romanischen Marienklagen*. Halle, 1893.

WOOLF, R., *The English Religious Lyric in the Middle Ages*. Oxford, 1968.

GENERAL STUDIES

BEVINGTON, D., *From Mankind to Marlowe*. Cambridge, Mass., 1962.

—— 'Popular and Courtly Tradition on the Early Tudor Stage', *Medieval Drama*, ed. N. Denny, Stratford-upon-Avon Studies 16 (London, 1973), pp. 91–107.

BEVINGTON, D., *Tudor Drama and Politics*. Cambridge, Mass., 1968.

CHAMBERS, E. K., *The Medieval Stage*. 2 vols., Oxford, 1903.

COFFMAN, G. R., 'The Miracle Play in England—Nomenclature', *PMLA* xxxi (1916), 448–65.

—— 'The Miracle Play in England: Some Records of Presentation, and Notes on Preserved Plays', *SP* xvi (1919), 56–66.

COLLIER, J. P., *The History of Dramatic Poetry to the Time of Shakespeare*. 3 vols., London, 1831.

CRAIG, H., *English Religious Drama of the Middle Ages*. Oxford, 1955.

CUSHMAN, L. W. *The Devil and the Vice in the English Dramatic Literature before Shakespeare*. *Studien zur englischen Philologie*, vi. Halle, 1900.

ECCLES, M., '*Ludus Coventriae*: Lincoln or Norfolk?' *MÆ* xl (1971), 135–41.

FRANK, G., *Medieval French Drama*. Oxford, 1954.

GARDINER, H. C., *Mysteries' End: An Investigation of the Last Days of the Mediaeval Religious Stage*. New Haven, 1946.

GARTH, H. M., 'Saint Mary Magdalene in Medieval Literature', *Johns Hopkins University Studies in Historical and Political Science*, lxvii (Baltimore, 1950), pp. 347–452.

GAUVIN, C., *Un Cycle du théâtre religieux anglais au Moyen Age*. Paris, 1973.

GRAY, D., *Themes and Images in the Medieval English Religious Lyric*. London, 1972.

HARDISON, O. B., JR., *Christian Rite and Christian Drama in the Middle Ages*. Baltimore, 1965.

HOSLEY, R., 'Three Kinds of Outdoor Theatre before Shakespeare', *Theatre Survey*, xii (1971), 1–33.

KAHRL, S., *Traditions of Medieval Drama*. London, 1974.

KOLVE. V. A., *The Play Called Corpus Christi*. Stanford, 1966.

MACKENZIE, W. R., 'The Origin of the English Morality', *Washington University Studies*, ii (1915), 141–64.

Magnyfycence, ed. R. L. Ramsay. EETS, ES 98 (1908, reprinted 1958).

MURRAY, J. T., *English Dramatic Companies*. 2 vols., London, 1910.

NELSON, A. H., *The Medieval English Stage*. Chicago, 1974.

PROSSER, E., *Drama and Religion in the English Mystery Plays*. Stanford, 1961.

ROSSITER, A. P., *English Drama from Early Times to the Elizabethans*. London, 1950.

SAXER, V., *Le Culte de Marie Madeleine en occident, des origines à la fin du Moyen-Age*. Paris, 1959.

SAXER, V., 'Les Saintes Marie Madeleine et Marie de Béthanie dans la Tradition Liturgique et Homilétique Orientale', *Revue des Sciences Religieuses*, xxxii (1958), 1–37.

SCHMITT, NATALIE C., 'Was There a Medieval Theatre in the Round? A Re-examination of the Evidence' I, *Theatre Notebook*, xxiii (1969), 130–42; II, xxiv (1969), 18–25.

SOUTHERN, R., *The Medieval Theatre in the Round*. London, 1957.

—— *The Staging of Plays before Shakespeare*. London, 1973.

STEVENS, M., 'The Theatre of the World: A Study in Medieval Dramatic Form', *Chaucer Review*, vii (1973), 234–49.

TEN BRINK, B., *History of English Literature*, ii. London, 1901.

THOMPSON, E. N. S., 'The English Moral Plays', *Transactions of the Connecticut Academy of Arts and Science*, xiv (1910), 291–414.

WARD, A. A., *A History of English Dramatic Literature*, i. London, 1899.

WICKHAM, GLYNNE, *Early English Stages 1300–1660*, i. London, 1959.

WILLIAMS, A., *The Drama of Medieval England*. East Lansing, Michigan, 1961.

—— 'The English Moral Play before 1500', *Annuale Medievale*, iv (1963), 5–22.

WILSON, F. P., (ed. G. K. Hunter), *The English Drama 1485–1585* (Oxford History of English Literature). Oxford, 1968.

WOOLF, R., *The English Mystery Plays*. London, 1972.

YOUNG, K., *The Drama of the Medieval Church*. 2 vols., Oxford, 1933.

PRESENTATION OF TEXTS

THE letters *u*, *v*, and *w* are as they appear in the MSS; *i* and *j* are retained except that capitals are given modern forms. The MS letter *ȝ* is retained where it is common in late medieval usage and will cause no confusion to the reader (e.g. *ȝ* for *y* as in *ȝe* or *ȝif*, *ȝ* for /g/ as in *ileȝant*, and *ȝ* for *gh*), but because of the idiosyncrasies of the *Mary Magdalen* scribe, we have replaced *ȝ* by the more common letters *þ* and *s* (e.g. MS *ȝe* for *þe* is printed as *þe*, and MS *pleȝant* is printed as *plesant*) where the scribe's practice elsewhere justifies the substitution, and *ȝ* is replaced by *z* where it seems warranted (e.g. MS *Laȝarus* is printed *Lazarus*, *ȝynȝyber* as *Zynzyber*, etc.). MS paragraph symbols are omitted. Capitalization, word division, and punctuation are modern. Where numbers are given in Roman numerals in an English context, we print in English words; where they are expressed in Roman numerals in a Latin context, we print in Latin words. Initial double *f* is printed as a capital *F* where appropriate, but otherwise is ignored. Directions from the MSS are italicized. Directions and place names added by the editors are bracketed. Editorial emendations are enclosed in square brackets except where whole words are altered or substituted, and these cases are explained in the textual notes; added words are enclosed in square brackets, and are noted, except when such additions are necessary because of scribal slips and have been accepted since Furnivall's edition. Angle brackets are used to indicate that words or letters have been lost through damage to the MSS. Speakers' names are consistently printed on the left regardless of where they appear in the MSS. All additions and corrections in the MSS themselves may be presumed to be in the hands of the original scribes unless otherwise indicated.

[The Conversion of St. Paul]

Myles Blomefylde[1]

POETA. *Rex glorie*, kyng omnipotent,
 Redemer of þe world by thy pouer diuine,
And Maria, þat pure vyrgy[n] quene most excellent,
 Wyche bare þat blyssyd babe Jhesu þat for vs sufferd payne,
 Vnto whoys goodnes I do inclyne,
Besechyng þat Lord, of hys pytous influens,   5
To preserue and gouerne thys wyrshypfull audyens.

Honorable frendys, besechyng yow of lycens
 To procede owur processe, we may [shew] vnder your correccyon,
The conuersyon of Seynt Paule, as þe Byble gyf experyens.
 Whoo lyst to rede þe booke *Actum Appostolorum*, 10
 Ther shall he haue þe very notycyon;
But, as we can, we shall vs redres,[2]
Brefly, wyth yowur fauour, begynyng owur proces.

[Jerusalem. First station.]   *Daunce*[3]

Here entryth Saule, goodly besene in þe best wyse,
lyke an aunterous knyth, thus sayyng:

SAULUS. Most dowtyd man I am lyuyng vpon the ground,
 Goodly besene, wyth many a ryche garlement!
My pere on lyue I trow ys nott found!   15
 Thorow þe world, fro þe oryent to þe occydent,
 My fame ys best knowyn vndyr þe fyrmament!
I am most drad of pepull vnyuersall—
They dare not dysp[l]ease me[4] most noble!   20

Saule ys my name—I wyll þat ye notyfy—
 Whych conspyreth the dyscyplys wyth thretys and menacys;
Before þe pryncys of prestys most noble and hye,[5]

Editions collated: Furnivall (F), Manly (M), Adams (A), and Bevington (B); M follows F except where noted, and A and B follow M except where noted.

 [1] *at top right of MS*
 [2] dresse *canc.*, re *written over caret, canc.*, redres *added*
 [3] *in later hand*   [4] *M; MS, F* my
 [5] *M; MS, F* hye and noble

I bryng them to punnyshement for ther trespace.   25
We wyll them nott suffer to rest in no place,
For they go abou3te to preche and gyff exemplis[1]   f. 3
To destroye oure lawes, sinagoges, and templis.

By the god Bellyall,[2] I schall make progresse
Vnto the pryncys, both Caypha and Anna,   30
Where I schall aske of them in suernes
To persue thorow all Dammask and Liba.
And thus we schall soone after than
Bryng them[3] þat so do lyff into Jerusalem,
Both man and child that I fynd of them!   35

*Her cummyth Sale to Caypha and Anna, prestys of þe
tempyll.*

Nobyll prelatys and pryncys of[4] regalyte,
    Desyryng and askyng, of your benyngne wurthynes,
Your letters and epystolys[5] of most souerente,
    To subdue rebellyous that wyll of frawardnes
    Agaynst our lawes rebell or transgresse,   40
Nor wyll not inclyne, but mak obiecc[y]on;
To pursue all such, I wyll do proteccyon.

CAYPHA. To your desyer we gyf perfyth sentens,
    Accordyng to your petycyons that ye make postulacyon,
Bycause we know your trewe delygens   45
    To persue all tho þat do reprobacyon
    Agayns owur lawes by ony redarguacyon.
Wherefor, shortly we gyf in commandment
To put down them þat be dy[s]obedyent.

ANNA. And by thes letturs þat be most reuerrent,   f.
    Take them in hand, full agre þerto,   51
Constreyne all rebellys by owur hole assent,
    We gyf yow full power so to doo.
    Spare not hardly for frend nor foo!
All thos ye fynd of þat lyfe in thys realme,   55
Bounde, loke ye bryng them into Jerusalem!

¹ *ll. 27–35 in different style, but probably same hand as bulk of text*
² all *inserted above* Belly   ³ of *canc. after* them
⁴ p *canc. after* of   ⁵ *first* y *over* e

Her Saule resayuyth ther letters.

SAULUS. Thys precept here I take in hande,
  To fullfyll after yowur wyllys both,
Wher I shall spare wythin þis londe
  Nother man nor woman—to þis I make an oth—[1]   60
But to subdue, I wyll not be loth!
Now folow me, knytys and seruauntys trewe,
Into Damaske, as fast as ye can sewe!

PRIMUS MILES. Vnto your commaundment I do obeysaunce.
  I wyll not[2] gaynsay nor make delacyon,   65
But wyth good mynd and harty[3] plesaunce
  I shall yow succede, and make perambulacyon
  Thorowoute Damaske wyth all delectacyon,
And all thoo[4] rebell and make resystens,
For to oppres I wyll do my delygens.   70

SECUNDUS MILES. And in me shalbe no neclygens,
  But to[5] thys precept myself I shall applye:
To do your behest wyth all conuenyens,
  Wythowt eny frowardnes or eny obstynacy—
  Non shall appere in me— but, verely,   75
Wyth all my mynd I yow insure,
To resyst tho rebellys I wyll do my cure!

SAULUS.[6] Truly, to me yt ys grett consolacyon   f. 38ᵛ
  To here thys report þat ye do avauns.
For your sapyencyall wyttys I gyf commendacyon!   80
  Euer at my nede I haue founde yow constant.
  But, knytys and seruuantys þat be so plesaunt,
I pray yow anon my palfray ye bryng,
To spede my jurney wythowt lettyng!

    Here goyth Sale forth a lytyll asyde for to make hym
    redy to ryde, the seruua[n]t[7] thus seyng:

---

[1] *ll. 59–60 trans.; scribe has marked order by labelling them* B *and* A
[2] not *over caret*
[3] *a second* harty *canc.*
[4] *MS, F, B; M emends to* that; *A emends to* thoo [who]
[5] to *underlined by later hand*
[6] *repeated from foot of f. 38ʳ*
[7] *only three minims for* uu *but it is not a* w; *and* stabylgrom *canc. after* seruuant

SERUUS. How, hosteler, how! A peck of otys and a botell of haye!   85
    Com of apase, or I wyll to another inne!
What, hosteler, why commyst not thy way?
    Hye þe faster! I beshrew þi skynne!
STABULARYUS. I am non hosteler, nor non hostelers kynne,
But a jentylmanys seruuant, I! þou dost know   90
Such crabyysh wordys do aske a blow!

SERUUS. I cry yow mercy, syr! I wyst well sumwhat ye were,
    Owþer a gentylman or a knaue, me thynkyth by your physnomy!
Yf on loke yow in þe face þat neuer se yow ere,
    Wold thynk ye were at þe next dore by!   95
    In good fayth, I wenyd yow had bene an hosteler, verely.
I sye suche another jentylman wyth yow a barowfull bare
Of horsdowng and doggys tordys, and sych other gere!

And how yt happenyd a mervelous chance betyde—
    Your felow was not suer of foote, and yet he went very brode,[1] 10
Butt in a cow tord both dyd ye slyde!
    And, as I wene, your nose þerin rode—
    Your face was bepayntyd wyth sowters code!
I sey neuer sych a syȝt,[2] I make God a vow!   f. :
Ye were so begrymlyd and yt had bene a sowe!   10

STABULARIUS. In fayth, þou neuer syest me tyll þis day!
    I haue dwellyd wyth my master thys seuen[3] ȝere and more.
Full well I haue pleasyd hym, he wyll not say nay,
    And mykyll he makyth of me therfore!
SERUUS. By my trowth, þan be ye changyd to a new lore?   11
A seruand ye are, and þat a good!
Ther ys no better lokyth owt of a hood!

STABULARIUS. Forsoth, and a hood I vse for to were,
    Full well yt ys lynyd wyth sylk and chamlett;
Yt kepyth me fro the cold, þat þe wynd doth me not dere,   11
    Nowther frost nor snow þat I therby do sett.

---

[1] wyde canc. after very; brode written above; all edns. brode except B, who prints wide
[2] sytt canc., syȝt written after
[3] vij

SERUUS. Yea, yt ys a dobyll hood, and þat a fett.[1]
He was a good man þat made yt, I warant yow—
He was nother horse ne mare[2] nor yet yokyd sow!

Here commyth þe fyrst knyth to þe stabylgrom, sayng:

PRIMUS MILES. Now, stabyllgrom, shortly bryng forth away   120
The best horse, for owur lorde wyll ryde!
STABYLARIUS. I am full redy! Here ys a palfray,
Ther can no man a better bestryde!
He wyll conducte owur lorde and gyde
Thorow the world; he ys sure and abyll   125
To bere a gentyllman, he [ys][3] esy and prophetabyll.

Her þe knyth cummyth to Saule wyth a horse.

PRIMUS MILES. Behold, Syr Saule! Your palfray ys comm,
Full goodly besene, as yt ys yowur desyer,
To take yowur vyage thorow euery regyon.
Be nott in dowt he wyll spede your mater,   f. 39ᵛ
And we, as your seruauntys, wyth glad chere   131
Shall gyf attendance. We wyll nott gaynsay,
But folow yow where ye go, be ny3t or day!

SAULUS. Vnto Damask I make my progressyon
To pursue all rebellyous[4] beyng froward and obstynate   135
Agayns our lawes be ony transgressyon.
Wyth all my delygens myself I wyll prepar[at]e,[5]
Concernyng my purpose to oppres and seperate;
Non shall reioyce that doth offend,
But vtterly to reproue wyth mynde and intende.   140

Her Sale rydyth forth wyth hys seruantys abowt þe
place, owt of þe pl⟨ace⟩.

CAYPHA. Now Saule hath takyn hys wurthy wyage
To pursue rebellyous, of what degre þei be,

---

[1] good *canc. before* fett   [2] *F; MS* nare
[3] *F*   [4] *probably superfluous abbreviation superscript over* ou (*or* on.²)
[5] *M; MS, F* prepare

He wyll non suffer to raygne nor haue passage
Wythin all thys regyon, we be in sertayn[te].[1]
Wherefor I commende hys goodly dygnyte,   14
That he thus aluay takyth in hande,
By hys power to gouerne thus all thys lande.

ANNA. We may lyue in rest by hys consolacyon.
He defendyth vs, wherefor we be bownde
To loue hym intyrely wyth our harttys affeccyon,   15
And honour hym as champyon in euery stownde.
Ther ys non such lyuyng vpon þe grownde,
That may be lyke to[2] hym, nor be hys pere,
Be est nor west, ferre nor nere!

Poeta—si placet.

Daunce[3]   *Conclusyon*

[POETA]. Fynally, of þis stac[y]on thus we mak a conclusyon.[4]   15
Besechyng thys audyens to folow and succede
Wyth all your delygens þis generall processyon;
To vnderstande þis matter, wo lyst to rede
The Holy Bybyll for þe better spede,
Ther shall he haue þe perfyth intellygens,   16
And þus we comyt yow to Crystys magnyfycens!

Finis istius stacionis et altera sequitur.

POETA. Honorable frendys, we beseche yow of audyens   f.
To here our intencyon, and also our prosses.
Vpon our matter, be your fauorable lycens,
Another part of þe story we wyll redres: 16
Here shalbe brefly shewyd, wyth all our besynes,
At thys pagent Saynt Poullys conuercyon.
Take ye good hede, and therto gyf affeccyon!

Here commyth Saule, rydyng in wyth hys seruantys.

---

[1] *M; MS, F* sertayn
[2] *inserted by later hand; no edn. prints*
[3] *in later hand in left margin*
[4] *letter blotted after* conclusyon, *superfluous suspension above*

SAULUS. My purpose to Damask fully I intende;
　　To pursewe the dyscypulys, my lyfe I apply!　　　170
For to breke down the chyrchys thus I condescende.
　Non I wyll suffer that shall edyfey—
　Perchaunce owur lawes they¹ my3te therby,
And the pepull also, turne and conuerte,
Whych shuld be gret heuynes vnto myn hart.　　　175

Nay, þat shall nott be butt layd apart!
þe prynces haue gouyn me full potestacyon—
All that I fynd, þei shall nott start,
　But bounde to Jerusalem, wyth furyous vyolacyon,
　Befor Cesar, Caypha, and Annas [have]² presentacyon.　　　180
Thus shalbe subduyd tho wretchys of þat lyfe,
That³ non shall injoy, nother man, chy[l]de, nor wyfe!

　　　Here comyth a feruent, wyth gret tempest, and Saule
　　　faulyth down of hys horse; þat done, Godhed spekyth
　　　in heuyn:

DEUUS. Saule, Saule! Why dost þou me pursue?
　　Yt ys hard to pryke agayns þe spore!
I am þi Savyour þat ys so trwe,　　　185
　Whych made heuyn and erth,⁴ and eche creature.
　Offende nott my goodnes; I wyll þe recure!
SAULUS.⁵ O Lord, I am aferd, I trymble for fere!　　　f. 40ᵛ
What woldyst I ded? Tell me here!

DEUS. Aryse, and goo þou wyth glad chere　　　190
　Into the cyte a lytyll besyde,
And I shall þe socor in euery dere,
　That no maner of yll xal betyde,
　And I wyll ther for the prouyde
By my grete goodnes what þou shalt doo.　　　195
Hy þe as fast thether as þou mast goo.

SAULUS. O mercyfull God, what aylyth me?
　I am lame, my leggys be take me fro!
My sygth⁶ lykwyse, I may nott see!

---

¹ than　　² M　　³ *blotted letter after* that　　⁴ r *added above*
⁵ *repeated from foot of f. 40ʳ*　　⁶ *also canc. after* sygth

I can nott tell whether to goo!   200
My men hath forsake me also.
Whether shall I wynde, or whether shall I pas?
Lord, I beseche the, helpe me of thy grace!

PRIMUS MILES. Syr, we be here to help the in þi nede—
   Wyth all our affyance we wyll nott sesse![1]   205
SAULUS. Than in Damask I pray yow me lede,
I[n] Godys name, accordyng to my promyse.
SECUNDUS MILES. To put forth yowur hand, loke ye dresse.
Cum on your way! We shall yow bryng
Into þe cyte wythowt taryng.   210

Here the knyghtys lede forth Sale into a place,
and Cryst apperyth to[2] Annanie, sayng:

DEUS. Ananie, Ananie! Where art þou, Ananie?

ANANIAS.[3] Here, Lord! I am here trwly!   f. 41

DEUS. Go thy way, and make þi curse
   As I shall assyng þe by myn aduysse,
Into þe strete, *qui dicitur rectus*,   215
   And in a certayn house, of warantyse,
Ther shall ye fynd Saule in humble vyse,
As a meke lambe þat a wolf before was namyd.
Do my behest! Be nothyng ashamyd!

He wantyth hys syth, by my punyshment constrayned;   220
   Prayeng vnto me, I assure þou shalt hym fynd.
Wyth my stroke of pyte sore ys he paynyde,
   Wantyng hys sygth, for he ys truly blynyde.
ANANIAS. Lord, I am aferd, for aluay in[4] my mynd
I here so myche of hys[5] furyous cruelte,   225
þat for spekyng of þi name to deth he will[6] þut me.

DEUS. Nay, Ananie, nay, I assure þe,
   He wulbe glad of thy cummyng!

---

[1] *MS* serse; *F, M emend to* seise   [2] to *inserted above*
[3] *repeated from foot of f. 40^v*   [4] in *inserted over caret*
[5] cruell *canc. after* hys; cl *canc. after* furyous   [6] *inserted over caret*

ANANIAS. A, Lord, but I know of a certayn[te][1]
That thy seyntys in Jerusalem to deth he doth bryng!   230
Many yllys of hym I haue bekennyng,
For he hath the poure of the pryncys alle,
To saue or spylle, do[2] which he schall.

DEUS. Be nothyng a-drad! He ys a chosen wessell,
To me assyngned by my Godly eleccyon.   235
He shall bere my name before the kyngys and chylder of Israell,
By many sharpe shourys sufferyng correccyon;
A gret doctor of benyngne conpleccyon,
The trwe precher of the hye deuynete,   f. 41ᵛ
A very pynacle of þe fayth, I ensure the.   240

ANANYAS. Lorde, thy commandment I shall fullfyll;
Vnto Saule I wyll take my waye.
DEUS. Be nothyng[3] in dowte for good nor yll.
Farewell, Ananie! Tell Saule what I do say.

Et exiat Deus.

ANANIAS. Blyssyd Lord, defende me as þou best may!   245
Gretly I fere hys cruell tyranny,
But to do þi precept, myself I shall applye.

Here Ananias goth toward Saule.

PRIMUS MYLES. I maruayle gretly what yt doth mene,
To se owur master in thys hard stounde!
The wonder grett lythtys þat were so[4] shene   250
Smett hym doune of hys hors to þe grownde,
And me thowt that I hard a sounde
Of won spekyng wyth voyce delectable,
Whych was to [vs][5] wonderfull myrable.

SECUNDUS MYLES. Sertenly thys lyȝt was ferefull to see,   255
The sperkys of fyer were very feruent!
Yt inflamyd so greuosely about þe countre,

---

¹ *M*; *MS, F* certayn   ² wich *canc. after* do
³ adrad *canc. after* nothyng   ⁴ se   ⁵ *M*

That, by my trowth, I went we shuld a bene brent![1]
But now, serys, lett vs relente
Agayne to Caypha and Anna to tell þis chaunce,   26
How yt befell to vs thys greuauns.

Her Saule ys in comtemplacyon.

SAULUS. Lord, of þi coumfort moch I desyre,
   þou myȝty Prynce of Israell, Kyng of pyte,
Whyche me hast punyshyd as þi presoner,
   That nother ete nor dranke[2] thys dayes thre.   f.
But, gracyos Lorde, of þi vysytacyon I thanke the;   26
Thy seruant shall I be as long as I haue breth,
Thowgh I therfor shuld suffer dethe.

Here commyth Anania to Saule, sayeng:

ANANIAS. Pease be in thys place and goodly mansyon!
   Who ys wythin? Speke, in Crystys holy name!   27
SALUS. I am here, Saule! Cum in,[3] on Goddys benyson!
   What ys your wyll? Tell, wythowten blame.
ANANIAS. From Almyghty God sertanly to the sent I am,
And Ananie men call me wheras I dwell.
SAULUS. What wold ye haue? I pray yow me tell!   27

ANANIAS. Gyfe me your hand for your awayle;
   For as I was commaundyd by hys gracyos sentens,
He[4] bad the be stedfast, for þou shalt be hayle.
   For thys same cause he sent me to þi presens.
Also, he bad the remember hys hye excellens,   28
Be þe same tokyn þat he dyd þe mete
Toward þe cyte, when he apperyd in þe strete.

Ther mayst þou know hys power celestyall,
   How he dysposyth euery thyng as hym lyst;
Nothyng may wythstand hys myȝte essencyall;   28
   To stond vpryght, or els[5] doun to thryste—
Thys ys hys powur, yt may not be myste,

---

[1] e *inserted above*   [2] y *of* drynke *blotted,* a *added above*
[3] on *canc. after* Cum   [4] *A, B; MS, F* And; *M emends to* [I byd]
[5] to *canc. after* els

For who þat¹ yt wantyth, lackyth a frende.
Thys ys þe massage þat he doth þe sende.

SAULUS.² His marcy to me ys ryght welcom!   f. 42ᵛ
I am ryght glad þat yt ys thus.   291

Hic aparebit Spiritus Sanctus super eum.

ANANIAS. Be of good chere and perfyte jubylacyon!
Discendet super te Sprytus Sanctus,
Whych hath wyth hys hye³ grace illumynyd vs.
Put fo[r]th þi hond, and goo wyth me—   295
Agayne to thy syght here I restore the!

SAULUS. Blyssyd Lord, thankys to yow euer bee!
The swame ys fallyn from my eyes twayne!
Where I was blynyd and cowd nott see,
Lord, þou hast sent me my syght agayne.   300
From sobbyng and wepyng I can not refrayne
My pensyue hart full of contryccyon;
For my offencys, my body shal haue punycyon.

And where I haue vsed so gret persecucyon
Of þi descyplys thorow all Jerusalem,   305
I wyll [ayd]⁵ and defende ther predycacyon,
That th[e]y dyd tech on all þis reme.
Wherefor, Ananie, at the watery streme
Baptyse me, hartely I þe praye,
Among your numbyr, that I electe and chosen be may!   310

ANANIAS. Onto þis well of mych vertu
We wyll⁴ vs hye wyth all our delygens!
SAULUS. Go yow before, and after I shall sewe,
Laudyng and praysyng our Lordys benevolens!
I shall neuer offend hys my3ty magnyfycens,   315
But aluay obserue hys preceptys, and kepe.   f. 43ʳ
For my gret vnkyndnes my hart doth wepe!

---

¹ who þat *in left margin, caret between* for *and* yt
² *repeated from foot of f.* 42ʳ
³ hys
⁴ F
⁵ we *canc. after* wyll

ANANIAS. Knele ye down vpon thys grownde,
　Receyuyng thys crystenyng wyth good intent,
Whyche shall make yow hole of your dedly wound　　　　32
　That was infecte wyth venom nocent.[1]
　Yt purgyth synne, and fendys pourys so fraudelent
It putyth asyde; where thys doth attayne,
In euery stede, he may not obtayne!

I crysten yow, wyth mynd full perfyght,　　　　32
　Reseyuyng yow into owur relygyon,
Euer to be stedfast, and neuer to flyt,
　But euer constant, wythowt varyacyon.
　Now ys fulfyllyd all our obseruacyon,
Concludyng, þou mayst yt ken,　　　　33
In nomine patris et filij et spiritus sancti, Amen.

SAULUS. I am ryght glad as foule on flyte
　That I haue receyuyd þis blyssyd sacrement!
ANANIAS. Com on your way, Saule, for nothyng lett!
　Take yow sum coumforth for your bodyes[2] noryschment.　　　　33
　Ye shall abyde wyth þe dyscyplys verament
Thys many dayes in Damask cyte,
Vntyll þe tyme more perfyt ye may be.

SAULUS. As ye commande, holy father Ananie,
　I full assent at yow[ur] request,　　　　34
To be gydyd and rulyd as ye wyll haue me,
　Evyn at your pleasur, as ye thynk best;
　I shall not offend, for most nor lest.
Go forth yowur way, I wyll succede　　　　f.
Into what place ye wyll me lede.　　　　34

Daunce[3]　　　　　　　　*Conclusyo*

POETA. Thus Saule ys conuertyd, as ye se expres,
　The very trw seruant of our Lord Jhesu.
Non may be lyke to hys perfy3t holynes,
　So nobyll[4] a doctor, constant and trwe;
　Aftyr hys conuersyon neuer mutable, but styll insue　　　　35

---

[1] -ys *suspension canc. after* nocent　　　[2] c *canc. after* bodyes
[3] *in left margin in later hand*　　　[4] co *canc. after* nobyll

The lawys of God to teche euer more and more,
As Holy Scrypture tellyth[1] whoso lyst to loke þerfore.

Thus we comyte yow all to þe Trynyte,
    Conkludyng thys stacyon as we can or may,
Vnder þe correccyon of them þat letteryd be;   355
    Howbeyt vnable, as I dare speke or say,
    The compyler hereof shuld translat veray
So holy a story, but wyth fauorable correccyon
Of my honorable[2] masters, of þer benygne supplexion.[3]

Finis istius secunde stacionis et sequitur tarcia.

POETA. The myght of the Fadirys potenciall Deite   360
    Preserue thys honorable and wurshypfull congregacyon,
That here be present of hye and low degre,
    To[4] vnderstond thys pagent at thys lytyll stacyon,
    Whych we shall procede wyth all our delectac[y]on,
Yf yt wyll plese yow to gyf audyens fauorable.   365
Hark wysely therto—yt ys good and profetable!

[*Jerusalem. Caypha and Anna in the temple. Enter the knights.*]

PRIMUS MILES. Nobyll prelatys, take hede to owur sentens!   f. 44ʳ
    A wundyrfull chaunce fyll and dyd betyde
Vnto owur master Saull when he departyd hens,
    Into Damaske purposyd to ryde.   370
    A meruelous lyȝt fro th'element dyd glyde,
Whyche smet doun[5] hym to grunde, both horse and man,
Wyth the ferfulest wether þat euer[6] I in cam!

SECUNDUS MILES. It rauysshid hym, and his spiritys did
                                                benomme!
    A swete dulcet voyce spake hym vnto,   375
And askyd wherfor he made suche persecucyon
    Ageynst hys dyscyplys, and why he dyd soo.
    He bad hym into Damaske to Ananie goo,

---

[1] M; MS, F tellyd
[2] MS f *altered to* h; *all edns. print* fauorable *but* M *queries* honorable
[3] MS benygne & supplexion; *all edns. ignore ampersand*
[4] w *canc. after* to   [5] doum
[6] þat euer *added in left margin, caret inserted before* I

And ther he shuld reseyue baptym truly;
And now clene ageyns owur lawys he ys, trwly!

CAYPHA. I am sure thys tale ys not trw!
  What, Saule conuertyd from our law?
He went to Damask for to pursue
  All the dyscyplys that dyd wythdraw
  Fro[1] owur fayth—thys was hys sawe!
How say ye, Anna, to thys mater? þis ys a mervelos chans!
I can not beleve þat thys ys of assurans!

ANNA. No, Caypha, my mynde trwly do [I][2] tell,
  That he wyll not turne in no maner wyse,
But rather to deth put and expell
  All myscreauntys and wretchys þat doth aryse
  Agaynst our lawes be ony enterpryse!
Say the trwth, wyth[owt] ony cause frawdelent,
Or els, for your talys, ye be lyke to be shent!

PRIMUS MILES. Ellys owur bodyes may [ye][3] put to payn![4]
  All þat we declare, I sye yt wyth my nye—
  Nothyng offendyng, but trwly do iustyfye!

CAYPHAS.[5] By the gret god, I do maruayle gretly!
  And thys be trw þat ye do reherse,
He shall repent hys rebellyous treytory,
  That all shalbe ware of hys falsnes!
  We wyll not suffer hym to obtayne, dowtles,
For meny perellys þat myght betyde,
By hys subtyll meanys on euery syde.

ANNA. The law ys commyttyd to owur aduysment,
  Wherfor we wyll not se yt decay,
But rather vphold yt, help and agment,
  That ony reprofe to vs fall may
  Of Cesar th'emproure by nyзt or day!
We shall to such maters harke and attende,
Accordyng to the lawes, our wyttys to spende!

---

¹ w canc. after Fro   ² F   ³ M
⁴ ys canc. after payn   ⁵ repeated from foot of f. 44ʳ

DIABOLUS[1]

(The following passage cancelled in manuscript)

Her apperyth Saule in a disciplis wede, sayeng:

SAULUS. That Lord þat ys shaper of see and of sond,
   And hath wrowth wyth hys woord all thyng at hys wyll,
Saue thys semely þat here syttyth or stonde,
   For hys meke marcy þat we do nott spyll.
   Grant me, good Lord, thy pleasure to fulfyll,   5
And send me suche speche that I þe trwth say,
My entencyons proph[e]table to meve yf I may.

Welbelouyd frendys, ther be seuen[2] mortall synnes,
   Whych be provyd pryncypall and pryncys[3] of poysonnes.
Pryde, þat of bytternes all bale begynnes,   10
   Wythholdyng all fayth, yt fedyth and foysonnes,
   As Holy Scryptur beryth playn wyttnesse:
'*Inicium omnium peccatorum superbya est*'—
That often dystroyeth both most and lest!

(End of cancelled passage)

Here[4] *to enter a dyvel wyth thunder and fyre, and to avaunce* f. 45ʳ
*hymsylfe, sayeng as folowyth, and hys spech spokyn, to syt
downe in a chayre:*

BELYALL. Ho, ho, beholde me, þe myȝte prynce of þe partys
                                 infernall!
Next vnto Lucyfer I am in magestye!
By name I am nominate þe god Belyall—
   Non of more myȝte nor of more excellencye!   415
   My powre ys pryncypall, and now of most soferaynte;
In þe templys and synagogys who[5] deneyth me to honore,
My busshopys, thorow my motyon, þei wyl hym sone devoure!

I haue movyd my prelatys, Cayphas and Anna,
   To persew and put downe by powre ryall,   420
Thorow þe sytyes of Damaske and Liba,
   All soch as do worship þe hye God supernall.

---

[1] *in left margin in later hand*   [2] vij   [3] n *written over* prycys
[4] *this direction and following scene (and to l. 515) are in the second principal hand*
[5] w *over caret*

There deth ys conspyryd wythowt any fauoure at all;
My busshopys hathe chosyne won most rygorus
Them to persew, howse name ys *Saulus*.   4

Ho! Thus as a god most hye in magestye
I rayne and I rule ouer creaturys humayne.
Wyth souerayne sewte sowȝte to ys my deyte;
Mans mynd ys applicant as I lyst to ordeyne!
My law styll encreasyth, wherof I am fayne!   4
Yet of late I haue hard of no newys, truly,[1]
Wherfor I long tyll I speke wyth my messenger Mercurye.

Here shall entere anoþer devyll callyd Mercury, wyth a f
fyeryng, commyng in hast, cryeng and roryng, and shall say
as folowyth:

MARCURY. Ho! Owȝt,[2] owȝt! Alas, thys sodayne chance!
Well may we bewayle þis cursyd aduenture!
BELYAL. Marcurye, what aylyst þou? Tell me thy grevaunce!   4
Ys þer any þat hath wrowȝte vs dyspleasure?
MERCURY. Dyspleasure inowgh, þerof ye may be sure!
Our law at lengthe yt wylbe clene downe layd,
For yt decayth sore, and more wyl, I am afrayd!

BELYAL. Ho, how can þat be? Yt ys not possyble!
Co[n]syder, þou foole, þe long contynuance!
'Decaye', quod-a! Yt ys not credyble!
Of fals tydyngys, þou makyst here vtterance!
Behold how the people[3] hath no pleasaunce
But in syn, and to folow our desyere,
Pryde and voluptuosyte þer hartys doth so fyre.

Thowȝe on do swauer away from our lore,
Yet ys our[4] powre of suche nobylyte,
To have hym agayne, and twoo[5] therfore,
þat shal preferre þe prayse of owre maiestye!
What ys þe tydyngys? Tell owt, lett vs see!
Why arte þou amasyd so? Declare afore vs,
What fury ys fallyn þat troblyth þe thus?

[1] e *over* truly   [2] ȝ *added above*
[3] *MS* o *added above; F* peple
[4] *added over caret*   [5] ij *added above*

MERCURY. Ho! Ow3t,[1] ow3te! He þat I most trustyd to,   f. 46ʳ
And he þat I thow3te wold haue ben to vs most specyall,   455
Ys now of late turnyd, and our cruell foo!
Our specyall frynd, our chosen Saull,
Ys becomme seruante to þe hye God eternall!
As he dyd ryde on our enemyes persecutyon,
He was sodenly strykyn by þe hye provysyon,   460

And now ys baptysyd, and promys he hath made
Neuer to vary, and soch grace he hath opteynyd
þat ondowtyd hys fayth from hym can not fade.
Wherfor to complayne I am constraynyd,
For moch by hym shuld we haue prevaylyd.   465
BELYAL. Ho! Ow3t, ow3t! What, haue we loste
Our darlyng most dere, whom we lovyd moste?

But ys yt of trowth þat þou doyst here specyfye?
MERCURY. Yt ys so, vndow3tyd! Why shuld I fayne?
For thow3te, I can do non oþer but crye!   470

Here þei shall rore and crye, and þen Belyal shal saye:

BELYAL. Ow3te! þis grevyth vs worse þan hell payne!
þe conuersyon of [a][2] synner certayne
Ys more payne to vs and persecutyon,
Than all þe furyes of þe infernall dongyon!

MERCURY. Yt doyth not avayl vs thus to lament,   f. 46ᵛ
But lett vs provyd for remedy shortlye!   476
Wherfor let vs both, by on assent,
Go to þe busshopys and moue þem pryvelye
þat by some sotyl meane þei may cause hym to dye.
Than shal he in our law make no dysturbaunce,   480
Nor hereafter cause vs to haue more greuaunce!

BELYAL. Wel sayd, Mercurye! Thy cowncel ys profytable.
Ho, Saul, þou shalt repent thy vnstablenes!
Thou hadyst ben better to haue byn confyrmable
To our law—for thy deth, dowtles,   485
Yt ys conspyryd to reward thy falsnes!
Thowgh on hath dyssayvyd vs, yet nowadays
Twenti[3] doyth gladly folow oure layes:

---

[1] 3 *added above*   [2] *M; A* [one]; *B does not emend*   [3] xxᵗⁱ

Some by Pryde, some thorowgh Envye;
Ther rayneth thorow my myght so moch dysobedyaunce,
Ther was neuer among Crystyans less charyte
Than ys at þis howre; and as for Concupysence,
[He]¹ rayneth as a lord thorow my violence!
Glotony and Wrath euery man doth devyse,
And most now ys praysyd my cosyn Covytyce!

Cum, Mercury, let vs go and do as we haue sayd;
To delate yt any lenger, yt ys not best!
MERCURY. To bryng yt abow3t, I wold be wel apayd!
Tell yt be done, let vs not rest!²
BELYAL. Go we than shortly! Let vs departe,
Hys deth to devyse, syth he wyl not revart!

Here þei shal vanyshe away wyth a fyrye flame, and a tempest.

[Damascus]

Here aperyth Saul in hys dyscyplys wede, sayng:

[SAULUS.] That Lord þat ys shaper of see and of sonde,
And hath wrow3t wyth hys worde al thyng at hys wyl,
Saue þis asemly þat here syttyth or stond,
For hys meke mercy, þat we do not spyll.
Graunte me, good Lorde, þi pleasure to fulfyll,
And send me soch spech þat I the truth say,
My ententyons profytable to meve yf I may.

Welbelovyd fryndys, þer be seuen³ mortal synnys,
Whych be provyd pryncypall and pryncys of poysons.
Pryde, þat of bytternes all bale begynnys,
Wythholdyng all fayth, yt fedyth and foysonnys,
As Holy Scrypture baryth playn wytnes:
'Initium omnium peccatorum su[per]bia est'—
That often dystroyth both man and best.⁴

¹ M
² *A line seems missing after l. 499; all edns. except Wickham number it l. 500,
but we do not*
³ vij
⁴ *end of the second principal scribe's work. F, M, and B print the text of the first
version of the two stanzas; A prints the first 8 lines of M's text*

Off all vyces and foly, pryde ys the roote;
   Humy⸱lyte may not rayn ner yet indure.
Pyte, alak, that ys flower and boot,
   Ys exylyd wher pryde hath socour.
    'Omnis qui se exaltat humiliabitur.'   520
Good Lord, gyf vs grace to vnderstond and perseuer,
Thys wurd, as þou bydyst, to fulfyll euer.

Whoso in pryde beryth hym to hye,
   Wyth mysheff shalbe mekyd as I mak mensyon.
And I therfor assent and fully certyfy   525
   In text, as I tell the trw entencyon
   Of perfyȝt goodnes and very locucyon:
    'Noli tibi dico in altum sapere sed time'.
Thys ys my consell: bere the not to hye!

But drede alway synne and folye   530
   Wrath, enuy, couytys, and slugyshnes;
Exeunt owt of thy syȝt glotony and lechery,
   Vanyte and vayneglory, and fals idylnes—
   Thes be the branchys of all wyckydnes.
Who þat in hym thes vyces do roote,   535
He lackyth all grace, and bale ys þe boote.

'Lern at myself, for I am meke in hart'—
   Owur Lorde to hys seruantys thus he sayth,
'For meknes I sufferyd a spere at my hart;
   Meknes¹ all vycys anullyth and delayeth;   540
   Rest to soulys ye² shall fynd in fayth:
    "Discite a me quia mitis sum et corde humilis,
Et invenietis requiem animabus vestris."'

So owur Sauyour shewyth vs exampls of meknes,
   Thorow grace of hys goodnes mekly vs³ groundys.⁴   545
Trwly yt wyll vs saue fro þe synnes sekenes,
   For⁵ Pryde and hys progeny mekenes confoundys.
    'Quanto maior es tanto humilia te in omnibus'—
The gretter þou art, the lower loke thu be;
Bere the neuer þe hyer for þi degre.   550

---

    ¹ *second* e *added above*   ² *M*; *MS, F, B* yt
    ³ *B*; *MS* ys; *M suggests* yt   ⁴ groundys *MS* s *over another letter*
    ⁵ Fror

Fro sensualyte of fleshe, thyself loke þou lede;
  Vnlefully therin vse not thy[1] lyfe!
Whoso therin delyteth, to deth he must nede.
  It consumyth nature, the body sleyth wythowt knyf;
  Also yt styntyth nott but manslawter and stryf.   5:
'*Omnis fornicator aut immundus non habet hereditatem Christi*':
Non shall in heuyn posses that be so vnthryfty!

Fle fornycac[y]on, nor be no letchour,
  But spare your speche, and spek nott theron:
'*Ex[2] habundancia[3] cordis os loquitur.*'   5(
  Who movyth yt oft, chastyte louyth non;
  Of þe hartys habundans, þe tunge[4] makyth locucyon.
What manys mynde ys laboryd, therof yt spekyth—
That ys of suernes, as Holy Scryptur tretyth.[5]

Wherfor I reherse thys wyth myn owyn mowthe: 5⦁
'*Caste viuentes templum Dei sunt.*'
Kepe clene your body from synne vncuth;
  Stabyll your syghtys, and look ye not stunt,
  For[6] of a sertaynte I know at a brunt,
'*Oculus est nuncius peccati—*'   5⸗
That the Iey ys euer þe messenger of foly.

SERUUS SACERDOTUM. Whate, ys not thys Saule þat toke hys vyage
  Into Jerusalem, the dyscyplys to oppresse?
Bounde, he wold bryng them, yf ony dyd rage
  Vpon Cryst—þis was hys processe—   5⸗
  To þe pryncys of prestys, he sayde, dowtles—
Thorow all Damask and also Jerusalem,
Subdwe all templys þat he founde of them.

SALUS. Yes, sertaynly, Saule ys my proper name,   f.
  That had in powr the full dominion—   5⦁
To hyde yt fro you, yt were gret shame,
  And mortall synne, as in my opynyon—
  Vnder Cesar and prystys of the relygyon,
And templys of Jues þat be very hedyous,
Agayns almyghty Cryst, þat Kyng so precyous.   5⦁

---

[1] self *canc. after* thy   [2] a *canc. after* Ex   [3] ia *over* y
[4] hart *canc.*, tunge *added above*   [5] n *canc. before* tretyth
[6] at *canc. after* For

SER[U]US SACERDOTUM. To Anna and Caypha ye must make your
                                                        recurse.
    Com¹ on your way, and make no delacyon!

SAULUS. I wyll yow succede, for better or wors,
    To the pryncys of prystys wyth all delectacyon!

SERUUS SACERDOTUM. Holy prystys of hye potestacyon,   590
Here ys Saule! Lok on hym wysely—
He ys another man than he was, verely!

SAULUS. I am þe seruant of Jhesu almyghty,
    Creator and maker of see and sonnd,
Whiche ys king conctypotent of heuyn glory,   595
    Chef comfort and solace, both to fre and bonde,
    Agayns whos power nothyng may stonde!
Emperowr he ys, both of heuyn and hell,
Whoys goodnes and grace althyng doth excell!

    *Recedit paulisper.*²

CAYPHA. Vnto my hart thys ys gret admyracyon,   600
    That Saule ys thus mervelously³ changyd!
I trow he ys bewytchyd by sum coniuracyon
    Or els the devyll on hym ys auengyd!
    Alas, to my hart yt ys dessendyd
That he ys thus takyn fro our relygyon!   605
How say ye, Anna, to thys conuercyon?

ANNA.⁴ Full mervelously, as in my concepcyon,   f. 49ᵛ
    Thys wnderfull case, how yt befell;
To se thys chaunce so sodenly don,
    Vnto my hart doth grete yll!   610
    But for hys falsnes we shall hym spyll!
By myn assent to dethe we wyll hym bryng,
Lest þat more myschef of hym may spryng.

CAYPHA. Ye say very trew! We myȝt yt all rewe!
    But, shortly, in thys we must haue aduysement,   615
For thus agayns vs he may nott contynew—

---

    ¹ Con   ² *added in right margin*
    ³ t *canc. after* mervelously   ⁴ *repeated from foot of f. 49*ᵛ

Perauentur, than, of Cesar we may be shent!

ANNA. Nay, I had leuer in fyer he were brent,
Than of Cesar we shuld haue dysp[l]easure,
For sych a rebell and subtyle fals treator!   620

CAYPHA. We wyll command the gatys to be kept aboute,
   And the wallys suerly on euery¹ stede,
That he may not eskape nowhere ow3te.
   For dye he shall, I ensuer yow indede!
ANNA. Thys traytour rebellyous, evyll mut he spede,   62
That doth þis vnhappynes agaynes all!
Now, euery custodyer, kepe well hys wall!

SERUUS SACERDOTUM. The gatys be shytt, he can note skape!
   Euery place ys kepte well and sure,
That in no wyse he may, tyll he be take,   630
   Gett owt of þe cyte by ony coniecture!
Vpon þat caytyf and fals traytour
Loke ye be auengyed wyth deth mortall,
And judge hym as ye lyst to what end he shall!

ANGELUS. Holy Saule, I gyf yow monycyon!   f.
   The pryncys of Jues entende, sertayn,   630
To put yow to deth! But by Goddys provysyon
   He wyll ye shall lyue lenger, and optayn!
And after thy deth þou shalt rayng
Above in heuyn wyth owur Lordys grace.   640
Conuay yowurself shortly into another place!

SAULUS. That Lordys pleasur euer mut be down,
   Both in heuyn and in hell, as hys wyll ys!
In a beryng baskett or a lepe anon,
   I shall me co[n]uay wyth help of the dyscyplys   64
      For euery gate ys shett, and kept wyth multytud of pepull[ys]²;
But I trust in owur Lord that ys my socour,
To resyst ther malyce and cruell furour!

---

¹ syde *canc. after* euery
² M

Conclusyo

POETA. Thus leve we Saule wythin þe cyte,
 The gatys kep by commandment of Caypha and Anna; 650
But the dyscyplys in þe ny3t ouer þe wall truly,
 As the Bybull sayeth: '*dim[i]serunt eum summitten[te]s*[1] *in sporta*'.
And Saule, after that, in Jerusalem *vera*,
Joyned hymself and ther accompenyed
Wyth þe dyscyplys wher þei were vnfayned. 655

Thys lytyll pagent thus conclud we
 As we can, lackyng lytturall scyens,
Besechyng yow all, of hye and low degre,
 Owur sympylnes to hold excusyd and lycens,
 That of retoryk haue non intellygens, f. 50ᵛ
Commyttyng yow all to owur Lord Jhesus, 661
To whoys lawd ye syng: '*Exultet celum laudibus!*'

Finis co[n]uercionis Sancti Pauli.

[1] M

[Saint Mary Magdalen]

[Rome]

INPERATOR. I command sylyns, in þe peyn of forfetur,
   To all myn avdyeans present general!
Of my most hyest and mytyest wolunte,
   I woll it be² knowyn to al þe word³ vnyversal
That of heven and hell chyff rewlar am I,
   To wos magnyfycens non stondyt egall!   5
For I am soveren of al soverens subjugal
Onto myn empere, beyng incomparable
Tyberyus Sesar, wos power is potencyall!
I am þe blod ryall most of soverente—
   Of all emperowers and kyngys my byrth is best,   10
And all regeouns obey my myty volunte!
   Lyfe and lem and goodys all be at my request!
   So, of all soverens, my magnyfycens most mytyest
May nat be agaynsayd of frend nor of foo,
   But all abydyn jvgment and rewle of my lyst.   15
All grace vpon erth from my goodnes commyt fro,
And þat bryngis all pepell in blysse so!
For þe most worthyest, woll I rest in my sete!

SERYBYL. Syr, from your person growyt moch grace!
INPERATOR. Now, for þin answer, Belyall blysse þi face!   20
Mykyl presporyte I gyn to porchase⁴—
   I am⁵ wonddyn in welth from all woo!
Herke þou, provost, I gyff þe in commandment
   All your pepull preserve in pesabyl possessyon.⁶   f.
Yff ony þer be to my goddys [dys]obedyent,   25
   Dyssevyr tho harlottys and make to me declaracyon.
      And I xall make all swych to dye,
   Thos precharsse of Crystys incarnacyon!

Editions collated: Furnivall (F), Lewis (L), and Bevington (B), and the editions of Pollard (P) and Adams (A); P. A, L, and B follow F except where noted.

  ¹ *in brownish ink at top of leaf*   ² be *over caret*
  ³ *the spelling of* world *used throughout*
  ⁴ *extra letter canc. between* c *and* h   ⁵ *added above*   ⁶ s *canc. before*

PROVOST. Lord of all lorddys, I xall gyff yow informacyon.   30
INPERATOR. Lo, how all þe word obeyit my domynacyon!
That person is nat[1] born þat dare me dysseobey!

Syrybbe, I warne yow, se þat my lawys
    In all your partyys have dew obeysavns!
Inquere and aske, eche day þat davnnys   35
    Yf in my pepul be fovnd ony weryouns
    Contrary to me in ony chansse,
Or wyth my goldyn goddys grocth or[2] grone!
I woll marre swych harlottys wyth mordor and myschanse!

Yff ony swyche[3] remayn, put hem in repreffe,   40
And I xall yow releff!

SERYBB. Yt xall be don, lord, wythowtyn ony lett or wythowt doth!
INPERATOR. Lord and lad to my law doth lowte!
Is it nat so? Sey yow all wyth on showte!

    Here answerryt all þe pepul at onys: '3a, my lord, 3a!'

INPERATOR. So ye[4] froward folkys, now am [I] plesyd!   45
    Sett wyn and spycys to my consell full cler.
Now have I told yow my hart, I am wyll plesyd.   f. 96ʳ
    Now lett vs sett don alle, and make good chyr!

[The Castle of Magdalen]

    Her entyr Syrus, þe fader of Mary Mavdleyn.

SYRUS. Emperor and ky[n]ggys and conquerors kene,
    Erlys and borons and knytys þat byn bold,   50
Berdys in my bower so semely to senne,
    I commav[n]d yow at onys my hestys to hold!
    Behold my person, glysteryng in gold,
Semely besyn of all other men!
    Cyrus is my name, be cleffys so cold!   55
I command yow all obedyent to beyn!

---

¹ nat *above caret*   ² *MS* on *altered to* or, *so A, L*
³ w *canc. before*   ⁴ *L; F, A* the

Woso woll nat, in bale I hem bryng,
  And knett swyche caytyfys in knottys[1] of care!
Thys castell of Mavdleyn is at my wylddyng,
  Wyth all þe contre, bothe lesse and more,   6
  And lord of Jherusalem! Who agens me don dare?
Alle Beteny at my beddyng be;
  I am sett in solas from al[2] syyng sore,
And so xall all my posteryte
Thus for to leuen in rest and ryalte.   6

I have her a sone þat is ful trew to me—[3]
  No comlyar creatur of Goddys creacyon;
To amyabyll dovctors full brygth of ble;
  Ful gloryos to my syth, an ful of delectacyon;
  Lazarus my son, in my resspeccyon,   f.
  Here is[4] Mary, ful fayur and ful of femynyte,   7
  And Martha, ful [of] bevte and of delycyte,
  Ful of womanly merrorys and of benygnyte.
þey haue fulfyllyd my hart wyth consolacyon.

Here is a coleccyon of cyrcumstance—   7
  To my cognysshon nevyr swych anothyr,
As be demonstracyon knett in contynens,
  Save[5] alonly my lady þat was þer mother!
Now, Lazarus my sonne, whech art þer brothyr,
The lordshep of Jherusalem I gyff þe aftyr my dysses,   8
  And Mary, thys castell alonly, an non othyr;
And Martha xall haue Beteny, I sey exprese.
Thes gyftys I gravnt yow wythowtyn les,

Whyll þat I am in good mynd!

LAZARUS. Most reuerent father, I thank yow hartely   8
  Of yower grett kyndnes[6] shuyd onto me!
Ye haue gravntyd swych a lyfelod worthy
  Me to restreyn from all nessesyte.
Now, good Lord, and hys wyll it be,
Gravnt me grace to lyue to thy plesowans,   9
  And aȝens hem so to rewle me,
Thatt we may haue joye wythowtyn weryauns.

---

[1] n *added above*   [2] al *added above*   [3] *MS, F* to me ful trew
[4] is *written above*   [5] of *canc.,* save *added in margin*   [6] d *added above*

MARY MAV[DLEYN]. Thou[1] God of pes and pryncypall covnsell,   f. 97[r]
  More swetter is þi name þan hony be kynd!
We thank yow, fathyr, for your gyftys ryall,   95
  Owt of peynys of poverte vs to onbynd.
Thys is a preseruatyff from streytnes we fynd,
From wordly labors to my covmfortyng,
For thys lyfflod is abyll for þe dowtter[2] of a kyng,

Thys place of plesavns, þe soth to seye!   100
MARTHA. O, ye good fathyr of grete degre,
  Thus to departe wyth your ryches,
Consederyng ower lowlynes and humylyte,
  Vs to save from wordly dessetres!
Ʒe shew vs poyntys of grete jentylnes,   105
  So mekly to meyntyn vs to your grace.
Hey in heuen awansyd mot yow be
  In blysse, to se þat Lordys face
Whan ye xal hens passe![3]
CYRUS. Now I reioyse wyth all[4] my mygthtys!   110
  To enhanse my chyldryn, it was my delyte!
Now, wyn and spycys, ʒe jentyll knyttys,
  Onto þes ladys of jentylnes.[5]

    Here xal þey be servyd wyth wyn and spycys.

[Rome]

INPERATOR. Syr provost, and skrybe, juggys of my rem,
  My massengyr I woll send into ferre cuntre,   115
Onto[6] my sete of Jherusalem
  Onto Herowdes, þat regent þer ondyr me,
And onto Pylat, juggys of þe covntre—   f. 97[v]
Myn entent I woll hem teche.
Take hed, þou provost, my precept wretyn be,   120
And sey, I cummavnd hem as þey woll be [wyth]owt[7] wrech,
Yf þer be ony in þe cuntre ageyn my law doth prech,

---

   [1] *L; MS, F* Thatt; *P had queried* Thou
   [2] *MS has wrong abbreviation,* -ys *for* -yr
   [3] *this line squeezed in right margin*   [4] h *canc. before*
   [5] *this line in right margin, as are the majority of tail-rhyming lines*
   [6] o *written over* v   [7] *MS* owt

Or ageyn my goddys ony trobyll tellys,
That thus agens my lawys rebellys,
As he is regent and in¹ þat reme dwellys,   12
    And holdyth hys crovn of me be ryth,
Yff þer be ony harlettys þat agens me make replycacyon,
Or ony moteryng aȝens me make wyth malynacyon.
PROVOST. Syr, of all thys they xall have informacyon,
    So to vphold ȝower renovn and ryte!   13

[INPERATOR]. Now, massengyr, wythowtyn taryyng,
    Have here gold onto þi fe.
So bere thes lettyrs to Herowdes² þe kyng,
    And byd hem make inquyrans in euery cuntre,
As he is jugge in þat cuntre beyng!   13
NVNCYUS. Soueren, your arend it xall be don ful redy
    In alle þe hast þat I may.
For to fullfyll your byddyng
    I woll nat spare, nother be nyth nor be day!

Here goth þe masengyr toward Herowdes.

[Jerusalem—Herod's Palace]

HEROWDES. In þe wyld, wanyng word, pes all at onys!   f.
No noyse, I warne yow, for greveyng of me!   14
Yff yow do, I xal hovrle of yower hedys, be Mahondys bonys,
As I am trew kyng to Mahond so fre!
Help! Help, þat I had a swerd!
Fall don, ye faytours, flatt to þe grovnd!   14
Heve of your hodys and hattys, I cummavnd yow alle!
Stond bare hed, ye beggars! Wo made yow so bold?
I xal³ make yow know your kyng ryall!
Thus woll I be obeyyd thorow al the word,
And whoso wol nat, he xal be had in hold,   15
And so to be cast in carys cold,
That werkyn ony wondyr aȝens my magnyfycens!
Behold these ryche rubyys, red as ony fyr,
Wyth þe goodly grene perle full sett abowgth!
What kyng is worthy, or egall to my power?   15

---

¹ *added above*   ² *letter canc. between* w *and* d   ³ *written above* make

Or in thys word who is more had in dowt
Than is þe hey name of Herowdes, Kyng of Jherusalem,
Lord of Alapye, Assye, and Tyr,
Of Abyron, Berȝaby, and Bedlem?
All thes byn ondyr my governouns!   160
Lo, all þes I hold wythowtyn reprobacyon!
No man is to me¹ egall, save alonly þe emperower
Tyberyus, as I have in provostycacyon!
How sey þe phylyssoverys be my ryche reyne?   f. 98ᵛ
Am nat I þe grettest governowur?   165
Lett me ondyrstond² whatt can ye seyn!

PHELYSOFYR. Soueren, and it plece yow, I woll expresse!
   Ye be þe rewlar of þis regyon,
And most worthy sovereyn of nobylnes
   That euyr in Jude barre domynacyon!   170
   Bott, syr, skreptour gevytt informacyon,
And doth rehersse it werely,
   That chyld xal remayn of grete renovn,
And all the word of hem shold magnyfy:

'*Et ambulabunt gentes in lumine [tuo], et reges*   175
In splendore³ ortus tui.'

HEROWDES. And whatt seyst thow?
SECUNDUS PHY[LOSOFYR]. The same weryfyyt my bok as how,

As þe skryptour doth me tell⁴
   Of a myty duke xal rese and reyn,   180
Whych xall reyn and rewle all Israell.
   No kyng aȝens hys worthynes xall opteyn,
The whech in profesy hath grett eloquence:

'*Non avferetur s[c]eptrum [de] Juda, et dux de*
Femore eius, donec veniet [qui] mitendus⁵ est.'   185

HEROWDES. A! Owt! Owt! Now am [I] grevyd all wyth þe worst! f. 99ʳ
   Ȝe dastardys! Ye doggys! þe dylfe mote yow draw!
Wyth fleyyng flappys I byd yow to a fest!

---

¹ *written above* egall   ² *letter canc. between* ondyr *and* stond
³ spelndore   ⁴ me *added above* tell   ⁵ *L; MS* imitendus

A swerd! A swerd! þes lordeynnys wer slaw!
Ye langbaynnys! Losellys! Forsake ʒe þat¹ word!
þat caytyff xall be cawth, and suer I xall hem flaw!
For hym many mo xal be marry[d]² wyth mordor!

PRIMUS MILIS. My sovereyn lord, dyssemay yow ryth nowt!
They ar³ but folys, þer eloquens wantyng;
For in sorow and care sone þey xall be cawt.
Aʒens vs þey can mak no dysstonddyng!

SECUNDUS MILES. My lord, all swych xall be browte before your
avdyens
And leuyn ondyr your domynacyon,
Or ellys dammyd to deth wyth mortal sentense,
Yf we hem gett ondyr⁴ ower gubernacyon!

HEROWDES. Now thys is to me a gracyows exsortacyon,
And grettly reioysyth to my sprytys indede!
Thow þes sottys aʒens me make replycacyon,
I woll suffer non to spryng of þat kenred;
Some woys in my lond shall sprede,
Prevely or pertely in my lond abowth.
Whyle I haue swych men, I nede nat to drede
But þat he xal be browt ondyr, wythowtyn doth!

*Her commyt þe emperowers [masengyr], þus sayyng to
Herowdes:*

MASENGYR. Heyll, prynse of bovntyowsnesse!
Heyll, myty lord of to magnyfy!
Heyll, most of worchep of to expresse!
Heyll, reytyus rewlar in þi regensy!
My sofereyn Tyberyus, chyff of chyfalry,
Hys soveren sond hath sent to yow here:
He desyrth ʒow and preyyt on eche party
To fulfyll hys commavndment and desyre.

Here he xall take þe lettyrs onto þe kyng.

---

¹ *added above*   ² *L; MS* marry
³ *added above*   ⁴ *letter canc. before* ondyr

HERAWDES. Be he sekyr I woll natt spare
    For [to]¹ complyshe hys cummavnddment,
Wyth sharp swerddys to perce þe[m] bare
    In all covntres wythin² thys regent,   220
For hys love to fulfyll hys intentt.

Non swych³ xall from ower handys stertt,
    For we woll fulfyll hys ryall juggement
Wyth swerd and spere to perce [þem] thorow þe hartt!

But, masengyr, reseyve thys lettyr wyth,   225
And ber ytt onto Pylattys syth!
MESENGYR. My lord, it xall be don ful wygth.⁴   f. 100ʳ
    In hast I woll me spede!

[Jerusalem—Pilate's palace]

PYLATT. Now ryally I reyne in robys of rych[e]sse,
    Kyd and knowyn both ny and ferre
For juge of Jherusalem, þe trewth to expresse,   230
    Ondyr⁵ the Emperower Tyberius⁶ Cesar!
þerfor I rede yow all bewarre
    Ye do no pregedyse⁷ aȝen þe law!
For and ȝe do, I wyll yow⁸ natt spare   235
Tyl ye⁹ haue jugment to¹⁰ be hangyd and draw!

For I am Pylat, pr[o]mmyssary and¹¹ pres[e]dent!
Alle renogat robber inperrowpent,¹²
    To put hem to peyn, I spare for no pete!
My serjauntys semle, qwat s[e]ye¹³ ye?   240
Of þis rehersyd I wyll natt spare!
    Plesauntly, syrrys, avnswer to me,
For in my herte I xall haue þe lesse care.

---

¹ *the bracketed words and letters here and to l. 224 are supplied from the similar*
passage in The Killing of the Children
  ² in *over caret*   ³ swych *repeated*
⁴ sond *canc. before*
⁵ O *over* V   ⁶ i *added above*
⁷ predy *canc. before*
⁸ *added above*   ⁹ *L, B; MS* he
¹⁰ *added above*
¹¹ *MS* ss *canc. before; B prints as* ser
¹² *L, B; MS* inper rowpent
¹³ *MS* sye; *L* sey

PRIMUS SERIUNT. As ye haue seyd, I hold it for þe best,
   Yf ony swych among vs may we know! 2.
SECUNDUS SERJAWNT. For to gyff hem jugment I holdd yt best,
   And so xall ye be dred of hye and low!

PYLAT. A, now I am restoryd to felycyte!

Her¹ comyt þe Emprorys masengyr to Pylat. f.

MASENGYR. Heyll, ryall in rem, in robis of rychesse!
   Heyl, present þou prynsys pere! 2.
Heyl, jugge of Jherusalem, þe trewth to expresse!
   Tyberyus þe Emprower sendyt wrytyng herre,
   And prayyt yow, as yow be hys lovyr dere,
Of þis wrytyng to take avysement
   In strenthyng of hys lawys cleyr, 2.
As he hath set yow in þe state of jugment.

Her Pylat takyt þe lettyrs wyth grete reverens.

PYLAT. Now, be Martys so mythy, I xal sett many a snare,
   Hys lawys to strenth in al þat I may.
I rejoyse of hys renown and of hys wylfare,
   And for þi tydynggys I geyff þe þis gold today. 2.
MASENGYR. A largeys, 3e, lord, I crye þis day,
   For þis is a 3eft of grete degre!
PYLAT. Masengyr, onto my sovereyn þou sey,
   On þe most specyall wyse recummend me!

Her avoydyt þe masengyr, and Syrus takyt hys deth.

[The Castle of Magdalen]

SYRUS. A, help, help! I stond in drede! 2.
   Syknes is sett ondyr my syde!
A, help! Deth wyll aquyte me my mede!
   A, gret God, þou be my gyde! f.
How I am trobyllyd, both bak and syde!
Now, wythly help me to my bede. 2.

¹ *y canc. after*

A! This rendyt my rybbys! I xall nevyr goo nor ryde!
The dent of deth is hevyar þan led!
A, lord, lord, what xal I doo þis tyde?
A, gracyows God, have ruth on me,
In thys word no lengar to abyde!   275
I blys yow, my chyldyrn, God mot wyth vs be!

Her avoydyt Syrus sodenly, and than sayyng Lazarus:

LAZARUS. Alas! I am sett in grete hevynesse!
þer is no tong my sorow may tell,
So sore I am browth in dystresse!
In feyntnes I falter for [þ]is fray fell!   280
Thys dewresse wyl lett me no longar dwelle,
But God¹ of grace sone me redresse!
A, how my peynys don me repelle!
Lord, wythstond þis duresse!

MARY MAGLEYN. The inwyttyssymus God þat euyr xal reyne,   285
Be hys help an sowlys sokor!
To whom it is most nedfull to cumplayn,
He to bry[n]g vs owt of ower dolor;
He is most mytyest governowre,
From soroyng vs to restryne.   290

MARTHA. A, how I am sett in sorowys sad,   f. 101ᵛ
That long my lyf Y² may nat indevre!
Thes grawous peynys make me ner mad!
Vnder clowyr is now my fathyris cure,
þat sumtyme was here ful mery and glad.   295
Ower Lordys mercy be hys mesure,
And defeynd hym from peynys sad.

LAZARUS. Now, systyrs, ower fatherys wyll we woll exprese;³
Thys castell is owerys wyth all þe fee!
MARTHA. As hed and governower, as reson is,   300
And on þis wyse abydyn wyth yow wyll wee.
We wyll natt desevyr, whattso befalle!

---

¹ me *canc. after*   ² *B omits*   ³ *added in right margin,* fulfylle *canc. before*

MARIA. Now, brothyr and systyr,[1] welcum 3e be,
And therof specyally I pray 3ow all!

[Stages of the World, Flesh and Devil, consecutively]

> *Her xal entyr þe Kyng of the Word, þe Flesch, and þe Dylfe,*
> *wyth þe Seuen Dedly Synnys, a Bad Angyll, an an Good*
> *Angyl, þus seyyng þe Word:*

[WORD.] I am þe Word, worthyest þat euyr[2] God wrowth,   30
   And also I am þe prymatt portature
Next heueyn, yf þe trewth be sowth,
   And that I jugge me to skryptur;
   And I am he þat lengest xal induere,
And also most of domynacyon!   31
   Yf I be hys foo, woo is abyll to recure?   f.
   For þe whele of fortune wyth me hath sett hys senture.

In me restyt þe ordor of þe metellys seuyn,
þe whych to þe seuen planyttys ar knett[3] ful sure:
Gold perteynyng[4] to þe sonne, as astronemere nevyn;   31
   Sylvyr to þe mone,[5] whyte and pure;
   Iryn onto þe Maris þat long may endure;
þe fegetyff mercury onto Mercuryus;
   Copyr onto Venus, red in hys merrour;
   The frangabyll tyn to Jubyter, yf 3e can dyscus;   32

On þis planyt Saturne, ful of rancure,
   þis soft metell led, nat of so gret puernesse;
Lo, alle þis rych tresor wyth þe Word doth indure—
   The seuyn[6] prynsys of hell, of gret bowntosnesse!
Now, who may presume to com to my honour?   32
PRYDE. 3e, worthy Word, 3e be gronddar of gladnesse

To þem þat dwellyn ondyr yower domynacyon!
COVETYSE. And whoso wol nat, he is sone set asyde
Wheras I, Couetyse, take mynystracyon!

---

[1] L; *MS* systyrs   [2] b *canc. after*
[3] n *added above*
[4] *altered from* perteynyt   [5] sonne *canc. before*
[6] vij

MUNDUS. Of þat I pray yow, make no declareracyon!   330
  Make swych to know my soverreynte,
And than þey xal be fayn to make supplycacyon,
  Yf þat þey stond in ony nesessyte.

    Her xal entyr þe Kynge of Flesch, wyth Slowth, Gloteny, f. 102ᵛ
    Lechery.

FLESCH. I, Kyng of Flesch, florychyd in my flowers,
  Of deyntys delycyows I have grett[1] domynacyon!   335
So ryal a kyng was neuyr borne in bowrys,
  Nor hath more delyth, ne more delectacyon!
For I haue comfortatywys to my comfortacyon:
  Dya galonga, ambra, and also margaretton—
Alle þis is at my lyst, aȝens alle vexacyon!   340

All wykkyt thyngys I woll sett asyde.
  Clary, pepur long, wyth *granorum paradysy,*
Zenzybyr and synamom at euery tyde—
  Lo, alle swych deyntyys delycyus vse I!

Wyth swyche deyntyys I have my blysse!   345
  Who woll covett more game and gle,
My fayere spowse Lechery to halse and kysse?
Here ys my knyth Gloteny, as good reson is,
  Wyth þis plesavnt lady to rest be my syde.
Here is Slowth, anothyr goodly of to expresse!   350
  A more plesavnt compeny doth nowher abyde!

LUXURIA. O ye prynse, how I am ful of ardent lowe,
  Wyth sparkyllys ful of amerowsnesse!
Wyth yow to rest fayn wold I aprowe,
  To shew plesavns to your jentylnesse!   355
ÞE FLESCH. O ȝe bewtews byrd, I must yow kysse!
  I am ful of lost to halse yow þis tyde!

    Here xal entyr þe prynse of dyllys in a stage, and helle ondyrneth f. 103ʳ
    þat stage, þus seyyng þe Dylfe:

             ¹ r over e

DYLFE. Now I, prynse pyrles, prykkyd in pryde,
  Satan, [ʒ]ower[1] sovereyn, set wyth euery cyrcumstanse,
For I am atyred in my towyr to tempt yow þis tyde!   36
  As a kyng ryall I sette at my plesavns,
  Wyth Wroth [and] Invy at my ryall retynawns!
The bolddest in bowyr I bryng to abaye,
  Mannis sowle to besegyn and bryng to obeysavns!
ʒa, [wyth] tyde and tyme I do þat I may![2]   36
For at hem I haue dysspyte þat he xold haue þe joye
  That Lycyfer with many a legyown lost for þer pryde.
þe snarys þat I xal set wher nevyr set at Troye!
  So I thynk to besegyn hem be every waye wyde—
  I xal getyn hem from grace whersoeuyr he abyde—   37
That body and sowle xal com to my hold,
    Hym for to take!
  Now, my knythtys so stowth,
  Wyth me ye xall ron in rowte,
  My consell to take for a skowte,   37
    Whytly þat we were went for my sake!
WRATH. Wyth wrath or wyhyllys we xal hyrre wynne!
ENVY. Or wyth sum sotyllte sett hur in synne!
DYLFE. Com of, þan, let vs begynne
    To werkyn hure sum wrake!   38

  Her xal þe Deywl go to þe Word wyth hys compeny.   f.

SATAN. Heyle, Word, worthyest of abowndans!
  In hast we must a conseyll take!
Ye must aply yow wyth all your afyavns,
  A woman of whorshep ower servant to make.

MUNDUS. Satan, wyth my consell I wyll þe awansse!   38
  I pray þe, cum vp onto my tent.
Were þe Kyng of Flesch her wyth hys asemlaunvs!
  Masengyr! Anon, þat þou werre went
    Thys tyde!
  Sey þe Kyng of Flesch wyth grete renown,   39
  Wyth hys consell þat to hym be bown,
  In alle þe hast þat euyr they mown,
    Com as fast as he may ryde!

        [1] *A, L, B; MS* ower   [2] d *canc. before*

MASENGYR. My lord, I am your servant, Sensvalyte!
   Your masege[1] to don, I am of glad chyr!   395
   Ryth sone in presens ȝe xal hym se,
   Your wyl for to fulfylle her!

Her he goth to þe Flesch, thus seyyng:

[MASENGYR]. Heyl, lord in lond, led wyth lykyng!
   Heyl, Flesch in lust, fayyrest to behold!
   Heyl, lord and ledar of emprore and kyng!   400
   þe worthy Word, be wey and wold,
   Hath sent for yow[2] and your consell!
   Satan is sembled wyth hys howshold,
   Your cov[n]seyl[3] to haue, most fo[r] aweyle.

FLESCH. Hens in hast, þat we þer wh[e]re!   f. 104ʳ
   Lett vs make no lengar delay.   406
SENSWALITE. Gret myrth to þer hertys shold yow arere,
   Be my trowth I dare safly saye!

Her comyt þe Kyng of Flesch to þe Word, þus seyyng:

[FLESCH]. Heyl be yow, soverens lefe and dere!
   Why so hastely do ȝe for me send?[4]   410
MUNDUS. A! We are ryth glad we haue yow here,
   Ower covnsell togethyr to comprehend!
     Now, Satan, sey your devyse!
   SATAN. Serys, now ye be set, I xal yow say:
   Syrus dyyd þis odyr day—   415
   Now Mary, hys dowctor, þat may,
     Of þat castel beryt þe pryse.

MUNDUS. Sertenly, serys, I yow telle,
   Yf she in vertu stylle may dwelle,
   She xal byn abyll to dystroye helle,   420
   But yf your cov[n]seyll[5] may othyrwyse devyse!

---

[1] ge *added above*
[2] *added above*
[3] *MS has wrong abbreviation,* -yr *for nasal*
[4] send *canc. before*
[5] *MS has wrong abbreviation,* -yr *for nasal*

FLESCH. Now ye,[1] Lady Lechery, yow must don your attendans,
For yow be flowyr fayrest of femynyte!
Yow xal go desyyr servyse, and byn at hure atendavns,
For ȝe xal sonest entyr, ȝe beral of bewte!   42.

LECHERY. Serys, I abey your covnsell in eche degre—
Stryttwaye þethyr woll I passe!
SATAN. Spiritus malyngny xal com to þe,
Hyre to tempt in euery plase.
Now alle þe six þat here be,   43

Wysely to werke, hyr fawor to wynne,   f. 1
To entyr hyr person be þe labor of lechery,
þat she at þe last may com to helle.

How, how, spiritus malyng—þou wottyst what I mene?
Cum owt, I sey! Heryst nat what I seye?   43.

BAD ANGYLL. Syrrys,[2] I obey your covnsell in eche degree;
Stryttwaye þethyr woll I passe!
Speke soft, speke soft, I trotte hyr to tene!
I prey þe pertly, make no more noyse!

[The Castle of Magdalen]
Her xal alle þe Seuyn[3] Dedly Synnys besege þe castell tyll
[Mary] agre to go to Jherusalem. Lechery xall entyr þe
castell wyth þe Bad Angyl, þus seyyng Lechery:

[LECHERY]. Heyl, lady most lavdabyll of alyauvns!   44
Heyl, oryent as þe sonne in hys reflexite!
Myche pepul be comfortyd be your benyng afyavuns.
Bryter þan þe bornyd is your bemys of bewte,
Most debonarius wyth your aungelly delycyte!
MARYA. Qwat personne be ȝe, þat þus me comende?[4]   44
LUXURYA. Your servant to be, I wold comprehende!

MARY. Your debonarius[5] obedyauns ravyssyt me to trankquelyte!
Now, syth ye desyre in eche degree,
To receyve[6] yow I have grett delectacyon!
ȝe be hartely welcum onto me—   45
Your tong is so amyabyll, devydyd wyth reson.

---

[1] *MS* yᵉ   [2] *first* r *added above*   [3] vij
[4] *F; MS* comendyd   [5] ius *added above*   [6] ve *added above*

MARY MAGDALEN

39

LUXURYA. Now, good lady, wyll ȝe me expresse   f. 105ʳ
  Why may þer no gladdnes to yow resort?
MARY. For my father I haue had grett heuynesse—
  Whan I remembyr, my mynd waxit mort.   455
LUXSURYA. Ȝa, lady, for all þat, be of good comfort,
For swych obusyouns may brede myche dysese.
  Swych desepcyouns potyt peynys to exsport;
Prynt yow¹ in sportys whych best doth yow plese!

MARY. Forsothe, ye be welcum to myn hawdyens!   460
  Ye be my hartys leche!
Brother Lazarus, and it be yower plesauns,
And ȝe, systyr Martha, also, in substawns
Thys place I commend onto your governons,
  And onto God I yow beteche!²   465

LAZARUS. Now, systyr, we xal do your intente,
In thys place to be resydent,
Whyle þat ȝe be absent,
  To kepe þis place from wreche!

              [Jerusalem—a Tavern]
  Here takyt Mary hur wey to Jherusalem wyth Luxsurya,
  and þey xal resort to a tavernere. þus seyy[n]g þe tavernere:

TAVERNER. I am a taverner, wytty and wyse,   470
  That wynys haue to sell gret plente!
Of all þe taverners, I bere þe pryse,
  That be dwellyng wythinne þe cete!
Of wynys I haue grete plente,   f. 105ᵛ
  Both whyte wynne and red þat [is] so cleyre.   475

Here ys wynne of Mawt and malmeseyn,
  Clary wynne, and claret, and other moo;
Wyn of Gyldyr, and of Gallys, þat made at þe Groine,³
Wyn of Wyan and Vernage, I seye also—
  Ther be no bettyr⁴ as ferre as ȝe can goo!   480

_____
    ¹ *another* yow *canc.*; d *before canc.* sportys
    ² L; *MS* betake
    ³ L; F grome; P *queries* grome, *suggests* groine
    ⁴ berttyr

LUXSU[R]YA. Lo, lady, þe comfort and þe sokower
  Go we ner and take a tast—
Thys xal bryng your sprytys to fawor!
Tavernere, bryng vs of þe fynnest þou hast!
TAVERNERE. Here, lady, is wyn, a repast,   48
To man and woman a good restoratyff.
ȝe xall nat thynk your mony spent in wast—
From stodyys and hevynes it woll yow relyff!

MARY. Ywys, ȝe seye soth, ȝe grom of blysse!
  To me ȝe be covrtes and kynde.   49

Her xal entyr a galavnt,¹ þus seyyng:

GALAVNT. Hof, hof, hof! A frysch new galavnt!
  Ware of thryst, ley þat adoune!
What?² Wene³ ȝe, syrrys, þat I were a marchant,⁴
  Becavse þat I am new com to town?
Wyth sum⁵ praty tasppysstere wold I fayne rownd!   f.
I haue a shert of reynnys wyth slevys peneawnt,   49
A lase of sylke for my lady constant!
A, how she is bewtefull and ressplendant!

Whan I am from hyre presens, Lord, how I syhe!
  I wol awye sovereyns, and soiettys I dysdeyne!   50
    In wyntyr a stomachyr, in somyr non⁶ att al;
      My dobelet and my hossys euyr together abyde.
  I woll, or euen, be shavyn for to seme ȝyng!
  Wyth here aȝen þe her I love mych pleyyng—
    That makyt me ileȝant and lusty in lykyng.   50
    Thus I lefe in þis word, I do it for no pryde!

LUXSURYA. Lady, þis man is for ȝow, as I se can,
  To sett yow i[n]⁷ sporttys and talkyng þis tyde!
MARY. Cal hym in, tavernere, as ȝe my loue wyll han,
  And we xall make ful mery yf he wolle abyde!   51

---

¹ of *canc. after*   ² w *canc.*, what *written above*
³ *MS* mene   ⁴ galavnt *canc. before*
⁵ *added above*   ⁶ wyn *canc. before*
⁷ *L; MS* i

TAVERNERE. How, how, my mastyre Coryossyte!
CORYOSTE. What is your wyll, syr? What wyl ȝe wyth me?
TAVERNERE. Here ar jentyll women dysyore your presens to se,
    And for to drynk[1] wyth yow thys tyde.

CORYOSTE.[2] A, dere dewchesse, my daysyys iee!   515
    Splendavnt of colour, most of femynyte,
    Your sofreyn colourrys set wyth synseryte!
Consedere my loue into yower alye,   f. 106v
    Or ellys I am smet wyth peynnys of perplexite!

MARI. Why, syr, wene ȝe þat I were a kelle?   520
CORIOSTE. Nay, prensses, parde, ȝe be my hertys hele,
So wold to God ȝe wold my loue fele!

MARI. Qwat cavse þat ȝe love me so sodenly?
CORIOSTE. O nedys I mvst, myn own lady!
Your person, itt is so womanly,[3]   525
I can not refreyn me, swete lelly!

MARI. Syr, curtesy doth it yow lere!
CORIOSTE. Now, gracyus gost wythowtyn pere,
    Mych nortur is þat ȝe conne.
But wol yow dawns, my own dere?
MARY.[4] Syr, I asent in good maner.   530
Go ȝe before, I sue yow nere,
    For a man at alle tymys beryt reverens.

CORIOSTE. Now, be my trowth, ȝe be wyth other ten.
Felle a pese, tavernere, let vs sen—[5]
    Soppys in wynne, how love ȝe [þos]?[6]   535
MARI. As ȝe don, so doth me.
I am[7] ryth glad þat met be we—
    My loue in yow gynnyt to close!

CORYOSTE. Now, derlyng dere, wol yow do be my rede?   f. 107r
We haue dronkyn and ete lytyl brede—   541
Wyll we walk to another stede?

---

[1] L, B; MS dryng   [2] repeated at top of f. 106v
[3] m written over canc.l   [4] Coriosite canc., Mary written before
[5] seyn canc. before   [6] no other edition emends   [7] added above

MARI. Ewyn at your wyl, my dere derlyng!
Thowe ȝe wyl go to þe wordys eynd,
I wol neuyr from yow wynd,   5
    To dye for your sake!

*Here xal Mary and þe galont awoyd, and þe Bad Angyll
goth to þe Word, þe Flych, and þe Dylfe, þus sayyng þe Bad
Angyl:*

[BAD ANGYL]. A lorges, a lorges, lorddys alle at onys!
    ȝe haue a servant fayur and afyabylle,
For she is fallyn in ower grogly gromys!
    ȝa, Pryde, callyd Corioste, to hure is ful lavdabyll,   5
    And to hure he is most preysseabyll,
For she hath gravnttyd hym all hys bonys!
    She thynkyt hys person so amyabyll,
    To here syte, he is semelyare þan ony kyng in tronys!

                                                                            5
DIAB[O]LUS. A, how I tremyl and trott for þese tydyngys!
    She is a soveryn servant þat hath hure fet in synne!
Go thow agayn and ewyr be hur gyde!
    þe lavdabyll lyfe of lecherry let hur neuyr lynne,
For of hure al helle xall make reioysseyng!

Here goth þe bad angyl to Mari agayn.

                                                                            5
REX DIABOLUS. Farewell, farewell, ȝe to nobyl kyngys þis tyde,
    For hom in hast I wol me dresse!   f.
MUNDUS. Farewell, Satan, prynsse of pryde!
FLESCH. Farewell, sem[l]yest alle sorowys to sesse!

*Here xal Satan go hom to hys stage, and Mari xal entyr into
þe place alone, save þe Bad Angyl, and al þe Seuen Dedly
Synnys xal be conveyyd into þe howse of Symont Leprovs,
þey xal be arayyd lyke seuen¹ dylf, þus kept closse; Mari
xal be in an erbyr, þus seyyng:*

¹ vij

MARI. A, God be wyth my valentynys,
My byrd swetyng, my lovys so dere!
For þey be bote for a blossum of blysse! 565
Me mervellyt sore þey be nat here,
But I woll restyn in þis erbyre,
Amons thes bamys precyus of prysse,
Tyll som lovyr wol apere 570
That me is wont to halse and kysse.

Her xal Mary lye doun and slepe in þe erbyre.

SYMOND LEPRUS. Thys day holly I pot in rememberowns,
To solas my gestys to my power;
I haue ordeynnyd a dynere of substawns,
My chyff freyndys þerwyth to chyre. 575
Into þe sete I woll apere,
For my gestys to make porvyawns,
For tyme drayt ny to go to dyner, f. 108ʳ
And my offycyrs be redy wyth þer ordynowns.

So wold to God I myte have aqueyntowns 580
Of þe Profyth of trew perfytnesse,
To com to my place and porvyowns;
It wold rejoyse my hert in gret gladnesse,
For þe report of hys hye nobyllnesse
Rennyt in contreys fer and nere—¹ 585
Hys precheyng is of gret perfythnes,
Of rythwysnesse, and mercy cleyre.

*Here entyr Symont into þe place, þe Good Angyll þus seyyng
to Mary:*

[GOOD ANGYLL]. Woman, woman, why art þou so onstabyll?
Ful bytterly thys blysse it wol² be bowth!
Why art þou aзens God so veryabyll?³ 590
Wy, thynkys þou nat God made þe of nowth?
In syn and sorow þou art browth,
Fleschly lust⁴ is to þe full delectabyll;
Salue for þi sowle must be sowth,
And leve þi werkys wayn and veryabyll! 595

¹ nye *canc. before*   ² *added above*   ³ a *added above*   ⁴ *altered from* lost

Remembyr, woman, for þi pore pryde,
How þi sowle xal lyyn in[1] helle fyre!
A, remembyr how sorowful itt is to abyde,
Wythowtyn eynd in angure and ir!
Remembyr þe on mercy,[2] make þi sowle clyre!   6
I am þe gost of goodnesse þat so wold þe gydde.

MARY. A, how þe speryt of goodnesse hat promtyt me þis tyde,   f.
And temtyd me wyth tytyll of trew perfythnesse!
Alas, how betternesse in my hert doth abyde!
I am wonddyd wyth werkys of gret dystresse.   6
A, how pynsynesse potyt me to oppresse,
That I haue synnyd on euery syde!
O Lord, wo xall put me from þis peynfulnesse?
A, woo xal to mercy be my gostly gyde?

I xal porsue þe Prophett wherso he be,   6
For he is þe welle of perfyth charyte.
Be þe oyle of mercy he xal me relyff.
Wyth swete bawmys, I wyl sekyn hym þis syth,
And sadly folow hys lordshep in eche degre.

*Here xal entyr þe Prophet wyth hys desyplys, þus seyyng
Symont Leprus:*

[SYMONT LEPRUS]. Now ye be welcom, mastyr, most of mag-
                                              nyfycens! 6
I beseche yow benyngly ȝe wol be so gracyows
Yf þat it be lekyng onto yower hye presens,
Thys daye to com dyne at my hows!

JHESUS. Godamercy, Symont, þat þou wylt me knowe!
I woll entyr þi hows wyth pes and vnyte.   6
I am glad for to rest þer grace gynnyt grow.
For wythinne[3] þi hows xal rest charyte,
And þe bemys of grace xal byn illumynows.
But syth þou wytystsaff a dynere on me,   f.
Wyth pes and grace I entyr þi hows.   6

---

¹ *added above*   ² ȝe *canc. before*   ³ ne *added above*

SYMOND. I thank yow, mastyr most benyng and gracyus,
　　That yow wol, of your hye soverente.
To me itt is a joye most speceows,
　　Wythinne my hows þat I may yow se.

Now syt¹ to þe bord, mastyrs alle!   630

　　Her xal Mary folow alonge, wyth þis lamentacyon:

MARY. O I, cursyd cayftyff, þat myche wo hath wrowth
　　Aȝens my makar, of mytys most!
I have offendyd hym wyth dede and thowth,
　　But in hys grace is all my trost,
　　Or ellys I know well I am but lost,   635

Body and sowle damdþnyd perpetuall!
ȝet, good Lord of lorddys, my hope [is]² perhenuall
　　Wyth þe to stond in grace and fawour to se;
Thow knowyst my hart and thowt in especyal—
　　Therfor, good Lord, aftyr my hart reward me!   640

　　Her xal Mary wasche þe fett of þe prophet wyth þe terrys of
　　hur yys, whypyng hem wyth hur herre, and þan anoynt hym
　　wyth a precyus noyttment. Jhesus dicit:³

　　　　[Symond looks on, doubtfully.]

[JHESUS]. Symond, I thank þe speceally
　　For þis grett r[e]past þat here hath be.
But Symond, I telle þe fectually,   f. 109ᵛ
　　I have thyngys to seyn to þe.
SYMOND. Mastyr, qwat your wyll be,   645
And it plese yow, I well yow here;
　　Seyth your lykyng onto me,
And al þe plesawnt of your mynd and desyyr.

JHESUS. Symond, þer was a man in þis present lyf,
　　The wyche had to dectours well suere,   650
þe whych wher pore, and myth make no restoratyf,
　　But stylle in þer dett ded induour.
　　þe on owt⁴ hym an hondyrd pense ful suere,

---

¹ syt *altered from* set　　　　² P　　　　³ *repeated at top of f. 109ᵛ*
⁴ *MS* t *superscript as for abbreviation*

And þe other, fefty, so befell þe chanse;
And becawse he cowd nat hys mony recure,
They askyd hym forȝewnesse, and he forȝaf in substans.

But, Symont, I pray þe, answer me to þis sentens:
Whych of þes to personnys was most beholddyn to þat man?
SYMOND.[1] Mastyr, and it plese your hey presens,
He þat most owt hym, as my reson ȝef can.
JHESUS. *Recte ivdicasti!* Þou art a wyse man,
And þis quessyon hast dempte trewly.
Yff þou in þi concyens remembyr can,
Ȝe to be þe dectours þat I of specefy.

Bnt, Symond, behold þis woman in all wyse,
How she wyth terys of hyr bettyr wepyng
She wassheth my fete and dothe me servyse,
And anoytyt hem wyth onymentys, lowly knelyng
And wyth hur her, fayur and brygth shynnyng,
She wypeth hem agayn wyth good entent.[2]

But, Symont, syth that I entyrd þi hows,
To wasshe my fete þou dedyst nat aplye,
Nor to wype my fete þou were nat so faworus;
Wherfor, in þi conscyens,[3] þou owttyst nat to replye!
But, woman, I sey to þe, werely,
I forgeyffe þe þi wrecchednesse,[4]
And hol in sowle be þou made þerby!

MARIA. O, blessyd be þou, Lord of euyrlastyng lyfe,
And blyssyd be þi berth of þat puer vergynne!
Blyssyd be þou, repast contemplatyf,
Aȝens my seknes, helth and medsyn!

And for þat I haue synnyd in þe synne of pryde,
I wol enabyte me wyth humelyte.
Aȝens wrath and envy, I wyll devyde
Thes fayur vertuys, pacyens and charyte.

---

[1] Jhesus *canc. before*
[2] in *before*
[3] e *added above*
[4] *altered from* wrecchednee

JHESUS. Woman, in contryssyon þou art expert,
 And in þi sowle hast inward mythe,
That sumtyme were in desert,
 And from therknesse hast porchasyd[1] lyth.
 Thy feyth hath savyt þe, and made þe bryth!   690
  Wherfor I sey to þe, 'Vade in pace'.

Wyth þis word seuyn dyllys xall dewoyde from þe woman,
and the Bad Angyll entyr into hell wyth thondyr.

[MARIA]. O þou, gloryus Lord, þis rehersyd for my sped,
 Sowle helth attys tyme[2] for to recure.
Lord, for þat I was in whanhope, now stond I in dred,
 But þat þi[3] gret mercy wyth me may endure.   695
My thowth þou knewyst wythowttyn ony dowth.
 Now may I trost þe techeyng of Isaye in scryptur,
Wos report of þi nobyllnesse rennyt fere abowt!

JHESUS. Blyssyd be þey at alle tyme
 That sen me nat, and have me in credens.   700
 Wyth contryssyon þou hast mad a recumpens
þi sowle to save from all dystresse.
 Beware, and kepe þe from alle neclygens,
And aftyr, þou xal be partenyr of my blysse!

Here devodyt Jhesus wyth hys desipyllys, þe Good Angyll
reioysyng of Mawdleyn:

BONUS ANGELUS. Holy God, hyest of omnipotency,   705
 The astat of good governouns to þe I recummend,
Humbylly besecheyng þyn inperall glorye
 In þi devyn[4] vertu vs to comprehend.

And,[5] delectabyll Jhesu, soverreyn sapyens,
 Ower feyth we recummend onto your pur pete,   710
Most mekely prayyng to your holy aparens,
 Illumyn ower ygnorans wyth your devynyte!

[1] l *canc. before*   [2] my *canc. before*
[3] I was *canc. before*   [4] dey *canc. before*
[5] ad *canc. before*

Ye be clepyd Redempcyon of sowlys defens,
Whyche shal ben obscuryd be þi blessyd mortalyte.
O *Lux Vera*, gravnt vs ȝower lucense,
That wyth þe spryte of errour I nat seduet be!

And, *Sperytus Alme*, to yow most benyne,
Thre persons in Trenyte, and on God eterne,
Most lowly ower feyth we consyngne,
þat we may com to your blysse gloryfyed from malyngne,
And wyth your gostely bred to fede vs, we desyern.

[Hell Stage]

REX DEABOLUS. A! Owt, owt, and harrow! I am hampord wyth
                                                        hate!
In hast wyl I set our[1] jugment to se![2]
Wyth thes betyll-browyd bycheys I am at debate!
How, Belfagour and Belzabub! Com vp here to me!

Here aperytt to dyvllys[3] before þe mastyr.

SECUNDUS DIABOLUS. Here, lord, here! Qwat wol ȝe?
REX DIABOLUS. The jugment of harlottys here to se,
Settyng in judycyal[4]-lyke astate.

How, thow bad angyll! Apere before my grace!
SPIRITUS MALIGNI. As flat as fox, I falle before your face!
REX DIABOLUS. Thow theffe! Wy hast þou don all þis trespas,
To lett yen woman þi bondys breke?
MALINUS SPIRITUS. The speryt of grace sore ded hyr smyth,
And temptyd so sore þat ipocryte!
REX DIABOLUS. ȝa, thys hard balys on þi bottokkys xall byte!
In hast, on þe I wol be wreke![5]

Cum vp, ȝe horsons, and skore awey þe yche,
And wyth thys panne, ȝe do hym[6] pycche!
Cum of, ȝe harlottys, þat yt wer don!

Here xall þey serva all þe seuyn as þey do þe frest.

[1] *MS* ou *with* r *added later in the same ink*; *F* on   [2] *over caret*
[3] v *added above*   [4] d *canc. before*   [5] *Schmidt*; *MS* wroke
[6] y *altered from* e

REX DIABOLUS. Now have I a part of my desyere!   740
  Goo into þis howsse, ȝe¹ lordeynnys here,
And loke ye set yt on afeyere—
  And þat xall hem awake!

Here xall þe tother deyllys sett þe howse on afyere, and make f. 112ʳ
a sowth, and Mari xall go to Lazar and to Martha.

REX DIABOLUS. So! Now have we well afrayyd þese felons fals!
They be blasyd, both body and hals!
Now to hell lett vs synkyn als,   745
  To ower felaws blake!

[The Castle of Magdalen]

MARI MAVGLEYN. O brother, my hartys consolacyown!
  O blessyd in lyff, and solytary!
The blyssyd Prophet, my comfortacyown,   750
  He hathe made me clene and delectary,
  The wyche was to synne a subiectary.
Thys Kyng, Cryste, consedyryd hys creacyown;
  I was drynchyn in synne deversarye²
Tyll þat Lord relevyd me be hys domynacyon.   755

Grace to me he wold nevyr denye;
  Thowe I were nevyr so synful, he seyd, '*Revertere*'!
O, I, synful creature, to grace I woll aplye;
  The oyle of mercy hath helyd myn infyrmyte.

MARTHA. Now worchepyd be þat hey name Jhesu,   760
  The wyche in Latyn is callyd Savyower!
Fulfyllyng þat word ewyn of dewe,
  To alle synfull and seke, he is sokour.
LAZARE. Systyr, ȝe be welcum onto yower towyre!   f. 112ᵛ
Glad in hart of yower obessyawnse,   765
  Wheyl þat I leffe, I wyl serve hym wyth honour,
That ȝe have forsakyn synne and varyawns.

---

¹ þe *canc. before*
² de *added above*

MARY MAGDALEN.[1] Cryst, þat is þe lyth and þe cler daye,
   He hath oncuryd þe therknesse of þe clowdy nyth,
Of lyth þe lucens and lyth veray,
   Wos prechyng to vs is a gracyows lyth,
   Lord, we beseche þe, as þou art most of myth,
Owt of þe ded slep of therknesse, defend vs aye!
   Gyff vs grace ewyr to rest in lyth,
In quyet and in pes to serve þe, nyth and day.

   Here xall Lazar take hys deth, þus seyyng:

[LAZAR]. A! Help, help, systyrs, for charyte!
   Alas! Dethe is sett at my hart!
A! Ley on handys! Wher are ȝe?
   A, I faltyr and falle! I wax alle onquarte!
   A, I bome above, I wax alle swertt!
A, good Jhesu, thow be my gyde!
   A, no lengar now I reverte!
I yeld vp þe gost, I may natt abyde!

MARY MAGDALEN. O, good brother! Take covmforth and myth,
   And lett non heuynes in ȝower hart abyde!
Lett away alle þis feyntnesse and fretth,
   And we xal gete[2] yow leches, ȝower peynys to devyde.

MARTHA. A, I syth and sorow, and sey, 'Alas'!
   Thys sorow ys apoynt to be my confusyon!
Jentyl systyr, hye we from þis place,
   For þe Prophe[t] to hym hatt[3] grett delectacyon.
   Good brothere, take somme comfortacyon

For we woll go to seke yow[er] cure.

   *Here goth Mary and Martha, and mett wyth Jhesus, þus
   seyyng:*

[MARY AND MARTHA]. O, Lord Jhesu, ower melleflueus swett-
                                                          nesse,
   Thowe art grettest Lord in glorie!
Lovyr to þe, Lord, in all lowlynesse,
   Comfort þi creatur þat to þe crye!
   Behold yower lovyr, good Lord, specyally,

---

   [1] *written twice, one canc.*   [2] *added above*   [3] *added above*

How Lazare lyth seke in grett dystresse.
  He ys þi lovyr, Lord, suerly! 800
Onbynd hym, good Lord, of hys heuynesse!

JHESUS. Of all infyrmyte, þer is non to deth.
For of all peynnys, þat is impossyble

To vndyrestond be reson; to know þe werke,
  The joye þat is in Jherusallem heuenly, 805
Can nevyr be compylyd be covnnyng of clerke— f. 113ᵛ
  To se þe joyys of þe Fathyr in glory,
The joyys of þe Sonne whych owth to be magnyfyed,
  And of þe Therd Person, þe Holy Gost, truly,
And alle thre¹ but on in heuen gloryfyed! 810

Now, women þat arn in my presens here,
  Of my wordys take awysement.
Go hom aȝen to yower brothyr Lazere—
  My grace to hym xall be sent.

MARY MAGDALEN. O, thow gloryus Lord² here present, 815
We yeld to þe salutacyon!
  In ower weyys³ we be expedyent.
Now, Lord, vs defend from trybulacyon!

   Here goth Mary and Martha homvard, and Jhesus devodyt.
    [Castle of Magdalen]

LAZARUS. A! In woo I waltyr as wawys in þe wynd!
  Awey ys went all my sokour! 820
A, Deth, Deth, þou art onkynd!
  A! A, now brystyt myn hartt! þis is a sharp showyr!
Farewell, my systyrs, my bodely helth!

   *Mortuus est.*⁴

MARY MAGDALEN. Jhesu, my Lord, be yower sokowre,
And he mott be yower gostys welth! 825

PRIMUS MILES. Goddys grace mott be hys governour,
  In joy euyrlastyng fore to be!
SECUNDUS MILES. Amonge alle good sowlys, send hym favour, f. 114ʳ
  As þi powere ys most of dygnyte!

¹ iij   ² c *canc. before*   ³ e *added above*   ⁴ L; *MS* mortuis est
F

MARTHA. Now, syn þe chans is fallyn soo,
   That deth hath drewyn hym don þis day,
We must nedys ower devyrs doo,
   To þe erth to bryng hym wythowt delay.
MARY MAGDALEN. As þe vse is now, and hath byn aye,
Wyth wepers to þe erth yow hym bryng.
   Alle þis must be¹ donne as I yow saye,
Clad in blake, wythowtyn lesyng.

PRIMUS MILES. Gracyows ladyys of grett honour,
   Thys pepull is com here in yower syth,
Wepyng and weylyng wyth gret dolour,
   Becavse of my lordys dethe.

   Here þe on knygth make redy þe ston, and other bryng in
   þe wepars, arayyd in blak.

PRIMUS MILES. Now, good fryndys þat here be,
   Take vp thys body wyth good wyll,
And ley it in hys sepoltur, semely to se;
   Good Lord hym save from alle manyr ille!

   Lay hym in. Here al þe pepyll resort to þe castell, þus seyyng
   Jhesus [in the place]:

[JHESUS]. Tyme ys comyn of very cognyssyon.
   My dyssyplys, goth wyth me
For to fulfyll possybyll peticion;
   Go we together into Jude,
   There Lazar, my frynd, is he.
Gow we together as chyldyurn of lyth,
   And, from grevos slepe, sawen heym wyll we!

DISSIPULYS. Lord, it plese yower myty volunte,²
   Thow he slepe, he may be savyd be skyll.
JHESUS. That is trew, and be possybilyte;
   Therfor, of my deth shew yow I wyll.

My Fathyr, of nemyows charyte,
   Sent me, hys Son, to make redemcyon,

---

¹ *added above*   ² w *canc. before*

Wyche was conseyvyd be puer verginyte,
 And so in my mother had cler incarnacyon;   860
 And þerfore must I suffyre grewos passyon
Ondyre Povnse Pylat, wyth grett perplexite,
 Betyn, bobbyd, skoernyd, crownnyd wyth thorne—
Alle þis xall be þe soferons of my deite.

I,[1] therfor, hastely folow me now,   865
 For Lazar is ded, verely to preve;
Whe[r]for I am joyfull, I sey onto yow,
 That I knowlege yow þerwyth, þat ye may it beleve.

Here xal Jhesus com wyth hys dissipulys, and on Jew tellyt
Martha:

[JEW]. A, Martha, Martha! Be full of gladnesse!
 For þe Prophett ys comyng, I sey trewly,   870
Wyth hys dyssypyllys in grett lowlynesse;
 He shall yow comfortt wyth hys mercy.   f. 115ʳ

Here Martha xall ronne aȝen Jhesus, þus seyyng:

[MARTHA]. A, Lord! Me, sympyl creatur, nat denye,
 Thow I be wrappyd in wrecchydnesse!
Lord, and þou haddyst byn here, werely,   875
 My brother had natt a byn ded—I know well thysse.

JHESUS DICIT. Martha, docctor, onto þe I sey,
 Thy brother xall reyse agayn!
MARTHA. Yee, Lord, ar þe last day,
 That I beleve ful pleyn.   880

JHESUS. I am þe resurreccyon of lyfe, þat euyr xall reynne,
 And whoso belevyt verely in me
Xall have lyfe euyrlastyng, þe soth to seyn.
 Martha, belevyst thow þis?
MARTHA. Ȝe, forsoth, þe Prynsse of blysch!   885
I beleve in Cryst þe Son of Sapyens,
 Whyche wythowt eynd ryngne xall he,
 To redemyn vs freell from ower iniquite!

---

[1] *B omits*

Here Mary xall falle to Jhesus, þus seyyng Mary:

MARY MAGDALEN. O, þou rythewys[1] regent, reynyng in equite,   f.
  þou gracyows Lord, þou swete Jhesus!   89
And þou haddyst byn here, my brothyr alyfe had be!
  Good[2] Lord, myn hertt doth þis dyscus!

JHESUS. Wher have ȝe put hym? Sey me thys.
MARY MAGDALEN. In hys mo[nv]ment, Lord, is he.
JHESUS. To that[3] place ȝe[4] me wys.   89
  Thatt grave I desyre to se.

Take of þe ston of þis monvment!

The agrement of grace here shewyn I wyll.

MARTHA. A, Lord, yower preseptt fulfyllyd xall be.
  Thys ston I remeve[5] wyth glad chyr.   90
Gracyows Lord, I aske þe mercy!
  Thy wyll mott be fullfyllyd here!

Here xall Martha put of þe grave ston.

JHESUS. Now, Father, I beseche thyn hey paternyte,
  That my prayour be reswondable to þi Fathyrod in glory,
To opyn þeyn erys to þi Son in humanyte.   90
  Nat only for me, but for þi pepyll, verely,
  That þey may beleue, and betake to þi mercy.
Fathyr, fore þem I make supplycacyon!
  Gracyows Father, gravnt me[6] my bone!

Lazer, Lazer! Com hethyr to me!   f.

Here xall Lazar aryse, trossyd wyth towellys, in a shete.

LAZAR. A, my Makar, my Savyowr! Blyssyd mott þou be!   91
  Here men may know þi werkys of wondyre![7]
Lord, nothy[n]g ys onpossybyll to the,
  For my body and my sowle was departyd asondyr!
  I xuld a rottytt, as doth þe tondyre,   9

---

[1] thow *canc. before*   [2] *second* o *added above*   [3] þat *and* o *canc. before*
[4] þe *canc. before*   [5] remembyr *canc. before*
[6] *added over caret*   [7] b *canc. between* n *and* d

Fleysch from þe bonys a-consumyd away![1]
Now is aloft þat late was ondyr!

The goodnesse of God hath don for me here,
    For he is bote of all balys to onbynd,
That blyssyd Lord þat here ded apere!   920

> *Here all þe pepull and þe Jewys, Mari and Martha, wyth*
> *on woys sey þes wordys: 'We beleve in yow, Savyowr, Jhesus,*
> *Jhesus, Jhesus!'*

[JHESUS]. Of yower[2] good hertys I have advertacyounys,
    Wherethorow in sowle, holl made 3e be.
Betwyx yow and me be nevyr varyacyounys,
    Wherfor I sey, '*Vade in pace*'.

> *Here devoydyt Jhesus wyth hys desypyllys; Mary and*
> *Martha and Lazare gon hom to þe castell, and here begynnyt*
> [þe Kyng of Marcylle] *hys bost:*

[Marcylle]

[KYNG OF MARCYLLE]. Awantt! Awant þe, onworthy wrecchesse!   f. 116ᵛ
    Why lowtt 3e nat low to my lawdabyll presens,   926
Ye brawlyng breellys and blabyr-lyppyd bycchys,
    Obedyenly[3] to obbey[4] me wythowt offense?

I am a sofereyn semely þat ye se butt seyld!
    Non swyche ondyr sonne, þe sothe for to say!   930
Whanne I fare fresly and fers to þe feld,
    My fomen fle for fer of my fray!
Ewen as an enperower I am onored ay,

Wanne baner gyn to blasse and bemmys gyn to blow!
    Hed am I heyest of all hethennesse holld!   935
Both kynggys and cayserys I woll þey xall me know,
    Or ellys þey bey[5] the bargayn, þat ewyr þey were so bold!
I am Kyng of Marcylle, talys to be told—
Thus I wold it were knowyn ferre and nere!
    Ho sey contraly, I cast heym in carys cold,   940
And he xall bey the bargayn wondyr dere!

---

[1] was *canc. between* a *and* way   [2] ower *canc. before*
[3] why lowtt ye natt lo *canc. before*   [4] y *canc. after*
[5] y *altered from* e

I have a favorows fode and fresse as the fakown,
  She is full fayur in hyr femynyte;
Whan I loke on þis lady, I am losty[1] as the lyon
    In my syth;
  Of delycyte most delycyows,
  Of felachyp most felecyows,
  Of alle fodys most favarows—
    O, my blysse in bevteus brygth!

REGINA. O of condycyons, and most onorabyll!
  Lowly I thank yow for þis recummendacyon—
The bovnteest and the boldest ondyr baner bryth,
  No creatur so coroscant to my consolacyon!
  Whan the regent be resydent, itt is my refeccyon.
Yower dilectabyll dedys devydytt me from dyversyte.
  In my person I privyde to put me from polucyon—
To be plesant to yower person, itt is my prosperyte!

REX. Now, Godamercy, berel brytest of bewte!
Godamercy, ruby[2] rody as þe rose!
Ye be so ple[s]avnt to my[3] pay, ӡe put me from peyn.
Now, comly knygthys, loke þat ӡe forth dresse
Both spycys and wyn here in hast!

  *Here xall þe knygtys gete spycys and wynne, and here xall
  entyr a dylle in orebyll aray, þus seyyng*:

[Hell Stage]

[DYLLE]. Owt, owt, harrow! I may crye and yelle,[4]
  For lost is all ower labor, wherfor I sey alas!
For of all holddys þat evyr hort, non so as hell!
  Owur barrys of iron ar all to-brost, stronge gatys of brasse!
  The Kyng of Joy entyryd in þerat, as bryth as fyrys blase!
For fray of hys ferfull banere, ower felashep fled asondyr![5]
  Whan he towcheyd it wyth hys toukkyng, þey brast as ony glase,
And rofe asondyr, as it byn wyth thondore!

---

[1] B; F, L lofty; *MS could be either*   [2] *MS* rubu
[3] 1 *canc. before*   [4] e *canc. before*
[5] y *altered from* e

Now ar we thrall þat frest wher fre,   f. 117ᵛ
  Be þe passyon of hys manhede.
O[n] a crosce on hye hangyd was he,
  Whych hath dystroyd ower labor and alle ower dede!
He hath lytynnyd lymbo, and to paradyse 3ede!   975
þat wondyrfull worke werkytt vs wrake!
  Adam and Abram and alle hyre kynred,
Owt of ower preson to joy were þey take!

All þis hath byn wrowth[1] syn Freyday at none!
  Brostyn don ower gatys þat hangyd were full hye!   980
Now is he resyn, hys resurreccyon is don,
  And is procedyd into Galelye!
Wyth many a temtacyon we tochyd hym to atrey,[2]
To know whether he was God ore non.
3e[t][3] for all ower besynes, bleryd is ower eye,[4]   985
For wyth hys wyld werke he hath wonne hem everychon!
    Now for þe tyme to come,
      þer xall non falle to ower chanse,
    But at hys deleverans,
    And weyyd be rythfull balans,   990
    And 3owyn be rythfull domme.
I telle yow alle *in sum*,[5] to helle wyll I gonne!

Here[6] *xall entyr þe thre*[7] *Mariis arayyd as chast women,* f. 118ʳ
wyth sygnis of þe passyon pryntyd ypon þer brest, þus seyyng
Mawdleyn :

[Place of Cruxifixion, and the Sepulchre.]

[MAWDLEYN]. Alas, alas, for þat ryall bem!
  A, þis percytt my hartt worst of all!
For here he turnyd a3en to þe woman of Jerusalem,   995
  And for wherynesse lett þe crosse falle!
MARY JACOBE. Thys sorow is beytterare þan ony galle,
  For here þe Jevys[8] spornyd hym to make hym goo,
And þey dysspyttyd þer Kyng ryall.
That clyvytt myn hart, and makett me woo.   1000

---

[1] wethe *canc.*, wrowth *added above*   [2] *letter canc. between* a *and* trey
[3] *F; MS* 3e   [4] ye *canc. before*
[5] *MS abbrev. can be either* in sum (*B*) *or* in fine (*F, L*)
[6] *red line drawn through first line of directions, but apparently not cancelling*
[7] iij   [8] *added above*

MARY SALOME. Yt ys intollerabyll[1] to se or to tell,
For ony creature, þat stronkg tormentry!
O Lord, þou haddyst[2] a mervelows mell!
Yt is[3] to hedyows to dyscry!

Al þe Maryys wyth on woyce sey þis folowyng :[4]

[THE THRE MARYYS]. Heylle, gloryows crosse! þou baryst þat   1c
                              Lord on hye,
Whych be þi mygth deddyst lowly bowe doun,
  Mannys sowle from all thraldam to bye,[5]
That euyrmore in peyne[6] shold a be [boun],[7]
  Be record of Davyt, wyth myld stevyn: 1(

'*Domine inclina celos tuos, et dessende!*'

MARY MAGDLEYN. Now to þe monument lett vs gon,   f.
  Wheras ower Lord and Savyower layd was,
To anoynt hym, body and bone,
  To make amendys for ower trespas.

[MARY JACOBE].[8] Ho xall putt doun þe led of þe monvment,   1(
  Thatt we may anoytt[9] hys gracyus wovndys,
Wyth hart and my[n]d to do ower intentt,
  Wyth precyus bamys, þis same stovnddys?
MARY SALOME. Thatt blyssyd body wythin þis bovndys.[10]
Here was layd wyth rvfull monys.   1
  Nevyr creature was borne vpon gronddys
þat mygth sofere so hediows a peyne at onys!

Here xall apere to[11] *angelys*[12] *in whyte at þe grave.*

[PRIMUS] ANGELUS. 3e women presentt, dredytt yow ryth nowth!
Jhesus is resun, and is natt here!
Loo, here is þe place þat he was in browth!   1
Go,[13] sey to hys dysypyllys and to Petur he xall apere.

[1] s *canc. after*   [2] hast *canc. before*   [3] *added above*
[4] yng *added above*; M Mavdleyn *canc. in margin*
[5] *MS* Mannys sowle to bye from all thraldam
[6] shold a be *canc. before, repeated after*   [7] *No other edition emends*
[8] *MS, F omit, but scribe has drawn red lines separating this speech, ll. 1015–18, from the preceding and following speeches, and Mary Jacobee is the logical speaker*
[9] *MS*   [10] v *canc. before*   [11] ij
[12] *MS scribe here and elsewhere abbreviates in error for* -us, *which F prints*
[13] Go *written above another canc.* Go

SECUNDUS ANGELUS. In Galelye, wythowtyn ony wyre,
þer xall ye se hym, lyke as he sayd.
Goo yower way, and take comfortt and chyr,
For þat he sayd xall natt be delayyd.   1030

Here xall þe Maryys mete wyth Petyr and Jhon.

MARY MAVDLEYN. O, Petyr and Jhon! We be begylyd!   f. 119ʳ
Ower Lordys body is borne away!
I am aferd itt is dyffylyd!
I am so carefull, I wott natt whatt to saye.
PETYR. Of þes tydynggys gretly I dysmay!   1035
I woll me thethere hye wyth all my myth!
Now, Lord defend vs as he best may!
Of þe sepulture we woll have a syth.

JHON. A, myn invard sowle stondyng in dystresse—
þe weche of my body xuld have a gyde—   1040
For my Lord stondyng in hevynesse,
Whan I remembyr hys wovndys wyde!

PETYR. The sorow and peyne þat he ded drye
For ower offens and abomynacyon!
And also I forsoke hym in hys turmentry—   1045
I toke no hede to hys techeyng and exortacyon!

*Here¹ Petyr and Jhon go to þe sepulcur and þe Maryys
folowyng.*

[PETYR]. A, now I se and know þe sothe!
But, gracyus Lord, be ower protexcyon!—
Here is nothyng left butt a sudare cloth,
þat of þi beryyng xuld make mencyon!   1050
JHON.² I am aferd of wykkytt opressyon!
Where he is becum, it can natt be devysyd,
But he seyd³ aftyr þe thrid⁴ day he xuld have resurrexyon.
Long beforn, thys was promysyd.   f. 119ᵛ

¹ *L, B, MS* How
² *repeated at top of f. 119ᵛ*
³ d *added above*   ⁴ iij ᵈ

MARY MAGDLEYN. Alas, I may no lengar abyde,   10
For dolour and dyssese þat in my hartt doth dwell.
                [Mary goes aside.]
PRIMUS ANGELUS. Woman, woman, wy wepest þou?
  Wom sekest[1] þou wyth dolare thus?
MARY MAGDLEYN. A, Fayn wold I wete, and I wyst how,
  Wo hath born away my Lord Jhesus!   10

    Hic aparuit Jhesus.

[JHESUS]. Woman, woman, wy syest thow?
  Wom sekest þou? Tell me þis.
MARY MAGDLEYN. A, good syr, tell me now
  Yf þou have born awey my Lord Jhesus,

For I have porposyd in eche degre   10
  To have hym wyth me, werely,
The wyche my specyall Lord hath be,
  And I[2] hys lovyr and cavse wyll phy.

JHESUS. O, O, Mari!

MARY MAGDLEYN. A! Gracyus Mastyr and Lord, yow it is þat I   10
                            seke!
  Lett me anoynt yow wyth þis bamys sote!
Lord, long hast þou hyd þe from my spece,
  Butt now wyll I kesse þou for my hartys bote!

JHESUS. Towche me natt, Mary! I ded natt asend
  To my Father in Deyyte, and onto yowers!   10
Butt go sey to my brotheryn I wyll pretende   f.
  To stey to my Father in heu[n]ly towyrs.

MARY MAGDLEYN. Whan I sye yow fyrst,[3] Lord, verely
  I wentt ye had byn Symov[n]d[4] þe gardener.
JHESUS. So I am, forsothe, Mary!   10
  Mannys hartt is my gardyn here.
þerin I sow sedys of vertu all þe ȝere.
  þe fowle[5] wedys and wycys I reynd vp be þe rote!
Whan þat gardyn is watteryd wyth terys clere,
Than spryng vertuus, and smelle full sote.   10

---

   [1] st *added above and canc.*   [2] *added above*   [3] fr *canc. before*
   [4] d *blotted before and* g *added above*   [5] *altered from* flowle

MARY MAGDLEYN. O, þou dereworthy Emperowere, þou hye
devyne!
To me þis is a joyfull tydyng,
And onto all pepull þat aftyr vs xall reyngne,
  Thys knowlege of þi deyyte,
To all pepull þat xall obteyne,   1090
  And know þis be posybyl[yt]e.
JHESUS. I woll shew to synnars as I do to þe,
Yf þey woll wyth veruens of love me seke.
  Be stedfast, and I xall evyr wyth þe be,
And wyth all tho þat to me byn meke!   1095

Here avoydyt Jhesus sodenly, þus seyyng Mary Magdleyn:

[MARY MAGDLEYN]. O, systyrs,[1] þus þe hey and nobyll inflventt
grace
  Of my most blessyd Lord Jhesus, Jhesus, Jhesus!   f. 120ᵛ
He aperyd onto me at þe sepulcur þer I was!
  þat hath relevyd my woo, and moryd my blysche!
Itt is innvmerabyll[2] to expresse,   1100
Or for ony tong for to tell,
  Of my joye how myche itt is,
So myche my peynnys itt doth excelle!

MARY SALOME. Now lett vs go to þe sette, to ower Lady dere,
  Hyr to shew of hys wellfare,   1105
And also to dyssypyllys, þat we have syn here—
  þe more yt xall rejoyse þem from care!

MARY JACOB. Now, systyr Magdleyn, wyth glad chyr!
  So wold þat good Lord we myth wyth hym mete!

[Jhesus appears again.]

JHESUS. To shew desyrows hartys I am full nere,   1110
  Women, I[3] apere to yow and sey, '*Awete!*'

SALOME. Now, gracyus Lord, of yowur nymyos charyte—
  Wyth hombyll hartys to þi presens complayne—
Gravntt vs þi blyssyng of þi hye deyte,
  Gostly ower sowlys for to sosteynne.   1115

[1] *MS* systyr   [2] v *over* u   [3] *over caret*

JHESUS. Alle tho byn blyssyd þat sore refreynne.
We blysch yow—Father, and Son, and Holy Gost—
  All sorow and care to constryne,
Be ower powyr of mytys most,

In nomine Patrys ett Felii et Spiritus Sancti, amen!

Goo ye to my brethryn, and sey to hem þer,
  þat þey procede and go into Gallelye,
And þer xall þey se me, as I seyd before,
  Bodyly, wyth here carnall yye.

  Here Jhesus devoydytt aȝen.

MAGDLEYN. O¹ þou gloryus Lord of heuen regyon,
  Now blyssyd be þi hye devynyte,
Thatt evyr thow² tokest incarnacyon,
  Thus for to vesyte þi pore servantys thre.
þi wyll, gracyows Lord, fulfyllyd xall be
As þou commavndyst vs in all thyng.
Ower gracyows brethryn we woll go se,
Wyth hem to seyn all ower lekeyng.

  *Here devoyd all þe thre³ Maryys, and þe Kyng of Marcyll
  xall begynne a sacryfyce.*

REX MARCYLL. Now, lorddys and ladyys of grett aprise,
  A mater to meve⁴ yow is in my memoryall,
þis day to do a sacryfyce
  Wyth multetude of myrth before ower goddys all,

Wyth preors in aspecyall before hys presens,

Eche creature wyth hartt demvre.

REGINA. To þat lord curteys and keynd,
  Mahond, þat is so mykyll of myth,⁵
Wyth mynstrelly and myrth in mynd,
  Lett vs gon ofer in þat hye kyngis syth.

  Here xall entyr an hethen prest and hys boye.

---

¹ *added in margin*   ² *first stroke of* v *or* w *canc. before*   ³ iij
⁴ ve *added above*   ⁵ t *written over* c

PRYSBY[TYR]. Now, my clerke Hawkyn, for loue of me,
Loke fast myn awter were arayd!
Goo ryng a bell, to or thre!   1145
Lythly, chyld, it be natt delayd,
For here xall be a grett solemnyte.
Loke, boy, þou do it wyth a brayd!
CLERICUS. Whatt, mastyr! Woldyst þou have þi lemman to þi
                                              beddys syde?
Thow xall abyde tyll my servyse is sayd!   1150

PRYSBY[TYR]. Boy! I sey, be Sentt Coppyn,
No swyche wordys to þe I spake!
BOY. Wether þou ded[1] or natt, þe fryst jorny xall be myn,
For, be my feyth, þou beryst Wattys pakke!

But syr, my mastyr, grett Morell,   1155
Ye have so fellyd yower bylly wyth growell,
þat it growit grett as þe dywll of hell!
Onshaply þou art to see!
Whan woman comme to here þi sermon,
Pratyly wyth hem I can houkkyn,   1160
Wyth Kyrchon and fayer Maryon—   f. 122ʳ
þey love me[2] bettyr þan þe!

I dare sey, and þou xulddys ryde,
þi body is so grett and wyde,
þat nevyr horse may þe abyde,   1165
Exseptt þou breke hys bakk asovndyre!
PRYSBY[TYR]. A, þou lyyst, boy, be þe dyvll of hell!
I pray God, Mahond mott þe quell!
I xall whyp þe tyll þi ars xall belle!
On þi ars com mych wondyre!   1170

BOY. A fartt, mastyr, and kysse my grenne!
þe dyvll of hell was þi emme!
Loo, mastyrs, of swyche a stokke he cam!
þis kenred is asprongyn late!
PRYSBY[TYR]. Mahovndys blod, precyows knave!   1175
Stryppys on þi ars þou xall have,
And rappys on þi pate!

    Bete hym.

          [1] *added over caret*   [2] *part of letter canc. after*

REX *dicitt.* Now, prystys and clerkys, of þis[1] tempyll cler,
Yower servyse to sey, lett me se.
PRYSBY[TYR]. A, soveryn lord, we shall don ower devyr.
Boy, a boke anon þou bryng me!

Now, boy, to my awter I wyll me dresse—
On xall my westment and myn aray.
BOY. Now þan, þe lesson I woll expresse,
Lyke as longytt for þe servyse of þis day:

Leccyo mahowndys, viri fortissimi sarasenorum:[2]
Glabriosum ad glvmandum glvmardinorum,
Gormondorum alocorum, stampatinantum cursorum,
Cownthtys fulcatum, congrvryandum tersorum,
Mursum malgorum, mararaʒorum,
Skartum sialporum, fartum cardiculorum,
Slavndri strovmppum, corbolcorum,
Snyguer[3] *snagoer werwolfforum*
Standgardum lamba[4] *beffettorum,*
Strowtum stardy strangolcorum,
Rygour dagour flapporum,
Castratum raty rybaldorum,
Howndys and hoggys, in heggys and hellys,
Snakys and toddys mott be yower bellys!
Ragnell and Roffyn, and other in þe wavys,
Gravntt yow grace to dye on þe galows!

PRYSBY[TYR]. Now, lordys and ladyys, lesse and more,
Knele all don wyth good devocyon.
Yonge and old, rych and pore,
Do yower oferyng to Sentt Mahownde,
And ye xall have grett pardon,
þat longytt to þis holy place,
And receyve ʒe xall my benesown,
And stond in Mahowndys grace.

REX *dicitt.* Mahownd, þou art of mytys most,
In my syth a gloryus gost—
þou comfortyst me both in contre and cost,
Wyth þi wesdom and þi wytt,

---

[1] *added above*   [2] *this line in red*   [3] Sy *canc. before*   [4] la *canc. before*

For truly, lord, in þe is my trost.
Good lord, lett natt my sowle be lost! 1215
All my cownsell well þou wotst,
    Here in þi presens as I sett.

Thys besawnt of gold, rych and rownd,
    I ofer ytt for my lady and me,
þat þou mayst be[1] ower covnfortys in þis stownd. 1220
    Sweth Mahovnd, remembyr me!

PRYSBY[TYR]. Now, boy, I pray þe, lett vs have a song!
    Ower servyse be note, lett vs syng, I say!
Cowff vp þi brest, stond natt to long,
    Begynne þe offyse of þis day. 1225
BOY. I home and I hast, I do þat I may,
Wyth mery tvne þe trebyll to syng.

    Syng both.

PRYSBY[TYR]. Hold vp! þe dyvll[2] mote þe afray,
For all owt of rule þou dost me bryng!

Butt now, syr kyng, quene, and knyth,[3] 1230
    Be mery in hartt everychon!
For here may ye se relykys brygth—
    Mahowndys own nekke bon!
And 3e xall se or ewer ye gon, f. 123ᵛ
    Whattsomewer yow betyde, 1235
And ye xall kesse all þis[4] holy bon,
    Mahowndys own yeelyd!
    3e may have of þis grett store;
And[5] ye knew þe cavse wherfor,
Ytt woll make yow blynd for ewyrmore, 1240
    þis same holy bede!

Lorddys and ladyys, old and ynge,
Golyas so good, to blysse may yow bryng,
    Mahownd þe [holy][6] and Dragon þe dere,

----

¹ o *canc. before* be
² *letter blotted before*
³ *red line separates ll.* 1229–30
⁴ mewyer ye *canc. before*
⁵ 3 *canc. before*
⁶ *MS* body

Wyth Belyall in blysse ewyrlastyng,   12
þat¹ ye may þer in joy syng
Before þat comly kyng
    þat is ower god in fere.

[Jerusalem—Pilate's Stage]

PYLATT. Now, ȝe serjauntys² semly, qwat sey ȝe?
    ȝe be full wetty men in þe law.   12
Of þe dethe of Jhesu I woll awysyd be—
    Ower soferyn Sesar þe soth mvst nedys know.

Thys Jhesu was a man of grett vertu,
    And many wondyrs in hys tyme he wrowth;
He was put to dethe be cawsys ontru,   12
    Wheche matyr stekytt in my thowth;   f.
And ȝe know well how he was to þe erth browth,
Wacchyd wyth knygths of grett aray.
    He is resyn agayn, as before he tawth,
And Joseph of Baramathye³ he hath takyn awey.   12

[PRIMUS] SERJANTT. Soferyn juge, all þis is soth þat ȝe sey,
    But all þis mvst be curyd be sotylte,
And sey how hys dysypyllys stollyn hym away—
    And þis xall be þe answer, be þe asentt of me!
SECUNDUS SERJANTT. So it is most lylly for to be!   12
Yower covncell is good and commendabyll;
    So wryte hym a pystyll of specyallte,
And þat for vs xall be most prophytabyll.

PYLATT. Now, masengyr, in hast hether þou com!
    On masage þou mvst, wyth ower wrytyng,   12
To þe soferyn emperower of Rome.
    But fryst þou xall go to Herodes þe kyng,
    And sey how þat I send hym knowyng
Of Crystys deth, how it hath byn wrowth.
    I charge þe make no lettyng,   12
Tyll þis lettyr to þe emperower be browth!

---

¹ t *altered from* e   ² xall *canc. before*
³ m *canc. before*

NVNCYUS PYLATUS. My lord, in hast yower masage to spede   f. 124ᵛ
  Onto þo¹ lordys of ryall² renown,
Dowth ȝe nat, my lord, it xall be don indede!
Now hens woll I fast owt of þis town!   1280

Her goth þe masengyr to Herodes.

Jerusalem—Herod's Palace]

NVNCYUS. Heyll, soferyn kyng ondyr crown!
þe prynsys of þe law recummende to yower heynesse,
  And sendytt yow tydyngys of Crystys passyon,
As in þis wrytyng doth expresse.

HERODES. A, be my trowth, now am I full of blys!   1285
þes be mery tydvngys þat þey have þus don!
Now certys I am³ glad of þis,
  For now ar we frendys þat afore wher fon.
Hold a reward, masengyr, þat thow were gon,
And recummend me to my soferens grace.   1290
  Shew hym I woll be as stedfast as ston,
Ferr and nere,⁴ and in every place!

Here goth þe masengyr to þe emperower.

[Rome]

NVNCYUS. Heyll be yow, sofereyn, settyng in solas!
  Heyll, worthy wythowtyn pere!
Heyll, goodly to gravntt all grace!   1295
  Heyll, emperower of þe word, ferr and nere!

Soferyn, and it plese yower hye empyre,
  I have browth yow wrytyng of grett aprise,   f. 125ʳ
Wyche xall be pleseyng to yower desyre,
  From Pylatt, yower hye justyce.   1300
He sentt yow word wyth lowly intentt;
In ewery place he kepytt yower cummavndement,
  As he is bovnd be⁵ hys ofyce.

¹ *MS* þat   ² 1 *canc. before*   ³ am *added above*
⁴ *letter canc. before*   ⁵ *added above*

EMPEROWER. A, welcum, masengyr of grett pleseavns!
  þi wrytyng anon lett me se!   1
My juggys, anon gyffe atendans,
  To ondyrstond whatt þis wrytyng may be,
  Wethyr it be good, are ony deversyte,
Or ellys natt¹ for myn awayll—
Declare me þis in all þe hast!   1

PROVOST. Syr, þe sentens² we woll dyscus,
  And it plese yower hye exseleyns;
The intentt of þis pystull is þus:
  Pylatt recummendytt to yower presens,
  And of a prophett is þe sentens,   1
Whos name was callyd Jhesus.
He is putt to dethe wyth vyolens,
For he chalyngyd to³ be kyng of Jewys.

þerfor he was crucyfyed to ded,
  And syn was beryyd, as þey thowth reson.   1
Also, he cleymyd hymsylf Son of þe Godhed!
  þe therd nygth he was stollyn away wyth treson,   f
  Wyth hys desypyllys⁴ þat to hym had dyleccyon,
So wyth hym away þey ȝode.
  I merveyll how þey ded wyth þe bodyys corupcyon—   1
I trow þey wer fed wyth a froward fode!

IMPERATOR. Crafty was þer connyng, þe soth for to seyn!
  Thys pystyll I wyll kepe wyth me yff I can,
Also I wyll have cronekyllyd þe ȝere and þe⁵ reynne,
  þat nevyr xall be forgott, whoso loke þeron.⁶

Masengyre, owt of þis town wyth a rage!
Hold þis gold to þi wage,
  Mery for⁷ to make!
NVNCYUS. Farewell, my lord of grett⁸ renown,
  For owt of town my way I take.

---

¹ it *canc. before*   ² *MS* sentellys *here and in l.* 1315
³ *added above*   ⁴ py *added above*   ⁵ *added above*
⁶ *scribe has tagged ll.* 1330-2 *as though they rhymed*
⁷ fo *canc. after*   ⁸ of *canc. before*

Her entyr Mawdleyn wyth hyr dysypyll, þus seyyng:

[Jerusalem]

MAVDLYN. A, now I remembyr my Lord þat put was to ded
Wyth þe Jewys, wythowttyn gyltt or treson!
þe therd nygth he ros be þe myth of hys Godhed;
Vpon þe Sonday had hys gloryus resurrexcyon,
And now is þe tyme past of hys gloryus asencyon;   1340
He steyyd to hevyn, and þer he is kyng.
A! Hys grett kendnesse may natt fro my mencyon!
Of alle¹ maner tonggys he ȝaf vs knowyng,

For to vndyrstond every langwage.
Now have þe dysypyllys² take þer passage   f. 126ʳ
To dyvers contreys her and ȝondyr,   1346
To prech and teche of hys hye damage—
Full ferr³ ar my brothyrn departyd asondyr.

Her xall hevyn opyn, and Jhesus xall shew [hymself].

[Heaven Stage]

JHESUS. O, þe onclypsyd sonne, tempyll of Salamon!
In þe mone I restyd, þat nevyr chonggyd goodnesse!   1350
In þe⁴ shep of Noee, fles of Judeon,
She was my tapyrnakyll of grett nobyllnesse,
She was þe paleys of Phebus brygthnesse,
She was þe wessell of puere clennesse,
Wher my Godhed ȝaff my manhod myth;   1355

My blyssyd mother, of demvre femynyte,
For mankynd, þe feynddys defens,
Quewne of Jherusalem, þat heuenly cete,
Empresse of hell, to make resystens.
She is þe precyus pyn, full of ensens,   1360
The precyus synamvyr, þe body thorow to seche.
She is þe mvske aȝens þe hertys of vyolens,
þe jentyll jelopher aȝens þe cardyakyllys wrech.

¹ l *canc. before*   ² L; MS dysyllpyllys
³ *added above*   ⁴ I *canc. before,* In *added in margin*

The goodnesse of my mothere no tong can expresse,
  Nere no clerke of hyre, hyre joyys can wryth.   13
Butt now of my servantt I remembyr þe kendnesse;
  Wyth heuenly masage I cast me to vesyte;   f.
Raphaell, myn angell in my syte,
To Mary Mavdleyn decende in a whyle,
  Byd here passe þe se be my myth,   13
And sey she xall converte þe land of Marcyll.

ANGELUS. O gloryus Lord, I woll resortt
  To shew your servant of yower grace.
She xall labor for þat londys comfortt,
  From heuynesse þem to porchasse.   13

  Tunc decendet angelus.

[ANGELUS]. Abasse¹ þe novtt, Mary, in þis place!
Ower Lordys preceptt þou must fullfyll.
  To passe þe see in shortt space,
Onto þe lond of Marcyll.

Kyng and quene converte xall 3e,
  And byn amyttyd as an holy apostylesse.   13
Alle þe lond xall be techyd alonly be the,
  Goddys lawys onto hem 3e xall expresse.
þerfore hast yow forth wyth gladnesse,
Goddys commav[n]ddement for to fullfylle.

                                                                  13

MARI MAWDLEYN. He þat from my person seuen² dewllys mad
                                                         to fle, f.
  Be vertu of hym alle thyng was wrowth;
To seke thoys³ pepyll I woll rydy be.
  As þou hast commavnddytt, in vertv þey xall be browth.

Wyth þi grace, good Lord in Deite,   1?
  Now to þe see I wyll me hy,
  Sum sheppyng to asspy.
Now spede me, Lord in eternall glory!
Now be my spede, allmyty Trenite!

        ¹ b *canc. between* a *and* basse
        ² vij
        ³ y *canc. before*

Here xall entyre a shyp wyth a mery song.

[The Place—near the 'Coast']

SHEPMAN. Stryke! Stryke!¹ Lett fall an ankyr to grownd!   1395
Her is a fayer haven to se!
Connyngly in, loke þat ye sownd!
I hope good harbarow have xal wee!

Loke þat we have drynke, boy þou!
BOY. I may natt, for slep, I make God a wow!   1400

þou xall abyde ytte, and þou were my syere!
SHEPMAN. Why, boy, we are rydy to go to dynere!
Xall we no mete have?
BOY. Natt for me, be of good² chyr,   f. 127ᵛ
Thowe ye be forhongord tyll ȝe rave,   1405
I tell yow plenly beforn!
For swyche a cramp on me sett is,
I am a poynt to fare þe worse.
I³ ly and wryng tyll I pysse,
And am a poyntt to be forlorn!⁴   1410

þE MASTYR. Now, boy, whatt woll þe þis seyll?
BOY. Nothyng butt a fayer damsell!
She shold help me, I know it well,
Ar ellys I may rue þe tyme þat I was born!
þE MASTYR. Be my trowth, syr boye, ȝe xal be sped!   1415
I wyll hyr bryng onto yower bed!
Now xall þou lern a damsell to wed—
She wyll nat kysse þe on skorn!

Bete hym.

þE BOY. A skorn! No, no, I fynd it hernest!
The dewlle of hell motte þe brest,   1420
For all my corage is now cast!
Alasse! I am forlorn!

---

¹ L, B; MS Skryke   ² *first* o *added above*
³ Cy *canc. before*   ⁴ lonr *canc. between* for *and* lorn

MAV[D]LEYN. Mastyr of þe shepe, a word wyth the!
MASTYR. All redy, fayer woman! Whatt wol ȝe?   f. 1
MARY. Of whense is thys shep? Tell ȝe me,   142
    And yf ȝe seyle wythin a whyle.
MASTYR. We woll seyle þis same[1] day,
Yf þe wynd be to[2] ower pay.
þis shep þat I[3] of sey,
    Is of þe lond of Marcyll.   143

MARY. Syr, may I natt wyth yow sayle?
And ȝe xall have for yower awayle.
MASTYR. Of sheppyng ye[4] xall natt faylle,
    For vs þe wynd is good and saffe.

              [Ship sails.]

Yond þer[5] is þe lond of Tork[y]e[6]   143
I wher full loth for to lye!
Yendyr is þe lond of Satyllye—
    Of þis cors we thar nat abaffe.[7]

      Now xall þe shepmen syng.[8]

SHEPMEN. Stryk! Beware of sond!
    Cast a led and in vs gyde!   144
Of Marcyll þis is þe kynggys lond.
    Go a lond, þow fayer woman, þis tyde,
    To þe kynggys place. Yondyr may ȝe se.

      [Mary goes ashore.]

þE BOY. Sett of! Sett of from lond!   144
All redy, mastyr, at thyn hand!   f. 1

      Her goth þe shep owt of þe place.

---

[1] m *over another letter*   [2] *added above*   [3] *added above*
[4] MS þe: *the scribe, however, frequently writes superscript* e *with* ye, *so that*
ye *and* þe *are often indistinguishable*
[5] Yond þer, *so F; MS could also be* Yondyr (B)
[6] MS Torke   [7] MS *reverses ll.* 1437–8
[8] *this direction appears in right margin between ll.* 1436–7, *but it would seem to*
refer to words and music not in the text; we insert the direction after the master's
speech which it would otherwise interrupt

MARY. O Jhesu, þi mellyfluos name
  Mott be worcheppyd wyth reverens!
Lord, gravnt me vyctore¹ aჳens þe fyndys flame,
  And yn þi lawys gyf þis pepyll credens!
    I wyll resortt be grett convenyens;   1450
  On hys presens I wyll draw nere,
    Of my Lordys lawys to she[w] þe sentens,
  Bothe of hys Godhed and of hys powere.

        Here xall Mary entyr before þe kyng.

[MARY]. Now, þe hye Kyng Crist, mannys redempcyon,
  Mote save yow, syr kyng, regnyng in equite,   1455
And mote gydde yow² þe [way] toward sauasyon.
  Jhesu, þe Son of þe mythty Trenite,
    That was, and is, and evyr xall be,
  For mannys sowle þe reformacyon,
    In hys name, lord, I beseche þe,   1460
  Wythin þi lond to have my mancyon.

REX. Jhesu? Jhesu? Qwat deylle is hym þat?   f. 129ʳ
  I defye þe and þyn apenyon!
Thow false lordeyn, I xal fell þe flatt!
  Who made the so hardy to make swych rebon?   1465
MARY. Syr, I com natt to þe for no decepcyon,
  But þat good Lord Crist hether me compassyd.
    To receyve hys name, itt is yower refeccyon,
  And þi forme of mysbele[f] be hym may be losyd!

REX. And whatt is þat lord þat thow speke of her?   1470
MARY. *Id est Salvator*, yf thow wyll lere,
þe Secunde Person, þat hell ded conquare,

And þe Son of þe Father in Trenyte!
REX. And of whatt powyr is þat God þat ჳe reherse to me?
MARY. He mad hevyn and erth, lond and see,   1475
  And³ all þis he mad of nowthe!

---

    ¹ vytory *canc.*, vyctore *written above*
    ² *MS* yow yow
    ³ *superfluous ampersand before*

REX. Woman, I pray þe, answer me!
  Whatt mad God at þe fyrst begynnyng?
Thys processe ondyrstond wol we,
  That wold I lerne; itt is my plesyng!

MARY.[1] Syr, I wyll declare al and sum,
  What from God fryst ded procede.
He seyd, '*In principio erat verbum*',
  And wyth þat he provyd hys grett Godhed!
He mad heuen for ower spede,
Wheras he sytth in tronys hyee;
  Hys mynystyrs next, as he save nede,
Hys angelus and archangyllys all the compeny.

Vpon þe fryst day God mad all þis,
  As it was plesyng to hys intent.
On þe Munday, he wold natt mys
  To make sonne, mone, and sterrys,[2] and þe fyrmament,
  The sonne to begynne hys cors in þe oryent,
And evyr labor wythowtyn werynesse,
  And kepytt hys covrs into þe occedentt.

The Twysday, as I ondyrstond þis,
  Grett grace for vs he gan to incresse.
þat day he satt vpon watyris,
  As was lykyng to hys goodnesse,
  As holy wrytt berytt wettnesse.
þat tyme he made both see and lond,
  All þat werke of grett nobyllnesse,
As it[3] was plesyng to hys gracyus sond.

On þe Weddysday, ower Lord of mythe
  Made more at hys plesyng:
Fysche in flod, and fowle in flyth—
  And all þis was for ower hellpyng.
On the Thorsday, þat nobyll Kyng
Mad dyverse bestys, grett and smale.
He yaff hem erth to ther fedyng,
And bad hem cressyn be hylle and dale.

---

[1] *MS speaker's name is followed at bottom of page by* Jhesu mercy *which F prints as a line (Sharp did not); from this point F's edition (and L's and B's) numbers one more line than ours*   [2] *on canc. after, ampersand added above* [3] *is canc.,* it *added above*

And on þe Fryday God mad man,
  As it plesett hys hynesse most,
Aftyr hys own semelytude than,
  And ȝaf hem lyfe of þe Holy Gost.   1515

O[n] þe Satyrday, as I tell can,
  All hys werkys he gan to blysse.
He bad them multyply and incresse than,
  As it was plesyng to hys worthynesse.

And on þe Sonday, he gan rest take,   1520
  As skryptur declarytt pleyn,
þat al shold reverens make
    To hyr Makar þat hem doth susteyn
    Vpon þe Sonday to leuen in hys servyse,
And hym alonly to serve, I tell yow pleyn.   1525

REX. Herke, woman, thow hast[1] many resonnys grett!
  I thyngk, onto my goddys aperteynyng þey beth!
But þou make me answer son, I xall þe frett,
  And cut þe tong owt of þi hed!

MARY. Syr, yf I seyd amys, I woll retur[n] agayn.   f. 130v
  Leve yower encomberowns of perturbacyon,   1531
And lett me know what yower goddys byn,
  And how þey may save vs from trevbelacyon.

REX. Hens to þe tempyll þat we ware,
  And þer xall thow se a solom syth.
Com on all, both lesse and more,   1535
  Thys day to se my goddys myth!

  Here goth þe kyng wyth all hys atendavnt to þe tempyll.

[REX]. Loke now, qwatt seyyst thow be þis syth?
  How pleseavnttly þey stond, se thow how?
Lord, I besech þi grett myth,   1540
  Speke to þis Chrisetyn þat here sestt[2] þou!
Speke, god lord,[3] speke! Se how I do bow!
Herke, þou pryst! Qwat menytt all this?
  What? Speke, good lord, speke! What eylytt þe now?
Speke, as thow artt bote of all blysse!   1545

---

[1] a *canc. before*   [2] *second* s *altered from* y   [3] *added above*

PRYSBITYR. Lord, he woll natt speke whyle Chriseten here is!

MARY. Syr kyng, and it plese yower gentyllnesse,
  Gyff me lycens my prayors to make
Onto[1] my God in heven blysch,
  Sum merakyll to shewyn for yower sake! 15
REX. Pray þi fylle tyll þen knees[2] ake!

MARY. *Dominus, illuminacio mea, quem timebo?*
Dominus, protecctor vite mee,[3] a quo trepedabo? f.

  Here xal þe mament tremyll and quake.

[MARY]. Now, Lord of lordys, to þi blyssyd name sanctifi-
                                              catt,
  Most mekely my feyth I recummend. 15
Pott don þe pryd of mamentys violatt!
  Lord, to þi lovyr þi goodnesse descend!
  Lett natt þer pryd to þi poste pretend,
Wheras is rehersyd þi hye name Jhesus!
  Good[4] Lord, my preor I feythfully send! 15
Lord, þi rythwysnesse here dyscus!

  Here xall comme a clowd from heven, and sett þe tempyl on
  afyer, and þe pryst and þe cler[k] xall synke, and þe kyng
  gothe hom, þus seyyng:

[REX]. A! Owt! For angur I am þus deludyd!
  I wyll bewreke my cruell tene!
Alas, wythin mysylfe I am concludytt!
  þou woman, comme hether and wete whatt I mene! 15
  My wyff and I together many ȝerys have byn,
And nevyr myth be conceyvyd wyth chyld;
  Yf þou for þis canst fynd a mene,
I wyll abey þi God, and to hym be meke and myld.

MARY. Now, syr, syn þou seyst so, 15
  To my Lord I prye wyth reythfull bone.
Beleve in hym, and in no mo,
  And I hope she xall be conceyvyd sone.

---

[1] *added above* [2] *letter canc. before* [3] q *canc. after*
[4] *second o added above*

REX. Awoyd, awoyd! I¹ wax all seke!
I wyll to bed þis same tyde! 1575
I am so wexyd wyth ȝen sueke, f. 131ᵛ
þat heth nere to deth me dyth!

*Here þe kyng goth to bed in hast, and Mary goth into an old
logge wythowt þe gate, þus seyyng:*

MARY. Now, Cryst, my creatur, me conserve and kepe,
þat I be natt confunddyd wyth þis reddure!
For hungore and thurst, to þe I wepe! 1580
Lord, demene me wyth mesuer!
As þou savydyst Daniell from þe lyounys rigur,
Be Abacuk þi masengyre, relevyd wyth sustynovns,
Good Lord, so hellpe me and sokore,
Lord, as itt is þi hye pleseawns! 1585

[Heaven Stage]

JHESUS. My grace xall grow, and don decend
To Mary my lovyr, þat to me doth call,
Hyr ass[t]att² for to amend.
She xall be relevyd wyth sustinons corporall.
Now, awngelys, dyssend to hyr in especyall, 1590
And lede hyr to þe prynssys chambyr ryth.
Bed hyre axke of hys good be weyys pacyfycal.
And goo yow before hyr wyth reverent lyth!

PRIMUS ANGELUS. Blyssyd Lord, in þi syth
We dyssend onto Mary.
SECUNDUS ANGELUS. We dyssend from yower blysse bryth— 1595
Onto yower cummavndement we aplye.

Tunc dissenditt angelus. Primus dyxit. f. 132ʳ

[PRIMUS ANGELUS]. Mary, ower Lord wyll comfortt yow send!
He bad, to þe kyng ye xuld take þe waye,
Hym to asay, yf he woll condesend, 1600
As he is slepyng, hem to asaye.
SECUNDUS ANGELUS. Byd hym releve yow, to Goddys pay,
And we xal go before yow wyth solem lyth;
In a mentyll of whyte xall be ower araye.
The dorys xall opyn aȝens vs be ryth. 1605

¹ a *canc. before*   ² L; MS assatt

MARY. O gracyus God, now I vndyrstond!
  Thys clothyng of whyte is tokenyng of mekenesse.
Now, gracyus Lord, I woll natt wond,
  Yower preseptt to obbey wyth lowlynesse.

Here goth Mary, wyth þe angelys before hyre, to þe kynggys
  bed, wyth lythys beryng, þus seyyng Mary:

[MARY]. Thow froward kyng, trobelows and wood,
  That hast at þi wyll all worddys wele,
Departe wyth me wyth sum of þi good,
  That am in hongor, threst, and chelle;[1]
God hath þe sent warnyngys felle!
I rede þe, torne, and amend þi mood!
Beware of þi lewdnesse, for þi own hele!
And thow, qwen, tvrne from þi good!

Here Mari woydyt, and þe angyll and Mary chongg[2] hyr
  clotheyng, þus seyyng þe kyng:

[REX]. A, þis day is com! I am mery and glad!
  The son is vp and shynyth bryth!
A mervelows shewyng[3] in my slep I had,
  That sore me trobelyd þis same nyth—
A fayer woman I saw[4] in my syth,
All in whyte was she cladd;
  Led she was wyth an angyll bryth,
To me she spake wyth wordys sad.

REGINA. I trow from Good þat þey were sentt!
  In ower hartys we may[5] have dowte.
I wentt ower chambyr sholld a brentt,
  For þe lyth þat þer was all abowth!
    To vs she spake wordys of dred,
    That we xuld help þem þat haue nede,
    Wyth ower godys, so God ded byd,
  I tell yow wythowtyn dowthe.

---

[1] *MS* cold
[2] *MS* woyd *canc. before; last letter of* chongg *partially lost in margin, but it is a* g *not an* e *as in F*
[3] is *canc. before*   [4] w *altered from* y   [5] *letter canc. before*

REX. Now, semely wyff, ȝe sey ryth well.
   A knyth, anon, wythowtyn delay!   1635
Now, as þou hast byn trew as stylle,
   Goo fett þat woman before me þis daye!
MILES. My[1] sovereyn lord, I take þe waye!
She xall com at [y]ower[2] pleseawns.
   Yower soveryn wyll I wyll goo saye—   1640
Itt is almesse hyr to awawns!

    Thunc transit[3] miles ad Mariam.   f. 133ʳ

[MILES]. Sped well, good woman! I am to þe sentt,
   Yow for to speke wyth þe[4] kyng.
MARIA. Gladly, syr, at hys intentt,
   I comme at hys own pleseyng!   1645

    Tunc transytt Maria ad regem.

[MARY]. The mythe and þe powyre of þe heye Trenyte,
   The wysdom of þe Son, mott governe yow in ryth!
The Holy Gost mott wyth[5] yow be!
   What is yowre[6] wyll? Sey me in sythe!
REX. Thow fayer woman, itt is my delyth,   1650
þe to refresch is myn intentt,
   Wyth mete and mony, and clothys for þe nyth,
And wyth[7] swych grace as God hathe me lentt.

MARIA. Than fullfylle ȝe Goddys cummavndement,
   Pore folk in mysch[ef] þem to susteyn!
REX. Now, blyssyd woman, reherse here presentt,   1655
   The joyys of yower Lord in heven.

MARY. A, blyssyd þe ower, and blyssyd be þe tyme,
   þat to Goddys lawys ȝe wyll gyff credens!
To yowerselfe ȝe make a glad pryme   1660
   Aȝens þe fenddys malycyows[8] violens!
From God above comit þe influens,   f. 133ᵛ
Be þe Holy Gost into þi brest sentt down,
   For to restore þi offens,
þi sowle to bryng to ewyrlastyng salvacyon.   1665

[1] I *canc. before*   [2] L, B; *MS* ower   [3] L, B; *MS* transiunt
[4] w *canc. before*   [5] *added above*   [6] ow *canc.,* yowre *written above*
[7] s *canc. before*   [8] l. *canc. before*

Thy wyffe, she is grett wyth chyld!

Lyke as þou desyerst, þou hast þi bone!

REGINA. A, ȝe! I fel ytt ster in my wombe vp and down!
  I am glad I have þe in presens!
O blyssyd womman, rote of ower savacyon,
  þi God woll I worshep wyth dew reverens!

REX. Now, fayer womman, sey me þe sentens,
I beseche þe, whatt is þi name?
MARY. Syr, aȝens þat I make no resystens!
Mary Mavdleyn, wythowtyn blame.

REX. O blyssyd Mary, ryth well is me,
  þat ewer I have abedyn þis daye!
Now thanke I þi God, and specyally þe,
  And so xall I do whyle I leve may.
MARY. Ȝe xall thankytt Petyr, my mastyr, wythowt delay!
He is þi frend, stedfast and cler.
  To allmythy God he halp me pray,
And he xall crestyn yow from þe fynddys powyr,
  In þe syth of God¹ an hye!

REX. Now, suerly ȝe answer me to my pay.
  I am ryth glad of þis tyddyngys!
Butt, Mary, in all my goodys I sese yow þis day,
  For to byn at yower gydyng,
  And þem to rewlyn at yower pleseyng
Tyll þat I comme hom agayn!
  I wyll axke of yow neythyr lond nore rekynyng,
But I here delevyr yow powere pleyn!

REGINA. Now, worshepfull lord, of a bone I yow pray,
  And it be pleseyng to yower hye dygnite.
REX. Madam, yower dysyere onto² me say.
  What bone is þat ȝe desyere of me?
REGINA. Now, worshepfull sovereyn, in eche degre,
þat I may wyth yow goo,
  A Crestyn womman made to be.
Gracyus lord, it may be soo.

¹ *added above*   ² *added above*

REX. Alas! þe wyttys of wommen, how þey byn wylld!
And þerof fallytt many a chanse!   f. 134ᵛ
A! Why desyer it yow, and ar wyth chyld?

REGINA. A, my sovereyn, I am knett¹ in care,
But ȝe consedyr now þat I crave,   1705
For all þe lowys þat ever ware,
Behynd yow þat ȝe me² nat leve!

REX. Wyff, syn þat ȝe woll take þis wey of pryse,
þerto can I no more seyn.
Now Jhesu be ower gyd, þat is hye justyce,   1710
And þis blyssyd womman, Mary Mavgleyn!

MARY. Syth ȝe ar consentyd to þat dede,
The blyssyng of God gyff to yow wyll I.
He xall save³ yow from all dred,
In nomine Patrys, et Filij, et Spiritus Sancti. Amen!   1715

    Ett⁴ tunc navis venit in placeam, et navta dicit:

                    [The 'Coast']

[NAVTA]. Loke forth, Grobbe, my knave,
And tell me qwat tydyngys þou have,
And yf þou aspye ony lond.
BOY. Into þe shrowdys I woll me hye!
Be my fythe, a castell I aspye,   1720
And as I ondyrstond!
NAVTA. Sett þerwyth, yf we mown,
For I wott itt is a havyn town
þat stondyt vpon a strond.

    Ett tuncc transitt rex ad navem, et dicit rex:

[REX]. How, good man, of whens is þat shep?   f. 135ʳ
I pray þe, syr, tell þou me.   1726
NAVTA. Syr, as for þat, I take no kepe!
For qwat cavse enquire ȝe?
REX. For cavsys of nede, seyle wold we,
Ryth fayn we wold owyr byn!   1730
NAVTA. ȝee, butt me thynkytt, so mote I the,
So hastely to passe, yower spendyng is thyn!

---

¹ n *altered from* e   ² *added above*   ³ fe *canc. before*   ⁴ tt *canc. after*

I trow, be my lyfe,
þou hast stollyn sum mannys wyffe!
þou woldyst lede hyr owt of lond!
Nevereþeles, so God[1] me save,
Lett se whatt I xall[2] have,
Or ellys I woll nat wend!

REX. Ten marke I wyll þe gyff,
Yf þou wylt set me vp[3] at þe cleyff
In þe Holy Lond!
NAVTA. Set of, boy, into þe flod!
BOY. I xall, mastyr! þe wynd is good—
Hens þat we were!

Lamentando regina.

[REGINA]. A, lady, hellp in þis nede,
þat in þis flod we drench natt!
A, Mary, Mary, flowyr of wommanned!
O blyssyd lady, forȝete me nowth!

REX. A,[4] my dere wyffe,[5] no dred ȝe have,
Butt trost in Mary Mavdleyn,
And she from perellys xall vs save!
To God for vs she woll prayyn.

REGINA. A, dere hosbond, thynk on me,
And save yowersylfe as long as ȝe may,
For trewly itt wyll no otherwyse be!
Full sor my hart it makytt þis day.
A, þe chyld þat betwyx my sydys lay,
þe wyche was conseyvyd on me be ryth—
Alas, þat wommannys help is away!
An hevy departyng is betwyx vs in syth,
Fore now departe wee!
For defawte of wommen here in my nede,
Deth my body makyth to sprede.
Now, Mary Mavdleyn, my sowle lede!
In manus tuas, Domine!

---

[1] *second o canc.*   [2] *repeated*   [3] I *canc. before*
[4] *added above in red*   [5] f *canc. before*

REX. Alas, my wyff is ded!
  Alas, þis is a carefull chans!
So xall my chyld, I am adred,
  And for defawth of sustynons.
      Good Lord, þi grace gravnte to me!   1770
      A chyld betwen vs of increse,   f. 136ʳ
      An it is motherles!
      Help me,[1] my sorow for to relesse,
        Yf þi wyl it be!

NAVTA. *Benedicite, benedicite!*   1775
Qwat wethyr may þis be?
  Ower mast woll all asondyr!
BOY. Mastyr, I þerto ley[2] myn ere,
It is for þis ded body þat we bere!
  Cast hyr owt, or ellys we synke ond⟨yr⟩!   1780

    Make redy for to cast hyr owt.

REX. Nay, for Goddys sake, do natt so!
  And ȝe wyll hyr into þe se cast,
Gyntyll serys, for my love, do—
Ȝendyr is a roch in the west—
As ley hyr þeron all above,   1785
  And my chyld hyr by.
NAVTA. As þerto I asent well.
  And she were owt of þe wessell,
  All we xuld stond þe more in hele,
    I sey yow, werely!   1790

    Tunc remiga[n]t ad montem et dicit rex[3]:

REX. Ly here, wyff, and chyld þe by.
  Blyssyd Mavdleyn be hyr rede!
Wyth terys wepyng, and grett cavse why,
  I kysse yow both in þis sted.
Now woll I pray to Mary myld   1795
    To be þer gyde here.

---

[1] *added above*   [2] *added above*
[3] *this is canc. after l. 1796; the scribe had written it in the wrong place, saw his*
error and canc., but forgot to write it in its proper place. No other edition prints

Tunc remiga[n]t a monte,[1] *et navta dicit:*

[NAVTA]. Pay now, syr, and goo to lond,   f.
    For here is þe portt ȝaf, I ondyrstond;
    Ley down my pay in my hond,
    And belyve go me fro!   18

REX. I gravnt þe, syr, so God me save!
    Lo, here is all þi connownt,
    All redy þou xall it have,
    And a marke more þan þi gravnt!

And þou, page, for þi good obedyentt,   18
I gyff yow, besyde yower styntt,
    Eche of yow a marke for yower wage!
NAWTA. Now he þat mad bothe day and nyth,
He sped yow in yower ryth,
    Well to go on yower passage!   18

[*Jerusalem. The ship stays at the 'coast'.*]

PETYR. Now all creaturs vpon mold,
    þat byn of Crystys creacyon,
To worchep Jhesu þey are behold,
    Nore nevyr aȝens hym to make waryacyon.

REX. Syr, feythfully I beseche yow þis daye: 18
    Wher Petyr þe apostull is, wete wold I!
PETYR. Itt is I, syr, wythowt delay!
    Of yower askyng, tell me qwy.

REX. Syr, þe soth I xall[2] yow seyn,
    And tell yow myn intentt wythin a whyle.   f.
þer is a woman, hyth Mary Mavdleyn,   18
    þat hether hath laberyd me owt of Marcyll—
    Onto þe wyche woman I thynk no gyle—
And þis pylgramage cavsyd me to take.
    I woll tell[3] yow more of þe stylle,   18
For to crestyn me from wo and wrake.

---

[1] *L; MS* a montem   [2] þe seyn *canc. after*   [3] *added above*

PETYR. O, blyssyd be þe¹ tyme þat 3e are falle to grace,
    And 3e wyll kepe yower beleve aftyr my techeyng,
    And alle-only forsake þe fynd Saternas,
    The commavndme[n]ttys of God to have in kepyng!   1830
REX. Forsoth, I beleve in þe Father, þat is of all wyldyng,
    And in þe Son, Jhesu Cryst,
    Also in þe Holy Gost, hys grace to vs spredyng!
    I beleve in Crystys deth, and hys vprysyng!

PETYR. Syr, þan whatt axke 3e?   1835
REX. Holy father, baptym, for charyte,
    Me to save in eche degre
    From þe fyndys bond!
PETYR. In þe name of þe Trenite,
    Wyth þis watyr I baptysse þe,   1840
    þat þou mayst strong be,
    A3en þe fynd to stond.

        Tunc aspargit illum cum aqua.

REX. A, holy fathyr, how my hart wyll be sor   f. 137ᵛ
    Of cummav[n]ddementt, and 3e declare nat þe sentens!
PETYR. Syr, dayly 3e xall lobor more and more,   1845
    Tyll þat 3e have very experyens.
    Wyth me xall 3e wall to have more eloquens,
    And goo vesyte þe stacyons, by and² by;
    To Nazareth and Bedlem, goo wyth delygens,
    And be yower own inspeccyon, yower feyth³ to edyfy.   1850

REX. Now, holy father, derevorthy and dere,
    Myn intent now know 3e.
Itt is gon full to 3ere
    þat I cam to yow owere þe se,
    Crystys servont, and yower to be,   1855
And þe lave of hym evyr to fulfyll.
    Now woll I hom into my contre.
Yower pvere blyssynd gravnt vs tylle—
    þat, feythfully, I crave!

¹ *added above*   ² *added above*   ³ e *added above*

PETRUS. Now in þe name of Jhesu,   1
    Cum Patre et Sancto Speritu,
    He kepe[1] þe and save!

    Et tunc rex transit ad navem, et dicit rex:

[REX]. Hold ner, shepman, hold, hold!
BOY. Syr, ӡendyr is on callyd aftyr cold!
NAVTA. A, syr! I ken yow of old!   1
    Be[2] my trowth, ӡe be welcum to me!

REX. Now, gentyll marranere, I þe pray,   f.
Whatsoewer þat I pay,
In all þe hast þat ӡe may,
    Help me owyr þe se!   1

NAVTA. In good soth we byn atenddawntt!
Gladly ӡe xall have yower gravnt,
Wythowtyn ony[3] connownt.
    Comme in, in Goddys name!
Grobbe, boy! þe wynd is nor-west!   1
Fast abowth þe seyle cast!
Rere vp þe seyll in all þe hast,
    As well as þou can!

    Et tunc navis venit adcirca placeam. Rex dicit:

[REX]. Mastyr of þe shyp, cast forth yower yee!
Me thynkyt þe rokke I gyn to aspye!   1
Gentyll mastyr þether vs gye—
    I xall qwyt yower mede.
NAVTA. I[n][4] feyth, it is þe same ston
þat yower wyff lyeth vpon!
Ye xall be þer even anon,   1
    Werely, indede!

REX. O þou myty Lord of heven region,
    Ӡendyr is my babe of myn own nature,
Preservyd and keptt from all corrupcyon!   1
    Blyssyd be þat Lord[5] þat þe dothe socure,
    And my wyff lyeth here, fayer and puer!

---

[1] ӡ *canc. after*   [2] b *canc. after*   [3] ow *canc. before*
[4] *MS* I   [5] ӡ *canc. before*

Fayere and clere is hur colour to se!
  A, good Lord, yower grace wyth vs indure,

My wyvys lyfe for to illumyn.   f. 138ᵛ
A, blyssyd be þat puer vergyn!   1895
  From grevos slepe she gynnyt revyve!
A, þe sonne of grace on vs doth shynne!¹
  Now blyssyd be God, I se my wyff alyve!

REGINA. O *virgo salutata*, for ower savacyon!
  O *pulcra et casta*, cum of nobyll alyavns!   1900
O almyty Maydyn, ower sowlys confortacyon!
  O demvr Mavdlyn, my bodyys sustynavns!
þou hast wr[a]ppyd vs in wele from all waryawns,
And led me wyth my lord i[n]to þe Holy Lond!
  I am baptysyd, as ye are, be Maryvs gyddavns,   1905
Of Sent Petyrys holy hand.

I sye þe blyssyd crosse þat Cryst shed on hys precyvs² blod;
  Hys blyssyd sepulcur also se I.
Whe[r]for, good hosbond, be mery in mode,
  For I have gon þe stacyounys, by and by!   1910
REX. I thanke it Jhesu, wyth hart on hye!
Now have I my wyf and my chyld both!
  I thank ytt Mavdleyn and Ower Lady,
And evyr shall do, wythowtyn othe.

    Et tunc remigant a monte, et navta dicit:

[NAVTA]. Now ar ye past all perelle—   f. 139ʳ
Her is þe lond of Marcylle!   1916
Now goo a lond, syr, whan ȝe wyll,
  I prye yow for my sake!
REX. Godamercy, jentyll marraner!
Here is ten³ poundys of nobyllys cler,   1920
And euer þe frynd both ferre and nere,
  Cryst save þe from wo and wrake!

----

¹ y *altered from* e
² *added above*
³ xli

Here goth þe shep owt of þe place, and Mavd[leyn] seyth:

[Marcylle.]

[MARY MAVDLEYN]. O dere fryndys, be in hart stabyll!
And [thynk] how dere Cryst hathe yow bowth![1]
A3ens God, be nothyng vereabyll—   19
Thynk how he[2] mad all thyng of nowth!
Thow yow in poverte sumtyme be browth,
[3]itte be in charyte both nyth and day,
For þey byn blyssyd þat so byn sowth,
For *'pavpertas est donum[3] Dei'*.   19

God blyssyt alle þo þat byn meke and good,[4]
And he blyssyd all þo þat wepe for synne.
þey be blyssyd þat þe hungor and þe thorsty gyff fode;
þey be blyssyd þat byn mercyfull a3en wrecched men;
þey byn blyssyd þat byn dysstroccyon[5] of synne—   19
Thes byn callyd þe chyldyren of lyfe,
Onto þe wyche blysse bryng both yow and me   f.
That for vs dyyd on þe rode tre! Amen.

Here xall þe kyng and þe quvene knele doun. Rex dicit:

[REX]. Heyll be þou, Mary! Ower Lord[6] is wyth the!
The helth of ower sowllys, and repast contemplatyff!   19
Heyll, tabyrnakyll of þe blyssyd Trenite!
Heyll, covnfortabyll sokore for man and wyff!

REGINA. Heyll, þou chosyn and chast of wommen alon!
It passyt my wett to tell þi nobyllnesse![7]
þou relevyst me and my chyld on þe rokke of ston,   19
And also savyd vs be þi[8] hye holynesse.

MARY. Welcum hom, prynse and prynsses bothe!
Welcum hom, yong prynsse of dew and ryth!
Welcum hom to your own erytage wythowt[9] othe,
And to alle yower pepyll present in syth!   19
Now ar 3e becum Goddys own knygth,

---

[1] both *canc. before*   [2] *added above*   [3] *L; MS* domum
[4] *later hand added* d   [5] ss *over another letter*   [6] *added above*
[7] *letter canc. between* nobyll *and* nesse   [8] *added above*
[9] b *canc. before*

For sowle helth salve ded ȝe seche,
   In hom þe Holy Gost hath take resedens,
And drevyn asyde all þe desepcyon of wrech.
   And now have ȝe a knowle[ge] of þe sentens,   1955
      How ȝe xall com onto grace!
   But now in yower godys aȝen I do yow sese.
   I trost I have¹ governyd þem to yower hertys ese.   f. 140ʳ
   Now woll I labor forth, God to plese,
      More gostly strenkth me to purchase!   1960

REX. O blyssyd Mary, to comprehend
   Ower swete sokor, on vs have pete!
REGINA. To departe from vs, why shovld ȝe pretende?
   O blyssyd lady, putt vs nat to þat poverte!

MARY. Of yow and yowers I wyll have rememberavns,   1965
   And dayly [y]ower bede woman for to be,
þat alle wyckydnesse from yow may have deleverans,
   In quiet and rest þat leve may ȝe!

REX. Now thanne, yower puere blyssyng gravnt vs tylle.
MARI. The blyssyn of God mott yow fulfyll.   1970

Ille vos benedicatt, qui sene fine vivit et regnat!

   Her goth Mary into þe wyldyrnesse, þus seyyng Rex:

REX. A! We may syyn and wepyn also,
   þat we have forgon þis lady fre—
It brynggytt my hart in care and woo—
   þe whech ower gydde and governor shovld a be!   1975
REGINA. þat doth perswade all my ble,
þat swete sypresse, þat she wold so.
   In me restytt neyther game nor gle
That she wold from owere presens goo.   f. 140ᵛ

REX. Now of hyr goyng I am nothyng glad!   1980
   But my londdys to gyddyn I mvst aplye,
Lyke as Sancte Peter me badde,
   Chyrchys in cetyys I woll edyfye;
   And whoso aȝens ower feyth woll replye,

¹ *added above*

I woll ponysch [s]wych personnys wyth perplyxcyon!   19
  Mahond and hys lawys I defye!
A, hys pryde owt of my love xall have polucyon,
And holle onto Jhesu I me betake!
    Mari in herimo.

[MARI]. In þis deserte abydyn wyll wee,
  My sowle from synne for to save;   19
I wyll evyr abyte me wyth humelyte,
  And put me in pacyens, my Lord for to love.
In charyte my werkys I woll grave,
And in abstynens, all dayys of my lyfe.
  Thus my concyens of me doth crave;   19
Than why shold I wyth my consyens st[r]yffe?
And ferdarmore, I wyll leven in charyte,
  At þe reverens of Ower Blyssyd Lady,
  In goodnesse to be lyberall, my sowle to edyfye.
Of wordly fodys I wyll leve all refeccyon;   20
  Be þe fode þat commyt from heven on hye,
Thatt God wyll me send, be contemplatyff.   f.

    [Heaven Stage]

JHESUS. O, þe swettnesse of prayors sent onto me
  Fro my wel-belovyd frynd wythowt waryovns!
Wyth gostly fode relevyd xall she be.   20
  Angellys! Into þe clowdys ye do hyr havns,
  þer fede wyth manna to hyr systynovns.
Wyth joy of angyllys, þis lett hur receyve.
  Byd hur injoye wyth all hur afyawns,
For fynddys frawd xall hur non deseyve.   20

PRIMUS ANGELUS. O þou redulent rose, þat of a vergyn
                  sprong![2]
  O þou precyus palme of wytory!
O þou osanna, angellys song!
  O precyus gemme, born[3] of Ower Lady!
Lord, þi commav[n]ddement we obbey lowly!   20
  To þi servant þat þou hast gravntyd blysse,
We angellys all obeyyn devowtly.
We woll desend to yen wyldyrnesse.

¹ *the scribe has skipped ff. 141ᵛ and 142ʳ; at top of f. 141ᵛ he has written* turne on þe othyr syde   ² sporng   ³ bornd *canc.* born *written above*

Here xall to angyllys desend into wyldyrnesse, and other to
xall bryng an oble, opynly aperyng aloft in þe clowddys; þe
to benethyn xall bryng Mari, and she xall receyve þe bred,
and þan go aʒen into wyldyrnesse.

SECUNDUS ANGELUS. Mari, God gretyt þe wyth hevenly
influens!

He hath sent þe grace wyth hevenly synys.   2020
þou xall byn onoryd wyth joye and reverens,
  Inhansyd in heven above wergynnys!   f. 142ᵛ
þou hast byggyd þe here among spynys—
God woll send þe fode be revelacyon.
  þou xall be receyvyd into þe clowddys,   2025
Gostly fode to reseyve to þi savacyon.

MARI. *Fiat voluntas tua* in heven and erth!
Now am I full of joye and blysse!
Lavd and preyse to þat blyssyd byrth!
  I am redy, as hys blyssyd wyll isse.   2030

Her xall she be halsyd wyth angellys wyth reverent song.
Asumpta est Maria in nubibus. Celi gavdent, angeli lavdantes
felium Dei, et dicit Mari:

[MARI]. O þou Lord of lorddys, of hye domenacyon!
In hewen and erth worsheppyd be þi name.
How þou devydyst me from hovngure and wexacyon!
  O gloryus Lord, in þe is no fravddys nor no¹ defame!
But I xuld serve my Lord, I were to blame,   2035
Wych fullfyllyt me wyth so gret felicete,
  Wyth melody of angyllys shewit me gle and game,
And have fed me wyth fode of most delycyte!

Her xall speke an holy prest in þe same wyldyrnesse, þus
seyyng þe prest:

[PREST]. O Lord of lorddys! What may þis be?
So gret mesteryys shewyd from heven,   2040
Wyth grett myrth and melody
  Wyth angyllys brygth as þe lewyn!   f. 143ʳ
Lord Jhesu, for þi namys sewynne,
As gravnt me grace þat person to se!

¹ added above

Her he xal go in þe wyldyrnesse and spye Mari in hyr
devocyon, þus seyyng þe prest:

[PREST]. Heyl, creature, Crystys delecceon!   2(
 Heyl, swetter þan sugur or cypresse!
Mary is þi name be angyllys relacyon;
 Grett art þou wyth God for þi perfythnesse!
þe joye of Jherusallem shewyd þe expresse,
þe wych I nevyr save þis thirty[1] wyntyr and more!   2(
 Wherfor I know well þou art of gret perfy[t]nesse,
I woll pray yow hartely to she[w] me of yower Lord!

MARI. Be þe grace of my Lord Jhesus
 þis thirty[2] wyntyr þis hath byn my selle,
And thryys on þe day enhansyd þus   2(
 Wyth more joy þan ony tong can telle
 Nevyr creature cam þer I dwelle,
Tyme nor tyde, day nore nyth,
 þat I can wyth spece telle,
But alonly wyth Goddys angyllys brygth.   2(
But þou art wolcum onto my syth,
 Yf þou be of good conversacyon.
As I thynk in my delyth,
 Thow sholddyst be a man of devocyon.   f.

PREST. In Crystys lav I am sacryed a pryst,   2(
 Mynystryyd be angelys at my masse.
I sakor þe body of ower Lord Jhesu Cryst,
 And be þat holy manna I leve in sowthfastnesse.
MARI. Now I rejoyse of yower goodnesse,
But tyme is comme þat I xall asende.   2(
PRYST. I recummend me wyth all vmbylnesse;
Onto my sell I woll pretend.

Her xall þe prest go to hys selle, þus seyyng Jhesus:

[Heaven Stage]

JHESUS. Now xall Mary have possessyon,
 Be ryth enirytawns[3] a crown to bere.

          [1] xxx   [2] xxx   [3] i *added above*

She xall be fett to evyrlastyng savacyon,[1]   2075
In joye to dwell wythowtyn fere.[2]
Now, angelys, lythly þat ȝe were ther!
Onto þe prystys sell apere þis tyde.
My body in forme of bred þat he bere,
Hur for to hossell, byd hym provyde.   2080

PRIMUS ANGELUS. O blyssyd Lord, we be redy,
    [3]Yower massage to do wythowtyn treson!
SECUNDUS ANGELUS. To hyr I wyll goo and make reportur,
    How she xall com to yower habytacyon.

> Here xall to[4] angellys go to Mary and to þe prest, þus seyyng
> þe angellys to þe prest:

ANGELLYS. Syr pryst, God cummav[n]dytt from heven region   2085
    ȝe xall go hosyll hys servont expresse,
And we wyth yow xall take mynystracyon   f. 144r
    To bere lyth before hys body of worthynesse.
PRYST. Angyllys, wyth all vmbyllnesse,
    In a westment I wyll me aray,   2090
To mynystyr my Lord of gret hynesse;
    Straytt[5] þerto I take þe way!

> In herimo.

SECUNDUS ANGELUS. Mary, be glad, and in hart strong
    To reseyve þe palme of grett wytory!
þis day ȝe xall be reseyvyd wyth angellys song!   2095
    Yower sowle xall departe from yower body.

MARI. A, good Lord, I thank þe[6] wythowt weryawns!
    þis day I am grovndyd all in goodnesse,
Wyth hart and body conclvdyd in substawns.
    I thanke þe, Lord, wyth speryt of perfythnesse!   2100

> Hic aparuit angelus et presbiter cum corpus domenicum.

[PRESBITYR]. þou blyssyd woman, invre in mekenesse,
    I have browth þe þe bred of lyf to þi syth,
To make þe suere from all dystresse,
    þi sowle to bryng to euyrlastyng lyth.

---

[1] damnacyon canc., savacyon written above   [2] e canc. before
[3] letter canc. before   [4] ij   [5] a added above   [6] added above

MARI. O þou mythty Lord of hye mageste,   21
þis celestyall bred for to determyn,
Thys tyme[1] to reseyve[2] it in me,
My sowle þerwyth to illumyn.   f.

Her she reseyvyt it.[3]

I thank þe, Lord of ardent love!
Now I know well I xall nat opprese.   21
Lord, lett me se þi joyys above!
I recummend[4] my sowle onto þi blysse!
Lord, opyn þi blyssyd gatys!
Thys erth at thys tyme fervenly I kysse!
In manus tuas, Domine!   21
Lord, wyth þi grace me wysse!
Commendo spiritum meum! Redemisti me,
Domine Devs veritatis!

PRIMUS ANGELUS. Now reseyve[5] we þis sowle, as reson is,
In heven to dwelle vs among.   21
SECUNDUS ANGELUS. Wythowtyn end to be in blysse!
Now lett vs syng a mery song!

Gavdent in celis.

PRYST. O good God, grett is þi grace!
O Jhesu, Jhesu! Blessyd be þi name!
A, Mary, Mary! Mych is þi solas,   21
In heven blysse wyth gle and game![6]
þi body wyl I cure from alle manyr blame,
And I wyll passe to þe bosshop of þe sete
Thys body of Mary to berye be name,
Wyth alle reverens and solemnyte.   21

Sufferens of þis processe, thus enddyt þe sentens   f.
That we have playyd in yower syth.

---

[1] tym *canc. before*
[2] ve *added above*
[3] *MS this stage direction parallel with l.* 2108; *F prints it before l.* 2108
[4] *MS* recumdmend
[5] s *altered from* r
[6] *Schmidt, L, B; MS* name

Allemythty God, most of magnyfycens,
  Mote bryng yow to hys blysse so brygth,
    In presens of þat Kyng!
    Now, frendys, thus endyt thys matere—
    To blysse bryng þo þat byn here!
    Now, clerkys, wyth woycys cler,
      'Te Deum lavdamus' lett vs syng!

  Explycit oreginale de Sancta Maria Magdalena.

Yff ony thyng amysse be,
Blame connyng, and nat me!
I desyer þe redars to be my frynd,
Yff þer be ony amysse, þat to amend.

Candlemes Day and the Kyllyng of þe Children of Israelle[1]

MDXij[2]   Anno Domini 1512[3]
                                              the vij booke[4]

POETA. This solenne fest to be had in remembraunce
  Of blissed Seynt Anne, modere to Oure Lady,
Whos right discent was fro kynges alyaunce—
  Of Dauyd and Salamon, winesseth the story.
  Hir blissid doughtere, that callid is Mary,   5
By Goddes provision an husbond shuld haue,
  Callid Joseph, of nature old and drye,
And she, moder vnto Crist, that alle the world shalle save.

This glorious maiden doughter vnto Anna,
  In whos worshippe this fest we honoure,   10
And by resemblaunce likenyd vnto manna,
  Wiche is in tast celestialle of savoure,
  And of Jerico the sote rose floure,
Gold Ebryson callid in picture,
  Chosyn for to bere mankyndes Savyoure,   15
With a prerogative aboue eche creature!

These grett thynges remembred, after oure entent,
  Is for to worshippe Oure Ladye and Seynt Anne.
We be comen hedere as seruauntes diligent,
  Oure processe to shewe you, as we can.   20
  Wherfor of benevolens we pray euery man
To haue vs excused that we no better doo—
  Another tyme to emende it if we can,
Be the grace of God, if oure cunnyng be thertoo.

Only the edition of Furnivall (F) is collated, the others being of no textual value.

     [1] *in a somewhat lighter ink, but in the hand of the main scribe*
     [2] *in the hand of the main scribe*
     [3] *apparently in the hand of the main scribe*
     [4] *in another hand, which F suggests (p. 1) is that of John Stow*

The last yeere we shewid you[1] in[2] this place   25
  How the shepherdes of Cristes birthe made letificacion,
And thre kynges that come[3] fro þer cuntrees be grace
  To worshippe Jhesu with enteere deuocion.
And now we purpose with hoolle affeccion   f. 146ᵛ
To procede in oure matere as we can,   30
  And to shew you of Oure Ladies purificacion
That she made in the temple, as the vsage was than.

And after that shalle Herowde haue tydynges
  How the[4] thre kynges be goon hoom another way,
That were with Jhesu and made[5] ther offrynges,   35
  And promysed Kyng Herowde without delay
  To come ageyn by hym—this is no nay;
And whan he wist that thei were goon,
  Like as a wodman[6] he gan to fray,
And commaundid his knyghtes for to go anoon   40

Into Israelle, to serche euery town and cite
  For alle the children that thei cowde ther fynde
Of too[7] yeeres age and within, sparyng neither bonde nor free,
  But sle them alle, either for foo or frende—
  Thus he commaundid in his furious wynde,   45
Thought that Jhesu shuld haue be oon.
  And yitt he failed of his froward mynde,
For by Goodes purviaunce, Oure Lady was into Egipte gon!

Frendes, this processe we purpose to pley, as we can,
  Before you alle here in youre presens,   50
To the honor of God, Oure Lady, and Seynt Anne,
  Besechyng you to geve vs peseable audiens!
  And ye menstrallis, doth youre diligens!
And ye virgynes, shewe summe[8] sport and plesure,
  These people to solas, and to[9] do God reuerens!   55
As ye be appoynted, doth your besy cure!

    Et tripident.

---

[1] y *altered from* þ   [2] b *canc. before*   [3] f *canc. before*
[4] that *canc. before,* thre *added above caret*   [5] t *canc. before*
[6] woman *with* d *added above,* wodman *added below*   [7] ij
[8] e *altered from* a   [9] d *canc. before*

[Jerusalem—Herod's Palace]

HERODES. Aboue alle kynges vnder the clowdys cristalle,   f. 1
  Royally I reigne in welthe without woo!
Of plesaunt prosperyte I lakke non at alle!
  Fortune, I fynde that she is not my foo!   60
I am Kyng Herowdes! I wille it be knowen soo!
  Most strong and myghty in feld for to fyght,
And to venquysshe my enemyes þat ageynst me do!
  I am most bedred, with my bronde bright!

My grett goddes I gloryfye with gladnesse,   65
  And to honoure them I knele vpon my knee,
For thei haue sett me in solas from alle sadnesse,
  That no conqueroure nor knyght is comparid to me!
Alle tho that rebelle ageyns me, ther bane I wille be,
  Or grudge ageyns my[1] goddes on hylle or hethe!   70
Alle suche rebellers I shalle make for to flee,
  And with hard punysshementes putt them to dethe!

What erthely wretches, with pompe and pride,
  Do ageyns my lawes, or withstonde myn entent,
Thei shalle suffre woo and peyne thurgh bak and syde!   75
  With a very myschaunce ther flesshe shalbe alle torent,
And alle my foes shalle haue suche commaundement,
  That they shalbe glad to do my byddyng ay!
Or elles thei shalbe in woo and myscheff permanent,
  That thei shalle fere me nyght and day![2]   80

[The following lines are cancelled.]

My messangere, at my commaundement come heder to me,   f. 1
  And take hed[3] what I shalle to the say!
I charge the loke abought thurgh alle my cuntre,
  To aspye if ony rebelles do ageynst oure lay,
  And if ony suche come in thy way,   5
Brynge hem into oure high presens,
And[4] we shalle se them correctid or thei go hens!

    [1] y *altered from* e
    [2] *another hand has written in the bottom right, vertically to the page,* dum sumus
in (*three minims follow and the rest is lost*)
    [3] what *canc.,* hed *written above, then canc.,* hed *and* what *then written again*
    [4] *in left margin the scribe has drawn an insertion symbol, but there is no indication
of what material was to be inserted after canc. l. 7*

WATKYN, MESSANGER. My lord, your commaundement I haue[1]
                                    fulfilled,[2]
    Evyn to the vttermest of my pore powere,
And I wold shew you more, so ye wold be contentid,[3]   10
    But I dare not, lest ye wold take it in angere!
For if it liked you not, I am sure my deth were nere,
    And therfor, my lord, I wole hold my peas!
HEROD. I warne the, thu traytour, that thu not seas

To shewe euery thyng thu knowist ageyns oure reuerence!   15
MESSANGER. My lord, if ye haue it in youre remembraunce,
    Ther were thre[4] straungere kynges but late in your presence,
That went to Bedlem to offre[5] with due obseruaunce,
    And promysed to come ageyn by you, without variaunce;
But by thes bonys ten, thei be to you vntrue,   20
    For[6] homward another wey thei doo[7] sue!

HEROD. Now, be my grett goddes that be so fulle of myght,
    I wille be avengid vpon Israelle[8] if thi tale be true!
MESSANGER. That it is, my lord, my trouth I you plight,
    For ye founde me neuer false syn ye me knewe!

            [End of cancelled passage]

HEROD. I[9] do perceyue, though I be here in my cheff cite,   f. 148[r]
    Callid Jerusalem, my riche royalle town,
I[10] am falsly[11] disceyvid by straunge kynges three!
    Therfor, my knyghtes, I warne you, without delacion,
That ye make serche thurghout alle my region—   85
Withoute ony tarieng, my wille may be seen—
    And sle alle tho children, without excepcion,
Of to yeeres of age þat within Israelle bene!

For within myself thus I haue concluded,
    For to avoide awey alle interrupcion,   90
Sythen theȝ thre kynges haue me thus falsly deluded,
    As in maner by froward collusion,

---

¹ shalle *canc.*, haue *written above*   ² d *added later by same hand*
³ and it were your wille *canc.*, so ye wold be contentid *written above*
⁴ iij   ⁵ make offryng *canc.*, offre *written above*
⁶ thei be departid and *canc. between* For *and* homward
⁷ thei doo *added over caret*   ⁸ *first* e *added above*
⁹ A now *canc. before*, do *added above* I   ¹⁰ Yitt *canc. before*
¹¹ I *canc. before*

And ageyn resortid hom into ther region—
But yitt, mavgre ther hertes, I shalle avengid be!
Bothe in Bedlem and my provynces¹ euerychone,   95
Sle alle the children, to kepe my liberte!

PRIMUS MILES. My lord, ye may be sure that I shalle not spare,
   For to fulfille your noble commaundement,
With sharpe sword to perse them alle bare,
   In alle cuntrees that be to you² adiacent!   10
SECUNDUS MILES. And for your sake, to obserue³ your com-
                              maundement!
TERCIUS MILES. Not on of them alle oure handes shalle astert!
QUARTUS MILES. For we wole cruelly execute youre judgement,
With swerde and spere to perse them thurgh the hert!

HEROD. I thanke you, my knyghtes, but loke ye make no tarieng!   10
   Do arme yourself in stele shynyng⁴ bright,
And conceyve in your myndes that I am your kyng,   f. 1
   Gevyng you charge þat with alle your myght,
   In conseruacion of my tytelle of right,
That ye go and loke for myn aduauntage,   11
   And sle alle the children þat come in your sight,
Wiche ben within too yeere of age!

Now beware that my byddyng ye truly obey,
   For non but I shalle reigne with equyte!
Make alle the children on your swordes to dey!   11
   I charge you, spare not oon for mercy nor pyte!
   Am not I lord and kyng of the cuntre?
The crowne of alle Jerusalem longith to me of right!
   Whosoeuer sey nay, of high or lowe degre,
I charge you sle alle suche⁵ þat come in your sight!   12

PRIMUS MILES. My lord, be ye sure accordyng to your wille,
   Like as ye charge vs be streigt commaundement,
Alle the children of Israelle doughtles we shalle kylle,
   Within to yeere of age—this is oure entent!

---

¹ MS in *canc. before*, al other *written above, then canc.*, my *added below*
² to you *added above caret*   ³ ob *added above caret*
⁴ fayr *canc. before*, s *altered from* and   ⁵ tho *canc. before*

SECUNDUS MILES. My lord, of alle Jurerye we hold you for chef 125
                                regent,
By titelle of enheritaunce, as your auncetours beforn;
  He that seith the contrary, be Mahound, shalbe shent,
And curse the tyme that euer [he] was borne!

HEROD. I thanke you, my knyghtes, with hoolle affeccion, 130
  And whan ye come ageyn I shalle you avaunce.
Therfor, quyte you wele in feld and town,
  And of alle tho fondlynges make a delyueraunce!

Here the knyghtes shalle departe from Herowdes to Israelle,
* and Watkyn shalle abyde, seyng thus to Herodes:*

WATKYN. Now, my lord, I beseche you to here my dalyaunce! f. 149ʳ
I wold aske you a bone, if I durst aright,
  But I were loth ye shuld take ony displesaunce— 135
Now, for Mahoundes sake, make me a knyght!

For oon thyng I promyse you: I wille manly fight,
  And for to avenge your quarelle I dare vndertake;
Though I sey it myself, I am a man of myght,
  And dare live and deye in this quarelle for your sake! 140
  For whan I com amonge them, for fere thei shalle quake!
And though thei sharme and crye, I care not a myght,
  But with my sharpe sworde ther ribbes I shalle shake,
Evyn thurgh the guttes, for anger and despight!

HEROWDES. Be thi trouthe, Watkyn, woldest thu be made a 145
                               knyght?[1]
Thu hast be my seruaunt and messangere many a day,
But thu were neuer provid in bataile nor in fight,
  And therfor to avaunce the so sodeynly[2] I ne may.
  But oon thyng[3] to the I shalle say,
Because I fynde the true in thyn entent: 150
  Forth with my knyghtes thu shalt take the way,
And quyte the wele, and thu shalt it not repent!

WATKYN. Now, a largeys, my lord! I am right wele apaid!
  If I do not wele, ley my hed vpon a stokke!
I[4] shalle go shew your knyghtes how ye haue seid, 155
  And arme myself manly, and go forth on the flokke

---

    [1] kyng *canc. before*   [2] shortly *canc. before*   [3] this *canc. before*
    [4] And *canc. before;* s *of* shalle *altered from another letter*

And if I fynde a yong child, I shalle choppe it on a blokke!
Though the moder be angry, the child shalbe slayn!
But yitt I drede no thyng more thanne a woman with a rokke!   f.
For if I se ony suche, be my feith, I come ageyn!   16

HEROWDES. What! Shalle a woman with a rokke drive the away?
Fye on the, traitour! Now I tremble for tene!
I have trosted the long and many a day—
A bold man, and an hardy, I went thu haddist ben!
WATKYN[1] MESSANGER. So am I, my lord, and that shalbe seen,   16
That I am a bold man, and best dare abyde!
And ther come an hundred women, I wole not fleen,
But fro morowe tylle nyght, with them I dare chide!

And therfor, my lord, ye may trust vnto me,
For alle the children of Israelle your knyghtes and I shalle kylle!   1'
I wylle not spare on, but[2] dede thei shalbe—
If the fader and moder wille lete me haue my wille!
HEROWDES. Thu lurdeyn! Take hede what I sey the tylle,
And high the to my knyghtes as fast as thu can!
Say, I warne them in ony wyse þer blood þat thei spille,   1'
Abought in euery cuntre, and lette for no man!

WATKYN.[3] Nay, nay, my lord! We wylle let for no man,
Though ther come a thousand on a rought,
For your knyghtes and I wille kylle them alle,[4] if we can!
But for the wyves, that is alle my dought,   18
And if I se ony walkyng abought,
I wille take[5] good hede tylle she be goon,
And as sone as I aspye that she is oute,
By my feith, into the hous I wille go anon!

And this I promyse you, that I shalle neuer slepe,   f.
But euermore wayte to fynde the children alone,   18
And if the moder come in, vnder the benche I wille crepe,
And lye stille ther tylle she be goon!
Than manly I shalle come out and hir children sloon!
And whan I haue don, I shalle renne fast away!   16
If she founde hir child dede, and toke me ther alone,
Be my feith, I am sure we shuld make a fray!

HEROWDES. Nay, harlott! Abyde stylle with my knyghtes, I warne
the,
   Tylle[1] the children be slayn, alle the hoolle rought!
And whan thu comyst home ageyn, I shalle avaunce the,   195
   If thu quyte the like a man whille thu art ought!
   And if thu pley the coward, I put the owt of dought,
Of me thu shalt neyther haue fee nor aduauntage!
   Therfor, I charge you, the contre be weelle sought,
And whan thu comyst home, shalt haue thi wage!   200

WATKYN. Yis, syre, be my trouthe, ye shalle wele knowe
   Whille I am oute, how I shalle aquyte me,
For I purpos to spare neither high nor lowe—
   If ther be no man wole smyte me!
   The most I fere, the wyues wille bete me!   205
Yitt shalle I take good hert to me, and loke wele abought,
   And loke that your knyghtes be not ferre fro me,
For if I be alone, I may sone get a clought!

HEROD. I say, hye the hens! That thu were goon!
   And vnto my knyghtes, loke ye, take the way,   210
And sey, I charge them that[2] my commaundement be don
   In alle hast possible, without more delay!
   And if ther be ony that wille sey you nay,   f. 150ᵛ
Redde hym[3] of his lyff out of hand, anon!
   And if thu quyte the weelle vnto my pay,   215
I shalle make þe a knyght aventururos whan þu comyst home!

     Et exeat.[4]

WATKYN. Syr knyghtes, I must go forth with you!
   Thus my lord commaunded me for to don,
And if I quyte me weelle whille I am amonge you,
   I shalbe made a knyght aventures whan I come home!   220
   For oon thyng I promyse you, I wille fight anon—
If my hert faile not whan I shal begynne!
   The most I fere is to come amonge women,
For thei fight like deuelles with ther rokkes whan þei spynne!

---

[1] t *and another letter canc. before*   [2] to do *canc.,* that *written above*
[3] MS *added above caret in later hand;* F him   [4] *added in right margin*

PRIMUS MILES. Watkyn, I loue the, for thu art euer a man!   22
  If thu quyte the weelle in this grett viage,
I shalle speke to my lord for the that I can,
  That thu shalt no more be neither grome nor page!
SECUNDUS MILES. I wylle speke for the, that thu shalt haue better
                                         wage,
  If thu quyte the manly amonge the wyves,   23
    For thei be as fers as a lyon in a cage,
Whan thei are broken ought, to reve[1] men of þer lives!

> *Here the knyghtes and Watkyn walke abought the place tylle*
> *Mary and Joseph be conveid into Egipt.*

> *Dixit angelus:*

ANGELUS. O Joseph, ryse vp, and loke thu tary nought!
  Take Mary with the, and into Egipt flee!
For Jhesu, thi sone, pursuyd is and sought,   23
  By Kyng Herowdes, the wiche of gret inyquyte   f.
  Commaundid hath thurgh Bedlem cite,
In his cruelle and furyous rage,
  To sle alle the children that be in that cuntre
That may be founde within to yeere of age!   24

Ther shalle he shewe in that region
  Diuerse myracles of his high regalye—
In alle ther temples the mawmentes shalle falle down,
  To shew a tokyn towardes the partie!
This child hath lordship, as prophetes do specifie,   24
And at his comyng, thurgh his myghty hond,
  In despight of alle idolatrie,
Euery oon shalle falle, whan he comyth into the lond!

JOSEPH. O good Lord, of thi gracious ordenaunce,
  Like as thu list for oure jorney provide[2]   25
In this viage with humble attendaunce,
  As God disposeth, and list to be oure gyde.
  Therfor, vpon them bothe mekely I shalle abide,
Praying to that Lord to thynk vpon vs three,
  Vs to preserue, wheder we go or ryde   25
Towardes Egipte, from alle aduercite.

---

         [1] v *altered from* w   [2] prov *canc. before*

MARY. Now, husbond, in alle hast I pray you, go we hens
   For drede of Herowdes, that cruelle knyght.
Gentylle spouse, now do youre diligens,
   And bryng your asse, I pray you, anon right,   260
   And from hens let vs passe with alle oure myght,
Thankyng that Lord so for vs doth provide   f. 151ᵛ
   That we may go from Herowdes, þat cursid wight,
Wiche wille vs devoure if that we abide!

JOSEPH. Mary, you to do plesaunce without ony lett,   265
   I shalle brynge forth your asse without more delay.
Ful sone, Mary, theron ye shalbe sett,
   And this litelle child that in your wombe lay;
Take hym in your armys, Mary, I you pray,
   And of your swete mylke lete hym sowke inowe,   270
   Mawgere Herowdes and his grett fray,
And as your spouse, Mary, I shalle go with you.

This ferdelle of gere I ley vp my bakke—
   Now I am redy to go from this cuntre.
Alle my smale instrumentes is putt in my pakke;   275
   Now go we hens, Mary, it wille no better be!

     *Et exeant.*¹

For drede of Herowdes apaas I wylle high me!
Lo, now is oure geere trussid, both more and lesse.
   Mary, for to plese you, with alle humylite,
I shalle go before, and lede forth youre asse.   280

   Here Mary and Joseph shalle go out of þe place, and þe
   goddes shalle falle,² and than shalle come in the women of
   Israel, with yong children in ther armys, and than the knyghtes
   shalle go to them, sayng as foluyth:

PRIMUS MILES. Herke ye, wyffys! We³ be come your housholdes
                                   to visite,
   Though ye be neuer so wroth nor wood,
With sharpe swerdes that redely wille byte,
   Alle⁴ your children within⁵ to yeere age in oure cruelle mood,
Thurgheout alle Bethleem to kylle and shed þer yong blood,   285

---

¹ *added in right margin*   ² *and þe goddes shalle falle added above caret*
³ w *altered from another letter*   ⁴ *added in left margin*
⁵ *MS* of *canc. after* children; within *added above by main scribe; F prints*
original reading Your children of to yer age

As we be bound be the commaundement of þe kyng!
  Who that seith nay, we shalle make a flood
To renne in the stretis, by ther blood shedyng!

SECUNDUS MILES. Therfor, vnto vs ye make a delyueraunce
  Of youre yong children, and that anone!   29
Or elles, be Mahounde, we shalle geve you a myschaunce!
  Oure sharpe swerdes thurgh your bodies shalle goon!
WATKYN. Therfor beware, for we wille not leve oon
In alle this cuntre that shalle vs escape!
  I shalle rather slee them euerychoon,   29
And make them to lye and mowe like an ape!

PRIMA MULIER. Fye on you traitours of cruelle tormentrye,
  Wiche with your swerdes of mortalle violens
SECUNDA MULIER. Oure yong children, that can no socoure but
                                 crie, 30
  Wylle slee and devoure in ther innocens!
TERCIA MULIER.[1] Ye false traitours! Vnto God ye do grett offens,
  To sle and mordere yong children þat in þer cradelle slumber!
QUARTA MULIER. But we women shalle make ageyns you resistens,
  After oure powere, youre malice to encomber!

WATKYN. Peas, you folysshe quenys! Wha shuld you defende 30
  Ageyns vs armyd men in this apparaile?
We be bold men, and the kyng vs ded sende
  Hedyr into this cuntre to hold with you bataile!
PRIMA MULIER. Fye vpon the, coward! Of the I wille not faile
  To dubbe the knyght with my rokke rounde! 31
  Women be ferse when thei list to assaile
Suche prowde boyes, to caste to the grounde!
WATKYN. Avaunt ye, skowtys! I defye you euerychone!
For I wole bete you alle, myself alone!

      Hic occident pueros.[2]

PRIMA MULIER.[3] Alas, alasse, good gossyppes! This is a
                        sorowfulle peyn, f.
  To se oure dere children that be so yong 31
With these caytyves thus sodeynly to be slayn!
  A vengeaunce I aske on them alle for this grett wrong!

    [1] Secunda *canc.*, Tercia *written above*   [3] *repeated at top of f.* 152^v
    [2] *added in right margin by another hand*

SECUNDA MULIER. And a very myscheff mut come them amonge,
Whersoeuer thei be come or goon,   320
For thei haue kylled my yong sone John!

TERCIA MULIER. Gossippis, a shamefulle deth I aske vpon
                                              Herowde oure kyng,[1]
  That thus rygorously oure children hath slayn!
QUARTA MULIER.[2] I pray God bryng hym to an ille endyng,[3]
  And in helle pytte to dwelle euer in peyn!   325
WATKYN.[4] What, ye harlottes! I haue aspied certeyn
That ye be traytours to my lord the kyng,
And therfor I am sure ye shalle haue an ille endyng!

PRIMA MULIER. If ye abide, Watkyn, you and I shalle game
  With my distaff[5] that is so rounde!   330
SECUNDA MULIER. And if I seas, thanne haue I shame,
  Tylle thu be fellid down to the grounde!
TERCIA MULIER. And I may gete the within my bounde,
  With this staff I shalle make the lame!
WATKYN. Yee, I come no more ther, be Seynt Mahounde!   335
For if I do, me thynketh I shalle be made tame!

PRIMA MULIER. Abyde, Watkyn! I shalle make the a knyght!
WATKYN. Thu make me a knyght? That were on the newe!
But for shame—my trouthe I you plight—
  I shuld bete you bak[6] and side tylle it were blewe!   340
  But be my god Mahounde that is so true,
My hert begynne to fayle and waxeth feynt,
  Or elles, be Mahoundes blood, ye shuld it rue!   f. 153ʳ
But ye shalle lose your goodes as traitours atteynt!

PRIMA MULIER. What, thu javelle! Canst not haue do?   345
  Thu and thi cumpany shalle not depart
  Tylle of oure distavys ye haue take part!
  Therfor, ley on, gossippes, with a mery hart,
And lett them not from vs goo!

---

[1] Kyng Herowde *canc. before,* Herowde oure kyng *written above*
[2] iiijᵃ *canc. in right margin and written again in left margin*
[3] and alle his blood *canc. and* to an ille endyng *written in right margin*
[4] Quarta Mulier *canc.,* Watkyn *written above*
[5] staff *canc.,* my distaff *written above caret*   [6] bak *canc., then written again*

Here thei shalle bete Watkyn, and the knyghtes shalle come
to rescue hym, and than thei go to Herowdes, þus sayng:

PRIMUS MILES. Honorable prynce of grett apparayle,   3
    Thurgh Jerusalem and Jude your wylle we haue wrought;
Fulle suerly harneysed in armour of plate and maile,
    The children of Israelle[1] vnto deth we haue brought!
SECUNDUS MILES. Syr, to werke your commaundement we lettid
                                  nought,
In the stretes of the children to make a flood!   3
    We sparid neithere for care nor thought
Thurgh Bethlem to shede alle the yong blood!
WATKYN.[2] In feyth, my lord, alle the children be dede,
    And alle the men out of the cuntre be goon!
Ther be but women, and thei crie in euery stede: 3
    'A vengeaunce take Kyng Herode, for he hath our children
                                    sloon!'
And bidde 'A myscheff take hym!' both evyn and morn;
For kyllyng of ther children on you thei crie oute,
And thus goth your name alle the cuntre abought!
HERODES. Oute! I am madde! My wyttes be ner goon!   3
    I am wo for the wrokyng of this werke wylde!
For as wele I haue slayn my frendes as my foon!
    Wherfor, I fere, deth hath me begyled!
Notwithstondyng syn thei be alle defyled,
And on þe yong blood of Bethlem wrought wo and wrake,   3
    Yitt I am in no certeyn of that yong child!
Now for woo myn herte gynneth to quake!
Alas! I am so sorowfulle and sett in sadnes![3]
    I chille and chevere for this orrible chaunce!   f.
I commaunde you alle, as ye wole stond in my grace,   3
    After this yong kyng to make good enqueraunce!
And he þat bryngeth me tydynges, I shalle hym auaunce.
Now, vnto my chambere I purpose me this tyde,
    And I charge you to my preceptes geve attendaunce,
In ony place where ye goo or ryde!   3

[1] Ira *canc. before*
[2] *this speech on a quarter-leaf tipped in between ff.* 152[v] *and* 153[r], *with symbols*
indicating point of insertion in the main page
[3] *MS* sett out of sadnes; out *canc., in* added *above and below by later hand;*
F prints original reading. A later hand has written Jhesu *at the foot of the page*

What! Out, out! Allas! I wene I[1] shalle dey þis day!
  My hert tremelith and quakith for feere!
My robys I rende ato, for I am in a fray,
  That my hert wille brest asundere evyn heere!
  My lord Mahound, I pray the[2] with hert enteere,   385
Take my soule into thy holy hande,
  For I fele be my hert I shalle dey evyn heere,
For my legges faltere, I may[3] no lengere stande!

Here dieth Herowde, and Symeon shalle sey as foluyth:

Vacat ab hinc[4]   [Jerusalem—the Temple]

SYMEON. Now, God, that art both lok and keye
  Of alle goodnesse and goostly gouernaunce,
So yeve vs grace thi lawys to obeye,   390
  That we vnto the do no displesaunce;
  Lett thi grace of mercifulle haboundaunce
Vpon me shyne, that callid am Symeon,
  So that I may without ony variaunce   395
Teche thi people thi lawis euerychon.

From the sterrid hevyn, Lord, thu list come down
  Into the closett of a pure virgyn,   f. 154[r]
Oure kynde to take for mannys saluacion!
  Thi grett mercy thu lowe lyst enclyne,   400
  Lyke as prophetys by grace that is divyne
Haue prophecied of the sythe longe afforn.
  It is fulfilled, I knowe be ther doctryne,
And of a chast maide I wete wele thu art born.

Now, good Lord, hertly I the pray,   405
  Here my requeste, grounded vpon right!
Most blissed Lord, lett me neuer dey[5]
  Tylle that I of the may haue a sight!
  Thu art so gloryous, so blissed, and so bright,
That thi presence to me shuld be gret solas!   410
  I shalle not reste, but pray bothe day and nyght,
Tylle[6] I may behold, o Lord, thi swete face!

    [1] *added above*   [2] *t altered from* w   [3] mak *canc. before*
    [4] *written in left margin by later hand*   [5] dye *canc. before*
    [6] Th *canc. before*

Here shalle Oure Lady come forth, holdyng Jhesu in hir
armys, and sey this language foluyng to Joseph:

MARIA. Joseph, my spouse, tyme it is we goo
Vnto the temple to make an offrynge
Of oure swete son—the lawe commaundith so—   4
And too¹ yonge dowys with vs for to bryng
Into a prestes handes, withoute tarieng;
I shalle presente for an obseruance
Oure babe so blissed wiche is but yonge.
With me to go, I pray you, make purviaunce.   4

JOSEPH.² Most blissed spouse, me list not to feyne—   f.
Fayn wold I plese you with hoolle affeccion.
Behold now, wyff, her³ are dowys tweyne,
Of wiche ye shulle make an oblacion
With oure child, of fulle grett devocion.   4
Goth forth aforn, hertly I you pray,
And I shalle folue, voide of presumpcion,
With true entent, as an old man may.

Here Maria and Joseph go toward the temple with Jhesu and
too⁴ dowes, and Oure Lady seith vnto Symeon:

MARIA.⁵ Heylle, holy Symeon, fulle of grett vertu!
To make an offryng I gan myself purveye   4
Of my souereigne sone, that callid is Jhesu,
With too⁶ yonge dowes, the lawe to obeye.
Toward this temple grace list me conveye,
Of Goddes sone to make a presentacion.
Wherfore, Symeon, hertly I you pray,   4
Into your handes take myn oblacion!

Her shalle Symeon receyve of Maria Jhesu and too⁶ dowis,
and holde Jhesu in his armys, expownyng 'Nunc dimittis',
et cetera, seyng thus:

SYMEON. Wolcome, Lord, excellent of powere!
And wolcome, Maria, with youre sone souereigne!

---

¹ ij   ² *repeated at top of f. 154ᵛ*   ³ r *added by later hand*
⁴ ij   ⁵ Symeon *canc.,* Maria *written under*   ⁶ ij

Your oblacion, of hoolle herte and enteere,
  I receyue with these dowys tweyn.   440
Wolcome, babe! For joye what may I seyn?
Atwen myn armys now shalle I the enbrace!   f. 155ʳ
  My prayer, Lord, was not made in veyn,
For now I se thy celestialle face!

  Here declare 'Nunc dimittis'.[1]

O blissed Lord, after thi langage,   445
  In parfight peas, now lett thy seruaunt reste,
Forwhy myn eyen haue seyn thi visage,
  And eke thyn helthe, thurgh my meke request.
Of the derk dungeon let the gates brest
Before the face of thyn people alle!   450
  Thu hast brought triacle and bawme of the best,
With souereigne sugere geyn alle bitter galle!

I mene thiself, Lord, gracious and benigne,
  That woldest come down from thyn high glorye,
Poyson to repelle. Thi mercy doth now shyne   455
  To chaunge thynges that are transitory.
  Thu art the light and[2] the hevynly skye!
To the relevyng of folk most cruelle,
  Thu hast brought gladnesse to oure oratorye,
And enlumyned thy people of Israelle.   460

  Here shalle Anna Prophetissa sey thus to þe[3] *virgynes:*

ANNA PROPHETISSA. Ye pure virgynes, in that ye may or can,
  With tapers of wex, loke ye come forth here,
And worship this child, very God and man,
  Offrid in this temple be his moder dere.

  *Her virgynes, as many as a man wylle, shalle holde tapers in
  ther handes, and the first seyth:*
                                                             f. 155ᵛ
PRIMA VIRGO. As ye comaunde we shal do oure devere,[4]   465
þat Lord to plese, echon for oure partye.
  He makyth vn[to] vs so comfortable chere,
þat we must nedes þis babe magnifie!

---

[1] *MS in right margin*   [2] *of canc. before,* and *added above*
[3] *MS barely legible, added above probably in the hand of the main scribe*
[4] *this line is the first of the passage written by the second principal scribe, who*
wrote ll. 465–548

SYMEON. Now, Mary, I shalle telle you how I am purposed.
 To worshippe þis Lord I wil go procession,   4
For I se Anna with virgynes disposed,
 Mekly as nowe to youre sonys laudacion.
MARIA. Blissed Symeon, with hertly affeccion,
As ye han seyd, I concent therto.
JOSEPH. In worshippe of oure child with gret devossion,   4
Abought þe tempille in ordire let vs go.

SYMEON. Ye virgynes alle, with feythfulle intent
 Dispose youresilf a song for to synge,
To worshippe this childe þat is here present,
 Whiche to mankende gladnes list bryng.   4
 In tokyn, oure hertes withe joye doth spryng!
Betwyn myn armys þis babe shalbe born.
 Now, ye virgynis, to this Lordes preysyng
Syngyth 'Nunc dimittis' of whiche I spak afforn.

Here shal Symeon bere Jhesu in his armys, goyng a procession
rounde aboute þe tempille, and al þis wyle þe virgynis synge
'Nunc dimittis' and whan þat is don, Symeon seyth:

SYMEON. O Jhesu, chef cause of oure welfare,   4
 In yone tapire ther be thyng thre:[1]
Wax, week, and light, whiche I shalle declare
 To þe apporpride by moralite—
Lord, wax betoknyth thyn humanyte,
And week betoknyth thy soule most swete;   4
 Yone lyght I lykene to þe Godhed of the,   f.
Brightere than Phebus, for al his fervent hete.

Pes and[2] mercy han set in the here swete,
 To slake[3] þe sharpnes, o Lord, of rigoure;
Very God and man gun togedire mete   4
 In the tabirnacle of thy modrys bowere.
 Now shalt þou exile wo and alle langoure,
And of mankende t'appese infernalle stryf;
 Record of prophetes, thou shalt be redemptoure,
And singulere repast of euerlastyng[4] lyf.   5

---

[1] iijᵉ   [2] *added above caret*
[3] sh *canc. before;* l *altered from* k   [4] l *altered from* e

as ye comaunde we shalde ony dewtes
y lord to plese echon for ony pryce
ho maketh our pes so comfortable chere
y so must nedys y babe magnifie

glori mary I shall tell you holl ye   Symeon
to worshipe y lord / I wilbe precious
for I so amme et gyngues disposed
mekly as nedys to your sonys landacion

blissed Symeon & heyrly affeccion   mary
as ye han seyd I consent therto
in worship of our child et gret devocion
abought y tempill in ordyr let vs go   Symeon

ye gyngues all / et feythfull intent
dispose your silf a song for to syng
to worshep this child y whes present
whiche to mankende gladnes hath bryng

in to kynd our flesh suche ioye doth spryng
bethynd mynd amys y babe shalbe born
now ye gyngues to this lord prysyng
syngyth nunc dimittis of whiche I spek aforn

— here shall Symeon bere hym in his armys goyng
a procession rounde abowte y tempill et al y wyle y
gyngues synge nunc dimittis et whan y is don Symeon
seyth   Symeon

O thu chef cause of our welfare
in yonge tayn theyr be thyngs in
say week et light whiche I shall declare
to y apropryd by moralite
lord say betokynth / thyn humanyte
et week betokynth / thy sonle most swete

Bodleian MS. Digby 133, f. 155ᵛ

My spretes joyen, þou art so amyable,
  I am nat wery¹ to loke on þi face.
Oure trewe entent, let it be acceptable
  To þe honor² of the, shewyd in this place.
For thy seruauntes, a dwellyng þou shalt purchase,   505
Brighter than beralle outhere clere cristalle.
  þe to worshippe as chef welle of grace,
On both my knees now doun knele I shalle.

MARIA. Now Semyon, take me my childe þat is so bright,
  Chef lodesterre of my felicyte,   510
And alle þat longyth to þe lawe of right
  I shalle obeye, as it lyth in me.
SYMEON. þis Lord, I take you knelyng on my kne,
Whiche shalle to blisse folk ageyn restore,
  And eke³ be called tonne of tranquylyte,   515
To yeve hem drynke þat han thrustyd sore.

  Here she receyveth hire sone, þus seyeng:

MARIA. Now is myn offryng to an ende conveyed,
  Wherfore, Symeon, hens I wole wende.
SYMEON. The lawes, Mary, ful welle ye han obbeyed   f. 156ᵛ
  In this tempille, with hert and mende.   520
  Nowe ferwelle, Lord, comfort to alle⁴ mankende!
Farwelle, Maria and Josephe on you waytyng.
JOSEPHE. Selestialle socoure oure sone mot you sende,
And for his high mercy, yeve you his blissyng.

  Here Maria and Josephe goyng from þe tempille seyng:

MARIA. Husbond, I thanke⁵ you of youre gentilnes   525
  þat ye han shewed onto me this day;
With oure child most gracious of godenes,
  Let vs go hens, hertly I you pray!
JOSEPHE. Go forthe afforn, my ovne wyf, I sey,
And I shalle come aftire, stil vpon þis ground.   530
  Ye shal me fynde plesaunt at euery assaye;
To cherysshe you, wyf, gretly am I bounde.

---

¹ worthy *canc. before*   ² on *canc. before*   ³ b *canc. before*
⁴ *added above caret*   ⁵ *MS* thenke

SYMEON. Nowe may I be glad in myn inward mende,
 For I haue seyn Jhesu[1] with my bodely eye,
Wiche on a cros shalle bey al menkende,
 Slayn by Jwes at þe Mount of Calvery;
And throwe devyn grace here I wille provysye[2]
Of blissed Mary howe she shalle suffre peyn,
 Whan hire swete sone shalle on a rood deye—
A sharpe sward of sorowe shalle cleve hire hert atweyn.

Anna Prophetissa, hertly I prey you nowe,
 Doth youre devire and youre diligent[3] laboure,
And take these virgynis euerychon with you,
 And teche hem to plese God, of most honoure.
ANNA PROPHETISSA. Lyke as ye say, I wille do[4] this houre.
Ye chast virgynis, with alle humylite,
 Worshippe we Jhesu, þat shalbe oure sauyoure—
Alle[5] at ones, come on, and folowe me.[6]

And[7] shewe ye summe plesure as ye can,
In the worshippe of Jhesu, Oure Lady, and Seynt Anne!

  Anna Prophetissa et [virgynes] tripident.

POETA. Honorable souereignes, thus we conclude
 Oure matere þat we haue shewid here in your[8] presens,
And though[9] oure eloquens be but rude,
 We beseche you alle, of youre paciens,
 To pardon vs[10] of oure offens,
For after þe sympylle cunnyng that we can,
 This matere we haue shewid to your audiens,
In the worshippe of Oure Lady and hir moder Seynt Anne.

---

¹ Jehesu *canc. before*   ² y *altered from* e
³ t *blotted, then written above*   ⁴ my *canc. before*
⁵ And *canc. before*
⁶ *following this line a speech-separation line is drawn and* finis *is written, ending the work of the second scribe; the first scribe returns, cancels* finis, *and adds the couplet of Anna's speech, the direction* Et tripident, *and the remainder of the lines, and the material on f.* 157ᵛ
⁷ And *canc. before, the abbreviation for* and *inserted before* shewe; ye *is added above in the hand of the principal scribe*
⁸ *added above caret*   ⁹ thurgh *canc. before*
¹⁰ oure *canc. before*

Now of this pore processe we make an ende,
   Thankyng you alle of your good attendaunce,   560
And the next yeer,[1] as we be purposid in oure mynde,
   The disputacion of the doctours to shew in your presens.
   Wherfor now, ye virgynes, er we go hens,
With alle your cumpany, you goodly avaunce!
   Also, ye menstralles, doth your diligens;   565
Afore oure departyng, geve vs a daunce!

Finis[2]

Anno domini millione CCCCCXII   f. 157ᵛ

   The namys of the pleyers

The poete
Kyng Herowde
firste knyght
the secunde knyght
thirde knyght
fourth knyght
Watkyn, Messanger
Symeon the bysshope
Joseph[3]   summa xvij
Maria
Anna Prophetissa
a[4] virgyn
Angelus
prima mulier
secunda mulier
tercia mulier
quarta mulier

Jhon Parfre ded wryte thys booke[5]

[1] yeer *added above caret*
[2] *at the foot of the page is written* Jhon Parfe ded wryte *in the same hand as the similar inscription at the foot of f. 157ᵛ*
[3] Maria *canc. beside* Joseph
[4] a *altered from* v
[5] *written in a later hand, the same as that of the aborted inscription on f. 157ʳ*

H

Wisdom

Fyrst entreth² Wysdam in a ryche purpylle cloth of gold, with³
a mantylle of the same ermyned within, havyng abought his
nek a ryalle hood furred⁴ with ermyn. Vpon his hed a cheveler
with browes, a berd of gold of Sypres⁵ curled. A ryche
imperialle crowne thervpon,⁶ set with riche⁷ stonys and
perlys.⁸ In his left hand, a balle of gold with a crosse þervpon,
and in his⁹ right hond a regalle sceptre, þus seyng:

[WYSDAM].¹⁰ If ye wylle wete the propyrte
    And the resoun of my name imp[er]ialle,
I am clepyd of hem that in erthe be
    Euerlastyng Wysdom, to my nobley¹¹ egalle,
    Wiche name accordith best in especialle,   5
And most to me is conuenyent.
    Allethough eche person of the Trinite be wysdam eternalle,
And alle thre, on euerlastyng wysdam togedyr present,

Neuertheles, forasmoche as 'Wysdom' is propyrly
    Applied to the Son be reson,   10
And also it fallith to hym specially
    Because of his highest¹² generacion,
    Therfor the belouyd Son hath this signyficacion,

The half-text of Wisdom *in MS Digby 133 is collated with the Macro full-text*
copy. We have also collated the transcription accompanying the Folger facsimile
edition of the Macro text. As with the other Digby plays, Wisdom *was edited by*
Sharp; the Macro text was also edited for the Abbotsford Club. Unless otherwise
noted our edition agrees with that of Furnivall, and Eccles follows Furnivall–
Pollard for the Macro text. When directions and words are noted as lost in the
Macro text, it is assumed that Furnivall–Pollard and Eccles supply them from
Digby, unless otherwise noted. Material in angle brackets in our text is supplied
from the Macro MS. The MSS will be designated by M for Macro and D for
Digby.

  ¹ *At the top of the page in Myles Blomefylde's hand*   ² *M* enteryde
  ³ with a mantylle of the *lost in M*   ⁴ ryalle hood furred *lost in M*
  ⁵ of Sypres *lost in M*
  ⁶ and in his right hand a ryall sceptre þus seyng *canc. after*
  ⁷ *MS* precious *canc.,* riche *added above; M* precyus; *E, B treat* precious *as*
uncanc. in D
  ⁸ and per *lost in M*   ⁹ *lost in M*   ¹⁰ *supplied in M*
  ¹¹ *M* noble; *E emends to* nobley   ¹² *M* hye

Customably Wysdam, now God, now man,
  Spowse of the chirche and verray patron,   15
Wyfe of eche chose sowle—thus Wysdam began.

> *Here entreth Anima as a mayde in a whight cloth of gold*
> *gy[n]tely*[1] *purfyled with menyver, a mantylle of blak,*
> *thervpon a cheueler*[2] *lyke to Wysdam, with a riche chapetelet*[3]
> *lasyd behynde, hangyng down*[4] *with too*[5] *knottes of gold and*
> *syde tasselys, knelyng down to Wysdam, þus seyng :*[6]

[ANIMA]. ' *Hanc amaui et exquisiui*'—
  Fro my yougthe[7] this haue I sought,
To haue to my spouse most specially
  For a louer of your shappe am I wrought.   20
  Above alle hele and bewte that euer was sought,   f. 158ᵛ
I haue louyd Wysdam as for my light,
  For alle goodnesse with hym he[8] brought.[9]
In[10] Wysdam I was made alle bewte bright!

Of your name the high felicite   25
  No creature knowith fulle exposicion.
WYSDAM. '*Sapiencia specialior est sole*'.
  I am founden light without co[m]parison,
  Of sterrys above alle the disposicion,
Forsothe, of light the very brightnesse,   30
  Meroure of the devyne domynacion,
And the image of his goodnesse.

Wysdam is better than alle wordly[11] precio[s]nesse,
  And alle that may desyred be
Is not in comparison to my lykenesse.   35
  The lengthe of the yeres in my right syde be,
  And in my lefte syde richesse, ioye, and prosperite.

---

[1] *MS* gytely *M* gytely; *E misreads as* gyedly *and B follows*
[2] r *lost in M*
[3] *M* chappetelot, *which E emends to* chappelet
[4] wn *lost in M*   [5] ij   [6] eyng *lost in M*
[7] *M* thowte; *E emends to* yougthe. *M scribe did not distinguish* þ *and* y—*see
also p. 138, n. 6 and Norman Davis's review of Bevington's facsimile of Macro in*
N. & Q. *ccxx* (*1975*), 79
[8] *M* ys   [9] b *canc. before*   [10] *M* I
[11] *MS; M* worldy *corr. to* worldly

Lo, this is the worthynesse of my name!
ANIMA. A, souereyn Wysdam! If your benygnyte
Wold speke of love, that were a game!   4

WYSDAM. Of my love to speke it is myrable.
Beholde now, Sovle, with ioyfulle mynde,
How louely I am, how amyable
    To be halsyd and kyssed of mankynde!
To alle clene sovles I am fulle hende,   4
And euer present where that thei be.
I love the[1] loueres withoutyn ende
That there loue have stedfast in me.

The prerogatyve of my love is so grett
    That who tast[2] therof the lest droppe sure   5
Alle lustes and lykenges wordely[3] shalle[4] lete;
    Thei shalle seme tylle[5] hym filthe and ordure.
    Thei that of the hevy burthen of synne hath cure,   f.
        My love dischargeth and purifieth clene.
It strengtheth the mende, the sovle makith pure,   5
    And yevyth wysdam to hem that perfight bene.
Who takith me to spowse may veryly wene—
    If above alle thyng ye[6] loue me specialle[7]
That rest and tranquyllite he shalle sene,
    And dey in sekyrnesse of ioye perpetualle.   6

The hey worthynesse[8] of my love
    Angelle nor man can telle playnly;
It may be felt in experience from[9] above,
    But not spoke ne told as it is veryly.
    The Godly love no creature can specyfie.   6
What wreth is that louyth not this love,[10]
    That louyth his louers euer so tenderlye,
That his sight from them neuer kan remove?

---

[1] *M* my   [2] *M* tastyt
[3] *M* worldly   [4] *M* xall *and so throughout*
[5] *M* to   [6] *MS; M* he
[7] *MS* specially *with* y *canc., and* ll *barred; M* specyally
[8] *MS* loue of my *subpuncted before*
[9] in experience from: *M* from experyens
[10] *line omitted in M; E emends* wreth *to* wrech

ANIMA. O worthy Spouse and Souereyne fayre.[1]
O swete amyke, oure joye, oure blisse!   70
To your love who doth repeyere,
Alle felicite in that creature is.
What may I yeve you ageyn for this,
O Creatour, louere of your creature?
Though be oure freelte we do amys,   75
Your gret mercy euer sparith reddure.

A, souereyn Wysdam, *sanctus sanctorum!*
What I may I yeve[2] to your most plesaunce?
WYSDAM. *'Fili, prebe michi cor tuum!'*
I aske not ellys of alle thi substaunce.   80
Thi clene hert, thi meke obeisaunce,
Yeve me that and I am content.
ANIMA. A, soueryen joy, myn[3] hertes affiaunce!
The fervoure of my love to you I represente,[4]

That mekith my herte your loue so feruent.   f. 195ᵛ
Teche me the scolys of your devenyte.   86
WYSDAM. Desire not[5] to sauour in cunnynges[6] to excellent,
But drede[7] and conforme your wille to me,
For it is the helefulle discyplyne that in wysdam may be;
The drede of God, that is begynnyng—   90
The wedys of synne it makith to flee,
And swete vertuose herbis in the soule spryng.

ANIMA. O endeles Wysdam, how may I haue knowyng
Of thi Godhed incomprehensible?
WYSDAM. By knowyng of yourselff ye may haue felyng   95
What God is in your soule sensyble.
The more knowyng of yourselff passible,
The more verily ye shalle God knowe.
ANIMA. O souereyn Auctoure most credible,
Your lesson I attende as I owe,   100

I, that represent here the soule of man.
What is a[8] soule, wylle ye declare?

---

[1] *M* father (faye *canc. before*)   [2] *M* may I yeue
[3] *M* my   [4] *M* present   [5] t *canc. before*
[6] *M* cunnynge   [7] *second* d *altered from* g
[8] *added above caret*

WYSDAM. It is the ymage of God that alle bygan,
   And not only ymage, but his lykenesse ye are.
Of alle creatures the fayrest ye were,   10
Into the tyme of Adamys offence.
ANIMA. Lord, syth we, thi soules, that[1] nought were thare,
Why of the first man bey we the violence?

WYSDAM. For euery creature that hath ben or shalle
   Was in nature of the first man, Adam,   11
Of hym takyng the fylthe of synne orygynalle,
   For of hym alle creatures cam.
Than be hym of reason ye haue blame,
And be made the brondes of helle.
When ye be bore first of youre dame,   f. 1
Ye may in no wyse in hevyn dwelle,   11

For ye be disfygured be hys synne,
   And dampnyd to derkeness from Goddes sight.
ANIMA. How doth grace thanne ageyn begynne?
   What reformyth the sovle to his first light?   12
WYSDAM. Wysdam, that was God and man right,
Made a fulle seth to the Fader of hevyn
   By the dredfulle deth to hym was dight,
Of wiche deth spronge the sacramentes sevyn,

Wiche sacramentes alle synne wasshe awey.   12
   Fyrst baptem[2] clensyth synne orygynalle,
And reformeth the soule in feith verray
   To the glorious lykenesse of God eternalle
   And makith it as fayer and as celestialle
As it neuer diffowled had be,   13
   And is Cristes owne specialle,
His restyng place, his plesaunt see.

ANIMA. In[3] a soule what thynges be,
   By wiche he hath his very knowyng?
WYSDAM. Tweyn parties. The on is the[4] sensualite,   13
   Wiche is clepyd the flesshly felyng.
The fyue[5] outward wittys to hym be seruyng;

---

[1] *MS; M* y^t   [2] *M* bapten   [3] *M* I
[4] *M omits* is the   [5] v

Whan thei be not rulyd ordynatly,
  The sensualite than, without lesyng,
Is made the ymage of synne then of his foly.   140

That[1] other parte, that is clepyd reson,
  And that is the ymage of God propyrly,
For by that the soule of God hath cognycion,
  And be that hym seruyth and louyth duly.
Be the nether parte of reason he knoweth discretly   145
Alle erthely thynges, how thei shalbe vsyd,   f. 160ᵛ
  What suffysith to his myghtys bodyly,
And what nedith not to be refusyd.

These tweyne do signyfie
  Your disgysyng and your araye,   150
Blak and whyte, fowle and fayr, verylye,
  Euery soule here—this is no naye;
Blak, by steryng of synne that comyth al day,
Wiche felyng comyth of sensualite,
  And white, be knowyng of reson verray   155
Of the blissed infinite Deite.

Thus a soule is both fowle[2] and fayre:
  Fowle as a best, be felyng of synne,
Fayr as[3] aungelle, of hevyn the hayr,[4]
  By knowyng of God by hys reson withinne.   160
ANIMA. Than may I sey thus and begynne
With fyue[5] prudent virgynes of my reme—
  Tho be the fyue[5] wyttys of my soule withinne—
'Nigra sum sed[6] formosa, filia Jerusalem'.

    Here entreth[7] fyue[8] virgynes in white kertelys[9] and mantelys
    with chevelers[10] and chapelyttes,[11] and syng: 'Nigra sum sed
    formosa, filia Jerusalem, sicut[12] tabernacula cedar et sicut
    pelles Salomonis'.[13]

[1] *M* The   [2] white *canc.*, fowle *added above caret*   [3] *M* as a
[4] *M* ayer   [5] v
[6] *MS* et; *M* sed. *We emend because it is merely a scribal slip—the D scribe gets*
it right in the following s.d.
[7] *M* enteryd   [8] v   [9] in white kertelys: *M* wᵗ kertylls
[10] elers *lost in M*   [11] y *altered from* e   [12] cut *lost in M*
[13] *in M later hand has written* va va va, *treated by B as an abbreviation for*
'vacat' (*it is omitted*), *but described as 'interlaced curves making a line-filler' by*
Norman Davis in his review of B in N. & Q. ccxx (1975), 79

ANIMA. The doughters of Jerusalem me not lak,   1[

   For this dyrke shadowe I bere of humanyte,

That, as the tabernacle of cedar without, it is blak,

   And withinne as the skynne of Salomon, fulle of bewte.

'*Quod fusca sum, nolite considerare me,*

Quia decolorauit me sol Jouis'.   1[

WYSDAM. Thus alle the soules, that in this lyve be

Stondyng in grace, be[1] lyke to this.

A, *quinque prudentes*—your wittes fyve—

   Kepe you clene, and ye shalle [n]euer[2] deface,

Ye Goddes ymage [n]euer shalle ryve,   f.

   For the clene soule is[3] Goddes restyng place.   1

   Thre myghtes euer[4] Cristen soule hase,

Whiche beth applyeth to the Trynyte.

MYNDE. Alle thre here, lo, byfore your face—

Mynde,

WYLLE. Wylle,

VNDERSTONDYNG. and Vnderstondyng, we thre!   1

WYSDAM. Ye thre declare thanne this,

   Youre signyficacion and your propyrte.

MENDE. I am Mende, that in the soule is

   The very figure of the Deite.

   Whan in myselve I haue mynde and se   1

The benefetes of God, and his worthynesse,

   How hole I was made, how fayr, how fre,

How glorious, and[5] how gentylle to his lyknesse,

This insight bryngeth to my mynde

   What grates I ough[6] to God[7] ageyn,   1

That thus hath ordeyned withouten[8] ende

   Me in his blisse euer for to reigne.

   Thanne myn insufficiens is to me peyn,

That I haue not whereof to yelde my dette,

   Thynkyng myselff creature most veyne.   1

Than for sorowe my bren I knette.

---

[1] M by   [2] M also euer, *but the sense is opposite and all editions emend*
[3] M omits; D has euer canc. *after*   [4] MS; M euery   [5] M omits
[6] M ought   [7] M omits to God   [8] M wythowt

Whan in my mynde I bryng togedyr
  The yeeres and dayes of my synfulnesse,
The vnstabylnesse[1] of my mynde hedyr and thedyr,
  Myn horrible fallynges[2] and freelnesse,   200
Myselff right nought than I confesse;
For be myselff I may not ryse
  Without specialle grace of Goddes goodnesse.
Thus, mynde makyth me myself[3] to dispise.

I seke and fynde nowhere comfort,   f. 161ᵛ
  But only in God, my creature;[4]   206
Than vnto hym I do resort
  And say, 'Haue mynde of me, my Sauyoure!'
Thus mynde to mynde bryngeth that fauoure;
Thus, be mynde of me, God I can knowe;   210
  Good mynde, of God it is the fygure,
And this mynde to haue, alle Cristen owe.

WILLE. And I of the soule am the wylle.
  Of the Godhed, lyknesse and a[5] fygure;
With[6] good wylle no man may spylle,   215
  Nor, withouten[7] good wylle, of blis be sure.
What soule wylle gret mede recure,
He must gret wylle haue in thought or dede,
  Vertuosly sett with conscience pure,
For in wylle onely standyth[8] mannys dede.   220

Wylle for dede oft is take;
  Therfor the wille must wele[9] be disposed.
Thanne ther begynnyth alle grace to wake,
  If it with synne[10] be not anosed.
Therfor[11] the wylle must be wele[12] apposed,   225
Or that it to the mevynges[13] yeve consent;
  The lybrary of reason must be vnclosed,
And after his domys to take entent.

---

[1] M sustabullnes   [2] M My oreble fallynge   [3] M meselff
[4] M also creature   [5] M omits   [6] M Wyt   [7] M wythowt
[8] M stondyt only   [9] nedys canc. before
[10] MS it with synne; M wyth synne yt   [11] for added above caret
[12] M wyll   [13] M mevynge

Oure wylle in God must be only sett,
　　And for God to do wylfully;[1]   2
Whan good wylle reysyth, God is[2] in vs knett,
　　And he performeth the dede veryly.
Of hym comyth alle wylle sett perfightly,
　　For of oureself we haue right nought
　　But synne, wrechednesse, and foly.   2
He is begynnere and grounde of wylle and thought.   f.

Than this good wylle seid before
　　Is behouefulle[3] to eche creature,
If he cast hym to restore
　　The soule that hath[4] take of cure,   2
　　Wiche of God is the fygure,
As longe as the figure is kept fayre,
　　And ordeigned euer to[5] endure
In blisse, of wiche is [he][6] the very hayr.

VNDERSTONDYNG. The thride[7] parte of the soule is vndyrstond-   2
　　　　　　　　　　　　　　　　　　　　　　　　　　　　　　yng.
For by vnderstondyng I behold what God is
In hymselff, begynnyng without begynnyng,
　　And ende withouten[8] ende, that shalle neuer mys.
Incomprehensible in hymselff he is;
　　His werkes in me I can not comprehende,   2
　　How shuld I holly hym[9] than, that wrought alle this?
Thus, by knowyng of me, to knowyng of God I ascende.

I know in aungelys he is desiderable,
　　For, hym to behold, thei[10] desire souereynly;
In his seyntes, most delectable,[11]   2
　　For in hym thei[12] joye assiduly;
　　In creatures his werkes ben most wonderfully,[13]
For alle this[14] is made by his myght,
　　Bi his[14] wysdam gouernyd most souereynly,
And be[14] his benygnyte, inspired alle soules with light.   2

[1] M wysly　　　　　　　　[2] is added above caret; h canc. after in
[3] M behoueable　　　　　 [4] M þat he hath　　　　 [5] M for to
[6] M; D omits　　　　　　　[7] iijde　　　　　　　　　[8] M wythowt
[9] added above caret　　 [10] M þe　　　　　　　　　[11] MS; F deleitable
[12] M þer　　　　　　　　　[13] M wondyrly　　　　　　[14] M omits

Of alle creatures he is louyd souereyne,
  For he is God of eche creature,
And thei be his people that euer shalle reigne,
  In whom he dwellyth as in[1] his temple sure.
  When I[2] of[3] this knowyng make reporture,   265
And se the loue he hath for me wrought,
  It bryngeth me to love that Prince most pure—   f. 162ᵛ
For, for loue, that Lorde made man[4] of nought.

This is that loue wiche is clepyd charite;
  For God is charite, as auctours telles,[5]   270
And who is in charite, in God dwellith he,
  And God, that is charite, in hym dwelles.
  Thus vnderstondyng of God compelles
To come to charite—than haue his lyknesse, lo!
  Blessed is that soule that this speche spelles: 275
'Et qui creauit me requieuit in tabernaculo meo'.

WYSDAM. Lo, these thre myghtes in o[6] soule be:
  Mynde, Wylle, and Vnderstondyng.
Be Mynde, of God the Fadyr knowyng haue ye;
  Be Vnde[r]stondyng, of God the Sone ye haue knowyng;   280
  By Wylle, wiche turnyth into[7] loue brennyng,
God the Holy Gost, that clepyd is Love—
  Not thre Goddes, but on God in beyng.
Thus, eche clene soule is simylitude[8] of God above.

Be Mynde, feith in the Fader haue we;   285
  Hope in oure Lorde Jhesu, by Vnderstondyng;
And be Wylle, in the Holy Gost, charite.
  Lo, these thre[9] princypalle vertues of you thre[9] sprynge!
  Thus[10] the clene soule standith as a kynge;
And above alle this ye haue fre wylle.   290
  Of that beware byfore alle thynge,
For if that peruert, alle this doth spylle.

---

[1] M omits   [2] altered from o   [3] M omits
[4] M a man   [5] M tell
[6] M on   [7] M omits to
[8] u altered from e   [9] iij
[10] M Thys

Ye haue thre¹ enemyes, of hem beware:
The Worlde, the Flessh, and the Fende.
Your fyue² wyttes from hem ye spare,
  That the sensualite thei bryng not to mynde.³
No thyng shuld⁴ offende God in no kynde,
And if ther do, se that the nether parte of reason
  In no wyse therto lende;
Than, the ouer parte shalle haue fre domynacion.

When suggestion to the Mynde doth appere,
Vnderstondyng, delyte not the⁵ thereinne!
Consent not, Wylle, ylle lessons to lere!
  And than suche sterynges be⁶ no synne;
    Thei⁷ do but purge the soule where is such contrauersie.
Thus in me, Wysdam, your werkes begynne;
  Fyght, and ye shalle haue the crowne of glorye,
That is euerlastyng⁸ ioye to be parteners therinne!

ANIMA. Souereigne Lorde, I am bounde to the!
When I was nought, thu made me thus glorious;
When I perisshed thurgh synne, thu sauyd me;⁹
  When I was in grett parelle, thu kept me, Christus;
  When I erryd, thu reducyd me, Jhesus;
When I was ignoraunt, thu taught me truthe;
  When I synnyd, thu correct me thus;
When I was hevy, thu conforted me⁹ be ruthe.

When I stonde in grace, thu holdest me that tyde;
  When I falle,¹⁰ thu reisest me myghtily;
When I go wele,¹¹ thu art my gyde;
  When I come, thu receyvist me most louyngly;
  Thu hast anoynted me¹² with the oyle of mercy;
Thy benefetys, Lord, be innumerable!
  Wherfor, laude endles to the I crye,
Recommendyng me to thi¹³ end[l]es powre durable!

¹ iij   ² v   ³ M yow byhynde
⁴ M xulde, and so generally for D shuld   ⁵ M ȝe   ⁶ M by
⁷ M The   ⁸ is euerlastyng; M euer ys lastynge
⁹ M omits   ¹⁰ f altered from w
¹¹ M wyll   ¹² M omits   ¹³ M þin

Here in þe goyng out, þe fyue[1] wyttes syng: 'Tota pulcra es,
etc.', thei goyng[2] before, Anima next, and hir folwyng,
Wysdam, and after hym, Mynde, Wylle,[3] and Vnderstondyng,
alle thre[4] in whit cloth of gold, chevelered and crestyd[5] in on[6]
sute. And after þe song, entreth Lucyfere in a deuely[7] aray[8]
without, and within as a prowde galaunt, seyng thus on this
wyse[9]:

[LUCYFER]. Out, herrowe, I rore!   f. 163ᵛ
For envy I lore.   326
My place to restore,
   God hath made man.[10]
Alle come thei not thore,
Woode and thei wore,   330
I shalle tempt hem so sore,
   For I am he that synne beganne!

I was aungelle[11] of light,
Lucifere I hight,
Presumyng in Gooddes sight,   335
   Wherfor I am lowest in helle!
In reformyng of my place is dight
Man, whan[12] I haue in[13] most dispight,
Euer castyng me with hem for[13] to fight,
   In that heuynly place that[13] he shuld not dwelle.   340

I am as wyly now as than;
The knowyng that I had, yet I can;
I know alle compleccions of man,[14]
   Whereto he is most disposed!
And therin I tempte hym ay-whan;   345
I marre his myndes to ther[15] wan,
That wo is hym God[16] hym bygan!
   Many an[17] holy man with me is mosed.[18]

---

[1] v	[2] oyng *lost in M*	[3] Wyll *lost in M*
[4] iij	[5] es *lost in M*	[6] M omits
[7] M dewyllys	[8] a *lost in M*	[9] se *lost in M*
[10] M a man	[11] M a angell	[12] M also
[13] M omits	[14] M a man	[15] MS thei; M þer
[16] that *canc. before*	[17] M a	

[18] *so apparently* M; *but both could be* inosed

Of God, man is the figure,
His symylitude, his pitture,   35
Gloryosest of ony creature
    That euer was wrought—
Wiche I wylle dysfygure
Be my false coniecture;
If he tende my reporture,   35
    I shalle bryng hym to nought!

In the soule be thre[1] parties, iwys:
Mynde, wylle, vnderstondyng[2] of blis—
Figure of the Godhed—I know wele this!
    And þe flessh of man that is so chaungeable,   36
That wille I tempte, as I gesse;
Though that I peruert, synne noon is
But if the soule consent vnto mys,[3]
    For in the wylle of the soule ben the dedes[4] dampnabylle.

To the mynde of the soule I shalle make suggestion,   36
And bryng his vnderstondyng to delectacion,
So that his wille make confirmacion;
    Than am I seker inoow
That dede[5] shalle sew of dampnacion;   f.
Than of the soule the devylle hath dominacion.   37
I wille go make this[6] examynacion,
    To alle the develis of helle[7] I make a vowe!

But,[8] for to tempt man in my likenesse,
It wold brynge hym to gret ferfulnesse!
I wille chaunge me into brightnesse,[9]   37
    And so hym to begyle.[10]
Syn, I shalle shew hym perfightnesse,
And vertu, prove[11] it wykednesse!
Thus vnder colours, alle thynge peruerse.
    I shalle neuer rest tylle the[12] soule I defyle!   38

[1] iij
[2] r *added above caret*
[3] *M* to þis
[4] ben the dedes: *M* the dedys ben
[5] *M* dethe
[6] *M* hys
[7] ll *lost in M*
[8] *M* For
[9] *M* bryghtne
[10] *M* begyl
[11] *MS* prove *altered from* prouyt; *M retains* provyt
[12] e *lost in M*

*Here Lucyfere devoydeth, and commyth in ageyn as a goodly
galaunt.*

MYNDE. My mynde is euer on Jhesu
That endued vs with vertu;
His doctryne to sue,
    Euer I purpose.
VNDERSTONDYNG. Myn¹ vnderstondyng is in trewe,   385
That with feith vs did renewe;
His lawes to pursewe
    Is swetter to me than the² sauour of the rose.

WILLE. And my wille is his wylle, verily,
That made vs his creatures so specialy,   390
Yeldyng vnto³ hym laude and glory
    For his goodnesse.
LUCYFERE. Ye fonnyd faders, founders of foly,
Vt 'quid hic statis tota die ociosi'?
Ye wille p[er]isshe⁴ or ye it aspy;   395
    The devylle hath accombred you expresse!⁵

Mynde, Mynde, sere, haue mynde of⁶ this!
MYNDE. He is not idylle that with God is!
LUCYFER. No, sere, I prove wele yis!⁷
    Lo,⁸ this is my suggestion: 400
Alle thynge hath dew tymes—
Prayer, fastyng, labour—alle thes;
Whan tyme is not⁹ kept, that dede is mys.¹⁰
    Be¹¹ more plenerly to your informacion,

Here is a man that levith wardly,   405
Hath wyff, children, and seruauntes besy,
And other charges that I not specify;
    Is it¹² leffulle to this man
To leve his labour vsyd truly?   f. 164ᵛ
His charges parisch, that God yave duly,   410
And yeve hym to prayere and ese of body?
    Whoso do thus, with God is not than!

---

¹ M My   ² M omits   ³ M omits to   ⁴ M also omits -er abbreviation
⁵ scribe separated this verse from l. 397 by a line, then cancelled the divider.
⁶ mynde of: M in mynde   ⁷ M thys   ⁸ M omits
⁹ t added above caret   ¹⁰ M amys   ¹¹ MS, M   ¹² Is it: M Yt ys

Martha plesid God gretly thore.

MYNDE. Ye, but Maria[1] plesid hym moche more!

LUCYFERE. Yit the lest had blisse for euermore!   41
    Is not that[2] inow?

MYNDE. Contemplatyfe lyff is sett before.

LUCYFERE. I may not beleve that in my lore,
For God hymselff, whan he was man bore,
    What lyff led he? Answere thu nowe!   42

Was he euer in contemplacion!

MYNDE. I suppose not, be my relacion.

LUCYFER. And alle his lyff was informacion
    And example to man!
Sumtyme with synners he had conuersacion,   42
Sumtyme with holy, also communycacion;
Sumtyme he labored, prayd; sumtyme, tribulacion.
    This was *vita mixta*, that God here began,

And that lyff shuld ye here sewe.

MYNDE. I can beleve that ye say is trewe.[3]   4:

LUCYFER. Contemplatyff lyff for to sewe,
    It is gret dred, and se cause why:
Thei must fast, wake, and pray euer newe,
Vse hard levynges,[4] and goyng with disciplyne dewe,
Kepe sylence, wepe, and surfettes eschewe;   4.
    And if thei faile of this, thei offend God highly.

Whan thei haue wastyd be feyntnesse,
Than febylle there wittes and fallyn to fondenesse,
Summe into dispeyr and summe into madnesse;
    Wete it wele, God is not plesid with this!   4
Leve, leve such synglere besynesse!
Be in the world! Vse thynges necesse!
The comon is best expresse.
    Who clymyth high, his falle grett is!   f.

MYNDE. Truly, me seme ye haue reson.   4
LUCYFER. Apply you than to this conclusion.

---

¹ *M* Mara   ² *M* þis
³ I can beleve that ye say is trewe: *M* I kan not belewe thys ys trew
⁴ *M* lywynge

MYNDE.[1] I can make no repplycacion,
   Your resons be grete![2]
I can not foryete this informacion.
LUCYFER. Thynke thervpon, it is your saluacion!   450
Now, and Vnderstondyng wold haue delectacion,
   Alle syngler deuocions he wold lete.

Your fyve[3] wittes abrode let sprede!
Se how comly[4] to man is precious wede;
What worshippe it[5] to be manffulle in dede—   455
   þat bryngeth in dominacion!
Of the symple, what profite it to take hed?
Behold how richesse distroyeth nede!
It makith man fayr, hym wele[6] for to fede!
   And of lust and lykyng comyth generacion!   460

Vnderstondyng, tendre ye this informacion?
VNDERSTONDYNG.In this I fele a[7] manere of delectacion!
LUCYFERE. A, ha, sere! Than there make a pawsacion.
   Se and behold the world abought!
Lytelle thyng suffysyth to saluacion;   465
Alle maner synnys distroyeth contricion;
Thei that despeyere mercy haue grett conpu[n]ccion—
   God plesyd best[8] with good wylle, no dowte!

Therfor Wylle,[9] I rede you inclyne;
Leve your stodyes, tho[10] be devyne—   470
Your prayers, youre penaunce, of ipocrytes the signe—
   And lede a comown lyff!
What synne is[11] in mete? In ale?[12] In wyne?
What synne is in richesse? In clothyng fyne?
Alle thyng God ordeigned to man to inclyne!   475
   Leve your nyse chastyte, and take a wyff!

Better is fayr frute than foule pollucion;   f. 165ᵛ
What seyth sensualite to this conclusion?

[1] *MS* Make; *M* Mynd   [2] *M omits this line*   [3] v
[4] *M* comunly   [5] *M* yt ys   [6] *added above caret; M* werkys
[7] *M* in   [8] b *altered from* v   [9] Wyll *altered from* Weyll
[10] *M* þow   [11] *M omits*   [12] *M* hale

WILLE. As[1] the fyve[2] wyttys yeve informacion,
  It semeth youre resons be good!   480

LUCIFER. The wille of the soule hath fre dominacion;
Dispute not to moche in this with reason;
Yitt the nethere parte to this takith summe instruccion,
  And so shuld the ouer parte, but he were woode!

WILLE. Me seme, as ye sey, in body and soule,   485
  Man may be in the world and be right good.

LUCYFER. Ya, sere, by Seynt Powle!
  But truste not these prechours, for thei be not good,
For thei flatere and lye as thei were wood;
There is a wolfe in a lombe[3] skynne!   490

WYLLE. Ya, I wylle no more row ageyn the flode—
I wylle sett my soule on[4] a mery pynne!

LUCYFERE. Be my treuthe, that[5] do ye wysely!
God louyth a clene soule and a mery!
Accorde ye thre[6] togeder by,   495
  And ye may not mysfare.[7]

MYNDE. To this suggestion agre me![8]

VNDERSTONDYNG. Delight therin I haue truly!

WYLLE. And I consent therto frely!

LUCIFERE. A, ha,[9] sere! Alle mery than, and[9] awey care!   500

Go in the world, se that abought!
Gete good frely, caste no dought!
To the riche ye se men lowly lought!
  Yeve to your body that is nede,
And euer be mery! Lett reuelle rought!   505

MYNDE. Ya, ellys I beshrewe my snowte!

VNDERSTONDYNG. And if I care, catche me[10] the gowte!

WYLLE. And if I spare, the deuylle me spede!   f. 1

LUCIFER. Go your wey, than, and do wysely.
Chaunge that syde aray!

MYNDE.   I it defye![11]   510

VNDERSTONDYNG. We wille be fressh, and it[12] happe[13] la plu joly!
  Farewele, penaunce!

---

[1] M At   [2] v   [3] M lombys   [4] M omits   [5] M than
[6] iij   [7] M omits this line   [8] M we   [9] M omits
[10] M I   [11] written as two lines in both MSS
[12] M omits and it   [13] M hamp

MYNDE. To worshippys I wylle my mynde applie!

VNDERSTONDYNG. Myn vnderstondynges[1] in worshepys and
                                        glorye! 515

WYLLE. And I in lustes of lechory,
  As was sumtyme gyse of Fraunce!

With 'why whyppe,
Farewelle', quod I, 'the deuylle is vp!'[2]

  Exiant.[3]

LUCIFERE. Of my desyre now haue I summe!
Were onys brought into custumme,   520
Than farewele, consciens, he were clumme!
  I shuld haue alle my wylle!
Reson I haue made both deff[4] and dumme;
Grace is out, and putt arome;
Whedyr I wille haue, he shalle cumme,   525
  So, at the last, I shalle hym spille!

I shalle now stere his mynde
To that synne made me a fende,
Pryde, wiche is ageyn kynde,
  And of alle[5] synnes hed.   530
So to couetyse he shalle wende,
For that enduryth to the last ende,
And vnto lechery, and I may hym rende!
  Than am I sekere the soule is ded!

That soule God made incomparable,   535
To his lykenesse most amyable,
I shalle make it most reprouable,
  Evyne lyke to a fende of helle.   f. 166ᵛ
At his deth I shalle appere informable,
Shewyng hym alle[6] hys synnys abhomynable, 540
Prevyng his soule dampnable,
  So with dispeyr I shalle hym quelle.

Whylle[7] clennesse is mankyn,
Verely, the soule God is within,

¹ *M* wndyrstondynge   ² *M has these two lines as one*
³ *MS* Exiā *added in later hand; not in M*   ⁴ *M* dethe
⁵ *M omits*   ⁶ *added above caret*
⁷ *E mistakenly records this as* Whygll

And whan it is in dedly synne,   54
  It is[1] veryly the deuelys place.
Thus by colours and false gynne[2]
Many a soule fro hevyn[3] I wynne;
Wyde to go, I may not blynne,
  With this false boy—God geve hym ille[4] grace!   55

*Here he takith a shrewede boy with hym and goth his way,
cryeng.*

MYNDE. Lo, me here in newe aray!
Whyppe, whyrre, care away!
Farewele, perfeccion!
Me semeth myself most lykly[5] ay.
It is but honest—no pride, no nay!   55
I wylle be fresshest be my fay,
  For that accordith with my complexion.[6]

VNDERSTONDYNG. And haue here one[7] as fressh as you!
Alle mery, mery and glad now!
I haue gete good, God wote howe!   56
  For joye I spryng, I skyppe!
Good makith on mery, to God a vowe!
Farewelle, conscience, I knowe not yowe!
I am at[8] ease, had I inowe.[9]
  Truthe on syde I lete hym slippe!   56

WILLE. Lo, here on as jolye as ye!
I am so lykyng, me seme I fle!
I haue atastid lust! Farewele, chastite!
  Myn[10] hert is euermore light!   f.
I am fulle of[11] felicite!   57
My delyte is alle in bevte!
There is no joye but that in me—
  A woman me semeth an[12] hevynly sight!

MYNDE. And these ben my synglere solace—
Kynde, fortune, and grace.   57

---

[1] *M omits*   [2] and false gynn: *M* gyane
[3] *MS* to hevyn *corr. by later hand to* fro hevyn; *M* to hell
[4] *M* euell   [5] *M* lyghtly   [6] *MS added above canc.* perfeccion
[7] *M* me   [8] *M* a   [9] *M* now   [10] *M* My
[11] *M repeats* full of   [12] *M* a

Kynde, nobley[1] of kynred me yovyn[2] hase,
　And that makyth me soleyne!
Fortune in worldes worsheppe me doth lace;
Grace yevith coryous elequence, and that mase
　That alle vnkunnynge I disdeyne!   580

VNDERSTONDYNG. And my joye is especialle
To[3] hurde vp rychesse for fere to falle,
To se[4] it, to handele it, to telle it alle—
　And[5] streightly[6] to spare!
To be hold ryche and ryalle!   585
I bost, I avaunt where I shalle!
Riches makyth a man equalle
　To hem sumtyme his souereignes were.

WYLLE. To me is joye most laudable[7]
Fresshe disgysynge to seme amyable,   590
Spekyng wordys delectable
　Perteynyng vnto loue!
It is joy of joyes inestimable
To halse, to kysse the affiable!
A louer is sone perceyvable   595
　Be the smylyng on[8] me whan it doth remove!

MYNDE. To avaunte[9] thus, me semeth no shame,
For galauntes now be in most fame.
Courtly persones men hem proclame—
　Moche we be sett bye![10]   600
VNDERSTONDYNG. The riche covetouse,[11] who dare blame f. 167ᵛ
Of govele and symonye, though he bere the name?
To be false, men reportith[12] it game!
　It is clepyd wysdam! ' "Whare that", quod Wyly'![13]

WYLLE. And of lechory to make avaunt,   605
Men forse it no more than drynke ataunt;

---

¹ M nobyll   ² M yewyn   ³ in left margin   ⁴ i canc. after
⁵ perteynyng vnto love canc. before   ⁶ M strenght   ⁷ M delectable
⁸ added above caret   ⁹ M a vaynte   ¹⁰ M omits this line
¹¹ M couetyse   ¹² M report
¹³ M Wyly with an I canc. before. See N. Davis's review of Bevington, N. & Q.
ccxx (1975), 79

These thynges be now so conuersaunt,
    We seme it no shame.
MYNDE. Coryous aray I wylle euer haunt!
VNDERSTONDYNG. And I, fal[s]nesse, to be passaunt!   610
WYLLE. And I in lust my flessh to daunt!
    No man dispise these—thei be but game!

MYNDE. In[1] reioyse of thes now let vs synge!
VNDERSTONDYNG. And if I spare, euylle joye me wrynge!
WYLLE. Haue at, quod I! Lo, howe[2] I sprynge!   615
    Lust makith me wondyr wylde!
MYNDE. A tenor to you both I brynge!
VNDERSTONDYNG. And I a mene for ony kynge!
WYLLE. And but a trebylle I out-wrynge!
    The deuylle hym spede that myrth exyled!   620

    Et cantent.

MYNDE. How be this trowe ye nowe?
VNDERSTONDYNG. At the best, to God a vowe!
WYLLE. As mery as the byrd on bowe,
    I take no thought!
MYNDE. The welefare[3] of this world is in vs, I avowe![4]   625
VNDERSTONDYNG. Let eche man telle his condicions how.
WYLLE. Begynne ye, and haue at yowe!
    For I am ashamyd of right nought!

MYNDE. This is cause[5] of my worshippe:
I serue myghty lorshippe,   630
And am in grete tendreshippe—
    Therfor moche folke me dredys.
Men sewe to my frendshippe
For meyntenaunce of here shenshippe;
I support hem by lordshippe   635
    For, to gete good, this a grete spede is!

VNDERSTONDYNG. And I vse jorourry,[6]
Enbrace questes of periury,

---

[1] M I   [2] M haue   [3] a *altered from* r   [4] M ma vowe
[5] M a cause   [6] M has the stanzas of ll. 637–52 reversed

Choppe and chaunge with symonye,
   And take large yiftes!
Be the case[1] neuer so try,
I preue it false—I swere, I lye!—
With a quest of myn affye;
   The redy wey this now to thrift is!   640

WYLLE. And[2] what trowe ye be me?   645
More than I take spende I thries thre!
Sumtyme I geve, sumtyme thei me,
   And am euer fresshe and gaye!
Fewe places now there be
But vnclennesse ye[3] shalle[4] ther se;   650
It is holde but a nysete—
   Lust is now comon as the[5] waye!

MYNDE. Lawe procedith not for mayntenaunce.
VNDERSTONDYNG. Trouthe recuryth not for abundaunce.
WYLLE. And lust is in so grete vsaunce,   655
   We forse it nought!
MYNDE. In vs the worlde hath most affiaunce.
VNDERSTONDYNG. Non thre be in so grett aqueyntaunce.
WYLLE. Fewe ther be out[6] of oure allyaunce—
   While the worlde is thus, take we no thought!   660

MYNDE. Thought! Nay, ther geyne[7] stryve I!
VNDERSTONDYNG. We haue that nedith vs, so thryve I!   f. 168ᵛ
WYLLE. And gyve[8] that 1 care, neuer wyve I!
   Let hem[9] care that hath for to sewe!
MYNDE. Who lordship shalle sue must it by!   665
VNDERSTONDYNG. Who wylle haue law must haue mony!
WYLLE. There pouert is the malewry,
   Though right be, he shalle neuer renewe.

MYNDE. Wronge is born vp boldly,
Though alle the world know it opynly;   670
Mayntenaunce is now so myghty,
   And alle is[10] for mede!

---

[1] M By þe cause   [2] M A   [3] MS added above caret; M we
[4] she altered from w   [5] MS thei, M þe   [6] M outhe
[7] M ageyn   [8] M yff   [9] M them
[10] MS i altered from f; M omits

VNDERSTONDYNG. The lawe is so coloured falsly
By sleightes and by periury,
Brybes be so gredy,
   That to[1] the pore trowthe is take right non[2] hede!   67

WYLLE. Who gete or lese, ye be ay wynnand!
Mayntenaunce and periury now stand—
There[3] were neuer so moche reynand
   Seth God was bore!   68
MYNDE. And lechory was neuer more vsande
Of lernyd and lewyd in this lande!
VNDERSTONDYNG. So we thre be now in hande!
WYLLE. Ya, and most vsyd euerywhere!

Va.[4]

MYNDE. Now wylle we thre do[5] make a daunce   68
Of tho that longe to oure retenaunce,
Comyng in be countenaunce—
   This were a disporte!
VNDERSTONDYNG. Therto I geve accordaunce
Of tho that ben of myn affyaunce.   69
WYLLE. Let se, betyme, ye[6] Meyntenaunce!
   Clepe in first your resort!

*Here entre six[7] disgysed in the sute of Mynde, with red berdes
and lyouns[8] rampaunt on here crestes, and iche a wardere
in his hand; hir menstralle, trumpes. Eche answere for his
name.*

MYNDE. Let se, com in Indignacion and Sturdynesse!   f.
Malyce also, and Hastynesse!
Wreche and Discorde expresse!   69
And the seuenth[9] am I, Mayntenaunce!
Seuen is a nombyr of discorde[10] and inperfightnesse;
Lo, here is a yomanry with love-day to dresse!
And the deuylle had swore it, thei wolde bere vp falsnesse,
   And mayntyn it at the best! This is the develys daunce!   70

---

[1] M omits   [2] M nought a   [3] so also M
[4] added in left margin by contemporary hand; M has va in same place
[5] added above caret
[6] M scribe does not distinguish between þ and y; E prints þe
[7] vj   [8] s lost in M   [9] vij[th]   [10] M dycorde

And here menstrellys be conuenyent,
For trompys shulld blowe to the jugement!
Of batayle, also, it is one instrument,
   Yevyng comfort to fight.
Therfor, thei be expedient   705
To these meny of mayntement.[1]
Blow! Lett[2] se, Madame Regent!
   And daunce, ye laddes, your hertes ben light!

Lo, that othere spare, this[3] meny wille spende!
VNDERSTONDYNG. Ye, who is hym shalle hem offende?   710
WYLLE. Who wylle not to hem condescende,
   He shalle haue thretys!
MYNDE. Thei spille, that lawe wolde amende!
VNDERSTONDYNG. Yit mayntenaunce no man dare reprehende.
WYLLE. These meny thre synnys comprehende: 715
   Pryde, Invy, and Wrathe in his hestys!

VNDERSTONDYNG. Now wylle I thanne begynne my traces.
Joroure in one hood berith[4] to faces:
Fayre speche and falsehed in on space is!
   Is it not ruthe?   720
The queste of Holborn come into this places;
Ageyne the right euer thei rechases;[5]
Of whom thei hold not, hard his grace is.
   Many a tyme haue dampnyd truthe.

Here entrith six[6] jorours in a sute gownyd with hoodes abowte f. 169ᵛ
her ⟨nekes⟩ hattes of mayntenaunce thervpon, vysered
diuersly, here mynstralle, a bag⟨pyp⟩.

VNDERSTONDYNG.[7] Let se, first, Wronge and Sleight!   725
Doblenesse and Falsehed,[8] shew your myght!
Now, Ravyne and Disceyte!
   Now holde you here togedyr!
This menyes conscyens is so streyte[9]
That report[10] as mede yevith beyte!   730

[1] *M* meyntnance   [2] *MS* l *altered from* s   [3] *M* thes
[4] *M* Jorowur . . . beer   [5] *M* rechase   [6] vj
[7] *MS* Mynde; *M also, but scribe has corrected to* Wndyrstondyng
[8] *M* Falsnes   [9] *first* e *added above caret*   [10] *M* þey report

Here is the quest of Holborn, an euylle endyrecte.[1]
Thei daunce alle this[2] londe, hyder and thedyr!

And I,[3] Periury, your foundoure!
Now daunce on, vs alle! The world doth on vs wonder!

Lo, here is a meyne loue welefare!   73

MYNDE. Ye, thei spende that true men spare!
WYLLE. Haue thei a brybe, thei haue[4] no care
      Who hath wronge or right!
MYNDE. Thei forse not to swere and stare,
WYLLE. Though[5] alle be false, lesse and mare,   74
VNDERSTONDYNG. Wiche wey to the wode wylle the hare?
      Thei knewe, and thei at[6] rest sett als tight!

Some seme hem wyse
For the fader of vs, Covetyse.

WYLLE. Now Mayntenaunce and Periury   74
Hath shewed the trace of her[7] company,
Ye shalle se a spryng of lechery,
      þat to me attende!
Here forme is of the stewys clene rybaldry!
Thei wene[8] sey soth whan that thei lye!   75
Of the comon thei synge, eche weke by and by!
      Thei may sey with tynkere, I[9] trowe, 'Late amende!'

Here entre[10] *six*[11] *woman in sute,* [*thre*][12] *disgysed as galauntes,*
and thre as mat[*rones*] *with wonderfulle vysers conregent,*[13]
here mynstrallys,[14] *an hornpype.*

(Here the Digby *Wisdom* ends.)

---

[1] *M also*   [2] *M* þe   [3] *M* A   [4] thei haue: *M* haue þey
[5] *M* Thouht   [6] *added above caret*   [7] *M* þer   [8] *M* veyne
[9] late *canc. before*   [10] *M* entreth   [11] vj   [12] *M also omits*
[13] *M also*   [14] *M* mynstrell

Alle that list to synge of love
Of crist that com till vs so lawe

Rede this treyte it may hym move
And may hym tho lightly tho avo
Off the sorow of mary stawgat to knawe
Vpon ynd friday aft none
Also of the apostolis also
And how maudleyne sorow cessit not son
And also
How Josephe of Aramathye
And other oxsons holye .
Mr Nichodeme worthely
how in thare garte hadno :
Fyrst lat vs mynde how and Josephe
On this wise wepte crist dothe .

Alasse that evir I levit this longe
This day to se so grete wronge .
So sell crueltee & paynes stronge
were now seyne or this .
Such envy . such ranco such malesse
Of crueli tormes such excesse
O pilate pilate in thy valesse
He that now did a antysse
this day was dampnyt o innocent bloode
Myst of sins myst thy acrose & ynde
this day stremyt out lik a floode
and lyk a ryvere grete
On calvery mownt on lenghe & brede
O calvery : thy greyn colore is tru nyd wede

The prologe of this treyte or meditation off the buryalle of Criste and mowrnyng þerat

A soule that list to singe of loue
  Of Crist that com tille vs so lawe,
Rede this treyte, it may hym moue,
  And may hym teche lightly with-awe
Off the sorow of Mary sumwhat to knawe,   5
  Opon Gud Friday afternone;
Also of the appostiles awe,
  And how Mawdleyn sorowe cessit not son;
    And also
      How Josephe of Aramathye   10
      And othere persons holye,
      With Nichodeyme worthely,
        How in thair harte had wo.

Fyrst lat vs mynde how gud Josephe
On this wise wepite Cristes dethe.   15

JOSEPHE. Alesse, that euer I levit thus longe!
This day to se so grete wronge!
So felle cruellitee and paynes stronge
  Were neuer seyn or this.
Such envy, such rancor, such malesse!   20
And[1] of cruelle tormentes such excesse!
O Pilate, Pilate, in thy palesse,
  He that neuer did amysse[2]

This day was dampnyt! O innocent bloode,
Most of vertue, most graciose and gude,   25
This day stremyt owt lik a floode,
  And lyk a ryvere grete,
On Caluery Mownt, on lenghe and brede.
O Caluery! Thy greyn colore is turnyd to rede
By a blessit lammes bloode, which now is dede.   f. 140ᵛ
  Alese! For faynt I swete,   31

Only the edition of Furnivall (F) has been collated, the earlier edition being of no textual value.   [1] *added in margin*   [2] *a blotted before*

Remembringe that so cleyne on[1] innocent shuld dye,
Which ledd his life the most perfitlye,
And wrought sich warkes wonderoslye,
      Ose Judea can recorde.
What mortalle creature that powre myght haue   3[*]
To make a dede man rise owt of his graue,
Lyinge therin iiij dayes tayve,
      But God, the gretist lorde?

A man to haue his sight, born starke blinde,   4[*]
From Adams creation where shalle we fynde?
Or what prophettes can ye calle to mynde
      Of whom may be verryfyed
So grete a miracle aboue naturs righte?
To many othere blind men he gaue the sighte   4[*]
And wrought many wounders by Godly myghte,
      As it is welle certifiede.

From the hylle I com bot now down,
Wher I left the holy women in dedly swoun.
O ye pepulle of this cetye and of this town,   5[*]
      Herd ye not the exclamation
And the grete brunte which was on the h[i]lle:
'Crucyfy hym! Crucify hym! Slo hym and kille!'?
Peace! Now harkyn, I pray you, stand stille!
      Me think I here lamentation.   5[*]

Off the wepinge of the thre[2] *Maries*[3]

(This is a play to be played, on part on Gud Friday afternone, and
þe other part opon Ester Day after the resurrection in the morowe,
but at ⟨the⟩ begynnynge ar certen lynes which ⟨shuld⟩ not be said
if it be plaied, which . . . [remaining words cut off at bottom])[4]

Thre Mariye sais alle togider in a voce:[5]   f.

---

[1] *inserted in red above caret*
[2] iij
[3] *this line written in red above two canc. lines:* Man, harkyn how Mavdleyn with
þe Maris ij° / Wepis and wringes thair handes os thay goo
[4] *this description added in red at foot of f. 140*[v]*; F prints at beginning of prologue*
[5] *this direction added in red at top of page*

Aiunt THRE MARIE. O most dolorose day! O tym of gretist sorowe!
MAVDLEYN. O sisters,[1] stand stille vntylle to-morowe!
  I trow I may not leue.[2]
JOSEPH. I[3] here the Mawdleyn bitterly compleyn.
What gud creature may hymself refrayn   60
  In this piteose myscheffe?[4]

PRIMA MARIA. O day of lamentation!
SECUNDA MARIA. O day of exclamatione!
THRID MARY. O day off suspiratione,
  Which Jewes shalle repent!   65
MAVDLEYN. O day most doloruse!
SECUNDA MARIA. O day paynfulle and tediose!
TERCIA MARIA. O pepulle most cruelle and furiose,
  Thus to slo an innocent!

SECUNDA MARIA. O Mawdleyn, your master dere,   70
How rewfully[5] he hinges here
  That set you first in ceile![6]
MAWDLEYN. A! Cesse, sisters, it sloes my chere,
His dulfulle deth I may not bere!
Devowt Josephe! I se hym here,   75
  Our cares for to keyle.

O, gud Josephe, approche to vs nere.
Behold hym wowndit with a spere,
  That louede yow so weylle.
JOSEPHE. O[7] Mawdleyn, said Joseph, I pray you here,   80
And your susters als, to be of gud chere.
MAGDAL⟨EYN⟩. O, frende Joseph, this prince had neuer[8] pere,
The welle of mercy that made me clere,   f. 141ᵛ
  And that wist ye weile.

---

[1] saide Mawdleyn *canc. in red after* sisters
[2] lefe *canc. before; following line* This hard holy Joseph standinge ryght gayn *crossed out in red*
[3] saide *crossed out in red before*
[4] *two following lines crossed out in red:* The Maries in that statione / Then saide *on this fascione*
[5] f *crossed out after* e
[6] *this line written in right margin*
[7] *following* gud *crossed out*
[8] no *crossed out,* neuer *inserted in red over caret*

Nay, gude Josephe, com nere and behold.   8
This bludy lammes body is starke and cold.
O, hadde ye seyn his paynes manyfold,
    Ye wald haue beyne right sory!
Josephe, luk bettere, behold and see,
In how litille space how many woundes bee!   9
Here was no mercee,[1] her was no pitee,
    But cruelle delinge paynfully!

O, goode Josephe, I am alle dysmayede[2]
To see his tendere fleshe thus rewfully arayed,
On this wise so wofully displayed,   9
    Woundit withe naylle and spere.
O dere Josephe, I feylle my harte wex cold,
Thes blessite fete thus bludy to behold,
Whom I weshid with teres manyfold,
    And wyped with my heare.[3]   1

O, how rewfulle a spectakille itt is!
Neuer hast bee seyn, ne shalle be after this,
Such cruelle rigore to the kinge of blisse,
    The Lord that made[4] alle.
Thus to suffere in his humanitee,   1
And that only for our iniquitee,
O, Makere of man, what loue and pitee
    Had thou for vs, so thralle!

O, gude Josephe, was ye not present here?
⟨J⟩oseph. Yis, Moder Mawdleyn, it changid my chere!   1
The wounder was so grete I yrkit to com nere,
    But I was not farre hence.   f
magdalena. O Josephe, if I told you euery circumstaunce
Of the moste merite and perseueraunce,
    Of hym þat neuer did offence—   ı
Thys highe kinge þat hinges befor our face,
Displayede on crosse in this piteos place—
    And telle you of his pacience,

---

    [1] mercye *altered to* mercee   [2] *first* e *inserted above*
    [3] *last part of* heare *obliterated,* are *written in later hand*
    [4] e *added*

Frende Josephe, this day am I sure
Scantly with force ye myght it indure,   120
   But your hart shuld tendere,
How he sufferte to be takid,
Sore scourgit and nakit,
   On alle his body sclender.

And notwithstondinge your manly hart,   125
Frome your ees the teres wald starte,
   To shew your hevynesse.
Com hithere, Josephe, and stande ner this rood!
Loo, this lamme spared not to shedd his¹ blude,
   With most paynfulle distresse!   130

Her was more rancore shewed than equitee,
Mich more malace than ony pitee,
   I reporte me—yourself behold and see!
   His payn passis alle othere,
Alle if he were the prince of peace,   135
Therfor my sorow haves no releace.
JOSEPHE. Gude Mawdleyn, of your mowrnynge cease,
   It ekes my doole, dere moder.²

MARIA JACOBI SECUNDA. Goode frende Josephe, what creatur
                            maye
But sorow to se this wofulle daye,   140
   The day of gretist payne?   f. 142ᵛ
MARIA SOLAMEE. Wo and³ sorow must nedes⁴ synke
Mor⁵ in our hartes than met and drinke,
   To se our Saueyoure slayne.

JOSEPHE. Alese, women, ye mak my hart to relente,   145
Beholdinge his body thus torne and rente,
   That inwardly I wepe.
But, gude Mawdleyn, shew vnto me
Where is Mary, his mothere so free?
   Who haues that maide to kepe?   150

¹ *inserted over caret*
² *following line crossed out in red:* The secund Mary began to saye
³ Wo and *inserted in red over caret,* The third Mary saide *crossed out in red*
before   ⁴ *inserted in red over caret*   ⁵ than *crossed out in red after* Mor

MAVDLEYN. A, Josephe, from this place is sho gone.[1]
To haue seyn hir, a harte of stone
    For ruthe wald haue[2] relente.
Right many tymes emanges vs here
Sche swownyd with most dedly chere,
    Ose mothere mekest kente.

With fulle longe prayere scant we myghte
Cause hir parte from this peteose sighte.
    Scho madde[3] many compleynte!
Ye saw neuer woman þis wise dismaide.
Zebedeus and John hase hir convaide.
    To spek of hire, I faynte.

Many men spekes of lamentacion,
Off moders and of their gret desolation,
    Which that thay did[4] indure
When that their childer dy and passe,
But of his peteose tender moder, alasse,
    I am verray sure[5]

The wo[6] and payn passis alle other.
Was ther neuer so sorowfulle a mother
    For inward thoȝt and cure!
When sho harde hym for his enmyse praye,
And promesid the thefe the blissis aye,
And to hirself no word wald saye,
    Sche sighid, be ye sure!

The sonne hynge and the moder stood,
And euer sho kissid the droppes of blood
    That so fast ran down.
Sche extendit hir armes hym to brace,
But sho myght not towch hym, so high was the place,
    And then sho felle in swoune.

---

[1] wente *crossed out in red before* gone
[2] *added in red above line*
[3] *second* d *over* e, e *added*
[4] *added in red over caret*
[5] *line written in right margin*
[6] passis all other *crossed out in red after* wo

JOSEPHE. A, gude Mawdleyn, who can hir blame,
To se hir awn son in so grete shame,
　　Withowt ony offence?
But, Mavdleyn, had he ony mynd on hir in his passion?　　185
MAVDLEYN. 3ee, yee, Josephe, of hir he had grete compassion,[1]
　　Os apperit by evidence.

For, hanginge on the crosse most petyfully,
He lukyd on that maide, his moder, rewfully,
　　And with a tender cow[n]tenaunce,　　190
As who say, 'Modere, the sorow of your harte
Makes my passion mor bitter and mor smarte;
　　Ye ben euer in my remembraunce.

Dere Modere, becawse I depart os nowe,
John, my cosyn, shalle waite on yowe,　　195
　　Your comforte for to bee'.
Loo, he had hyr[2] in his graciose mynd,
To teche alle chi[l]deren to be kind
　　To fader and modere of dewtee.

This child wald not lefe his moder alone,　　200
Notwithstandinge hir lamentabille mone　　f. 143ᵛ
　　And hevynesse.[3]
⟨JO⟩SEPH. A, gud lady, fulle wo was shee.
But can ye telle what wordes saide hee
　　There in that grete distresse?　　205

⟨M⟩AVDLEYN. O Josephe,[4] this lame most meke,
In his cruelle tormentes and paynfulle eke,
　　But fewe wordes he hadd,
Saue that in grete agonye
He saide thes wordes: 'I am thrustye',　　210
　　With chere demure and sadd.

---

[1] com crossed out before
[2] inserted in red over caret
[3] this line written in right margin; following line Than saide Josephe right
peteoslee crossed out in red
[4] Mawdleyn saide crossed out in red at beginning of line, O Josephe inserted
in red over caret

I

⟨J⟩OSEPH. Mawdleyne, suppose ye his desire was to drinke?
⟨M⟩AVDLEYN. Nay, verrelye, frende Joseph, I think
    He thrustide no lyquore.
His thruste was of charitee.   215
For our faithe and fidelitee
He ponderite the rigore

Off his passion done so cruellye.
For the helth of mannys saulle cheflye
He thrustid and desirede.   220
And then, after tormente longe,
And after paynes felle and stronge,
    This mekist lam expyrede.

For wikkit synners þis lamm is dede!
Alese, my¹ hart wex hevy os lede,   225
    Myndinge my writchitnesse!
Wher was euer a mor synfulle creature
Than I myself? Nay, nay, I am sure
    Was none of mor offencesse!

O, what displesur is in my mynd,   230
Rememberinge that I was so vnkynd   f. 1
    To hym that hinges here,
That hinges here so piteoslye
For my synnes done owtragioslye—
    Mercy, Lorde, I require!   235

Notwithstondinge the gre[t] enormitee
Of my fowle synnes, and of his humylitee,
    This lambe, this innocent,
For my contrition he forgaue mee
Only of his fre mercifulle pitee;   240
    Neddes must my harte relente!

This is the sacrifice of remission.
Crist, alle synners havinge contrition,
    Callith to mercy and grace,
Sayinge thes swete wordes: 'Retorn to mee,   245
Leve thy syn, and I shal be with thee,
    Accepte in euery place'.

¹ mo *crossed out in red before*

Had not beyne his most mercyfulle consolatione,
I, wreche of alle wretches,[1] into[2] desperation[3]
   Had fallen right dangeroslye.   250
My dedes were dampnabille of righte,
But his mercee accepte my harte contrighte,
   And reconsiled me gracioslye.

O, mekeste lambe hanginge here on hye,
Was ther none othere meyn but þou must nede dy,   255
   Synners to reconsyle?
A, sisters, sisters! What sorow is in me,
Beholdinge my master on this peteose tree!
My harte fayntes, I may no longer dree!
   Now lat me pawse[4] a whyle.[5]   260

O, where shalle ony comfurth com to mee,   f. 144v
And to his modere, that maid so free?
   Wald God here I myght dye![6]

TWO[7] MARIES. Gud Mawdleyn, mesure youre distillinge teres!
⟨M⟩AVDLEN. O, sisters,[8] who may hold theire cheres?   265
Thes are the swete fete I wipet with heris,
   And kissid so deuowtlye.
And now to see tham thyrlite with a nayle,
How shulde my sorowfulle harte bot fayle,
   And mowrn contynually?   270

Cum hithere, Joseph, beholde and looke,
How many bludy letters beyn writen in þis buke—
   Smalle margente her is![9]
⟨JO⟩SEPHE. Ye, this parchment is stritchit owt of syse!
O, derest Lorde, in how paynfulle wise   275
   Haue ye tholit this!

---

[1] had fallen *crossed out in red after* wretches
[2] to *inserted above caret*
[3] s *inserted above caret*
[4] *capital* A *crossed out following*
[5] *corr. from* wele
[6] *three following lines crossed out:* Ose Mawdleyn thus sore did wepe / The othere two Maryes tuk gude kepe / And saide righte soberlye
[7] ijᵒ   [8] saide sho *crossed out in red following*
[9] *following line* Than said Josephe, a nobille man of prise *crossed out in red*

O, alle the pepille that passis here by,
Beholde here inwardlye[1] with your ees gostly,
  Consider welle and see,
Yf that euer ony payn or torment   28
Were lik vnto this which this innocent
  Haues suffert thus meklee!

Remembere, man! Remembere welle, and see
How liberalle a man this Lord was and free,
  Which to saue mankind,   28
On droppe of blude haues not kepit ne sparid!
Fulle litille for ease or plesure he carid,   f.
  By reason ye may finde,

Which on dropp of blood hase not resaruyd.
O Lord, by thy deth we beyn preseruyd!   29
  By deth, thou hast slayne deth!
Was neuer no love lik vnto thyn,
That to this meknes thyselfe wald inclyn,
  And for vs to yelde thy brethe!

Thou knew ther were no remedy[2] to redeym syn   29
But a bath of þi blude to bath mans saule in,
  And thou were welle[3] assent
To let it ren owt most plenteosly.
Where wer euer sich love? Neuer, verrely,
  That such wise wald content!   30

To his Fadere for vs he made a surerender.
Loo, euery bone ye may nowmbere of his body tender!
  For vntollerabille paynes,
The tormentours sparede no crueltee,
With sharp scowrges te-terre his fleshe, ye may see,   30
  With thorns thrust in his braynes;

Grete nayles drevyn the bones alle to-brake;
Thus in euery parte the nayles thay did wrake.[4]
  O cruelle wikkitnese!
From the crowne of the hede vnto the too,   31
This blessit body was wrappit alle in woo,
  In payn and distresse.

---

              [1] *corr. from* inwardlee   [2] *corr. from* redmedy
             [3] *following word* content *crossed out*   [4] r *added above*

In this displaied body, wher may it be found,
On spott, or a place, bet ther is a wound,
   Owther mor or lesse?   315
Se his side, hede, handes and fete!   f. 145ᵛ
Lo, alle his body with blude is wete,
    So paynfulle was his presse.

On yche parte he is paynede sore,
Saue only the tunge, which euer more   320
    For synners did prayee.¹
⟨MA⟩VDLEN. Who saw euer a spektacle more pitevs?
A more lamentable sight and dolorus?
    A! A, this wofulle daye!

Alese, this sorow that I endure   325
With grete inwarde hevynes and cure!
    Alesse, þat² I do not dye,
To see hym dede, made me of noghte,
And with his deth thus haves me boughte.
    O cruelle tormentrye!   330

O, dere Master, be ye not displeasid,
Yf I myght dy with yow, my hart wer wel easid.
    O faynt, and faynt it³ is!⁴
⟨JO⟩SEPH. What meyn ȝe, women, in Goddis name?
Moder, to mych sorow ȝe mak, ye be to blame!   335
    I pray yow, leve alle this!

He that hingeth here, of his humilite,
From deth shalle aryse, for right⁵ so saide hee.
    His wordes must nedes be trewe.
This is the finale cavse and conclusion,   340
To bringe our mortalle enmy to confusion,
    And his powere to subdewe.

For this cawse he descendit from þe hevynly place,   f. 146ʳ
Born of þe mekist virgyn, alle fulle of grace,
    Which now most sorowfulle is.   345

¹ *following line* To that word Mavdlen awnswert thus *crossed out in red*
² *added above line in red*   ³ *added over caret*
⁴ *following line* Holy Josephe awnswerit to this same *crossed out in red*
⁵ *added in red over caret*

For that cawse he did our natur take,
Thus by deth to sloo deth for mannes sake,
   And to restor hym to blysse.

Wherfor, good women, your self comforte;
Amongest vs agayn he shalle resorte,   3.
   I trust verrelye.
I pray yow, compleyn not thus hevylee.[1]
MAVDLE⟨N⟩. Nedes must I compleyn, and that most bitterlee,
   And I shalle telle yow whye.

Insensibille creaturs beyn trovblid, ʒe see;   3!
The son had lost his sight, eclippid was hee;
   Th'erth tremblide ferfullye!
The hard flynt and stone is brokyn in sundre!
Yf resonable creaturs be trowblid, it is no wonder!
   And emange alle, speciallye,   3⬤

I, a wrechit woman! A wrech! A wreche!
Behold these bludy welles! Her may þou feche
   Balme more preciose than golde.
O, ye welles of mercy, dyggide so depe!
Who may refrayn? Who may bot wepe,   3⁶
   These bludy streymys to beholde?

O fontains flowinge with water of life,
To wash away corrupcion of wondes infectyfe
   By dedly syne grevose!
Alle with meknese is mesured this ground, without dowte,   f.
Wherin so many springes of mercy flowes owte,   37
   Beholde, how so plenteose![2]

ALTERA MARIA. Mawdleyne,[3] your mowrnynge avaylis nothinge.
Lat vs speke to Josephe, hym hertely desiringe
   For[4] to finde some gude waye   37
This crucified body down to take,
And bringe it to sepulcre and so lett make
   Ende of this wofulle daye.[5]

---

[1] *following line* Than said Mawdleyn A Josephe free *crossed out in red*
[2] *following line* The othere Mary myldly gafe awnsweringe *crossed out in red*
[3] *preceding two words* And saide *crossed out in red*
[4] *added in red in left margin*
[5] *following line* Than saide Josephe Gude women and worthye *crossed out in red*

⟨J⟩OSEPH. 3e shalle vnderstand yit more, that I
Haue beyne with the juge Pilat instantlye   380
   For this same requeste,
To berye this most holy bodye,¹
Ande he grauntid me fulle tenderlye
   To do os me thought beste.

I haue spokene with Nichodemus also;   385
Ye shalle se hyme takyn down or ye go.
   That he taryes so longe, I mervelle.
A, I se hym now com vpward the hille!
Cesse of² youre wepinge, I pray you, be stille!
   I trust alle shal be welle.³   390

Nichodemus, come nerre! We haue longe for you thou3t!

   ⟨Ni⟩codemus venit.⁴

[NICHODEMUS]. O worthy Lorde, who made alle thinge of noght,
With the most bitter payn to deth is thou broughte.   f. 147ʳ
   Thy name blessit bee!
O, how a⁵ pitefulle sight is this,   395
To se the prince of euerlastinge blisse
   To hinge here on this tree,

To hinge here thus soo piteoslye!
O, most lovinge Lorde, thy gret mercy
   To this havese the constreynyd!   400
Why wold thyn awn pepille, þi awn flokke,
Thus crucyfy the, and naylle tille a stokke?
   Why haves thou not refreynyd?

For fourty yere in wildernesse,
Theire olde faders in theire progresse   405
   Thou fed with angelles foode,
And brought tham in to the land of promission,
Wher they fand lond in euery condischon,
   And alle thinge that was goode.

A! A, is this theire gramercy? Is this theire reward?   41
Thy kindnesse, thy gudnese, can they regard
　　No better but thus?
Notwithstondinge the vesture of þi humanyte,
That þou were the verrey Son of God, þay myȝt see
　　By myracles most gloriose.   41

JOSEPH. Gude¹ brothere, of your compleinte² cesse!
Ȝe renewe agayne grete hevynesse
　　Now in thes women here.³
NICODEM⟨E⟩. Nay,⁴ gret comfurthe we may haue alle,
For, by his Godly powere, arise he shalle,   f.
　　And the thride daye apere.   42

For ons he gaue me leue with hym to reasone,
And he shewet of this deth and of this treasone,
　　And of this crueltee,⁵
And how for mankynd he com to dye,   42
And that he shuld arise so glorioslye
　　By his myghtee maiestee,

And with our flesch in hevyn tille ascend.
Many swete wordes it plesit hym to spend,
　　Thus speking vnto me,
That no man to hevyn myght clym,
But if it were by grace of hym   43
　　Which com down to make vs free:
'Nemo ascendit in celum nisi qui descendit de celo'.

　　　*Joseph, redy to tak Crist down, sais:*⁶

[JOSEPH]. To tak down this body, lat vs assaye.   43
Brother Nichodemus, help, I yow praye.
　　On⁷ arme I wald ye hadd,
To knokk out thes nayles so sturdy and grete.
O, Safyoure! They sparid not your body to bete!
　　Thay aught now to be sadd.   44

---

¹ Then saide Joseph *crossed out in red before*
² of your compleinte *added in red over carets*
³ *following line* Nay saide Nicodeme it may befalle *crossed out in red*
⁴ *added in red in left margin,* That *crossed out after*   ⁵ *corr. from* crueltyee
⁶ *From this point on, names of speakers and 'stage' directions are neatly spaced
in MS. When speakers' names are included in directions but not repeated in margins,
we add them in brackets beside the speeches*   ⁷ h *crossed out after*

MAWDLEYN. Gude Josephe, handille hym tenderlye!
JOSEPHE. Stonde ner, Nichodemus, resaue hym softlye.
Mawdleyn, hold ye his fete.
MAWDLEYNE. Haste yow, gude Josephe, hast yow whiklye!   f. 148ʳ
For Marye, his moder, wille com, fer I.   445
A, A, that virgyne most swete!

NICHODEMUS. I saw hir benethe on the othere sid;
With John, I am sure sho wille not abid
Longe frome this place.

> Mary, Virgyn and Mother [with John Euaungeliste]¹ com
> then sayinge:

[MARY VIRGIN]. A! A, my dere sone Jhesus! A! A, my dere sone   450
                                                        Jhesus!
JOHN EUAUNGELISTE. Gude Marye, swete cosyn, mowrn ye not
                                                          thus!
Ye see how stondes the case.

MAWDLEYNE. Allese! Scho commys. A, what remedye?
Gud Joseph, comfurth hire stedfastlye,

That virgyne so fulle of woo.   455

> Mary Virgyn sais, falles in swown:

[MARY VIRGYN]. Stonde stille, frendes, hast ye not soo!
Haue ye no fere of mee!
Lat me help to tak my dere son down!
MARY MAWDLEYN. Lo, I was sure sho walld falle in a swown!
Her on euery sid is pitee.   460

JOSEPHE. Help, Mawdleyn, to revyue hir agayn!
A! A! This womans harte is plungid with payn!
Hir sorowe sho cane not cesse.
JOHN EUAUNGELISTE.² A, A, dere ladee, wherfore and why   f. 148ᵛ
Fare ye on this wise? Wille ye here dy?   465
Leyf of this hevynesse!

¹ As John clearly enters with the Virgin, we add the bracketed direction
² repeated from foot of f. 148ʳ

Ye promesit me ye wold not do thus.
MAWDLEYN. Speke, ladye, speke for the loue of Jhesus,
Youre swete sone, my master[1] here.
MARYE VIRGYN. A, A, Mawdleyn, Mawdleyn, your master so dere!
TWO[2] MARIES. Most meke modere, be now of gude chere!

JOHN EUAUNGELISTE. Wipe awaye that rynnys owte so faste!
From your remembraunce, rayse owt at þe last
  Of his passione the crueltee.
JOSEPHE. Tak comfurthe, Marye; this wailinge helpes nothinge.
Your dere son we wille to his sepulcre bringe,
  Als it is alle oure dewtee.

MARY VIRGYN. God reward yow of your tendernese!
I shalle assiste you with alle humylnesse.
  But yit, or he departe,
Suffere me my mynd for to breke,
How-be-it fulle scantly may I speke,
  For faynte and febille harte.

A! A, Cosyn John, what shalle I saye?
Who saw euer so dolfulle a daye?
  So sorowfulle a tym as this?
This wofulle moders sorow, who cane itt expresse,
To se hir own chyld sleyn with cruelnesse?
  Yit, myn own swet son, your woundes wold I kysse!

O, Gabrielle, Gabrielle!
Of gret joy did ye[3] telle,
  In ȝour[4] first salutation.
Ye saide the Holi Gost shuld co[m] in mee,
And I shuld consaue a child in virginitee,
  For mankind saluation.

That ye said truthe, right welle knaw I;
But ye told me not my son shuld dye,
  Ne yit the thought and care

---

[1] dere *following crossed out and* here *written after*   [2] ijᵒ
[3] *added above caret, preceding* thou *crossed out, another* ye *added above and also crossed out*
[4] they *crossed out,* ȝour *added above*

Of his bitter passion which he suffert nowe.
O, old Symeon, fulle suthe said yowe—   500
   To spek, ye wold not spare.

Ye saide the sword of sorow suld enter my hart.
Ye, ye, juste Symeon, now I felle it smarte
   With most dedly payn!
Was there neuer moder that felit so sore?   505
Iwise, John, I felle it alway more and more!
   Help! Help now, Mawdleyn!

     et cadit in extas⟨ia⟩.

MAWDLEYN. Mek moder and mayde, leve your lamentation!
Ye swown stille on pase with dedly suspiration.
   Ye mare yowreself and vs.   f. 149ᵛ
JOHN EUAUNGELIST. Ye shuld lefe of your paynfulle afflictione, 511
Callinge to your mynd his resurrection,
   Which sal be so glorivse.
This knaw ye, and þat¹ beste.
MARY VIRGYN. I knaw it welle, or ellis in reste   515
   My harte shuld neuer bee.
I myght not leve nore endure
On mynnate, bot I am sure
   The thrid day ryse² shalle hee;

But yit havinge remembraunce   520
The gret cruelty and felle vengance
   Of the Jues so vnkind,
Which thus wikkitly has betrayed
Goddes Son, born of me, a mayd,
   Most sorowfulle in my mynd.   525

O, Judas, why didist thou betraye³
My son, þi master? What can þou saye,⁴
   Thyself for tille excuse?
Of his tender mercyfulle charite,
Chase he not the on his twelue⁵ to bee?   530
   He wald not þe refuse.

---

¹ *added in red over caret*   ² *corr. from* rese   ³ *corr. from* betrayye
⁴ sy *crossed out before*   ⁵ xij

Callyt not he þe to his supere and last refection?
Cowth þou not put owt þi pesyn and infection[1]
　　Saue thus only,　　　　　　　　　　　　　　　　f.
Vnto thy master to be so vnkind?　　　　　　　　5
Was his tender gudnese owt of thy mynd
　　So vnnaturallye?

Gaue he not to[2] the his body in memorialle,
And also in remembraunce perpetualle
　　At his suppere there?　　　　　　　　　　　　5
He that was so comly and fayre to behold,
How durst thou, cruelle hert, to be so bold
　　To cawse hym dy thus here?

By thy treson my son here is slayn,
My swete, swetist son! How suld I refreyn,　　　5
　　This bludy body to behold?
JOSEPHE. Gud dere Marye, git you hence!
We shalle bery hym with alle reuerence,
　　And ly hym in the mold.

Haue hir hence, John,[3] now I desire.　　　　　5
JHOANNES EUANGELISTE. Com on, swete lady, I ȝow[4] reqwire.
　　I shalle gife yow attendance.
JOSEPHE. On of yow women, ber hir companye.
ALTERA MARIA. I shalle wayte on hir. Go we hence, Marye;
　　Put alle this from your remembrance.　　　　5

MARIE VIRGYN. What meyn ye, frendes? What is your mynd?
Towardes me be not so vnkinde!　　　　　　　　f.
　　His moder[5] am[6] not I?
Wold ye haue the moder depart hym fro?
To lefe hym thus I wille not so,　　　　　　　　5
　　But bide and sitt hym bye.

Therfore, gud Joseph, be content!
JOSEPHE. A, A, Marye! For a gud consent,
　　We wald not haue you here.

---

[1] s crossed out before c, n added in red　　　　[2] added over caret
[3] added in red over caret　　　　　　　　　　　[4] added over caret
[5] that I crossed out after moder　　　[6] a second I crossed out in red after am

MARIE VIRGYN. Wold ye renewe mor sorow in me?   565
JOSEPHE. Nay, gud lady, that were pitee!
MARYE VIRGYNE. Than late me abide hym nere!

John, why spek ye not for my comforte?
Mi dere sone bad me to you resorte,
    And allway on you calle.   570
Ye knaw welle, her is my tresure,
Whom I loue beste, whom alle my plesure
    Is, and euer be shalle.

Her is my likinge and alle my loue.
Why wald ye than me hens[1] remoue?   575
    I pray yow hartly, cesse!
Departe I may not, bot by fors constreynyd.
Remembringe departinge, ales, my hert is paynid
    Mor then I may expresse!   f. 151[r]

Now, dere swete coysyn, I you praye!   580
Myn awn dere loue, which on Thursdaye,
    Of his[2] grace specialle,
Of his lovinge mynd and tendernesse,
And of verrey inward kindnesse,
    At suppere emanges you alle,   585

He admyttid you frendly for to reste,
And slepe on his holye Godly breste,
    For a[3] specialle prerogatife,
Because of your virginite and clennesse;
Der cosyn, encrease not myn hevynesse,   590
    Yf ye desire my life!

But, gud frendes, here intreyt not ye,
But be content, and suffere mee
    Ons yit for to hold,
For to holde here in this place,   595
And in myn armys for to enbrace,
    This body, which now is cold,

---

[1] *added above in red*   [2] *added in red over caret*   [3] *added above in red*

This bludy body woundit so sore,
Of my swet son—John, I aske no more!

JOHN EUAUNGELISTE. Lady, if ye wille haue moderation   60
Of youre most sorowfulle lamentacion,
  Do as ye list in this case.[1]
MARIE VIRGYNE. John, I shalle do os ye thinke gude.
Gentille Josephe, lat me sit vnder your rude,   f.
  And holde my son a space.   60

NICHODEMUS. Let vs suffere the modere to compleyn
Hir sonnes dethe in verrey certeyn,
  Tille ease hir and content.
JOSEPHE. Ye, so shalle hir sorowfulle harte
Alway to suffere smarte,   61
  And we can bot repente.

MARIE VIRGYN. O sisters, Mawdleyn, Cleophe, and Jacobye!
Ye see how pitefulle my son doth lye
  Here in myn armys, dede.
What erthly mother may refreyn,   61
To se hir son thus cruelly sleyn?
  A, my harte is hevy os lede!

Who shalle gife me water sufficient,
  And of distillinge teris habundance,
That I may wepe my fille with hart relent,   62
  After the whantite of sorofulle remembrance,

For his sak that made vs alle,
  Which now ded lyes in my lappe?
Of me, a mayd, by grace specialle,
  He pleside to be born and sowket my pape.   62
  He shrank not[2] for to shew the shape   f.
Of verreye man at his circumcision,
  And þer shed his blude for mannys hape.
Also at my purification

----

[1] cease *crossed out before*
[2] He shrank not *repeated from foot of f. 151ᵛ*

Of hym I made a fayre oblation,   630
  Which to his Fader was most plesinge.
For fere than of Herodes persecution,
  In-tille Egipe¹ fast I fled with hym.
  His grace me gidid in euery thinge;
And now is he dede. That changes my chere!   635
  Was neuer child to moder so lovinge!
Who þat cann not wepe, at me may lere.

Was neuer deth so cruelle as this,
  To slo the gyvere of alle grace!
Son, suffer me your woundes to kisse,   640
  And your holy blude spilt in this place.
  Dere son, ye haue steynyd your face,
Your face so frely to behold.
  Thikk bludy droppes rynnes down apace:
'Speciosus forma', the prophet told.   645

But, alese, your tormentes so manyfold
  Hase abatid your visage so² gloriose!
Cruell Jewes, what mad yow so bold
  To commyt þis crym most vngraciose,
  Which to yourself is most noyose?   650
Now shalle alle the cursinges of your lawe
  Opon yow falle most myschevose,   f. 152ᵛ
And be knawen of vagabundes ouer-awe!

He and I com both of your kyn,
  And that ye kithe vncurteslye.   655
He com for to fordoo your syn,
  But ye forsuke hym frowardly.
  Who can not wepe, com sit me bye,
To se hym that regnyd in blisse,
  In hevyn with his Fader gloryoslye,   660
Thus to be slayn, in alle giltlesse.

Son, in your handes ar holes wid,
  And in your fete that so tender were;
A gret wounde is in your blessit sid,
  Fulle deply drevyn with a sharpe spere.   665
  Your body is bete and brussid here—

_____
¹ F emends to egip[t]e   ² added over caret

On euery sid, no place is free!
Nedes muste I wepe with hevy chere!
Who can not wepe, com lern at me,

And beholde your Lorde, myn awn der son,   67
Thus dolfulye delt with, ose ye see.
Se how his hede with thornys is thronge!
Se how he naylit was tille a tree!
His synows and vaynes, drawne so straytlee,
Ar brokyn sonder by payns vngude.   67
Who can not wepe, com lern at me,
And beholde hym here þat hange on rude!

Se alle abowte the bludy streynes!   f.
O, man, this suffert he for thee!
Se so many felle and bitter peynes!   68
This lamme shed his blude in fulle plentee.
Who can not wepe, com lern at mee!
Se alle his frendes is from hym fled!
All is but blude, so bett was hee,
Fro the sole of his fute vnto þe hed.   68

O, swete child, it was nothinge mete—
Saue your sufferance, ye had no pere—
To lat Judas kisse thes lippes so[1] swete,
To suffer a traytor to com so nere,
To betray his master, myldist[2] of chere.   69
O, my swete child, now suffer yee
Me, your moder, to kisse yow here!
Who can not wepe, com lern at me!

To kisse, and swetly yow imbrace;
Imbrace, and in myn armes hold;   69
To hold, and luke on your blessit face;
Your face most graciose to behold;
To beholde so comly, euer[3] I wold!
I wold, I wold stille with yow bee,
Stille with yow, to ly in mold!   70
Who can not wepe, com lern at me!

---

[1] *added above in red*   [2] y *written over* i   [3] *corr. from* eyer

My wille is to dy; I wald not leve.
   Leve, how suld I, sithen dede ar yee?
My lif were ye, noght can me greve,   f. 153ᵛ
   So¹ þat I may in your presence bee.   705
   Me, your wofulle moder, her may ye se;
Ye see my dedly sorow and payn.
   Who can not wepe, com lern at mee,
To see so meke a lambe her slayn,

Slayn of men that no mercy hadd.
   Had they no mercy? I reporte me, see!   710
To se this bludy body, is not your hart sadd?
   Sad and sorowfulle? Haue ye no pitee,
   Pite and compassion, to se this crueltee?
Crueltee! Vnkindnese! O men most vnkind!   715
   Ye that can not wepe, com lern at mee,
Kepinge this crucifixe stille in your mynd.

When ye war born of me, a mayde² myld,
   I sange 'lullay'³ to bringe you on slepe.
Now is my songe 'Alese, ales, my child!'   720
   Now may I wayle, wringe my handes, and wepe!
   Who shal be my comforth? Who shalle me kepe?
Save at your departinge, ye segnyte to mee
John, your cosyn,⁴ most virtuus and ȝepe.
Who that can not wepe, com and lern at mee!   725

O, derest childe, what falt haf ye done?
   What was your trispace? I wald knav it fayn,
Wherfor your blessid blude is forsid forth to rone.
   Haue murtherid any person, or ony man slayn,
   That your avn pepille þus to yow dose endeyn?   f. 154ʳ
Nay, nay, nay! Ye neuer did offence!⁵   731
Was neuer spote of syn in your clere conscience!

---

    ¹ *written in left margin,* Fro *crossed out*
    ² a *added over caret*
    ³ a *added over caret*
    ⁴ *following phrase* standinge in þis place *crossed out.* most virtuus and ȝepe
written in red above
    ⁵ did of offence

And notwithstandinge their felle indignation,
  Only of gud wille and inward charitee,
Also for loue,[1] and mannes saluation,   735
  3e haue suffert alle this of your humylitee.
Of your large mercee gret was þe whantite,
Grete was þe multitude of your merites alle,
Thus for mannes sake to tast þe bitter galle.

Sonn, helpe, help your moder in this wofulle smarte!   740
  Comfurth your wofulle moder þat neuer was vnkind!
In your conception ye reyoyet my harte;
  But now of dedly woo so gret cawse I find,
That þe joy of my haylsinge is passit fro my mynd.
Yit suffer me to hold yow her on my lape,   745
Which sumtym gafe yow mylk of my pape!

O, swete, swetist child! Woo be vnto[2] me!
  O, most wofulle woman, your awn moder, loo!
Who shalle graunt it[3] me with you fore to dee?
  The son is dede! What shalle the moder doo?   750
  Where shalle sho resorte? Whider shalle sho goo?
Yit suffere me to hold yow a while in my lap,
Which sumtym gafe yow[4] mylk of my pap.

O crewelle Deth! No lenger thou me spare!
  To[5] me thou wer welcom, and also acceptabille!   755
Oppresse me down at ons! Of the I haue no care!   f. 15
  O my son, my Saueyour, and joye most comfortabille,
  Suffere me to dy with yow, most merciabille,
Or at lest lat me hold you a while in my lape,
Which sumtym gaue yowe þe milk of my pape.   760

O, ye wikkit pepille, without mercy or pitee,
  Why do ye not crucyfye and hinge me on þe crosse?
Spare not your nayles! Spare not your crueltee!
  Ye can not make me to ron in greter losse
Than to lesse my son þat to me was so dere.   765
Why sloo ye not þe moder, which is present here?

---

[1] ye *crossed out before*   [2] vn *added over caret*   [3] *added above in red*
[4] me *crossed out,* yow *added in red over caret*
[5] *preceding partial line* O my son my saveyour *crossed out*

Dere sone, if the Jwes yit wille not sloo me,
 Your gudnes, your grace, I besech and praye,
So calle me to your mercy of your benignitee.
 To youre mek suters ye neuer saide yit naye;   770
 Then may ye not your moder in this cavse delaye.
The modere with the child desires for to reste.
Remembere, myn awn son, þat ȝe sowket my breste!

Remember, when your fleshe was soft os tender silke,
 With the grosse metes then yow I wold not fede,   775
But gaue yow the licour¹ of a maydyns mylke;
 Tille Egipe² in myne³ armes softly I did yow lede;
 But your smylinge contenaunce, I askit non other mede.
Then be content that I with yow may riste.
Remembere, my der son, þat ȝe sowkit my briste.   780

At your natiuitee, remember, my dere son,
 What vesselle I brochit to your nobille grace.
Was þer neuer moder that brochit sich a ton!   f. 155ʳ
 From my virgyne pappes⁴ mylk ran owt apasse.
 To your Godly power natur gaf a place;   785
Ye sowkit maydens milke, and so did neuer none,
Nore herafter shalle, saue yourself alone.

When ye sowkid my brest, your body was hole and sound;
 Alese! In euery place now se⁵ I many wound!
Now help me, swet Mawdleyn, for I falle to þe ground!   790
 And me, wofulle Mary, help now, gud John!
JOHN EUAUNGELISTE. Than, gude swete lady,⁶ lef your gret mon!
MARY VIRGYN. A! A, Mawdleyn, why devise ye nothinge
To this blessid body for to gif praysinge?

Sum dolorose ditee express now⁷ yee,   795
In þe dew honour of þis ymage of pitee!

MAWDLEYN. To do ȝour biddynge, lady, [we] be rightt⁸ fayn,
But yit, gud lady, your teres⁹ ȝe refreyn!

---

¹ *written over caret,* mylke *crossed out below* ² *F emends to* Egip[t]e
³ myns   ⁴ *corr. from illegible word, suspension mark crossed out above*
⁵ *a word blotted out after* ⁶ d *written over* y ⁷ *corr. from* noy
⁸ *word blotted out before, superscript* a *above blotted word*
⁹ *added in red over caret*

JOSEPHE. Now, Mary, deliuer that blessit body tille vs.
MARY VIRGYN. Wille ȝe tak from me myn own son Jhesus?   80

NICHODEMUS. Gud lady,[1] suffere[2] vs to bringe hym to his grave.[3]
MARY VIRGYNE. Swete frendes, suffer me mor respit to haue!   f.
Haue compassion of me, frendes, I ȝou praye!
So hastely fro me tak hym not away.

Yf to his sepulcre nedes ye wille hym bere,   80
Bery me, his moder, with myn awn son here!

When he was lyvynge, to leve I desirid;
Now, sithen he is ded, alle my joye is expirid.

Therfor, lay the moder in grave with the child.
JOHANNES EUANGELISTA. O, Mary, modere and maiden most   81
                                                                                        myld,
Ordere yourselfe[4] os reson doth requere!
JOSEPHE. Com on, lat vs bery this body that is here!

MARY VIRGYN.[5] O, now myn harte is in a mortalle dred!
Allas! Shalle I not kep hym nothire whik ne ded?
    Is ther no remedye?[6]   81
Yit, Josephe, agayn the cloth ye vnfold,
That his graciose visage I may ons behold,
    I pray yow interlye!

JOSEPHE. Pece, gude Marye! Ye haue had alle your wille!
MARY VIRGYN. Ales! This departinge my tender hart doth kille!   82

Gud coysyn John, yit spek a word for mee!
JOHNE EUAUNGELIST. Be content, swet Mary, for it may nott bee.

MARY VIRGYN. A! A! Toward me ye be verreye cruelle!   f.
Yit lat me bid ons myn own son farwelle!
    Ye may it not denye.   82
Now, farewelle, only joye of alle my harte and mynd,
Farewelle! The derest redemption of mankind
    Suffert most bitterlye!

[1] corr. from laidy   [2] MS has second r after
[3] last part of word blotted, ave written above   [4] l inserted above
[5] speaker's name changed from Mawdleyn   [6] corr. from redmedye

JOHNE EUAUNGELIST. Com one, gud¹ Mary, com!

NICHODEMUS. Some of you women, ber hir companye!   830

TWO MARIES. We shalle gife hire attendance,
Faithfully, with humble reuerance.

Exeunt.

JOSEPHE. Now in his grave, lat vs ly hym down,

Sepelit[ur].

And then resorte we agayn to the town,
    To her what wille men saye.   835
Mawdleyn, ye must hense departe.²
MAWDLEN. Ye, and that with a sorowfulle harte,
    Mowrnynge nyght and daye.

Farewelle, swete lambe! Farwelle, most innocent!
Wrichit Mawdleyn, with most hartly intent,   840
    Commendes hir to your grace.
Farwelle, der master! Farwelle, derest Lord!
Off yowr³ gret mercye, ȝe shalle þe warld record,
    Herafter in ylk place.

Summe preciose balmes I wille go bye   f. 156ᵛ
Tille anoynt and honour this blessit body,   846
    Os it my dewty is.
Fayre Josephe, and gude Nichodemus,
I commend ȝou⁴ to the kepinge of Jhesus!
    He wille whit ȝou alle this.   850

JOSEPHE. Farewelle, Mawdleyn, to yourself comfurth take.
Of this blessit berialle, lat vs ane end make.

    ¹ *added in red over caret*
    ² *red line between ll. 836–7 marks division into two speeches; second speaker's*
name, Mawdlen, *added in right margin*
    ³ r *added in red above*
    ⁴ t *crossed out before* ȝou

Here now is he gravid and here lyes hee,
Which for loue of man, of his charite
  Suffert bitter passion.   85
Gret comforthe it is vnto vs alle
That the thride day aryse he shalle,
  In the most gloriose fassion!

The tyme drawethe fast and approchis nere;
Schortly, I truste sum gud tidinges to here.   86

Devowte Nichodemus, departe we as nowe.[1]

NICODEMUS. Gladly, frende Joseph, I wille go with ȝowe.

Thus Her Endes the Most Holy Berialle of þe Body of Crist Jhesu.

[1] *red line between ll. 861–2 marks division into two speeches; second speaker's*
name, Nicodemus, *added in left margin.*

Her Begynnes His
Resurrection on Pas[c]he Daye at Morn[1]

Pascha *Mawdleyne begynnes, sayinge:*[2]

[MAWDLEYNE]. O, this grete hevynese and payn!
Alese, how longe shalle it remayn?
  How longe shalle it endure,
And rist within my most carfulle hart?
How longe shalle I feyle this dedly smarte?   f. 157ʳ
  Who shalle my sorowe cure?   5

How longe shalle I lef in desolation?
When shalle þe houre com of consolation,
  That my master I maye see,
Which opon the Friday laste,
Was crucified and nailit fast,   10
  Peteosly tille a tree?

So pyteose a sight and lamentabille,
So dolorose and miserabille,
  I hop ye shalle neuer fynd!
Cursid Kayn was verrey cruelle,   15
And slew his awn brothere Abelle,
  Of a maliciose mynd;

Yit was he not so maliciose
Ose the cruelle Jewes most owtragiose   20
  Which here has slayn my Lord!
The sonnes of Jacob gret envy had
Agayns þer brother Joseph, ӡonge, wise, and sad,
  Os scriptur doth record.

---

  [1] *these four lines underlined in red*
  [2] *this direction mistakenly bracketed by scribe to rhyme with the following two*
lines of text; Pascha is written in red in left margin before direction

Thay intendit to slo hym malishosly,   25
And yit þay did not soo cruelly,
    Os wrought thes Jewes wild!
Few ȝeres past, Herod the kinge
Put to deth many ȝonglinge,
    And many moders child,   30

Here in the land off Israelle;   f.
But of such cruelte harde ye neuer telle
    Ose done was one Fridaye,
When so grete rigore and tyrannye
Was in theire hartes to garre hym dye,   35
    Which was so graciose aye.

Abelle and Josephe wer gude and graciose,
But theire dedes wer not so gloriose,
    Nor of so vertuose kynd,
Ose of hym which in his humanitee   40
Wrought grete¹ myracles in his diuinitee,
    Als ye may calle to mynd.

For alle his werkes so welle devyside,
Emange tham thus to be dispised,
    And with cruellty slayn!   45
Ales, when I remembere his woo,
Scantly may I spek or goo,
    In harte I haue such payn.

I haue bought here oyntmentes preciouse²
To ensalue his body most graciose,   50
    To doo it reuerence.
My sister Cleophe saide that shee
To the sepulcre wald goo with mee,
    And doo hir diligence.

Of the thrid day this is þe mornynge,   55
And of my dere master yit herd I nothinge,
    Wherfor I am moste hevee.
Alese, felishipe her is noon!   f.
Rathere then I faile, I wille go alone.
    A, dere Lorde, your mercee!   60

¹ *added in brown ink over red caret*   ² *written over* graciose *which is crossed out*

Secund Marye commys in and sais:

[SECUND MARYE]. A, my harte, what þou art faynt!
How longe shalle we thus mak complaynt?
    So sorowfulle tym neuer was!
When shalle comforth com of our desire?
What woman is this þat lyes here?   65
    It is Mawdleyn, alese!

Sister Mawdleyn, why waile ye on this wise?
Gud sister, we pray ʒou, stand vp,[1] arise!
    Comforth yourself wyslye!
MAWDLEYN. Off your commynge, sister, I am glade.   70
Iwise, I knaw welle þat ʒe be sadd;
    Ye haue cawse os welle os I!

SECUND MARYE. Ther is no gud creatur, dar I saye,
But inwardly sorowe he may,
    And compleyn bitterlye,
To remembere the felle torment,   75
And cruelle payne of this innocent,
    Which levit so vertuoslye.

Of his meknese hymself he offred,
Whatsoeuer payn to hym was profred,
    This lambe, God[es][2] Sonn so[3] free;   80
Nothinge ragid he, ne was vnpaciente,
But euer most mekly tille his payn he went,   f. 158�v
    With bayne benignitee.

From the tym of Abrahame,   85
And þat our faders from Egip[4] cam,
    Or when sorow was maste,
I am suere was neuer day so piteouse,
So doolfulle and so dangerouse,
    Ose Friday that is paste,   90

[1] and *crossed out after* vp: a *in red over caret before* rise
[2] þat *is blotted out before* God
[3] *written in red above*
[4] *F emends to* Egip[t]

When alle the crueltye was owt sought,
To distroy hym made alle thing of noght,
   To sloo hym that gyves life?
Owt of my mynd this neuer goo shalle,
That for man diete the maker of alle,
   By his manhed passyve.

MAWDLEYN. So doolfulle a day was neuer befor this!
But go we to the monyment where his sepulcre is,
   To anoynte his body there.
SECUND MARYE. Sister, I com for that sam intent;
Ther is nothinge can me better content;
   To go, I haue no fere.

MAWDLEYN. Then, gude sister, lat vs goo devowtlee.
SECUNDE MARYE. Abide! Yonder commes Marye Jacobee!
   I trow with vs sho wille goo.[1]
       Thride Marye commys in.

[THRIDE MARYE]. O, gude sisters, how is it with ʒowe?
MAWDLEYN. A, dere sister, neuer soo eville os nowe!
THRID MARYE. Gud Mawdleyn, say not soo!

This is the third day, ʒe remember welle.
MAWDLEYN. Ye, bot of my master and Lorde I her not telle,
   Therfore I can not cease.
We were goynge to [the] monyment
Wheros lyeth that swete innocent.
   Loo, here, oyntmentes of swetnese!

THRID MARYE. Gude sisters, on yow shalle I wayte.
SECUNDE MARYE. Then let vs tak þe way furth strayte.

MAWDLEYN. Sisters, I perceyve the place is her bye.
Lat vs ordeyn our oyntmentes accordinglye,[2]
   With alle humylite.
Here lyes he þat was mercifulle to synners alle;
Here lyese he most piteose when we did calle;
   Com nerr, sisters, and see!

---

[1] *F numbers l. 105 as two lines, his ll. 971–2*   [2] *g written over y*

Lo, here is the place wher þe body was laid,
Which born was of a virgyn and a cleyn maid.
  Tille honour it, grete cawse haue wee.
Gud sisters, be we not affrayd
  To do hym reuerence and dewtee.

f. 159ᵛ
126

Here he lyeth whose¹ lif surmountes alle oþer,
Which raysed from deth to lyve Lazarus my broþer,
  Now a levinge man.
He lyese here, which by his powre devyn,
In Chana Galilee turnyde water to wyn,
  Ose many testyfy can.

130

The angelle spekes:
[ANGELLE]. Whom seke ye, women sanctifiede?

Three Maryes togider sais:
[THREE MARYES]. Jhesus of Nazareth crucified,
  The redemer of mankind.
ANGELLE. He is resyne! He is not here!
To his disciples he shalle apere—
  In Galilee thay shalle hym fynd!

135

Mulier, quid ploras? Woman, why wepis þou soo?
MAWDLEN. For myn harte is fulle of sorow and woo.
My Lorde, þat was the kinge of blisse,
Is takyn away; I² wat not wher he is.

140

ANGELLE. Com hidder, women, approche mor nere!
Be of gude comfurth and of gud cher,
  For so gret cawse ye haue!
He that ye seke so beselye,
With gude mynd so faythfullye,
  Is resyn here from his grave!

145

f. 160ʳ

The Son of Gode in his humanite
Sufferde deth, and by his diuinitee
  Is resyn the thrid daye.
For redemption of man was he born,
Displayede on the crose, and alle to-torn,
  In right piteose araye.

150

155

¹ whose whose   ² we *crossed out in red after* I

The batelle is done and victorye renuyd!
The grete enmy of man þerby is subduyd,
　That most hatid mankynd.
Com hidder, and behold with your eye
The place where þe body did lye.
　Be joyeos[1] now of mynd!

Loo, here is the cloth droppid blud,
Which was put on hym takyn of þe rud,
　Ose yourself did see.
For a remembrance tak it yee,
And hy yow fast to Galilee—
　For ther apper shalle hee!

MAWDLEYN. Yit must myn herte wepe inwerdlye!
Yit must I mowrn contynuallye,
　Myndinge my master dere.
O, what myn harte is hevy and lothe
When I beholde this piteose clothe,
　Which in my hande is here!

This cloth with blude þat is so stayned,
Of a maydens child so sor constraynid,
　On cross when he was done!
O rygore vnright! O crueltee!
O wikkit wylfullnese! O peruersitee!
　O hartes harde os stone,

To[2] put to deth a lamb so meke!
Welle may the teres ron down your cheke!
　Welle may your hertes relent,
Myndinge the payn my Lord and master felte!
O, in my body my herte now dothe melte!
　To dy I were content.

SECUND MARYE. Sister Mawdlen, to blame ye are,
With this dedly sorow yourself to marre,
　Yourself thus to torment!
Ye torment your selfe and crucifye!
Ye haue cawse to tak gladnes, and whye,
　Ye haue proue evident

---

[1] *second o written over caret*　　　[2] *in margin*

That your master and oures, by his Godly myght,
Is resen from deth to lyfe! An angelle bright
　　Schewes thes tidinges tille vs,
And shewed vs the place wher his body laye,   195
Which is not ther! Forþi, let passe a waye
　　Our sorow most grevouse!

THRIDE MARYE. Sister Mawdleyn, in your hart be stabille.
We shalle here tidinges right comfortabille,
　　And þat, I trust, shortlye,   200
For that is suth veritabille,
　　Saide so afore suthlye.

MAWDLEYN. A! A, sisters! My slewth and my necligence!   f. 161ʳ
I haue not don my dewty ne my diligence,
　　Ose vnto me did falle!
At my masters sepulcre if I hade gifen attendance,   205
And waytid wisely with humble affiance,
　　Os I was bound most of alle,

I shuld haue seyn his vprisinge gloriose
Of my swete Lorde, of þe which desirose
　　I am, and nedes must bee.   210
Alese, sisters! I was to tidiose,
　　That holy sight to see!¹

Than I shuld haue had comforth vncomparabille,
Of the which joye to speke I am not abille!
　　Than I hade seyn my Lorde   215
To haue resyn from his sepulture
With his bludy woundes; of hym I had ben sure!
　　Ales, when I record

How I myghte haue had a sight of your presence,
Who then aught of verrey congruence   220
　　To be mor glad than I,
Which ye haue callid by your grace onlee,
Beynge gretist synner, vnto your large mercee,
　　And that most curtesly?²
　　　　　　　　　　　　　　　　　　　　　　　　　　　　　225

¹ these lines, ll. 212–13, omitted and added at bottom of page, the place of
insertion marked by red crosses   ² graciosly or crossed out before curtesly

Whoso wille not wayte when þat tym is,
When faynest he wold, therof shalle he mysse—
   So it faris by mee.
O, wold to God I had made more haste!
My slewthfulle werke is now in wast!
   3it, gud Lord, haue þou pitee!

When Symon to dyner did hym calle,
Amonges the gestes and straungers alle,
   With meknese soberlye,
I com in with mynde contrite,
For I hade levid in fowlle delite,
   In syn of licherye.

Notwithstandinge the gret abhomynation
Of my grete synnes fulle of execration,
   Yit of his benignite,
As with alle mercy he was replete,
He sufferte me with teris to wesh his fete!
   Loo, his mercyfulle pitee!

My synfulle lippes, which I did abuse,
To towch his blessit fleshe he wald not refuse.
   And ther right oppenlye,
Off his most piteouse tendernese,
The pardoun of my synnes and gret excesse
   He gaue to me hoolye!

Now may I wringe, both wepe and wayle,
Myndinge on Friday his gret bataile
   He had on crosse of tree,
And tuk opon hym for vs alle
To ouercom the fend þat made vs falle!
   A, sisters, welle mowrn may wee!

SECUND MARYE. Sister Mawdleyn, it is bot in vayn
Thus remedilesse to mak compleyn.
   Therfor it is the best,
Ych on of vs a diuerse way to take;
His apperinge joyfulle may vs make,
   And set ouir hartes in reste.

THE THRIDE MARYE. Ye, to sek and inquere, let vs faste hye,
Sister Mawdlen! This is next remedye,
  And þerfore departe wee!
MAWDLEYN. O, Lorde and master, help vs in hye   265
  To haue a sight of thee!¹

    Tunc exeunt hee tres Marie.
    Petrus intrat, flens amare.

[PETER]. O, allmyghty God, which with thyn inward ee
  Seest the depest place of mannys conscience,
And knowest euery thinge most cler and perfitlee,
  Haue mercy, haue pitee, haue þou compatience!
   I confess and knowlege my most gret offence,   270
My fowle presumption and vnstabilnesse.
Let þi mekille mercy ouerflowe my synfulnesse!

And yit I knaw welle,
No erthly thinge can telle,
  Nor ȝit it expresse,   275
My fawtes and gret syn,
Which I am wrappid in
  With dedly² hevinesse!

Ther may not be lightly a greter trispesse
  Then the seruaunt the master to denye!   280
His owne master!³ His own kind master, alesse!
  I mak confession here most sorowfullye
  That I denyed mayster, and þat most vnkindlye!
For when thay did enquere if þat I did hym knoo,   f. 162ᵛ
I saide I neuer sawe hym! Alesse! Why did I soo?   286

With teres of contrition,
With teres of compassion,
  Welle may I mowrnynge make!
What a fawte it was,
The seruaunte, alas,   290
  His master to forsake!

¹ *ll. 265–6 and preceding speaker's name omitted and supplied at foot of page,
the place of insertion marked by red crosses*
² mo *crossed out in red before* dedly   ³ kind *crossed out before*

When his grace callid me fro warldly besines,
    And of a poore fishere his disciple chas mee,
I was callit Symon Bariona, playnly to expresse.
    But he namid me 'Petrus'—Petra was hee![1]
    Petra is a ston, fulle of stabilitee,
Alway stedfaste! Alase! Wherfor was I
Not stabille accordinge to my nam, stedfastlye?

O, my febille promesse!
O, my gret vnkindnesse,
    To my shame resaruyd!
O, mynde so vnstabille!
Thou hast made me culpabille!
    Deth I haue deseruyd!

It plesid thy gudnese gret kindnese to shew mee,
    Callinge me to þi grace and gudly conuersation;
And when it pleasid thi Godhed to tak but three
    To beholde and see the highe speculation
    Of thy Godly maiestye in thy transfyguration,
Thy specialle grace did abille me for on,
With the gud blessid James, and þi cosyn John.

Alese, þat I was so vnkind
To hym, so tender of mynd
    To me, most vnworthye!
Ales, the paynes ar smarte,
Which I fele at my harte,
    And that so bitterlye!

O Lorde, what example of meknesse shewed yee!
    On Thursday after supere, it pleasid your grace
To wesh your seruauntes fete. Who euer are did see
    More perfite meknese shewet in any case?
    I myself was present in the same place.
Alese! Of myself why presumyd I,
Consideringe your meknese, don so stedfastlye?

---

[1] *added in red in margin*

A, myn vnkinde chaunce!
When it commys to remembrance,
    In my mynde it is euer!
I fele owt of mesure
Dedly payn and displesure,   330
    That I can not desseuere.

O mercyfulle redemer, who may yit recownte
    The paynes which þiself for vs did endure?
Vnworthy if I were, I was with þe in þe mount,
    Where þou swet bludy droppes man saule to recure.   335
    In that gret agonye, I am right verrey sure,
Stony hartes of flint, þou wald þam haue mevid,
Seynge thy tendernese to man, by þe relevid!

O, that passion was grete,   f. 163ᵛ
When blud[y] droppes of swet   341
    Ran down apace!
That was excedinge payne
In euery membere and vayn,
    As apperit by his face.

Of Judas thow were betrayede by and bye,   345
    Which was thy discipulle, and familiere with the;
It grevid the more, I knew it certanlye,
    He was fede at þi burde of þi benignitee,
    And ȝit [thow] were betrayed by his iniquitee!
Yf a straunger had don þat dede so trayterouse,   350
It had beyn mor tolerabille and not so greuowse.

Dauid did say in prophecye,
'Homo pacis mee, in quo speraui,
    Supplantauit me'.
O Lord, your pacience¹ may be perceyvid,   355
Which suffert so to be betrayed
    Of Judas! Woo is hee!

¹ mercy crossed out before
K

Fulle of wo may I bee, sorowfulle and pensyve,
Complenynge and wepinge with sorow inwertlee,[1]
And wep bitter teres alle þe days of my life!   36ᴏ
My vnstabille delinge is euer in myn ee.
I saide I wald not leve my master for to dee;
He said I shuld forsak hym or þe cok crow[2] thris.
But I was presumptuose, vnware, and vnwise!

Afterwerd, when hee   36ᵴ
Lokid opon mee
    With a myld cowntenaunce,
Ose he stude on the ground,[3]   f. 1
Emange his enmyse bownd,
    O, I wepit abundaunce!   37ᴄ

Then my teres continuelly
Ran down most sorowfully,
    And yit thay can not cesse;
How may I cesse or stynte?
Yf my harte wer of flinte,   37ᵴ
    I haue caus to wepe, dowtlese!

O caytife! O wofulle wreche!
From thy harte þou may feche
    Sore and sighes depe!
O, most vnkind man!   38ᴄ
What creatur may or can
    The from sclaunder kepe?

To forsake þi master so tender and soo gud,
Which gaue to þe[4] þe keyes of alle holy kirke,
And morouer for thy sake shed his own blud!   38ᵴ
    O synfulle caytyfe! Now aught I sore tille irke!

Ales, John! Why did not I
Folow my master so tenderlye
    Os ȝe did, to the ende?
But for ye delt soo stedfastlye,   39ᴄ
My master gaue you Marye
    To kep in your commend.

---

[1] corr. from inwertlye
[2] o added above   [3] appears also at foot of f. 163ᵛ as catch-phrase
[4] first þe added in red over caret

Yf this dedly woo¹ and sorowe
Endure with me vnto tomorowe,
   Myn hart in sunder wille breke!   395
Now, Lorde, for þi tender mercyes alle,   f. 164ᵛ
Reconcyle me to grace, and to þi mercy calle!
   Ales, I may not speke!

     Et sic cadit in terram, flens amare. [*Andreas et Iohannes*
     intrant.]² *Andreas, frater Petri, dicit.*

[ANDREAS]. A, brothere Peter, what nedes alle þis?
I se welle,³ good cowncelle wille yow mysse.   400
   Dry vp your teres and rise!
Comforth yourselfe, I require yow, and praye!
We shalle haue gud tidinges! This is þe thrid day!
   Sorow not in this wise!

JOHANNES EUANGELISTA. Stand vp, gud brothere, and mesur   405
                                 your hevynese!
This gret contrition of your hart, dowtlese,
   To God is plesant sacrifice.
PETRUS. A, gud brethere Andrewe and John,
Was neuer creatur so wobegon
   Os I, wrech most vnwyse!   410

For, rememberinge the infinite gudnese
Of my Lorde, and my most vnkyndnese
   Don so writchitlye,
At my hart sorow sittes so sore
That my dedly payn encresis mor and more!   415
   Alese, my gret folye!

ANDREAS. Gud brothere Peter, yourself ȝe⁴ comfort!
   Ther is none of alle bot comfurth may he hafe,
For emonges vs agayn our Lorde shalle resorte!   f. 165ʳ
   By his passion his purpasse was mankind to saue.   420
   This is the thrid daye, in which from his graue
He shalle arise fro deth, I haue no dowte.
Therfor, lett comfurth put this sorowe owt!

---

¹ soo *crossed out before* woo
² *As Andrew and John clearly enter at this point, we so indicate in brackets;*
we take the apostrophe to John in l. 387 to be rhetorical
³ *added in red over caret*   ⁴ *added in red above*

Brothere Peter, þe verrey truth to saye,
    Few of vs alle hade perfit stedfastnesse,   42
But sumwhat dowtid, and wer owt of the waye,
    Notwithstandinge of his Godhed the clernesse,
    Schewed by his miracles, with alle perfitnese.
And yf ye remember, brothere, in his last oblation
He spak of our vnstabilnesse, and of his desolation,   43

Saynge '*Omnes vos scandalum patiemini*'—
    'Alle ye shalle suffer sclaunder for me'—[1]
Os who say, 'Ye shalle forsak me alonly;
    The hird-man shal be strikyn, and þe flokk'—which we bee—
    'Schal be disperbilit, and away shalle flee'.   43
Loo, gud brother Peter, he knew our frealtes alle;
Our gude master is mercifulle and graciose withalle.[2]

And yow, brother Peter, the most specialli
    Hase cause of comfurth, for of his church þe hed
He chace you by order, by his grace frelye;   44
    Forþi, from your harte put þis fere and dred!
    Yf ye remember, he said to yow indede,
'Thy faith shalle neuer faile, whatsoeuer befalle'.
Therfor, haue gud hope, and comforth spiritualle!

Ye askit hym ons a whestion, wherwith he was content,   44
    How oft to your brother synn ye shuld relese.
Ye thought seuen tymmes were verrey sufficient,
    But he said sevynty tymes and seuen ye suld forgif, dow[t]les.
    A gret now[m]ber, it plesit hym tille expresse[3]
The gret frelty of man he saw in his Godly mynd—   f.
Forthy for your trispace pardon may ye find.   4!

Howbeit, of yourself to presume, to blame[4] ye[5] were;
Man, þat is freale, of hymself suld haue fere.

---

    [1] onlyee *crossed out after* me
    [2] *ll. 433–7 omitted on f. 165ʳ and added at foot of f. 164ᵛ, with red crosses
marking point of insertion*
    [3] *following this line* Amen *crossed out in bottom right margin*
    [4] *added in red over caret*
    [5] *corr. from* þe e *added in red, though superscript* e *remains*

Your pennance [and] contrition acceptabille must bee;
   Therfor, in your harte rejoye ye may be fayn,   455
Rememberinge he has put [yow] in gret auctoritee.
   That¹ he has saide ons, he wille neuer calle agayn;
    '*Quodcumque ligaueris*', he said—þes wordes ar playn—
And gaue yow þe keyes of hevyn and of helle,
So to lowse and to bynd—this can we alle telle!   460

JOHANNES EUANGELISTA. Gude brother Peter, marke ye welle,
                                    and note;
   The wordes of Andrewe beyn sadd and ponderose.
In your conscience I knaw welle is noȝt so great² mot,
   But that mercy may clere it, of hym that is so graciose.
   Perauenter it was þe wille of our master Jhesus   465
That ȝe shuld not be present his passion to see,
Which he hade on the hille in þe most crueltee.

Peter, if ye had seyn your mastere at þat poynt,
   I trov þat syȝt had beyn to hevy to yow tille endure.
He had torment opon torment in euery vayn and joynt,   470
   He was so harde nailet to þat paynfulle lure;
   His flesh þat was so tender, born of a mayden pure,
And was wont to be towchid with virgyns handes swet,³
Was al totorn most piteosly from hede to þe fet,

When his body was halid and stritchid with ropes,   475
   To caws his armes and fet to þe holes extend,   f. 166ʳ
Then þe nayles dreffyn in, and of þe blude dropes
   Ran owt so plentuosly; his wille it⁴ was to spend
   Alle his precios blude, mannes sor tille amend.
Withowt compleint he suffert the nayles and þe spere;   480
But gretist payn þat he had was for his moder dere.

He sufferd patiently
To be betrayed vnkindly,
To be accusid falsly,
To be intraytid cruelly,   485
To be scornyd most dedenynglye,

---

¹ at *added in red above caret*   ² t *added in red above caret*
³ *ll. 472–3 reversed, but scribe marks correct order by red crosses*
⁴ *added in red over caret*

To be juged wrangfully,
To be dampnyt to deth dolfully,
  With other paynes sere;
To be crucified piteosly,   490
To be woundid vniuersally,
  With scowrges, nayles, and spere.

For thes causes he wald be born of a maid most obedient.
  Now the gret rawnson is paied which was requirid
For redemption of man of the Fader omnipotent.   495
  The tyme of desolation is now expirid;
  The tym of grace is commen, so longe of vs desirid!
Hevyn ȝeates, so longe closid for gret syn,
  Our Saueyour gafe yow the keyes to open and to lat in.

He knew welle, for his deth we shuld be afrayed,   500
  And þerfor ose ȝe remembere, he told vs afore.
His Godhed saw welle þat we shuld be dismaid;
  Of his resurrection he comfortid vs therfore,   f. 1
  He saide he shuld arise, and live eueremore!
This is the thride daye: therfor, dowt nothinge,   505
But shortly we shalle here of his gloriose vprisinge!

Brether, I wolde tarrye with yow longer here,
  But nedes I must go to the virgyn mylde.
Most sorowfulle is hir hart, most hevy is hir chere;
  Alle joye and comfurthe from hir is exilde;   510
  Alle hir rememberance is of hir dere childe.
My master assignyt me to gyve hir attendance,
And that is my dewtye, with alle humblye obseruance.

Hir sorow increacyse aye,
As welle nyght os daye,   515
In most piteose araye;
  For I dar say suerlye,
Sen hir son was betrayed,
And in his grave layde,
The maid hase me dismaid,   520
  For sorow inwerdlye,

That¹ sho nowther tuk rist ne slepe,
Ne from hevynese hirself cowth kepe,
But euermore stille dose sho wepe,
    That I am verrey sure   525
Hartes harder then stone
Wold be² mollyfyed³ anone,
And melte to⁴ see hire mone,
    That sho dose endure.

To here hir mourn so moderlye,   f. 167ʳ
To se hir wep so tenderlye,   531
    Alle myn hert, it fayles;
Now sho spekes of the scornes,
Now sho remembers þe thornes,⁵
    And the grete sturdy nayles!   535

Now sho spekes of his pacience,
Now sho myndes his obedience,
    That vnto deth was.
Now of his visage spekes shee,
Defilid with deformyte,   540
    Of fowlle spittinge, alasse!

Now of his woundes dos sho speke,
And of the sper which did breke
    Hir sonnes blessid sid.
Thus is sho alle comfurthlesse,   545
Replet with alle dulfulnesse—
    Therfor, I may not bide.

As for this tym, I wille departe.
Brother Peter, be of gud harte,
    For other cause haue ye none.   550
Now farwelle for a starte,
    I shalle ȝow mete anon.

PETER. Praye fore me, brother, for Goddes sake!
JOHANNES EUANGELISTA. Brothere, to yow no discomfurth take,
    But truste euer faithfullye!   f. 167ᵛ

¹ a *over* e *in* That, *final* t *added in red over caret*   ² *added in red above*
³ d *added in red*   ⁴ *added above*   ⁵ s *canc. before*

We shalle haue comforth, ȝoure sorowe to slake,   55
  And that, I trust, shortlye.

  Tunc exit Iohannes et dicit Petrus:

[PETER]. Brothere Andrewe, God reward ȝoue euer speciallye!
  For John and ye, with youre swete wordes of consolation,
Hase easid my mynd with comforte stedfastlye.   56
  I am in trewe faith and hope without desperation,
  In my saule now havynge spiritualle iubilation,
Trustinge on the mercy of my master and Lord,
Of whose infinite gudnese I shalle euer record.

Let the dew of mercy falle opon vs: 56
'*Ostende faciem tuam et salui erimus!*'
  Schewe thy powere, gud Lord, and to vs appere!
  Let beames of thi grace approche to vs nere,
Super nos, writchit synners!

      [*Exeunt Petrus et Andreas*]
      Intrat Maria Magdalena.

[MAWDLEYN]. O, I, writchit creature, what shalle I doo?   57
O, I, a wofulle woman, whidere salle I goo?
  My Lorde, wher shalle I find?
When shalle I se that desirid face,
Which was so fulle of bewty and grace,
  To me, the most vnkind?   57

I haue sought and besely inquerid
Hym whom my harte alleway[1] has desired,
  And so desiries stille.
'*Quem diligit anima mea, quesiui;
Quesiui illum, et non inueni!*'
  When shalle I haue my wille?   58
                                          f.

I haue sought hym desirusly,
I haue sought hym affectuosly,
  With besines of my mynd.
I haue sought hym with mynd hartely,   58
The tresure wherin my hart dose lye.
  O Deth, thou arte vnkind!

  [1] *corr. from* alle was; way *added in red under* was; w *of* was *blotted and* h *added above*

On me vse thou and exercise
The auctorite of thyn office!
   My bales thou may vnbind!   590

What offence, Deth, haue I don to the,
Which art so ouer-vnkind to mee?
   Nay, nay, Deth, be not soo!
Filie Jerusalem, wheros ye goo,
Nunciate dilecto meo   595
   Quia amore langueo!

Of Jerusalem, ye virgyns clere,
Schew my best loue that I was here,
   Telle hym, os he may prove,
That I am dedly seke,   600
   And alle is for his loue.

     Jhesus intrat, in specie ortulani, dicens:
[JHESUS]. *Mulier, ploras? Quem queris?*
Woman, why wepis thou? Whom sekes thou thus?
   Telle me whome thou wald haue.

MAWDLEN. I sek my master and swete Lorde, Jhesus,   605
   Which her was layd in grave.

JHESUS. Woman, thou mournest to piteoslye,   f. 168ᵛ
And compleynist the most hevilye;
   Thy mynd is not content.
Thyn hart is trowblit, welle I see,   610
Alle fulle doloruse os thinkes mee;
   Thou has not thyn intente.

MAUDLEYN. Myn intent, that knawes hee
On whom my hart is set, and ay shal bee.
   Gardener, I yowe praye,   615
Schew vnto me, if ye can,
Yf that ye did¹ see here ony man
   Tak his body awaye.

     Jhesus dicit: 'Maria!'
     Mawdleyn awnswers: 'Raboni!'²

¹ *added over caret*
² *these two lines of direction are in the middle of the page and not bracketed, so we
do not number.*

JHESUS. *Noli me tangere!*
Mary, towche me not now! 6
But into[1] Galilee go thowe,
 And to my brether saye,

And to Peter, which sorowfulle is,
That I am resen from dethe to lif ay in blisse,
 Renynge perpetuallye! 6
Exhort tham to be of gud chere,
And hastely wylle I to tham aper,[2]
 To comfurth joefullye!

 Exit Jhesus.

MAWDLEYN. O, myn harte, wher hast thou bee?
Com hom agayn, and leve with mee! f.
 My gret sorow is past! 6
Now may thou entone a mery songe,
For he, whom thou desirid so longe,
 I haue foun now at laste! 6

I thanke your grace with hert intere,
That of yowre gudnese to me wald apere,
 And make my hert thus light.

 Secund Marye intrat cum tercia.

[SECUND MARYE]. *Soror, nuncia nobis!*[3]
Gud Mawdleyn! Sister, how standes with yow?
MAWDLEYN. Dere sisters, neuer so welle os nowe! 6
 For I haue hade a sight

Of my Lorde and master, to my comfurth specialle!
To his Godhed I render thankes immortalle,
 Os I am bound of dewtee.
THRID MARYE. It apperis, suster, by your cowntenaunce, 6
That the gret sorow is owt of remembraunce,
 And so, by your sawe, gret cause haue yee!

---

 [1] to *added in red above*
 [2] ap *crossed out before* aper
 [3] *though this Latin line does not rhyme, the scribe has bracketed it, and we print it as a numbered verse*

MAWDLEYN. I haue gret cause, sisters, I knaw it welle!
For of my joye he is the springe and welle,
  And of my lyfe sustenaunce.   650
SECUNDE MARYE. Haue ye seyn our Lord, sister? Ar ye sure?
MAWDLEN. Sister, I haue seyne my gretist tresure,   f. 169ᵛ
  My hartly joye and plesaunce!

THRIDE MARY. A, sister, gret comfert may your hart inflame!
MAWDLEN. Ʒe, gude sister, he callit me 'Mary', by my name,   655
  And spak with me homlye.
I saw hym bodely, in flesh and bloode,
Our Redemere, which for vs hang on the roode;
  He shewed hyme gratioslye,

And bade me go to his disciples sone,   660
Thaime to certifye of his resurrectione,
  And so wille I shortly doo.
SECUND MARIE. A, A, Mawdleyn, right happee ye were!
Ye spente not in vayn so many bitter tere!
  Gret grace is lent yow too!   665

*Tunc venit Jhesus et salutat mulieres istas tres. Tamen
mulieres nil dicunt ei, sed procidunt ad pedes eius.*

[JHESUS]. *Auete!* Hayle, blessit women leve!
My blessinge here I youe geve!
Let sorow no more youre harte meve,
  But haue comfort allwaye!
I am resene fro deth, so may ye telle;   670
I haue deliuert my presoners frome helle,
  And made tham sure for aye!

  [*Exit Jhesus.*]

MAWDLEYN. Now, gud sisters, be no more sadd!
Ye haue cause os welle os I to be gladd!   f. 170ʳ
  Oure Lorde, loo, of his gudnese,   675
Of his heghe and Godly excellence,
Haves shewede vs here his joyefulle presence,
  With wordes of swetnese!

My wordes wer not fantasticalle, sisters, yee see!
I told youe no lesinge, sisters, report mee!
    Ye haue seyn with your eye.
THRID MARY. Oure spirites ben revivid, our hartes beyn light!
O, Mawdleyn, this was a gloriose sight,
    Schewed to vs gracioslye!

SECUND MARYE. Blessid be that Lorde! Blessit be that Kinge,
That haues comfurth vs thus with his vprisinge,
    So sone and glorioslye!
MAWDLEN. Susters, in joye of this joyfullnese,
A songe of comforte lete vs expresse,
    With notes of armonye:
'*Victime paschali laudes immolant Christiani!*'[1]

> *Tunc hee tres cantant idem, id est, '*Victime pascha⟨li⟩*'—*
> *totum vsque ad '*Di⟨c nobis⟩*'[2] in cantifracto vel saltum in*
> *pallinodio. Tunc occurent eis apostoli, scilicet Petrus, Andreas,*
> *et Johann⟨es⟩, cantantes hoc, scilicet: '*Dic nobis, Maria,*
> *quid vidisti in vi⟨a⟩?' Respondent mulieres, cantantes:*
> *'*Sepulcrum Christi viue⟨ntis⟩*', et cetera, vsque ad '*Credendum
> est*'. Apostoli, respondentes, cantant: '*Credendum est magis
> soli Marie veraci quam Judeorum turbe fallaci*'. Mulieres*
> *iterum cantant: '*Scim⟨us⟩ Christum surrexisse[3] vere*'. Apostoli*
> *et mulieres s⟨imul⟩ cantant quasi concredentes: '*Tu nobis
> Christe rex misere⟨re⟩*'. Amen. Post cantum dicit Petrus.*
>   *Sufficit si cantetur eisdem notis et cantibus vt habetur in*
> *sequentia predicta.[4]*
>   *Petrus dicit post cantum.*

[PETER]. How is it now, Marye, can ye telle
Any newes which may lik vs welle?
    Blithe is youre countenaunce!
MAWDLEYN. Peter, in youre mynde be fast and stabille!
I can shew youe tydinges most comfortabille,
    Trust it of assurance!

---

[1] *this Latin line is bracketed by scribe with preceding stanza, and we number.*
[2] totum vsque ad 'Di⟨c nobis⟩' *added in red above its line; beginning with*
Respondent mulieres *the scribe uses red ink for directions and black ink for the words of the sequence*
[3] re *blotted before* surrexisse   [4] *this direction added in red at foot of page*

PETERE. Gude Marye, of hym I wold knawlege haue.
MAWDLEYN. Peter, oure master is resyn from his grave!
  He apperit vnto vs three   700
In fleshe and bone in a gloriose wise!
He hase restorid Adam and his into paradise,
  Which were in helles captiuitee!

PETER.[1] God graunte youre wordes war not in vayn!
MAWDLEN. Peter, that[2] I saye is trew and certayn,   705
  And therfor dowt no more!
SECUND MARYE. Brother, we saughe our Lord face to face!
He apperit to vs in this same place,
  And bad vs mowrne not so sore!
THRIDE MAR[Y]E. He bade vs testify and telle   710
That he was resyn in flesh and felle,
  And dy he shalle no more!

PETERE. A, Mary, gret grace to youe is lent,
To whom our Lord was so content   f. 171ʳ
  Befor other tille apere.   715
MAWDLEN. He said ye alle shuld see hym in Galilee,
And, Peter, youreselfe expresly namyd hee.
  Therfore, be of gud chere!

ANDREWE. Yit to his sepulcre lat vs go and see,
To satisfye our myndes from alle perplexitee!   720
PETER. So cownselle I we doo!
     Tunc ibunt. Precurrens, Johannes dicit.

[JOHN]. Brothere Peter, com hither and behold!
It is no fabille that Marye vs hase[3] told!
  This thinge is certen, loo!

How say ye, brother, be ye satisfied?   725
PETRUS. Brothere John, I am fully certifyed
  To gife credens hertoo.
Now shalle the suth be verefied
  Of hym that most may doo!

       [1] *added in left margin*
       [2] which *blotted out after* That
       [3] *added above in red*

O, myche ar we bound, gud Lord, to your highnes!   73⁰
  For vs wer ye born, and also circumcised;
For vs were ye tempid in the wildernese;
  Now crucyfied to deth, most shamfully dispised!
Yit alle this, gude Lorde, had vs not sufficyed,
But ye had resen fro deth, by your Godhed gloriuse!   73.
Your resurrection was most necessarye for vs!

Youre meknese suffert deth for our saluation,   f. ⊺
And now are ye resen for oure justification—
  Youre name euer blessit bee!
ANDREWE. This resurrection to alle þe warld is consolation,   74⁰
For of oure fayth it is trew consolation,¹
  Approvid by his diuinitee!

JOHANNES EUANGELISTA. Brether, joy and comfurth and
                                          inward jubilation,
  And gostly gladnese in vs alle encrease may!
We haue passid the tym of dole and desolation,   74.
  And also, I am sure, and right welle dare I saye,
  The joyfulle tresure of our hart we salle se þis daye!
Honour, joy, and glory be to hym without end,
Which after sich sorow comfurte can send!

To laude and prayse hym, lat vs be abowt!   75⁰
To loue hym, and lofe hym, and lawly hym lowt,
  With mynd and mowth devowtlye!
Ther, brethere, with joyfulle harte,
And, devowt sisters, on your parte,
  Enton sum ermonye!   75.

    *Tunc cantant omnes simul: 'Scimus Christum', vell aliam
    sequentiam aut ympnum de resurrectione. Post cantum dicit
    Joh[an]nes, finem faciens.*

[JOHANNES]. Loo! Down fro hevyn euermor grace dos springe!
  The gudnese of God is incomparabille, yee see!
Her was sorow and mourniynge,² lamentacion and wepinge;
  Now is joy and gladnese, and of comfurth plentee!

    ¹ *probably an error for* confirmation
    ² w *crossed out before* mourniynge

Joyfully depart we now owt of this place,   f. 172ʳ
Mekly abidinge the inspiration of grace,   761
 Which we belefe
Schalle com to vs this nyght!
Now, farwelle, euery wighte!
We commend yow alle¹ to his myght,   765
 Which for vs suffert grefe!

Explicit.

¹ *added in red over caret*

NOTES

THE CONVERSION OF ST. PAUL

11–12 This reads like a translation of *Lectio* ix of the matins for the feast of St. Paul (30 June): 'Quod si rebus ipsis id ita fieri videre desideras, lege. Actuum Apostolorum librum, perspicies profecto.'

23 *thretys and menacys*: The rhyme would require the singular, to which Manly emends; the MS has clear *-ys* suspensions, but the scribe may have confused final *e*'s in his exemplar. Since, however, the rhyme is close enough for the poet, and since the words reflect Caxton's phrase in *The Golden Legend*, we have not emended.

30 *pryncys . . . Caypha and Anna*: This attribution arose from a misunderstanding of 'principem sacerdotum' of Acts 9: 1, 21.

32 *Liba*: Libya, but this apparently is a confusion in which Lydda (Acts 9: 32, 35, 38) is confused with Libya (Acts 2: 10), Cyrenian Libya, named in Acts as a place from which some Jews had come who heard Peter preach at Pentecost; it had nothing to do with Saul's persecutions.

33 This line does not rhyme; the original may have ended with *tha* rather than *than*, but we are insufficiently convinced to emend. Cf. *OED* Tho *adv.* (*conj.*) 1. a.

36–8 Acts 9: 2.

42 *proteccyon*: The meaning of *do proteccyon* is unclear; it may mean 'act with diligence', but Saul seems to be asking legal sanction for his persecution, suggested also by his asking for *letters and epystolys*.

56 Acts 9: 2.

69 *And all thoo* (who) *rebell and make resystens*.

112–19 There are various possible interpretations of what seems to be an elaborate joke about the hood, but probably it means just 'among mankind'.

172 *that shall edyfy*: i.e. those that shall build up (the church).

173 *they*: Our emendation of *they* for MS *than* makes passable sense of the passage, for *they* has clear antecedents in *Non* and *that* of the preceding line; the sense of the MS is extremely tortuous.

183 Acts 9: 4.

184 Acts 9: 5.

188–9 Acts 9: 6.

190–6 Acts 9: 7.

204–10 Acts 9: 8.

211–12 These lines are an isolated couplet. Furnivall in a note says (p. 35) of ll. 212–14 that 'the rymes get mixt', but he is confused by the couplet here, for ll. 213–26 are two ordinary rhyme royal stanzas. The sense is drawn from Acts 9: 10.

213–15 Acts 9: 11.

217–18 Cf. *Lectio* of the matins for the feast of the conversion of St. Paul (25 January) taken from St. Augustine's *Sermo de Sancti*, No. 14: 'Prostravit enim Christus persecutorum, ut faceret Ecclesiae doctorem; percutiens eum, et sanans; occidens et vivificans; occisus agnus a lupis et faciens agnos de lupis' (*PL* xxxix, col 2098). The wolf-into-lamb figure was widely used, e.g. *The Golden Legend*.

221 Acts 9: 11.

223 *blynyde*: Good rhyme would require *blynde*, and perhaps we should emend, but the scribe does not apparently distinguish between the adjectival and past participial use, and spells the word the same way in l. 299.

224–6 Acts 9: 13–14.

231 *bekennyng*: The MS is *be kennyng*, and Furnivall and Manly so print. Adams suggested that the word was a noun, and cited *OED*; there Wyclif is quoted: 'þei tellen more bi þer owne bekenyng . . . þan þei don bi Goddis heestis.' Though *MED* does not recognize the word, Adams's suggestion that it is a noun meaning knowledge, and should be written as one word, seems convincing to us.

234–40 Acts 9: 15.

265 Acts 9: 9.

276–82 Acts 9: 17.

278 MS *And bad the be stedfast* . . . so violently contorts the syntax that Manly was forced to emend to *I byd the be stedfast*. The sense is that Ananias is giving to Saul a message from God (*For as I was commaundyd by hys gracyos sentens*); Manly's emendation is not very satisfactory, and Adams's suggestion of *He* for *And* makes somewhat better sense.

291 s.d. *Hic aparebit Spiritus Sanctus super eum*: Cf. John 1: 32.

293 See previous, and Acts 9: 17.

298–310 Acts 9: 18.

395–7 A curious *abb* stanza fragment, which may be the remnant of a rhyme royal stanza which had been divided between the speeches of the first and second soldiers.

490–1 Awkward syntax: *Ther rayneth thorow my myght* . . . (that)/*Ther was neuer*. . . .

502 The long sermon that follows is in illustration of Acts 9: 20.

514 Ecclus. 10: 1–15; Eccles. 10: 13.

520 Luke 14: 11, 18: 14; cf. Matt. 23: 12.

528 Rom. 11: 20.

537 Matt. 11: 29.

539 *For mekues I sufferyd a spere at my hart*—apparently the poet's own, though it is of course paralleled by lines in many lyrics.

542–3 Matt. 11: 29.

548 Cf. Ecclus. 3: 20.

554 Cf. *The Castle of Perseverance*, l. 1124.

555 A rather awkward sentence that seems to mean that sensuality leads to manslaughter and strife.

556 Eph. 5: 5.

558 1 Cor. 6: 18.

560 Matt. 12: 34.

566 *Caste viuentes, templum Dei sunt*: a commonplace, cf. *Wisdom*, ll. 543–4.

570 *Oculus est nuncius peccati*: a commonplace, cf. John 9: 41.

572 Derived from Acts 9: 21. The confusion about Jerusalem stems from a misreading: '. . . Nonne hic est, qui expugnabat in Jerusalem eos qui invocabant nomen istud: et huc ad hoc venit ut vinctos illos duceret ad principes sacerdotum?'

589 At this point St. Paul clearly goes somewhere with the servant of the priests. We must not imagine the playwright's conception of the action to have been literal; St. Paul is in Damascus and the priests are in Jerusalem, yet St. Paul addresses them and they in turn comment on his behaviour. At the same time St. Paul clearly remains in Damascus, for it is that city that has its gates shut against his escape, and later, when he escapes, Poeta tells us, he goes to Jerusalem. For the playwright, the chief antagonists are St. Paul and the priests, who are, to him, Caiphas and Anna. It would not have done to introduce new priests in Damascus, nor does he imagine that Caiphas and Anna have gone to Damascus. For the playwright the question was simply a matter of St. Paul and the priests' servant walking the twenty or thirty feet from the 'place' (Damascus—Heaven on its other side) to the Jerusalem stage. That the playwright was not terribly clear on the distinctiveness of the location is indicated by his confusion in l. 573, and would perhaps indicate that Damascus itself was not a stage, but a general playing area beyond the 'place' where Saul is blinded by God.

MARY MAGDALEN

1–19 Our division of this speech into stanzas is, of course, speculative, but the passage would seem originally to have been two double quatrains.

4 *word*—the spelling throughout of 'world'.

19 Speaker's name, *Serybyl*. It is difficult to imagine what the writer considered this character to be; it is apparently the same as that called

Syrybbe in l. 33. Perhaps the writer thought the Sibyl was a functionary of the Roman court; but the title is also likely to be a confusion of 'Sibyl' and 'scribe', for it is probably the same character who is the *skrybe* of l. 114. The writing of our scribe illustrates how the confusion could have arisen, for *serybyl* and *skrybe* are very similar. At any rate, the 'Sibyl' and the philosophers of ll. 164–85 are likely echoes of the *Ordo Prophetarum*.

20–3 It would seem that the second four (or three) lines of this stanza are missing, though, given the rambling nature of the passage, it is impossible to say that any sense is missing.

23 *wonddyn in welth from all woo* is a common sort of tag, cf. *The Castle of Perseverance*, l. 699, 'Worthy World in welthys wonde'. *Mary Magdalen* is particularly rich in these line-fillers, e.g. *sett in solas from al syyng sore*, l. 63.

49 s.d. *Her entyr Syrus, þe fader of Mary Mavdleyn*: The account of Mary's family is that of *The Golden Legend*, though her mother, Eucharia, is not named in the play:

Marye Magdalene had her surname of Magdalo a castel and was borne of a right noble lygnage and parentes which were descended of the lignage of kynges and her fader was named Sirus and her moder Eucharie. She with her broder Lazare and her syster Martha posseded þe castel of Magdalo, whiche is two mile from Nazareth, and Bethanye þe castel which is nygh to Jherusalem, and also a grete parte of Jherusalem whiche al these thynges they departed amonge them in suche wyse þat Mary had þe castell Magdalo wherof she had her name Magdalene. And Lazare had þe parte of þe cyte of Jherusalem and Martha had to her parte Bethanye. (Caxton's trans., London, Wynkyn de Worde, 1527), f. clxvii verso.

55 *be cleffys so cold*: another common tag, cf. *The Play of the Sacrament*, 'be þe clyffys cold', l. 100.

63 Cf. l. 291.

66 *full trew to me*: the MS is *to me ful trew*, so printed by all editions; this is possibly the original reading, but *trew* and *ble* (l. 68) are so imperfect a rhyme and the inversion so plausible a scribal error, that we have emended.

75–8 A difficult passage. Furnivall's and Adam's printing of *incontynens* makes no sense. A probable reading is: 'Here is a group of qualities (*cyrcumstance*) which clearly (*be demonstracyon*) are united (*knett*) in modest behaviour (*in contynens*); the only other example known to Cyrus of such a paragon was their mother.'

80–2 Cf. *The Golden Legend* on the division of property.

93–9 A rare rhyme royal.

100–13 A fourteen-line bob-and-wheel stanza.

120-8 An apparently incomplete sentence. One is tempted to emend with a verb, for no lines appear missing and the stanzaic structure seems complete, e.g. (Report) *yf þer be ony in þe cuntre* . . .

121 Though previous editors have not emended *owt* to *wythowt*, the latter seems clearly implied, i.e. 'I command them (that) as they will be wythowt wrech (harm)', etc., with the meaning that they will obey his commands if they know what is good for them. The unstated command is to inform the Emperor.

131 [Inperator] We, like Furnivall, have supplied the speaker's name because it seems clearly to be Tiberius rather than the Provost speaking. The next speaker, Nuncius (l. 136), replies directly to Tiberius rather than to the Provost.

140 *wanyng*: Probably 'decreasing' as in 'waning moon' is meant, as a version of the phrase 'in the wild waniand', which has lost the word 'moon'. See *OED*.

140-66 Although quatrains and a double quatrain may be seen in this jumbled passage, it seems impossible to reconstruct by emendation the original stanzaic pattern.

151 *carys cold*: another common tag of the East Anglian drama, cf. *The Castle of Perseverance*, l. 3052, 'For þe I clynge in carys colde'.

154 *grene perle*: *grene* may be a miscopying of 'grey'.

158 ff. The lists of places, like the rhetorical lists elsewhere in the play, are part of the ranting tradition of the religious drama, cf. the Towneley *Magnus Herodes*, and is found in folk drama as well.

163 *as I haue in provostycacyon* is a polysyllabic but concise way of saying 'whom I serve in the office of provost'.

167-92 The usual scene in the Herod play in which the 'philosophers' or advisers have the temerity to quote scripture on the coming of the Messiah, cf. the Towneley *Magnus Herodes*.

173 *That chyld*: a bit confusing; perhaps the original was *A chyld*.

175-6 Cf. Isa. 60:3.

180 *Of a myty duke* (that) *xal rese and reyn*.

185 Gen. 49: 10.

187 The variation of our scribe's spelling of 'devil' is unusually rich: *deylle, deywl, dylle, dyvyll, dywll, dylf, dylfe*, etc.

188 *fleyyng flappys*: 'flaps' could mean 'blows', but more probably here 'whips'. The term appears in *The Castle of Perseverance*, l. 225, 'Fele folke on a flokke to flappyn and to flene', and in l. 1888, 'with flappys felle and fele'. That devils in the plays were equipped with whips or other objects to swing is attested by the churchwardens' accounts book of Chelmsford (cf. W. A. Mepham, 'The Chelmsford Plays of the Sixteenth Century', *Essex Review*, lvi [July 1947], 149. The accounts book reference is Essex Record Office ERO D/P 94/5/1, f. 20ʳ.

189 (would that) *þes lordeynnys wer slaw!*

190 *word*: here literally the word, i.e. the prophecies that have just been read.

194 *eloquens wantyng*: i.e. their eloquence lacking sense or point.

205 (Lest) *some woys in my lond shall sprede.*

208 *he*: Christ.

215 An awkward sentence: 'he desires and prays that in every particular you fulfil his commandments.'

219–24 Cf. the almost identical speech in *The Killing of the Children*, ll. 97–104.

225–8 Probably the second four lines of an eight-line, tail-rhyming stanza are missing, perhaps Herod's response to the messenger.

237 A line following was probably dropped; the stanza was clearly a double quatrain *ababbcbc*, the missing line being the first *b*.

238 *inperrowpent*: an obscurity which has defied editors; possibly it is the scribe's misreading 'in peril pent'. Adams suggested (p. 229) 'in pressure pent'. Mr John Reidy, of the *MED*, has privately suggested to us that the word is a scribal error in which the tail of the first *p* is crossed instead of that of the second. The word originally would have been *inprowperent*, a participial form of the verb 'improperate', meaning to rebuke, or revile. The sentence would then have read 'Rebuking all runagate robbers, to put them to pain I spare for no pity', or, possibly, 'I will punish all insulting robbers, etc.'.

240 *qwatt*: the scribe spells this out only a handful of times, and divides his practice between *qwat* and *quat*; we expand to *qwat*.

250 *present.* this makes only awkward sense, 'Hail, (one) present, thou princes peer'. It seems probably to be a scribal error for *presedent*, which has appeared as one of the titles of Pilate, in l. 237, but we are not sufficiently certain to emend.

258 *strenth in*: most previous editors have printed this as *strenthin* (strengthen); *strenth* is, however a common infinitive form, and we have treated *in* as a preposition: *to strenth* (to strengthen) *in al þat I may* (in every way that I can). The writer uses the same verb as a present participle in l. 255, *strenthyng*.

285 *inwyttyssymus*: Furnivall glossed this as *infinitissimus*; Pollard correctly saw it as *invictissimus*.

288 *He* should perhaps be *Hym*, but the poet's grammar, as filtered through our scribe, would allow for such awkwardnesses.

304 s.d. *Her xal entyr þe Kyng of the Word*, etc. An interesting direction in that the three sets of characters are introduced at once, perhaps indicating that they all played within the same area, probably in small pavilions on either side of the Hell stage. The direction does not group the characters, but as the action makes clear, two of the sins, *Pryde* and

Covetyse, accompany the World; another three, *Sloth*, *Gloteny*, and *Lechery*, accompany the Flesh; and *Wroth* and *Invy*, the Devil. This is not the usual grouping, which gave only Covetousness to the World, and Pride, Wrath, and Envy to the Devil (cf. *Ancrene Riwle*, Part IV), but accounts differed. There is some confusion in *The Castle of Perseverance* which, in the vexillatores' speech, has Pride and Covetousness with the World, but which in the play itself associates Pride, Wrath, and Envy with the Devil (Belial).

306 *prymatt portature*: i.e. chief bearer, or supporter, who was created by God second only to heaven.

308 *I jugge me to skryptur*: I call scripture to witness.

305–33 The stanzaic form of these lines is difficult to perceive; they are dominated by *-ure* and *-yon* rhymes, and may be divided in a number of ways. Our division into two eights, a six, and a seven seems reasonable.

313–24 The relation of the Seven Deadly Sins to the metals through the planets is discussed briefly by M. W. Bloomfield, *The Seven Deadly Sins* (East Lansing, Michigan, 1952), pp. 234 ff. Our poet's assigning of the metals to planets is a traditional account. They are equated with the Seven Deadly Sins (ll. 323–4), though the syntax of the passage is not beyond dispute. Lewis suggests (p. 123) that the Sins may have been arrayed in crowns corresponding to the metals, rather like the gods in *The Assembly of Gods*. At any rate, these seven princes of hell are probably also intended to be the seven devils cast out of Mary Magdalen (f. l. 691).

328 Almost certainly a *b* rhyme of the double quatrain is missing, which would have fallen as l. 330.

334 *florychyd in my flowers*: cf. *The Castle of Perseverance*, l. 237, 'I am mankyndys fayre Flesch, florychyd in flowrys'.

338 *comfortatywys*: Furnivall prints this as *comfortat ywys*, or 'comfort, certainly', instead, as Adams pointed out, of 'comfortatives'.

339–43 Some of the spices and medicines found in this list are also in similar lists, cf. *The Play of the Sacrament*, ll. 173–88, and *The Foure PP*, ll. 604–43, and are paralleled in many folk play texts. *Dya galonga* is a compound of galingale. 'Dia' is a Greek preposition which, placed before a noun, signified a compound. *Ambra*, of course, is amber, and *margaretton* is a compound of pearls. *Dya* is perhaps intended to prefix all three nouns. *Clary* is a labiate plant (not claret) cultivated for medicinal purposes. *Pepur long* is a pepper prepared from the immature fruit spikes of *Piper officinarum* and *Piper longum*. *Granorum paradysy* or grains of paradise (or Guinea grains) are capsules of *Amomum Meleguetta* of Western Africa used as both spice and medicine. *Zenzybyr* is probably ginger, and *synamom*, cinnamon.

346 Possibly a line preceded l. 345 and ended with a word rhyming with *gle*; if so, the following stanza was an ordinary double quatrain.

347 (Than) *my fayere spowse Lechery to halse and kysse*.

358 *prynse pyrles, prykkyd in pryde* is another tag found elsewhere, cf. *The Castle of Perseverance*, l. 159: 'Precyous prinse, prekyd in pride' and l. 209, 'Pryde in my prince in perlys ipyth'; *Mundus et Infans*, l. 216, '. . . I am a prynce peryllous yprovyd' (Manly notes, p. 360, that 'peryllous' is probably 'peerless'). The peerless (or pearl-attired, or perilous) prince pricked in pride was, in any case, a popular line. Furnivall unfortunately misread *pyrles* as *pyrked*, and has been followed by all other editors but Devlin.

367 *Lycyfer*: the poet seems uncertain whether his speaker really is Satan, as he is also called, or a chief devil.

368 *wher nevyr set at Troye*: a common analogy and allusion, cf. *Sir Gawain and the Green Knight*, l. 1.

377 *Wyth wrath or wyhyllys we xal hyrre wynne*: Furnivall and Lewis printed *or wyhyllys* as two words and read the line as meaning 'By wrathful force or by wiles we shall her win'; Adams and Bevington read instead *orwyhylles* as an adverb, i.e. 'By wrath sometimes we shall her win'. The latter argument appears supported by the next line '*Or wyth sum sotyllte sett hur in synne!*' which provides *sotyllte* as the alternative for *wrath*; but the force of the alliteration compels us to Furnivall's view. There is just the possibility that *orwyhyllys* may be our poet's spelling of *orguillous*, proud. Another curiosity involves *hyrre*; there is no antecedent, nor is there any clear indication until l. 416 that they are speaking of Mary.

407 *Senswalite*: the name of the Messenger.

428 *Spiritus malyngny*: Furnivall printed *spirits*. The scribe uses the normal Latin abbreviation for *spiritus*, which we take to mean the Latin word (particularly with *malyngny*), which may be either singular or plural, but here clearly singular, cf. the Bad Angel.

431–3 Three unrhymed lines which we see no possibility of fitting into stanzas.

436–7 These lines are probably a slip of the scribe, who repeats them from ll. 426–7. We do not omit because it is just possible that the repetition is deliberate, and that *passe* and *noyse* are intended to rhyme. We think the lines an error, and that the passage (with last line corrected) was originally a simple quatrain:

> How, how, spiritus malyng—þou wottyst what I mene?
> Cum owt, I say! Heryst nat what I seye?
> BAD ANGYLL. Speke soft, speke soft, I trotte hyr to tene!
> Make no more noyse, pertly I þe prey!

438 *trotte hyr to tene*: 'hurry to torment her.'

439 s.d. f. The successful siege of the castle is the allegorical dumb-show of the spiritual action ordered by Satan (l. 432).

458 This line is obscure; possibly it means 'Take pains to dismiss such disappointments'.

459 *prynt yow in sportys*: i.e. 'express yourself in pleasurable pursuits'.

462-4 cf. *The Golden Legend*:

And whan Mary gaue herselfe to all delyces of þe body and Lazare entended all to knighthode Martha whiche was wyse gouerned nobly her brothers parte and also her systers and also her owne. . . . Than whan Magdalene habounded in rychesses and bycause delyte is felowe to rychesses and haboundaunce of thinges, and for so moche as she shone in beaute gretly and in rychesses, so moche þe more she submysed her body to delyte and therfore she lost her ryght name and was called customably a synner (f. clxvii verso).

465 *beteche*: Furnivall prints MS *betake*, suggesting *beteche* as the original. Schmidt argued that *betake* was right, and that the rhyme word *wreche* in l. 469 should instead be *wrake* ('Die Digby-Spiele', *Anglia*, 390). This, however, overlooks a third rhyme, *leche* (l. 461), which would seem decisive for *beteche*. Cf. *The Castle of Perseverance*, ll. 3457–63, with the same rhymes, 'wreche', 'leche', and 'beteche'.

470 ff. See the discussion of the rhetoric in this scene by R. H. Bowers, 'The Tavern Scene in the Middle English Digby Play of Mary Magdalene', . . . *All These to Teach* (Gainesville, Fla., 1965), pp. 15–32.

470 *wytty and wyse*: cf. *Mundus et Infans*, l. 267.

475 A curious unrhymed line which defies emendation.

476 In the obligatory fashion of these plays, nearly every new character other than Christ or Mary, boasts upon entry, and much of the boast takes the form, as in the folk plays, of a list of places, abilities, possessions, etc. Rarely is it as appropriate as the taverner's wine-list. His *wynne of Mawt* is most probably Maltese wine. *Malmesyn* was wine of Monemvasia in Greece, though it was made elsewhere in the Mediterranean. *Clary* was a mixture of wine, honey, and spices (cf. Chaucer's 'The Former Age', l. 16). *Claret* (f. F. *clair*) was the name given to light yellowish or red wine (only much later did it come to be restricted to red wine). *Gyldyr* is wine imported from the Dutch wine centre Guelder; *Gallys* is wine from Spanish Galicia; wine made at the *Groine* was from the Spanish province of Coruña; *wyan* was wine from Guienne in France; and *vernage* was a white Italian wine (cf. *The Play of the Sacrament*, l. 428).

489-90 A pair of unrhymed lines which would seem originally to have been an independent couplet.

491 *Hof, hof, hof*: a common entrance tag for a boisterous fellow, cf. Skelton's *Magnyfycence*, l. 745, where Courtly Abusyon says 'Huffa, huffa . . .'. Galavnt is, of course, 'Coryoste', and is an aspect of Pride, as the Bad Angyll tells us (l. 550).

493-4 Somewhat similar to the stabularius scene in *The Conversion of St. Paul*, ll. 85–119

500 An awkward line which seems to say that 'I disdain subjects, and vie with kings themselves'. The previous line seems to conflict with this sense, but it is the culminating line of the previous stanza, and is not really contradictory.

501–6 The sense of these lines is not always clear, but Galavnt (Coryoste) seems to be saying that he dresses in the highest fashion, his doublet and hose are always matching; he shaves possibly twice a day so that the growth of beard will not add years to his age, and that he loves an intimate encounter of hair against hair.

506 *I do it for no pryde*: seems to suggest that this is simply his way of life, that he does not deliberately attempt to be fashionable; he is just being honest. A common delusion of pride, cf. *Wisdom*, l. 555; *Nature*, ll. 772–3; *Ludus Coventriae* XXVI, prologue, ll. 111–12. See G. R. Owst, *Literature and Pulpit in Medieval England* (Cambridge, 1937), p. 314.

517 *colourrys*: probably an error for *semlynes* which would fit the alliteration; *colour* is in the preceding line.

520–6 What we have printed as a triplet and a mono-rhyming quatrain was probably originally an eight-line, tail-rhyming stanza.

534 *wyth other ten*: possibly an error for *worth other ten*, but perhaps as Adams suggests, *with other things grieved*.

535 *Felle a pese*: 'fill a pece (i.e. a wine-cup)'.

536 [*þos*]: this emendation seems logical, but we must point out that the scribe nowhere writes either *þose* or *þos*; his adjectival form is *þo*, and the pronoun is not found. At any rate, l. 536 is the line that would have been written in the right margin (like l. 539) of the scribe's exemplar, and hence could easily have lost its final word; the stanza, ll. 534–9, would appear to have been a six-line, tail-rhyming stanza.

542 A line has apparently been lost after this, for the stanza was probably an eight-line, tail-rhyming stanza, and the line rhyming with l. 546 would have been written in the right margin, as l. 546 is, and such lines are several times lost by our scribe (or a predecessor).

548 *afyabylle*: 'affable, courteous' rather than 'betrothed', cf. *Wisdom*, l. 594.

549 We are unable to offer good sense for *grogly gromys*; the words would appear to mean something malicious, or 'grudge-ful men' (grom or groom)' with *gromys* bearing something like the meaning of 'henchmen'. But the phrase will not permit this meaning; the poet may well have been employing a traditional alliterative phrase with no clear idea of its sense. His use would require the sense of 'in our grips' or 'in our snares'. It may have had its origin in the phrase 'grisley grome', as in the Chester *Antichrist*, l. 607.

550 The guise of Pryde as a gallant is paralleled by the disguise of Lucifer as a gallant in *Wisdom*, l. 324, s.d. following.

555 *tremyl and trott*: a common tag, meaning 'shake and jump for joy' (cf. *The Castle of Perseverance*, l. 457).

563 *semlyest . . . sesse*: 'the most appropriate to end all sorrows.'

572–91 The action of the following seems to be partially drawn from the interpretative tradition represented by *The Golden Legend*:

And whan our lord Jesu Chryst preched there and in other places she was enspyred with the holy ghoost, and went into þe hous of Simon Leprous where as our lord dyned. Than she durst not bycause she was a synner appere tofore the iuste and good people but remayned behynde at þe feet of our lord and wasshed his feet with the teres of her eyen and dryed them with þe heere of her heed and enoynted them with precious oyntment, for þe inhabytantes of þat regyon vsed baynes [baymes] and oyntmentes for the ouer grete brennynge and hete of the sonne. And bycause þat Symon þe pharisee thought in hymselfe that yf our lord had ben a very prophete he wolde not haue suffred a synfull woman to haue touched hym. Than our lord (f. clxviii recto) repreved hym of his presumpcyon and forgaue þe woman al her synnes.

The Golden Legend, however, does not contain the parable of the two debtors by which Jesus demonstrates Simon's presumption, nor Jesus' lecture. The story is in Luke 7: 36–50. The name, 'Simon Leprus', is the result of a confusion of this episode in Luke with episodes involving Simon the Leper in Matt. 26: 6–16 and Mark 14: 3–11.

581 *profyth*: i.e. the prophet Jesus.

613 *swete bawmys*: Mary was represented in iconography as holding a box of ointment, and this would probably have been a part of her stage 'character', together with her finery.

637–9 These lines are very awkward; even with Pollard's emendation to *my hope [is] perhenuall* the passage remains difficult. The meaning is probably: 'My perennial hope is to stand in thy grace and see thy favour.'

640 s.d. f. No indication is given in the play of the reason for Christ's lecture to Simon; however the story in Luke is quite clear (7: 39) that Simon in his heart began to doubt that Christ was a true prophet because he allowed a sinful woman to touch him; we add the stage direction because, no matter how well the audience could have been expected to know the story, the actor playing Simon would undoubtedly have made a great show of suspicion.

649–64 Luke 7: 41–3.

661 *Recte ivdicasti*: Luke 7: 43.

670 This last unrhymed line suggests strongly that, with another line now missing, it formed the last two lines of a rhyme royal.

680–5 The doctrine of equivalent penances, whereby the virtues are set against the sins, cf. E. Prosser's brief discussion in *Drama and Religion in the English Mystery Plays* (Stanford, Calif., 1961), p. 35, n.

688 *That sumtime were in desert*: a little puzzling; Bevington glosses the line as 'That deserves future grace', but it seems possible that it means literally 'that before were in the desert', i.e. the wasteland of the spirit, for the emphasis of the passage is on the contrast of before and after: you are now expert in contrition that before wandered, you have purchased light from darkness.

690–1 Luke 7: 50.

691 s.d. f. The seven devils are those 'kept closse' in Simon's house, as described in the stage direction following l. 563; the seven devils expelled from Mary Magdalen were traditionally equated with the Seven Deadly Sins, cf. *Jacob's Well*, ed. A. Brandeis, EETS, os 115 (London, 1900), p. 185.

694 *now stond I in dred*: i.e. she fears that now that she is in a state of grace, she may be unable to continue so.

697 Cf. Isa. 11: 1–2, and perhaps 9: 6–7.

699 A short unrhymed line that suggests a final phrase with rhyme word has been skipped by the copyist. Lines 699–700 seem to refer to the statement by Christ (reported in John 10: 29) which was made to Thomas; it is not entirely applicable to Mary.

705–21 As Lewis observes (p. 132), the rejoicing of the Good Angel takes the form of a tripartite hymn to the Holy Trinity of a kind which was common in the Middle Ages. The imagery, treating each person of the Trinity in succession, is much the same throughout the hymns.

710 *pur pete*: 'pure pity' seems the probable meaning of the phrase which previous editors have printed as one word; Furnivall glosses it as 'pure pity', though Lewis thinks it means 'perpetuity', and Bevington glosses it as 'care'.

711 *aparens* here would seem to mean your state of being heir apparent, the Son, or second person of the Trinity.

725 *Belfagour, Belzabub*: Balfagour is probably the Moabite divinity Bel (or Baal) Peor (Num. 25: 3–18); Belzabub is found variously throughout the New Testament (e.g. Matt. 12: 24–8, Luke 11: 15–20). Although no stage direction is given, Satan is on top of Hell stage, as is made clear in the command (l. 725) *com vp here to me!*

727 The MS calls for this speech to be spoken by *Tercius Diabolus*, and Furnivall so prints (but Adams and Lewis emend to 'Satan'), though the speech assigned to him is clearly Satan's reply. The real speech of the third devil was probably, like that of the second devil, a one-line *a* rhyme in the eight-line, tail-rhyming stanza, and was missed by the scribe. The scribe's confusion also may account for his referring to Satan as *Primus Diabolus* instead of Satan or *Rex Diabolus* (the name which he is given preceding the speech beginning l. 722). The 'bad angyll', the first of the seven to be presented, probably is Pride.

730 Cf. *The Castle of Perseverance*, l. 668.

735 *balys*: scourges, cf. *Mankind*, l. 807 (*MED baleis*).

736 *wreke*: Schmidt suggested ('Die Digby-Spiele', *Anglia*, 390), that MS *wroke* should be *wreke* for a rhyme with *breke*, l. 732, the other *b* rhyme of the tail-rhyming stanza; since the spelling and pronunciation of this past participle must have been variable, we have emended.

737–8 The *yche* and *pycche* are confusingly bracketed by the scribe with *byte*, l. 735, and *don*, l. 739. Apparently three lines are missing, the second half of a six-line, tail-rhyming stanza. L. 737's *skore awey þe yche* is usually read as 'score away the itch', but may possibly be 'score away ye each'; since the *ye* does have a superscript *e*, in this case we have printed *þe*, but the scribe's practice is extremely erratic.

743 In the stage direction following this line, the *howse* is apparently that of Simon, not the tower of hell as Bevington suggests (p. 713).

744–7 Four lines of an eight-line, tail-rhyming stanza are missing, whether dropped by the scribe, or, as is possible in view of the fairly complete nature of Satan's speech, cancelled by the author.

748 The epithets following apply to the Prophet, Christ.

757 *Revertere*: Isa. 44: 22: 'revertere ad me, quoniam redemi te.'

762 *word*: i.e. the prophecies in which the ideas of God and salvation are linked, e.g. Isa. 12: 2.

768–75 Lewis points out (p. 134) that Mary's prayer takes the form of a compline hymn, and quotes as an example

> Christe, qui lux es et dies,
> noctis tenebras detegens,
> lucifer lucem proferens,
> vitam beatam tribue.
>
> Precamur sancte domine,
> defende nos in hac nocte,
> sit nobis in te requies,
> quietam noctem tribue.

(F. J. Mone, *Hymni Latini Medii Aevi*, i, 92.)

775–845 *The Golden Legend* does not expand on the raising of Lazarus: 'And for þe loue of her he reysed Lazare whiche had ben iiij dayes deed . . . .' (f. clxviii recto). The details of the story are drawn from John 11: 1–44.

802 John 11: 4.

804–10 A seven-line stanza which was probably originally a double quatrain; the repetition of the *b* line is missing after l. 807. The sense is not impaired, for the missing line was probably a clause modifying *þe joyys of þe Fathyr in glory*.

805–6 Cf. 1 Cor. 2: 9.

849–52 Cf. John 11: 7, 9–11.

856–68 In this rather difficult passage Christ makes an analogy between his own death and resurrection and that of Lazarus. The last two lines apparently mean that 'I am pleased to tell you that Lazarus is dead; my foreknowledge of this you may accept as evidence of my divinity'.

863 *Betyn, bobbyd, skoernyd, crownyd wyth thorne*: a common pattern found in the religious lyric, cf. 'Who cannot weep come lern of me', *Religious Lyrics of the Fifteenth Century*, pp. 17–18.

865 *I*: 'Aye' (?). The meaning is unclear, and Bevington omits.

876 John 11: 32.

879–80 John 11: 24.

881 John 11: 25.

884 *Martha belevyst thow þis?*: Furnivall's emendation *þis* [*truly*] has much to recommend it, for obviously rhyme words are missing in the passage, but it would not solve the problems of what was probably one double quatrain stanza, for there is no rhyme for *Sapyens*, and none for *blysch* if Furnivall is followed.

893 John 11: 34.

897 John 11: 39.

897–8 Two unrhymed lines which are likely to have been a couplet rhyming on *wyll*.

903–10 John 11: 41–4.

915 *tondyre*: Furnivall understood the word as 'tender', for he did not place a comma after it, i.e. *þe tondyre / Flesch*; Lewis reads it as 'tinder', with the sense 'I would have rotted as does the tinder, flesh consumed from the bones'. Since clearly the sentence contains an analogy, Lewis's reading seems correct, for if the sense is 'tender flesh', the comparison is without point.

924 Luke 7: 50.

925 MS has *þe*, which Furnivall prints; but the scribe frequently does not distinguish between *ye* and *þe* (except when using ȝ), writing superscript *e* in unquestionable cases of *ye*, and since the address here is plural, we print *ye*.

938 *talys to be told*: another of the many line-filling alliterations, but one which has a kind of meaning, i.e. of whom tales can be told.

942–9 R. L. Greene sees in these lines (and ll. 58–9) a parody of the sort of alliterative love poetry represented in his *A Selection of English Carols* (Oxford, 1962), pp. 158–60; see his discussion, pp. 252–3.

945 *in my syth*: a line filler like *here present* but possibly meaning 'in my power'.

950 The rhyme word is missing; a possibility is 'lyth'.

958–62 A peculiar passage of five unrhymed lines in succession; they do not seem to have been intended to form a stanza.

992 *in sum*: the MS abbreviation could be either *in fine*, as Furnivall and Lewis print it, or *in sum* as Bevington has it; we think that the interior rhyming possible on *domme* and perhaps *gonne* suggest *in sum* as the more appropriate expansion.

992 s.d. *Here xall entyr þe thre Mariis . . . wyth sygnis of þe passyon pryntyd vpon þer brest,* cf. *Mankind,* l. 322.

995 *þe woman of Jerusalem:* Luke 23: 27–8.

998–9 Matt. 27: 30, Mark 15: 19.

1005–10 As Lewis points out (p. 140), this passage takes the form of a hymn to the cross, of which a large number existed with similar themes and imagery; a reasonable parallel is found in:

Salve crux sancta,	Quam praesignavit
Salve lignum triumphale,	lex testamenti veteris,
in qua pependit	quam praegustavit
Christus patris salutare,	rex dans exemplum ceteris.

(Mone, i, p. 137).

The passage in our play is confused, and our emendations are far from certain, but, we think, they are very plausible. The MS reading of the first four lines is:

Heylle, gloryows crosse! þou baryst þat Lord on hye
Whych be þi mygth deddyst lowly bowe doun,
Mannys sowle to bye from all thraldam,
That euyrmore in peyne shold a be . . .

That the scribe was confused is made clear by his having first written *shold a be* before *peyne.* The original form of the passage would appear to have been a quatrain and a concluding couplet.

1009–10 Cf. Ps. 143: 5.

1015 Cf. Mark 16: 3. The speaker here is clearly in her turn Mary Jacobee, and though the speaker's name is omitted, the scribe has drawn the usual red lines separating this speech from the preceding and following speeches.

1023–9 Cf. Mark 16: 6–8.

1040 *The weche . . .:* 'which should have guidance of my body.'

1046 s.d. The traditional race between Peter and John (John 20: 4) is apparently not used here, though it might have been stage business.

1047–54 Cf. John 20: 6–8.

1055–7 Cf. John 20: 11–13.

1057–60 Cf. John 20: 13.

1060 s.d. Jesus is probably dressed as a gardener (cf. *Christ's Resurrection,* l. 601, s.d.).

1061–8 Cf. John 20: 15.

1068 *cavse wyll phy:* the last word has caused some trouble (Lewis emended the phrase to *cavse I'll qwy).* But *phy* is 'fie' (a. F. *fier),* meaning 'to trust'.

1069–70 Cf. John 20: 16.

1072 *spece:* the word is probably 'speech', causing a strained rhyme.

1074–7 Cf. John 20: 17.

1078–85 The figure of Christ as the gardener of souls was widely used; Lewis (p. 143) cites a hymn:

> Aestimavit hortulanum
>   et hoc sane credidit,
> semenabat enim granum,
>   quod in mentem cecidit,
> linguam novit et non manum,
>   lingua Jhesum indidit.

(Mone, iii, p. 418)

1079 Cf. John 20: 15.

1081–3 Cf. *Wisdom*, ll. 91–2.

1086–98 A curious group of lines which we have printed as one ten-line stanza, with ll. 1086–8 rhyming imperfectly.

1090–1 *To all pepull* . . . 'to all people who follow and know this (truth) to be possible.'

1100 *innvmerabyll to expresse*: incapable of being expressed in numbers, quantity (perhaps verses also?).

1111 Matt. 28: 9.

1120 Cf. Matt. 28: 19.

1132 *ower lekeyng*: Lewis suggests (p. 144) plausibly enough that a better reading is *ȝower*, but the sense is sufficient as it stands.

1137 *hys*: the apparent antecedent is *goddys* of the preceding line, and Lewis emends *hys* to *þer*. We, however, keep the MS reading because of the emphasis of the line—*Wyth preors in aspecyall before hys presens*— which would seem to refer to the primary god, 'Mahond', the *þat lord* of l. 1139.

1149 This line has lost its rhyme; probably the original was something like 'have þi lemman com to þe?'

1151 *Sentt Coppyn*: perhaps, but not probably, St. James (Jacob, or Cobbin, diminutive), and possibly, as Lewis notes (p. 144) the Jewish Copin hanged for the murder of St. Hugh of Lincoln. The name was apparently used for an impostor, as in the Towneley Play 'The Buffeting of Christ', ll. 165–7: 'Therfor I shall the name / that euer shall rew the, / kyng copyn in our game / thus shall I indew the, for a fatur.' England and Pollard suggest that Kyng Copyn meant 'King Empty-Skein' (*The Towneley Plays*, EETS, ES 71, London, 1897, p. 233). But A. C. Cawley, *The Wakefield Pageants in the Towneley Cycle* (Manchester, 1958), p. 120, suggests more plausibly that it is derived from 'cop' meaning the crest on the head of a bird (*OED* Cop sb.² d), and thus would mean 'coxcomb'.

1154 *Wattys þakke*: a proverbial saying, apparently meaning that one is fat, or that one is deceived in love; in this instance, probably both, as cause and effect. See B. J. Whiting, *Proverbs and Proverbial Sayings* *mainly from English Writings before* 1500 (Cambridge, Mass., 1968), p. 625.

1155 *Morell*: a common name for a black horse, particularly a draught horse, and hence appropriate for the fat priest.

1160 *houkkyn*: to hook, steal; here perhaps to fornicate with (a pun on Hawkyn?).

1176-7 Probably a *c* rhyme line missing from this tail-rhyming stanza.

1185-201 This mock *'lectio'* in its dog-Latin (the genitive plural added to a series of nouns) has many parallels elsewhere, e.g. the Towneley *Processus Talentorum*, ll. 1-46 (though the Latin is more straightforward there). Various phrases emerge dimly from the passage after the clear 'Lesson of Mahound, the mightiest of the Saracens'. Line 1189 is clearly obscene, as is l. 1191; the *Snyguer snagoer* business of l. 1193 is found elsewhere (Skelton's *Magnyfycence*, l. 1155), and the notion of werewolves standing guard over the lambs emerges from l. 1194, a common figure for the careless priest. The passage would probably have been a little clearer in its punning if scribal variations had not interfered. The general theme would seem to be slippery, smooth-talking priests who fornicate with parishioners' wives, mislead their flocks for their own gain, not caring whether their souls go 'ablackberyed', as Chaucer's Pardoner observed.

1198 A roundabout way of saying hell-hounds and hedgehogs.

1200-1 Pollard (Pollard, *English Miracle Plays*, p. 196) calls our attention to passages in other plays where *Ragnell* and *Roffyn* are found as the names of demons, the Chester plays of 'Antichrist' and 'The Fall of Lucifer':

'The Fall of Lucifer', ll. 239-40: 'Ruffian, my frend fayre and free, / Loke that thou kepe mankinde from bliss!' 'Antichrist', ll. 653-6: 'Helpe, Sathanas and Lucifier! / Belzebub, bould Bachler! / Ragnell, Ragnell, thou art my deere! / Now fare I wonder evill!'

1200 *in þe wavys*: 'in the waves' is possible, but the original word was probably *wayys*, i.e. the ways or paths; it is also possible that *wavys* may represent our scribe's variant spelling of *wayys*.

1225 ff. Probably a traditional farcing of a part of a real Latin service.

1229-30 The scribe has drawn a red line between these verses, perhaps indicating that ll. 1230-48 were to be spoken by the Boy rather than by the priest.

1229 *owt of rule*: out of tune, or, at any rate, out of the 'line' of the melody.

1242-8 What was probably originally an eight-line, tail-rhyming stanza has dropped one of its *a* lines. The MS has ll. 1243-4 reversed. What probably happened was that l. 1244 was, like l. 1248, written in the right margin of our scribe's exemplar, as these tail-rhyming lines normally were, but its exact place in the order of the stanza was probably obscured by inaccurate bracketing or none at all (inaccurate bracketing of rhyming lines occurs many times in our MS).

1244 *holy*: the MS reading is *body*; we have emended to *holy* because *body* makes no good sense as a parallel epithet to *dere*; *holy* alliterates with Mahownd (stress on 'hownd') as does *dere* with *Dragon*. The words *holy* and *body* are very similar in the handwriting of the period and easily confused. *Dragon* is almost certainly 'Dagon', but it does not seem to be a scribal error.

1252 *know*: the original spelling was probably *knaw*, but the rhyme seems close enough.

1260 A confusing line; *hym* would seem to make better sense than MS *he*, but we cannot be certain what was in the writer's mind. He may have had reference to the tradition in the Gospel of Nicodemus that Joseph had been imprisoned following the burial of Christ and that subsequently Christ released him and returned him to Joseph's house.

1288 *that afore wher fon*: see Luke 24: 12 for the enmity between Pilate and Herod, but there is nothing in the play to account for it.

1304–10 We have printed this as a seven-line stanza, *ababbcb*; it would appear to be the remnant of a double quatrain, with one line missing and a rhyme botched in l. 1309 or 1310, or a rhyme royal with the *c* rhymes confused.

1314 *recummendytt*: recommends (himself).

1326 A puzzling line; it is perhaps a reference to the Last Supper, which to the Nuncius would have been *froward* (i.e. evil, or here perhaps magical), and so made them able to bear with the corruption of the body, or perhaps it means that they must have had a difficult meal (a perverse difficulty) of it.

1334 Certainly a *c* rhyme line is missing here, probably a preceding line in which the Nuncius thanked the emperor for his gift.

1335 s.d. No subsequent speech is given to this character, her disciple.

1343–4 Cf. Acts 2: 1–12.

1345–9 Cf. Acts, *passim*.

1349–65 A collection of common epithets for the Virgin, found in many hymns, sequences, and prayers. We have found no single source, however, of which this passage may be a translation. Lewis observes (p. 148) that many of the epithets are found in the Litany of Loreto, which, however, was not formalized until the mid-sixteenth century. Most were used in the religious lyric as well, e.g. 'Marye, mayde mylde and fre', *Religious Lyrics of the Fourteenth Century*, ed. C. Brown (Oxford, 2nd edn. 1952), pp. 46–9.

1355 A line rhyming with this one is missing after l. 1353; as these lines are simply parallel clauses, the scribe's error is understandable.

1366–71 This motivation for Mary's journey differs radically from the account in *The Golden Legend*, in which she, Lazarus, Martha, Martha's chamberer Marcelle, St. Maximian, and St. Cedony are cast adrift by the Jews. Instead of a tragic scene of her embarkation, we have the comedy of Mary and the shipman and his boy, ll. 1395–438.

1380–5 These six lines may be the remnant of a rhyme royal which would have had a seventh line rhyming with *fullfylle*.

1395–445. The shipman scenes are dominated by tail-rhyming eights in keeping with the custom in the drama of using a 'less elevated' stanzaic structure for the comic scenes.

1400 *I may natt for slep*: 'I am too tired and sleepy to do it.'

1411–22 An unusual twelve-line tail-rhyming stanza.

1418 *She*: i.e. the whip.

1435–8 The master is giving a running commentary on their journey which would, of course, have had a comic effect as the ship sailed around the playing area.

1455 *regnyng in equite*: Christ, that is, not the Kyng of Marcyll.

1458 Cf. Rev. 22: 13.

1471 Cf. Matt. 1: 21.

1472 There would appear to be a tail-rhyming line missing after l. 1472, but no sense seems lost and the syntax is good.

1480 At the bottom of f. 129ʳ the scribe has written *Jhesu mercy*; this is centred in the page, and would seem to have been an exclamation rather than a line of the play. The scribe has just for the second successive page written the speaker's name at the bottom without having left any space for the first line of the speech; this, we think, provoked his pious outburst.

1481–525 The sermon from Genesis with which Mary tries to convert the king is much elaborated upon *The Golden Legend*:

And whan the blyssed Mary Magdalene sawe the people assembled at this temple for to sacrefyce to the ydolles she arose vp peasybly wyth a gladde visage and discrete tongue and wel spekyng and began to preche the fayth and lawe of Jesu Chryst and withdrewe them fro the worshyp-pyng of the ydolles (f. clxviii recto).

1483 Cf. John 1: 1.

1520–5 A six-line *ababcb* which has clearly lost at least one line, but there is apparently no sense missing.

1552–3 Ps. 27: 1.

1565–671 Cf. *The Golden Legend*:

. . . it happed þat the prynce . . . and his wyfe made sacrefyce to the ydolles for to have a chylde and Mary Magdalene preched to them of Jesu Chryst and forbade them tho sacrefyces and after þat a lyttel whyle Mary Magdalene appered in a vysyon to the lady sayenge, Wherfore hast þou so moche rychesse and suffrest þe poore people of our lorde to dye for hungre and for colde? And she doubted and was aferde to shewe this

vysyon to her lorde. And than the seconde nyght she appered to her
agayn and sayd in lyke wyse and added therto menaces yf she warned
not her (f. clxviii verso) husbond for to conforte the poore and nedy and
yet she sayd no thynge therof to her husbonde. And than she appered to
her the thyrde nyghte . . . and to her husbonde also with a frownynge and
angry vysage like fyre. . . .

Following this, Mary preaches them a sermon. At another, later, time
the king strikes a bargain with Mary whereby he will convert if his wife
may have a child. The play has the king's plea and Mary's nocturnal
visitations in reverse order.

1576 *wyth ʒen sueke*: 'with that illness'? or 'caused by that deceiver'?

1582–3 Cf. Dan. 14: 30–42.

1610–17 Of the three appearances of Mary in visions as related in *The
Golden Legend*, our playwright has used only the third, in which she
appears to both the queen and the king.

1613 *chelle*: the MS word *cold* fails to rhyme in this otherwise normal
double quatrain, and the requirement is for a rhyme with *wele* and *felle*.

1641 *Itt is almesse hyr to awawns*: it is an act of charity to assist her.

1660 *pryme*: the canonical hour is probably a metaphor of a new
beginning.

1666–7 Probably originally a rhyming couplet, though possibly a part of
the preceding stanza.

1667–9 Cf. *The Golden Legend*:

And than Mary Magdalen . . . prayed unto our lorde þat he wolde vouche-
safe of his grace to gyue to them a sone And our lord herd her prayers
and the lady conceyued (f. clxviii verso).

1684 A curious single line which seems to fall between two stanzas, with
neither of which it could plausibly fit.

1680–715 Cf. *The Golden Legend*:

Than her husbonde wolde go to Saynt Peter to wyte yf it were true þat
Mary Magdalen had preched of Jesu Chryst. Than his wyfe sayd to hym,
What wyll ye do syr, wene you to go without me? Nay, whan thou shalt
departe I shal departe with the, and whan þou sholt returne agayn I shall
return. . . . To whome her husbonde answered and sayd, Dame it shall
not be so for thou art grete with chylde and the perylles of þe see ben
without nombre. . . .And this lady for no thynge wold not chaunge her
purpose. . . . And so at the last he consented. Than Mary Magdalene set
þe sygne of the crosse on theyr sholdres to the ende that the fende shold
nat . . . lette them in theyr journey. Than they charged a shyppe haboun-
dauntly . . . and lefte all theyr thynges in the kepyng of Mary Magdalene.
. . . (f. clxviii verso).

The playwright has reversed the order in which they give Mary their
goods for keeping and quarrel over whether the queen should accompany

the king. And, of course, the mariner and Grobbe are totally of the author's imagination.

1701–3 A line missing from what was clearly a quatrain.

1704 *knett in care*: cf. l. 58, *And knett swych caytyfys in knottes of care.*

1715 Mary in blessing them would have made the sign of the cross; she may have placed on their backs a cross as well, as in *The Golden Legend*, but this is not indicated in the play.

1722 *sett þerwyth*: 'set our course therto.'

1744 The rhyme word is missing.

1745–96 Cf. *The Golden Legend*:

And whan they had . . . sayled a daye and a nyght there arose a grete tempest and orage and the wynde encreased and grewe ouer hydous, in suche wyse that this lady whiche was grete and nygh the tyme of her chyldynge, began to wexe feble . . . and was delyuered of a fayre sone . . . and in her chyldynge dyed . . . (f. clxix recto). And þe maryners than sayd this deed body must be cast in to þe see or els we all shall perysshe. . . . And whan they had taken the body for to cast it into þe see the husbonde sayd abyde . . . and whyles he thus spake to them the shipmen espyed a mountayne not ferre fro þe shyppe and than they sayd þat it was best to set the shyppe toward the londe and to bury it [the body] there. . . . And they lefte þe body there lyenge and covered it with a mantell and þe fader layde his lytel sone at þe brest of þe deed moder (f. clxix verso).

1790 s.d. f. The scribe because of the similarity of this direction with the one that follows l. 1796 confused them and wrote this one after l. 1796, saw his error, crossed it out and wrote the second, but neglected to re-write the first in its proper place. He also left the error *a montem* in the second direction. The two as they appear together in the manuscript are:

> *Tunc remigant ad montem et dicit rex*
> *Tunc remigat a montem et navta dicit*

The latter stage direction is written correctly when it once more appears after l. 1914. The *mons* is, of course, the rock of Peter as well as the mountain (of which *rock* is the translation) in the play.

1792 *be hyr rede*: not only the common formula pleading for intercession, but a foreshadowing of Mary's function as the physical benefactor of wife and child.

1796, 1800 These are apparently the two 'tail' lines in the tail-rhyming part of the stanza, but something has got confused.

1796 *gyde*: The Virgin Mary, of course, serves as their guide through the stations (paralleling the king's adventures) as well as their spiritual overseer.

1798 *ʒaf*: Furnivall thought that this was a conjunction, but J. Zupitza pointed out in *The Academy*, xii (1882), 281, that it is Jaffa, the port; this was promptly accepted by Furnivall. Bevington misinterprets it as the verb 'gave' but corrects the error in his revised edition.

1811–62 Cf. *The Golden Legend*:

And whan he came to Saynt Peter the holy saynt Peter came agaynst hym and whan he sawe þe sygne of the crosse vpon his sholder he demaunded of hym what he was and wherfore he came. And he tolde to hym all by ordre. [In *The Golden Legend* Peter tells the king that his wife is only asleep and that God will let no harm come to her; the king does not receive this assurance in the play.] Than Peter ladde hym into Jherusalem and shewed to him all the places where Jesu Chryst preched and dyd myracles, and þe place where he suffered deth and where he ascended into heuen (f. clxix recto).

1832 Something seems to have gone wrong with this line and with the rhyme pattern of the stanza.

1844 *Of cummavnddement . . . sentens*: 'If you don't declare the meaning of God's commandments.'

1850–1 Probably the king and Peter have walked apart for a time to signify the passage of the two years.

1851–62 An unusual twelve-line *ababbcbcdeed* stanza, with the *d* lines written in the right margin.

1864 *callyd aftyr cold*: a formula, rather like *by clyffys cold*. Bevington suggests that the Boy has deliberately confused *hold* with *cold* for comic effect, but this seems unlikely.

1879–922 Cf. *The Golden Legend*:

. . . he tooke his shyppe for to return agayne into his countree and as he sayled by þe see they came by þe ordynaunce of God by the roche where þe body of his wyf was left and his sone. . . . And whan they came they sawe þe lytel chylde playenge with stones on the see syde . . . and whan the childe sawe them whiche neuer had seen people tofore was aferde and ran secretly to his moders brest and hydde him under the mantell. And then the fader . . . toke of þe (f. clxix recto) mantell and founde the chylde which was ryght fayre soukynge his moders brest . . . þe woman respyred and toke lyfe. . . . I lyue and am now fyrst come from þe pylgrymage fro whens þou art come. And all in lyke wyse as Saynt Peter ladde the in Jherusalem and shewed to þe al þe places where our lord sufferd deth, was buryed and ascended to heuen. . . . I was with you with Mary Magdalen which ladde . . . me and shewed to me all þe places. . . . And than þe good pylgrym receyued his wyfe and his chylde and went to shyppe and soone after they came to the port of Marselle. . . . (f. clxix verso).

1899–901 An address to the Virgin, not as Bevington supposes, to Magdalen; the queen's address to the Magdalen begins with the latter's name at l. 1902; the double address is made clearer in l. 1913.

1914 s.d. *Et tunc remigant a monte*: Bevington emends to *a[d] monte[m]*, apparently thinking the rock and the *mons* are different places.

1920 The reference to ten pounds of nobles may perhaps indicate that the original play is pre–1500, for though the term noble was used throughout the sixteenth century, it was generally used to indicate an amount of money (except for the punning use), much as 'guinea' is used today, rather than the specific coin. The rose-noble of Edward IV was the last noble minted for general use (though Henry VIII experimented with a 'George' noble, which was withdrawn almost at once).

1930 *pavpertas est donum Dei*: cf. 2 Cor. 13: 9; the phrase appears in *Piers Plowman*, B XIV, l. 275.

1931–8 A condensation of the Sermon on the Mount, cf. Matt. 5: 3–11.

1936 *chyldyren of lyfe*: perhaps originally *chyldyren of lyth* but the rhyme in this stanza went wrong (probably it was an *ababbcbc*).

1984–5 The king as a Christian is not much less blustering than he was as a pagan.

1989–2038 Cf. *The Golden Legend*:

In this meane whyle the blyssed Mary Magdalene desyrous of souerayn contemplacyon sought a ryght sharpe deserte, and toke a place whiche was ordeyned by þe aungell of God and abode there by the space of thirty yere without knowlege of any body, in which place she had no comforte of rennynge water ne solace of trees ne of herbes. And þat was bycause our Redemer dyd so shewe it openly that he had ordeyned for her refeccyon celestiall and no bodyly metes. And euery daye at euery houre canonycall she was lyfte vp in the ayre of þe aungels and herde þe gloryous songe of þe heuenly companyes . . . and than was brought agayne by the aungels vnto her propre place . . . (f. clxix verso).

2002 *be contemplatyff*: we do not attempt an emendation, but this may have originally been *be contemplacyon*; something, however, is still missing in ll. 2001–2, which makes the syntax difficult, though the general sense is clear: she will live in contemplation by the physical means of the spiritual food that God will send her from heaven.

2027 Cf. Matt. 6: 10.

2043 *namys sewynne*: cf. the Towneley *Secunda Pastorum*, l. 190. This probably just means 'all thy names', for there is little indication that the names of God were ever systematically formulated as seven in Hebrew or Christian tradition (see E. R. Curtius, 'Nomina Christi', *Mélanges Joseph de Ghellinck*, Gembloux, 1951, pp. 1029–32).

2039–44 Cf. *The Golden Legend*:

It happed that a preest which desyred to lede a solytary lyfe toke a cell . . . a twelve forlonge from þe plase of Mary Magdalene. On a daye our lorde opened the eyen of þat preest and sawe with bodyly eyen in what maner the aungelles descended in to þe place where þe blyssed Magdalene dwelled and how they lyfted her into the ayre . . . (f. clxix verso).

The playwright does not use the miraculous weakness which subsequently overcomes the priest when he attempts to approach Mary's cell.

2050 *save*: *sawe*.

2053–64 Cf. *The Golden Legend*:
I am she that by the space of thirty yere haue ben here without wyttynge of ony persone . . . (f. clxx recto).

2070 Cf. *The Golden Legend*:
. . . it is shewed to me by our Lorde þat I shall departe out of this worlde (f. clxx recto).

2081 A short line, missing the rhyme with l. 2083.

2083 Cf. *Wisdom*, l. 265.

2092 An echo of the response of Lechery to the devil's summons in l. 427.

2101–18 The priest performs here the function of several priests and a bishop (Maximian) in *The Golden Legend*.

2109–18 A curious stanza, apparently *ababbbcbcb*.

2115, 2117–19 Cf. Ps. 31: 5.

2122 s.d. f. *Gavdent in celis*: As *Primus* and *Secundus Angelus* together would not make much of a heavenly host, this stage direction would seem to presume at least a small choir.

2131–8 In spite of the fact that the serious scenes of the play are almost exclusively in quatrains or double quatrains, whereas the bob-and-wheel and tail-rhyming stanzas are reserved for the comic scenes, the playwright ends his drama with the speaker's fervent prayer for salvation and for the approval of the audience cast in a nine-line bob-and-wheel. Perhaps he simply wanted to break the steady pattern of quatrains and double quatrains to have a more distinctive final speech. We are in some doubt whether this speech was in fact spoken by the priest; it seems more likely to have been the speech of a 'Poeta', or some such character, but for lack of evidence we refrain from tampering with the MS.

2139 *explycit oreginale de Sancta Maria Magdalena*: an indication that the scribe is working from an 'official' copy, the play-book, not that the present MS is the 'official' copy.

2139 *Te Deum lavdamus*: the traditional hymn sung at the end of so many mystery plays, an echo perhaps of the distant origin of the religious drama in the matins observances of monasteries. As Lewis suggests (p. 163), its theme of conclusion and beginning made an ideal 'final curtain'.

2140–3 These lines, though we have numbered them, form no part of the play, but are the scribe's addtess to his 'redars', i.e. the people who have caused him to write the copy.

THE KILLING OF THE CHILDREN

Candelmes Day and the Kyllyng of þe Children of Israelle: Furnivall states (p. 1) that this is in a later hand, but it appears to us to be in the hand of the main scribe of the play.

the vij booke: comparison of this brief phrase with John Stow's writing lends support to Furnivall's statement that the inscription is by Stow, but the example is so short that we prefer not to assert this as a fact. For the inconsistency of the use of the word 'booke' in the early sixteenth century, see T. B. Blatt, *The Plays of John Bale* (Copenhagen, 1968), p. 103, n. 102.

1–2 *This solenne fest . . . Of blissed Seynt Anne*: 26 July.

1–18 These lines of Poeta must be taken as a series of declarations, for the whole passage has no proper verbs, and the pattern is too consistent to admit emendation.

4 *David and Salomon.* Cf. Matt. 1: 1–20; Luke 1: 27.

7 *old and drye*: the usual characterization of Joseph in the plays.

11–13 Manna and the 'sweet rose of Jericho' are traditional epithets for the Virgin.

14 *Gold Ebryson*: pure gold, i.e. *aurum obryzum*, cf. 2 Chron. 3: 5: *Laminas auri obrizi affixit*; Job 28: 15: *Non dabitur aurum obrizum.*

16 Cf. Luke 1: 30, 42.

21–4 The usual modest disclaimer, cf. the conclusions of *The Conversion of St.Paul* and *Mary Magdalen.*

29–48 Poeta has the events of the play in reverse order; see our discussion in the introduction.

35 Matt. 2: 11.

43 *of too yeeres age*: cf. Matt. 2: 16.

45 *in his furious wynde*: cf. prologue, l. 217, to *Ludus Coventriae.*

46 This is the closest the play comes to stating the reason for the slaughter of the innocents; the specific prophecy which causes the slaughter is nowhere referred to.

53 It is worth noting that the minstrels and dancers, though a part of the performance, are distinct from the players, and are not mentioned in the cast of the plays on f. 157^v.

58 *Royally I reigne in welthe without woo*: the usual alliterative rant, cf. *Mary Magdalen*, l. 23.

67 *sett . . . in solas from alle sadnesse*: a common alliterative phrase, cf. l. 373, *sett in sadnes*, and *Mary Magdalen*, l. 63.

70 *grudge ageyns my goddes*: cf. *Mary Magdalen*, l. 38: '. . . or wyth my goldyn goddys grocth or grone.'

80–1 See the discussion of these cancelled rhyme royal stanzas of f. 147^v in our introduction.

97–104 Cf. the almost identical passage in *Mary Magdalen*, ll. 217–24, and our discussions in the introduction.

114 *reign with equyte*: a common phrase, cf. *Mary Magdalen*, l. 889, 'reynyng in equite' (there used of Christ). The technical sense of law in reason and nature is, of course, ironic in our context, if, indeed, the playwright had any idea of its meaning.

127 *be Mahounde*: as in the mystery plays, Herod and his court were considered pagans, worshippers of the god 'Mahound'.

244 *partie*: i.e. the people.

245 *prophetes*: i.e. the Old Testament prophets, particularly Isa. 7: 14.

262 . . . *that Lord* [that] *so for vs doth provide*.

276 s.d. *et exeant*: as the subjunctive mood would indicate, Mary and Joseph are to begin moving out of the place while Joseph speaks the last four lines of his speech.

280 s.d. *and þe goddes shalle falle*: a similar stage effect, apparently, to that in *Mary Magdalen*, l. 1561, s.d., following, but no indication is given here as to how it is achieved.

322–8 The scribe has taken considerable liberty with this passage, creating an *ababbaa* rhyme royal where a normal *ababbcc* had existed. The stanza originally read:

TERCIA MULIER Gossippis, a shameful deth I aske vpon Kyng Herowde
That thus rigorously our children hath slayn.
QUARTA MULIER I pray God bryng hym and all his blood
And in helle pytte to dwelle euer in peyn!
WATKYN What, ye harlottes, I haue aspied certeyn
That ye be traytours to my lord the kyng,
And therfor I am sure ye shalle haue an ille endyng!

The phrase *Kyng Herowd* has been changed by the principal scribe to *Herowde our kyng*, and *and alle his blood* altered to *to an ille endyng*, thus making the *a* rhymes duplicates.

365–88 The death of Herod is not explained in the play, except as a result of an excess of rage and the fulfilment of the wives' prayers (ll. 322–5); the playwright used neither the motive of remorse for Herod's own children being accidentally slain (except perhaps in the oblique reference to *frendes and foon*, l. 367), nor that of the hideous disease that overtakes Herod, both of which figure largely in *The Golden Legend*'s account.

366 *wrokyng*: probably *working*, but perhaps confused with *wrake*, l. 370.

373 *sett in sadnes*: the original reading was *sett out of sadnes*, altered by a later hand to *sett in of sadnes*; the corrector apparently forgot to eliminate *of*, but we think that his instinct was correct, for *sett in sadness* (or *sett in solas*) is the common phrase, and *sett out of sadnes* makes no clear sense. Furnivall, as we note, prints *sett out of sadnes*.

388 f. *Vacat ab hinc* ('from here it is omitted') is written in another hand. This would seem to indicate that on at least one occasion the second part of the play was omitted in performance.

397–404 Cf. Luke 2: 25.

401 Cf. Isa. 7: 14.

407–8 Cf. Luke 2: 26.

415–16 *the lawe*: cf. Lev. 12: 1–8; Luke 2: 24.

417 *voide of presumpcion*: i.e. without pride, but specifically without pretence of paternity.

436 s.d. f. *nunc dimittis*: Luke 2: 28–32: Nunc dimittis seruum tuum, Domine, secundum verbum tuum in pace, Luke 2: 29. Used after the gradual of the mass for the Feast of the Purification of the Blessed Virgin, 2 February.

449–50 i.e. the Harrowing of Hell.

461 s.d. f. *Anna Prophetissa* is found in Luke 2: 36–8, but the virgins derive from a medieval tradition illustrated by the account in *The Golden Legend* of a vision which a good lady had in a dream, in which the virgins appeared bearing candles for a mass attended by the Virgin herself:

And her semed that she was in a chirche and sawe come into the chirche a grete company of virgynes. . . . And whan they were al set . . . entred one that bare a burthen of candelles and to eche of them by ordre he gaue one. . . . And two yonge aungels began the Introyte of þe masse and all þe company of the virgyns songe the masse. . . . (Caxton's trans., London, 1527, f. lxxxvii verso.)

486–92 The *wax, week, lyght* are explained in *The Golden Legend* in this way:

This feest [the feast of the Purification] is called candelmas and is made in remembraunce of þe offrynge þat Our Lady offred in þe temple. . . . And euerychon beryth this day a candell of waxe brennyng whiche representeth our Lord Jesu Chryst, lyke as the candell brennynge hath thre thynges in it . . . the waxe, the weyke and the fyre. . . . Ryght so be thre thynges in Jesu Chryst . . .the body, the soule, and þe godhede. . . . For the waxe signyfyeth þe body of our Lorde . . . and the fyre of þe candell signyfyeth þe diuynite of Jesu Chryst whiche enlumyneth all creatures (f. lxxxviii recto).

The wax-wick figure is, of course, found elsewhere, cf. *Piers Plowman*, B Text, ed. G. Kane and E. T. Donaldson (London, 1975), Passus xvii, ll. 206–51.

540 *sharp sward of sorowe*: Luke 2: 35.

The namys of the pleyers: see the discussion in the introduction.
Jhon Parfre ded wryte thys booke: see the discussion in the introduction.

WISDOM

These few notes are merely supplementary to the annotation in Eccles's edition of the Macro text. For all commentary on the sources and parallels of particular passages the reader is referred to that edition.

206 *Creature*: Also the Macro spelling. Eccles emends to *Creator*, but this does not reflect the spelling habits of either of the scribes; they did not distinguish between the spelling of the two words, and *creature* can clearly be either *creature* or *creator*. This is true generally of East Anglian writers (cf. *Mary Magdalen*, l. 1578).

379 *colours*: i.e. pretences, but probably colours of rhetoric as well.

500 Cf. *Mundus et Infans*, l. 522: 'What, hey now, care awaye!'

511 *and it happe la plu joly*: see our discussion of *happe* versus *hamp* or *hanip* in the introduction. The phrase means that 'we should be fresh and ready should opportunity for pleasure come our way'.

517–18 An isolated couplet, which apparently was never part of a stanza.

551–2 Both Digby and Macro have only a couplet instead of the usual triplet here of the tail-rhyming stanza; it is possible that a line is missing, but no sense appears lost.

555 Cf. *Mary Magdalen*, l. 506, 'I do it for no pryde'.

685 f. *va* (for *vacat*, 'it is omitted'). The Digby text, like the Macro, was apparently an acting text of which parts were on occasion omitted in performance. The omitted section here, as we know from the Macro text, ended at l. 784; the deletion was therefore of the dumb show of Maintenance, the jurors, and the whores.

722 *thei rechases*: the original was probably *ther rechase is*: the final *r* of *ther* was easily confused with *i*, for almost invariably both scribes, and probably the scribe of their exemplar, used the secretary *r* as a final letter. The MS reading is not impossible, but would seem improbable.

731 *endyrecte*: Eccles may be correct in his emendation of *endyrecte* in Macro to *entyrecte*, which he takes as the same word as *Entret* in l. 796 of the Macro version, and which would mean salve or plaster; the word in this context would then mean an evil of bribery (i.e. salving or greasing the palm).

CHRIST'S BURIAL

1–15 These opening lines are those ... *which ⟨shuld⟩ not be said if it be plaied* ... It is interesting to note that the prologue is in the 'bob-and-wheel' stanza (with a loose couplet), which is also the stanza of the concluding lines of *CR*. Only one other stanza in the plays, ll. 482–92 of *CR*, has this form.

36–9 John 11: 1–44.

40–7 John 9: 1–12.

53 Luke 23: 21.

70–84 These fifteen lines are really one stanza, being bound by both *a* and *b* rhymes.

80 Our writer forgets in his revision to cross out *said Joseph*, as he forgets a few other narrative elements.

93–6 The conjunction of the *dismayede–arayed–displayed* rhymes suggest an echo of the rhymes of a stanza, No. 47, of the poem 'Who can not

wepe, come lern at me' published as 'De arte lacrimandi' by R. M.
Garrett in Anglia, xxxii (1909), 269–94. That poem, however, generally
does not, except for the refrain, resemble any of the planctūs in CB, and
the rhymes are, of course, almost inevitable.

97 John 12: 2–3; Luke 7: 36–9.

194–6 John 19: 27

210 'I am thrustye': John 19: 28—'Sitio'.

245–7 'Retorn to mee': This might be suggested by the famous 'revertere'
passage of the S. of S. 6: 12, but it is much more probable that the reference is to Isa. 44: 22: 'Revertere ad me, quoniam redemi te.' A carol
attributed to Ryman, 'Reuert, reuert, reuert, reuert,/O synfull man geve
me thyn hert', printed by R. L. Greene, Early English Carols, No. 269,
p. 199, would seem to be a likely parallel.

261–3 The three lines of the narrative excised after l. 263 were the last
three lines of a normal aabccb stanza.

271–6 This figure turns, of course, on the idea of Christ as Agnus Dei.
The sheepskin used for manuscripts was often damaged in preparation,
and red was a common ink colour, and so the figure of a sheepskin
stretched and torn, marked with bloody letters, was a natural monkish
conceit for the body of Christ, the Lamb of God, who is the Charter of
Salvation. Rolle used a similar figure in Meditations on the Passion, ed.
H. E. Allen in English Writings of Richard Rolle (Oxford, 1931), p. 36.
We have already observed the same figure elsewhere in MS e Museo 160.
See the discussion of the figure in Woolf, The English Religious Lyric,
pp. 212–13, and in Gray, Themes and Images, pp. 129–30.

328 made me of noghte, i.e. (that) made me of noghte.

355–8 Matt. 27: 51–2. This speech of description and justification is
usually assigned to the Virgin, as in the Bernardine Quis dabit: 'Tunc
terra tremuit, et sol sua lumina clausit. Merebantque poli, merebant
sidera cuncta. . . . Petrae durissimae scissae sunt. . . . Cogitare nunc libet
quantus dolor tunc fuit matri, cum sic dolebant, quae insensibilia erant.'
Opera Omnia, ii (Venice, 1516), ff. 303ᵛ–304ʳ.

362–3 The figure of the wounds as wells of mercy is widespread, e.g. the
short poem, No. 100, in C. Brown, ed., Religious Lyrics of the Fifteenth
Century, p. 49.

379–84 John 19: 38–9

391–7 The cancelled four lines following l. 391 (see Textual Notes) were
lines 2–5 of a curious aababaa stanza; the excision left three a rhymes,
which then fitted with a following group of four, ll. 394–7, in a new
aaabccb group.

434 John 3: 13.

456–8 Cf. Meditationes, 'Nolite amici mei, tam cito filium meum occipere,
vel me cum ipso sepelire', Sancti Bonaventurae Opera, xii (Venice, 1756),

p. 500, and the *Quis dabit*, 'Nolite quaeso eum tam cito tradere sepulture, sed ipsum reddite mihi . . . ', f. 305^r.

467–71 A curious five-line stanza, *aabbb*, with no short lines, but bracketed as a stanza by the writer.

472 The antecedent of the relative *that*, i.e. 'the tears' is understood.

487–8 Cf. *Quis dabit*: 'Dicat qui potest, cogitet quantum potest, quae doloris immensitas tunc materna cruciabat', f. 304^v.

500 Luke 2: 34.

500–3 Cf. *Quis dabit*: 'O verum eloquium iusti Simeonis, quem promisit gladium sentiebat doloris', f. 304^r.

515–19 Cf. ll. 1006–15, *Meditations on the Supper of Our Lord and the Hours of the Passion*, ed. J. M. Cowper, EETS, os 60 (London, 1875), p. 32.

520–4 Cf. *Quis dabit*: 'Cogitabat mirabilia facta vnici sui, et durissima opprobria, et tormenta, que viderat oculis suis, et auribus audierat, reuoluebat in mente, quis videlicet, qualis, et quantus fuerat, quem ipsa virgo concepit. . . .', f. 304^v.

592–7 Cf. *Quis dabit*: 'Reddite, vel saltem nunc maestissimae matri extinctum filium', f. 304^r.

612–17 Cf. *Meditations on the Supper of Our Lord*, ll. 809–18.

613–14 Cf. *Quis dabit*: 'In gremio meo nunc te mortuum teneo', f. 304^v.

618–21 Cf. *Quis dabit*: 'Quis dabit capiti meo aquam, et oculis meis fontem lacrymarum, vt possim flere per diem, et noctem. . . .', f. 302^v. This adaptation from Jer. 9: 1 is also used in the pseudo-Anselm *Dialogus* (*PL* clix, col. 275). From this point in the play until near the end the basic *rime couée* stanza is replaced by the eights and sevens of the three *planctūs*.

624–35 Cf. *Quis dabit*: 'Ipsa eum portauit regem gloriae, illum omni petenti datura. Ipsa genuit eum, lactauit eum, die octaua circumcidit, et quadragesima praesentauit in templo. . . . Fugiens ab Herode, ipsum portauit in Aegyptum, lactans eum, et nutriens, curam illius habens, sequens cum fere quocumque pergebat', f. 302^v.

637 The refrain *Who þat cann not wepe, at me may lere* perhaps echoes ll. 24440–1 of the *Cursor Mundi* (Cotton MS), 'Qua ne wist forwit quat weping were / Do list to me and þai mai here', as suggested by G. C. Taylor, 'The English "Planctus Mariae"', *MP*, iv (1907), 29. The *Cursor* passage is found in Part v, ed. R. Morris, EETS, 68 (London, 1878), p. 1398. For references to other poems with similar passages and refrains, see our introduction and notes.

640–1 Cf. *Quis dabit*: 'Stabat iuxta crucem Maria . . . et in oscula eius ruens ea parte, qua vnda preciossimi sanguinis defluebat', f. 304^r.

642–7 Cf. *Quis dabit*: 'De vultu illius pulchritudo effluxerat omnis, et qui erat prae filiis hominum speciosus forma (Ps. 45 : 2), videbatur omnium indecorus. Videbam quod complebatur illud propheticum in eo: Vidimus eum, et non erat ei species, neque decor' (Isa. 53: 2), f. 303ʳ.

662–7 Cf. *Quis dabit*: 'Aspiciebat illud reuerendissimum caput coronae spineae diris aculeis perforatum, manus illas, et pedes sacros clauis ferreis crudelissime perforatos, latusque suffossum lancea, cum ceteris membris laceratis. . . .', f. 304ʳ.

694–715 G. C. Taylor, 'The English "Planctus Mariae"', pp. 27–9, suggests that the *Cursor Mundi* provides a parallel for the incremental repetition in these lines. The parallels offered by Taylor are interesting, but they are scattered over a wide area instead of being concentrated as here, and do not bind line to line as in *CB*.

722 Cf. *Quis dabit*: 'Quo vadam charissime? Vbi me vertam dulcissime? Quis mihi de cetero consilium . . .?', f. 303ᵛ.

726–31 Cf. *Quis dabit*: 'O fili mi dulcissime, quid fecisti? Quare crudelissimi Iudaei te crucifixerunt? Quae causa mortis tuae? Commisistine scelus, vt tali morte damnareris? Non, fili, non, fili, sed sic tuos redimere dignatus es, vt posteris exempla relinquas', ff. 304ʳ–304ᵛ.

739 A subject appears to be missing, but the writer probably felt the *ȝe* of l. 736 to be carried forward.

740–4 Cf. *Quis dabit*: 'Vae mihi fili mi, in quantum dolorem, et tristitiam versum est illud tam magnificum gaudium? Succurre mihi fili mi, et spiritum sanctum mihi interim infunde, quia iam gaudii illius, quod in obumbratione, et angelica salutatione concepi, fere prae dolore immemor deficio', f. 304ᵛ.

745–6 ff. The obvious *lappe–pape–hape–shape* rhymes of this *planctus* are found frequently, e.g.:

> For he is ded þat soke my pappe—
> His corsis graue I come nowe fro,
> þat sumtym lay quyke on my lappe

of 'Filius Regis Mortuus Est' in Lambeth MS 853, printed by Furnivall in *Political, Religious, and Love Poems*, EETS, os 15 (London, 1866), p. 206. The better-known MS Douce 78 version of the poem, printed in *Religious Lyrics of the Fifteenth Century*, No. 6, pp. 8–13, lacks the stanza containing these lines. Another poem (from Porkington MS 10) published in Brown's collection, p. 2, has similar rhymes:

> Alas dyre son, sowerov now ys my happe;
> To see my chyld þat sovkys my pappe
> So rwthfully takyn ovt of my lape.

749 Cf. *Quis dabit*: 'Vae mihi, vae mihi! Quis dabit mihi vt ego moriar pro te fili mi (2 Kgs. 18: 33)? O misera quid faciam? Moritur filius meus. Cur scelum non moritur haec maestissima mater eius? Mi fili, mi fili, amor vnice fili, dulcissime, noli me derelinquere post te, trahe me ad teipsum, vt et ego moriar tecum . . .', f. 303ʳ. The pseudo-Anselm *Dialogus*, col. 286, also makes use of the plea of David, 'Quis mihi det ut ego moriar pro te?'

751 Cf. note to 722.

754–60 Cf. *Quis dabit*: 'O mors misera, noli mihi parcere, tu mihi sola prae cunctis places, exaggera vires, trucida matrem, matrem cum filio perime simul . . .', f. 303^r.

761–3 Cf. *Quis dabit*: 'O Iudaei impii, O Iudaei miseri, nolite mihi parcere. . . . Cur ego viuit mater post filium in dolore? Tollite, suspendite matrem cum pignore. Non parcitis proli, non parcatis et mihi!', f. 303^v.

764–5 Cf. *Quis dabit*: '. . . et nil [mihi] certe amarius, quam viuere post tuam mortem . . .', f. 303^v.

767–72 Cf. *Quis dabit*: 'O fili charissime, O benignissime nate, misere matri tuae, et suscipe preces eius. Desine nunc mihi esse durus, qui cunctis semper fuisti benignus. Suscipe matrem tuam in cruce, vt viuam tecum post mortem semper . . .', f. 303^v.

767–80 After the intervening six-line stanza, ll. 761–6, another rhyme royal *planctus* begins, with the refrain 'Remembere, myn awn son, þat ȝe sowket my breste'. A somewhat similar refrain is found in No. 10, *Religious Lyrics of the Fifteenth Century*, pp. 18–12.

802–17 Cf. *Quis dabit*: 'Miseremini mei, miseremini mei, saltem vos amici mei. Illum adhuc paululum mihi relinquite, vt faciem ipsius sublato velamine valeam contemplari, et prae amore ipsius aliquantulum videndo consolari. Nolite quaeso eum tam cito tradere sepulture, sed ipsum reddite mihi miserae matri suae, vt illum mecum habeam saltem vel defunctum aut si illum in sepulchro reconditis, ibidem me miseram matrem cum ipso sepelite, quia male post ipsum superero. . . .', f. 305^r.

829 This is not rhymed; l. 830 is bracketed to the last rhyme of the preceding stanza, rhyming *companye* with *bitterlye*.

CHRIST'S RESURRECTION

92 A relative is understood, i.e. *To distroy hym* (that) *made alle thing of noght*.

123–7 The five-line stanza, *aabab*, here and elsewhere, is similar to the stanza scattered in the Towneley 'Creation' and 'The Killing of Abel'.

131–3 John 2: 1–10.

134–9 As always, this part of a resurrection play has as its seed the *Quem quaeritis* trope from which medieval liturgical drama apparently began. There are many variations of the words, put together from the Gospels, Luke 21: 5–6; Mark 16: 6–7; Matt. 28: 5–7. K. Young, *The Drama of the Medieval Church*, i (Oxford, 1933), *passim*, has an extremely full discussion of these developments.

140 John 20: 13. The '*Quid ploras?*' is found, of course, in the *De Maria Magdalena*, p. 292.

150–64 Much of this passage is suggested by the '*Victime Paschali*' itself, as well as by the famous Easter hymn '*Aurora lucis rutilat*', which is printed by F. J. E. Raby, No. 38, in *The Oxford Book of Medieval Latin Verse* (1959).

203–18 Mary's self-accusation of sloth and negligence perhaps echoes Christ's 'O stulti et tardi corde' to the Wayfarers (Luke 24: 25), and seems here to be derived from the passage 'Quare monumentum tunc perseveranter non custodiui' of the *De Maria Magdalena*, p. 293.

209–13 Another short stanza of five, confused by the writer's dropping out two lines and adding them at the bottom of the page. He brackets the rhymes as if they were a normal six, obscuring the rhyme pattern of the following stanza.

216 '*Than I hade seyn my Lorde*'—i.e. 'should have seen'.

232–49 Luke 7: 36–51.

266 The directions following, *Petrus intrat, flens amare*, are derived from Matt. 25: 75 and Luke 22: 62, and were given further emphasis in Peter Comestor's *Historia Scholastica* (*PL*, cxcviii, col. 1624).

267 ff. Another rhyme royal is introduced, and alternates with a new variety of the *aabccb* six, which has lines generally of a length, with three stresses. The rhyme royal stanzas are basically five-stress, but lines may contain as many as fifteen syllables and seven stresses.

293–5 Matt. 4: 18–20.

308–12 Matt. 17: 1–4; Mark 9: 2.

320 John 13: 5.

353–4 A somewhat garbled version of Ps. 41: 9: 'Etenim homo pacis meae, in quo speravi, qui edebat panes meos magnificavit super me supplantationem.'

362–3 Matt. 26: 34; Mark 14: 30; Luke 22: 34; John 12: 38.

390–2 John 19: 26–7.

431–5 Matt. 26: 31: 'Tunc dicit illis Iesus: "Omnes vos scandalum patiemini in me in ista nocte. Scriptum est enim: Percutiam pastorem, et dispergentur oves gregis" '.

443 Luke 22: 32.

445–53 Matt. 18: 21–2.

452–3 An added couplet to the rhyme royal stanza.

458 Matt. 16: 19: 'Et quodcumque ligaveris super terram, erit ligatum et in coelis; et quodcumque solveris super terram, erit solutum et in coelis.'

471 *lure*. This is a very condensed figure, if, indeed, the writer meant much by it. It would seem to suggest the sort of analogy that one finds in such a poem as the Vernon MS 'Mercy Passes All Things', No. 95 in Brown's *Religious Lyrics of the Fourteenth Century*, 2nd edn., G. V. Smithers (Oxford, 1952), pp. 125–9. Here a merlin catches a bird and takes it into a tree, but later releases it in an act of mercy. The poet sees an analogy between the hawk and God. It might, then, be that behind the *lure* figure is the idea of Christ as both hawk and bird, the releaser and the released.

482–92 A most unusual stanza of eleven lines, rhyming *aaaaaaabaab*; perhaps it was inspired by certain litany patterns.

565–9 A curious *aabba* stanza; the rhyme of the last *a* is very imperfect, and perhaps the poet meant to write 'synneres', but in any case he meant the rhyme for the scribe brackets the *a* lines.

566 S. of S. 2: 14: '. . . ostende mihi faciem tuam, sonet vox tua in auribus meis. . . .'

579 S. of S. 3: 1–2: 'In lectulo meo per noctes quaesivi quem diligit anima mea: quaesivi illum, et non inveni.' The application of these phrases to the laments may be seen in the *De Maria Magdalena*: 'Quaesivi eum in monumento et non inveni . . . inveniam illum quem diligit anima mea', p. 293, and in the *Quis dabit*: 'Quaesiui, et non inueni illum', f. 305ʳ.

594 S. of S. 5:8: 'Adjuro vos, filiae Jerusalem si inveneritis dilectum meum, ut nuncietis ei quia amore langueo.' The Bernardine *Quis dabit* assigns this language of the wound of love to the Virgin, and is a bit closer to the Song's phrasing than is that of the pseudo-Origen *De Maria Magdalena*, e.g.: 'Filiae Ierusalem, nunciate dilecto, quia amore langueo', *Quis dabit*, f. 305ʳ, and 'Quaeso nunciate illi quia amore langueo', *De Maria Magdalena*, p. 293. In addition to the Virgin and the Magdalen, Christ is also assigned this language in the literature of meditation, e.g. the lyric 'In the vaile of restles mynde' of MS Camb. Univ. Lib. Hh. 4. 12, printed by Furnivall in *Political, Religious, and Love Poems*, pp. 150–9.

597–601 The five-line stanza has the fourth line unrhymed, *aabcb*. Very probably a *c* rhyme line is missing, but as two or three other lines are unrhymed elsewhere, we think it best not to assume a missing line and number a ghost.

601 The directions following this line (*Jhesus intrat, in specie hortulani*) derive from John 20: 15. This, and the cancelled line of f. 141ʳ, *The Maries in that stacione*, are the only references to physical 'stage' details that the two plays contain.

602 John 20: 15.

613–22 Another curious stanza, a ten-liner based on the *rime couée*, *aabccbbddb*. The writer has bracketed the *Noli me tangere* with the *now* and *thowe* rhymes of the following stanza, and the rhyme of l. 622 with the *b* rhymes of the preceding part of the stanza. We assume, however, that he meant *tangere* to rhyme with *praye*, *away*, and *saye*. The 'directions' which intervene between ll. 618 and 619 are placed in the middle of the page and not bracketed as being in the stanzaic pattern; ll. 618 and 622 are bracketed around the directions. It is very probable, however, that, either in the writer's source or in his previous intention, the *Jhesus dicit*:

'*Maria*' / *Mawdleyn awnsers: 'Raboni*!' lines of the directions were verses perhaps 'Marie', rhyming with 'Raboni'), being the first two *a* rhymes of a *rime couée* stanza. We would then have had two six-line normal *rime couée* stanzas instead of the ten-line curiosity broken by directions. But we have followed the clear intentions of the writer's spacing and bracketing.

619 John 20: 17.

629–30 S. of S. 6: 12. This passage seems to echo the *De Maria Magdalena*'s 'Reuertere dilecte mi, reuertere votorum meorum', p. 293, and the 'Reuertere, ergo dilecte mi . . .' of the *Meditationes*, p. 509. At least two late medieval English lyrics use this theme in the Song of Songs tradition, the carols 'Reuertere, reuertere / The quen of blysse and of beaute' (*Early English Carols*, No. 140, p. 96), and 'Com home agayne, com home agayne, / Min owine swet hart, com home agayne' (*Early English Carols*, No. 270, pp. 192–3). There is also a *chanson d'aventure* using the 'Reuertere', printed by Furnivall in *Hymns to the Virgin and Christ*, EETS, os 24 (London, 1867), pp. 91–4.

638 Though this Latin line does not rhyme, it is bracketed in the MS with ll. 639–40, and we have printed it as a verse.

665 The Latin directions following this line are derived from Matt. 28: 9.

666 '*Auete*': Matt. 28: 9.

691 The entire *Victime Paschali* sequence according to the Use of York, divided into the traditional parts described by Young, *Drama of the Medieval Church*, i, pp. 273–88, is as follows:

THREE MARYS:	Victime Paschali laudes
	Immolant Christiani.
	Agnus redemit oues:
	Christus innocens Patri
	Reconciliauit peccatores.
	Mors et vita duello
	Conflixere mirando
	Dux vite mortuus
	Regnat viuus.
APOSTLES:	Dic nobis, Maria,
	Quid vidisti in via?
THREE MARYS:	Sepulchrum Christi viuentis
	Et gloriam vidi resurgentis
	Angelicos testes
	Sudarium et vestes.
	Surrexit Christus, spes nostra,
	Precedet vos in Galileam.
APOSTLES:	Credendum est magis soli
	Marie veraci
	Quam iudeorum
	Turbe fallaci.

THREE MARYS: Scimus Christum
                        Surrexisse a mortuis vere.

ALL: Tu nobis Christe rex miserere.
                        Amen.

This text is taken from the *Missale ad Vsum Ecclesie Eboracensis* printed by Francis Regnault (Paris, 1533), *Feria tertia post Pascha.*

721 The directions following this line are derived from John 20: 3–4.

GLOSSARY

THIS glossary is intended primarily to explain words and senses now unfamiliar and to elucidate special contextual meanings, and is therefore by no means complete. The great variety of spelling in the texts, particularly in *Mary Magdalen*, has made it desirable, however, to enter a good number of words still common but which may be disguised orthographically. Inflexional forms are given where they may be of interest or are spelled misleadingly; also set phrases in which some common words appear are collected.

In our arrangement we have placed 3 after *g*, but treated þ as *th*; we have treated vocalic *y* as *i*, but put consonantal *y* in its usual place; we have treated consonantal *i* as *j*; we have separated *u* and *v* according to function. We have noted in 'The Presentation of Texts' that because of the unusual spelling practices of the *Mary Magdalen* scribe, we have silently altered 3 to þ, 3 to *s*, and 3 to *z* where the spelling conventions of the age or the scribe's own practice elsewhere would seem to justify it; these instances are so numerous that we have not marked them with an asterisk, but other emendations found in the glossary are so marked. The sign ~ stands for the headword in any of its forms.

The numbers refer to the lines of the texts; in two plays we have printed passages that are cancelled in the MS, and these are indicated parenthetically, e.g. K (canc.) 20. The identifying letters are: S = *The Conversion of St. Paul*; K = *The Killing of the Children*; M = *Mary Magdalen*; W = *Wisdom*; CB = *Christ's Burial*, and CR = *Christ's Resurrection*. The abbreviation 's.d.' refers to a stage direction following the line number given.

a see **haue**
abaffe *v.* turn back M 1438.
abaye see **obbey**.
abasse *imp. refl.* fear M 1376.
abey see **obbey**.
abhomynation, abomynacyon *n.* loathsome sin M 1044, CR 238.
abydyn, abyde *v.* await K 253, remain S 336, M 301; endure M 1401; *pr. pl.* submit (to) M 16; **abide** *imp.* stay K 337, CR 104; *pr. subj.* live M 370; **abidinge** *pr. p.* awaiting CR 761; **abedyn** *pp.* lived (until) M 1677.
abyll *adj.* suitable M 99.

abille *v.* enable, make worthy CR 311.
abyte *v.* clothe M 1991 [OED *habit* v.³], see **enabyte**.
abought, abou3te, abowgth, abowth *adv.* around K 181, M 154; on every side K 206, S 27, M 206, W 464, CB 678; *be* ~ be busy CR 750; *prep.* around K 476, S 257; see **bringe**.
abowndans, haboundaunce, habundans *n.* plenty M 381, K 393, S 562.
acceptabille *adj.* agreeable CB 755; worthy of acceptance CR 454.

accepte *adj.* welcome CB 247.

accepte *pa. sg.* received CB 252.

accombred *pp.* hindered W 396.

accorde *imp.* agree W 495; **accordith** *pr. 3 sg.* is fitting W 5; **accordinge** *pr. p.* according CR 299, S 44, K 121.

aconsumyd *pp.* destroyed M 916.

admyttid *pa. sg.* allowed CB 586.

adrad, adred *adj.* afraid S 234, M 1768.

aduenture *n.* occurrence S 434.

aduys(e)ment *n.* care S 405; counsel S 615; **avysement, awysement** notice M 254, 812. *See* **take.**

aduysse *n.* direction, command S 214.

advertacyounys *n. pl.* observations, evidence M 921.

afeyere *adj.* afire M 742.

aferd *adj.* afraid S 188, M 1033.

affectuosly *adv.* ardently, eagerly CR 583.

affiable *adj.* as *n.* loved one W 594; **afyabylle** *adj.* willing M 548.

affia(u)nce, affya(u)nce, afyawns *n.* loyalty S 205, M 383, CR 207; reliance W 83, 657; trust M 442; faith M 2009; *of myn* ~ dependent on me W 690.

affye *n.* trust: *of myn* ~ trusted by me W 643.

af(f)orn *adv.* previously K 484; ahead K 529.

afray *v.* harry M 1228; **afrayyd** *pp.* harassed M 744.

aftire, aftyr *adv.* afterwards K 530; *prep.* about K 376; in accordance with K 17, S 58, M 640, W 228, CB 621.

agaynsayd *pp.* contradicted M 15.

ageyn, aȝen *adv.* once more K 514, S 449; back K 37, S 260, CB 834; in return W 73.

(a)geyn, aȝen(s), agens, ageynst, ȝeyn(e) *prep.* against K 63, 452, S 40, M 122, W 491, CR 23;

with respect to M 91; to M 1605; toward M 872 s.d.; ther ~ *adv.* against that W 661.

agre *pr. subj.* assent to M 439 s.d.; *pp.* agreed S 51.

agrement *n.* covenant M 898.

ay(e) *adv.* always K 78, M 773, W 554, CB 173, CR 36; ~ *whan* whenever W 345.

al(l)yaunce, alya(u)vns *n.* family connection K 3, M 1900.

alye *n.* kinship: *into yower* ~ allied with you M 518.

alyfe *adj.* alive M 891.

all(e), al *adv.* entirely K 99, S 135, M 501, etc.; as *conj.* although W 329; ~ *if conj.* although CB 135.

alle-only, alonly *adv.* completely M 1829, CR 433; only M 78.

almesse *n.* alms M 1641.

als *adv.* also M 746, CB 81.

als *conj.* as CR 42.

althyng *pro.* everything S 599.

aluay *adv.* always S 146.

ambra *n.* ambergris M 339.

amend(e) emende *v.* correct, mend K 23, M 1588, W 713, CR 479; *imp.* M 1615.

amendys *n. pl.* amends M 1014.

amerowsnesse *n.* passion M 353.

amyabyll, amyable *adj.* worthy of love K 501, M 68, W 43; pleasant M 451.

amyke *n.* friend W 70.

amys(se) *adv.* wrongly M 1530, CB 23; sinfully W 75; *adj.* wrong M 2140.

amyttyd *pp.* admitted, accepted M 1381.

amons, emange(s), emonges *prep.* among M 569, CB 154, CR 44, 419.

an, and *conj.* if S 399, M 89, W 330; as if S 105.

ankyr *n.* anchor M 1395.

anon(e), anoon *adv.* at once, immediately K 184, S 83, M 388, CR 527.

anosed *pp.* harmed W 224.

apaas, apace, apas(s)e, on pace, a-pace *adv.* apace, quickly K 277, S 86, CB 509, CR 341.

apaid, apayd *pp.* rewarded K 153, S 498.

aparens *n.* nobility (state of being heir to heaven MED sb.⁵) M 711.

apart *adv.* aside S 176.

apenyon *n.* opinion M 1463.

aperteynyng *pr. p. adj.* relevant M 1527.

apoynt *adv.* likely M 789 (cf. a poynt M 1408).

apostylesse *n.* woman apostle M 1381.

applicant *adj.* docile S 429.

applie, apply(e) *v.* offer M 672; dedicate S 170, M 1981; comply S 72, W 446; apply M 758, W 513; **aplye** *pr. pl.* comply M 1597; **applied, applyeth** *pp.* assigned W 10, 178.

apporpride *pp.* assigned (a property) K 488.

apposed *pp.* examined W 225.

aprise *n.* worth M 1133.

aprowe *v.* commend M 354.

aqueyntaunce, aqueyntowns *n.* acquaintance M 580; familiarity W 658.

aquyte *v.* reward M 267; *refl.* give account of K 202.

aray(e) *n.* clothing M 1183, W 551; condition CR 155.

arayed *pp.* treated CB 94.

are see **or, er(e)**.

arend *n.* errand M 136.

arere *v.* raise M 407.

arome *adv.* apart, at a distance W 524.

as, os(e) *conj.* as, in the way that K 32, S 10, M 179, W 64, CB 35, CR 24; if M 121; as though W 130; ~ *we* (I) *can* as well as we (I) can K 20, S 13; *where* ~ where CR 594; *prep.* ~ *for* for W 22.

asemlaunvs *n.* assembly M 387.

asemly, semely *n.* assembly S 504, S (canc.) 3.

ashamyd *pp.* frightened S 219.

aspy(e), asspy *v.* see K (canc.) 4, M 1880; *pr. 1 sg.* K 183, M 1720; *pr. 2 sg.* W 395; *pr. subj.* M 1718; **aspied** *pp.* K 326.

asprongyn *pp.* originated M 1174.

as(s)aye *v.* test M 1600, CB 435.

assaye *n.* testing K 531.

assent *pp.* agreed CB 297.

assiduly *adv.* continuously W 256.

assyng *v.* assign S 214; **assignyt** *pa. sg.* directed CR 512; **assyngned** *pp.* S 235.

ass[t]att, astat(e) *n.* state, condition M 1588; estate M 706; pomp M 728.

assurans *n.* credibility S 387.

astert *v.* escape K 102.

at, att *prep.* at (the time of) K 246, S 81, etc.; from S 537, CB 669; in M 478, CR 317; subject to S 503, M 13; against M 366; ~ *alle* entirely K 59, S 423; ~ *the best* in the best way W 622; ~ *þe last* finally M 433, W 526, CB 473; ~ *length* finally S 438; ~ *lest* at least CB 759; ~ *rest* in rest W 742.

atastid *pp.* tasted W 568.

ataunt *adv.* excessively W 606.

atenda(v)ns, attenda(u)nce *n.* attention K 560, M 422; company CB 831, CR 512; *gyf, gife yow* ~ attend S 132, CB 552; *don your* ~ M 422.

atenddawntt *adj.* on duty M 1871.

ato *adv.* in two K 383.

atrey *v.* test M 983.

attayne *v.* have effect S 323.

atteynt *pp.* condemned K 344.

attende *v.* pay attention to S 410; *pr. 1 sg.* W 100; *pr. pl.* await W 748.

attys *prep.* at this M 693.

atweyn *adv.* in two K 540.

atwen *prep.* between K 442.

auctoure *n.* creator W 99; auctours *pl.* authorities W 270.

audiens, avdyeans, hawdyens
n. hearing K 52, S 162; audience
S 7, M 2; presence M 460.

auncetours *n. pl.* ancestors K 126.

aungelly *adj.* angelic M 444.

aunterous *adj.* venturous, bold S
14 s.d.

avayl *v.* profit S 475; avaylis *pr.*
3 sg. CB 373.

avaunce, awansse *v.* promote K
130; come forth K 564; bring
forward S 79, M 1641; awansyd
pp. elevated M 107.

avaunt(e), awant(t) *interj.* out,
away K 313, M 925.

avaunt *v.* boast W 605; *pr. 1 sg.*
W 586.

aventures *adj.* adventurous K 220.

avoide *v.*: ∼ *awey* remove K 90;
avoydyt *pr. 3 sg.* leaves M 276
s.d.; awoyd *imp.* go away M
1574.

awayle, awayll, aweyle *n.* help
S 276, M 404; advantage M 1309.

awansse see avaunce.

awe *adj.* see withalle.

awete *interj.* hail M 1110. [Lat.]

awye *v.* vie with M 500.

awysyd *pp.* advised M 1251.

awter *n.* altar M 1144.

axke *v.* ask M 1691; *pr. 2 sg.* M
1835.

bagpyp *n.* bagpiper W 724 s.d.

bayne *adj.* ready, willing CR 84.

bale *n.* evil, suffering S 511, M 57;
balys *pl.* M 919, CR 590.

balys *n. pl.* whips, scourges M 735.

bamys see bawme.

baptem, baptym *n.* baptism S
379, M 1836, W 126.

bargayn *n.* price M 937; see bey.

baryst, baryth see bere.

barowfull *n.* wheel-barrow full S
97.

bar(r)e see bere.

bawme *n.* balm K451; bawmys *pl.*
M 613; bamys trees of balm M
569.

be *prep.* see by.

be, bee, beyn *v.* be K 1, S 61 etc.
be(e) *pr. subj.* S 549, M 89, CR
126; ys, isse *pr. 3 sg.* S 17, M
2030; ar(e), arn, ben(e), beyn,
byn, beth *pr. pl.* K 112, S 335, M
194, 811, 1527, W 178, CB 662,
CR 462; ware, wher *pa. pl.* M
651, 1706; wer(e), werre, wore
pa. subj. S 92, M 388, 520, W 330,
CB 332, CR 185; be(e), bene,
beyne, byn *pp.* K 46, S 105, M
891, CB 88, 102, CR 469.

bede *n.* prayer M 1241; ∼ *woman*
n. woman who prays for someone
M 1966.

bedred *pp. adj.* feared K 64.

begrymlyd *pp. adj.* covered with
grime S 105.

behouefulle *adj.* necessary W 238.

bey, bye *v.* redeem K 535, M 1007;
suffer W 108; ∼ *the bargayn* pay
the price M 937; bowth *pp.*
bought M 589.

bekennyng *n.* knowledge S 231.

belefe *pr. pl.* believe CR 762;
belevyt *pr. 3 sg.* M 882.

beleve *n.* belief M 1828.

belyve *adv.* quickly M 1800.

belle *v.* swell M 1169 [OE *belgan*];
poss. bellow, break wind [OE
bellan].

bem *n.* beam, tree or the Cross M
993.

bemys, beames *n. pl.* rays of light
M 443, CR 568.

bemmys *n. pl.* trumpets M 934.

benesown, benyson *n.* blessing S
271, M 1208.

benignite(e), benygnyte *n.* kindness M 73, W 39, CB 769, CR
84.

benyngly *adv.* kindly M 616

benomme *v.* become numb S 374.

bepayntyd *pp.* painted S 103.
beral(le), **berel** *n.* beryl, a jewel K 506, M 425.
berdys see **byrd**.
bere *v.* bear, carry K 484 s.d., S 126 etc.; give birth to K 15; endure CB 74; bear *pr. 1 sg.* M 472, W 166; **beryst** *pr. 2 sg.* M 1154; **baryth, berith, beryth, beryt(t)** *pr. 3 sg.* S 513, M 417, W 718; **beryt** possesses M 533; **bere** *pr. subj.* bear W 602; *pr. pl.* M 1779; **ber(e)** *imp.* S 529, M 226, CB 553; **baryst** *pa. 2 sg.* M 1005; **bare** *pa. sg.* S 97, M 170; **bore, borne** *pp.* born K 404, M 32, W 115, CB 40, CR 124.
bery(e) *v.* bury M 2129, CB 382; *imp.* CB 806; **beryyd** *pp.* M 1320.
beryyng. *n.* burial M 1050.
beryng *adj.* bearing: ~ *baskett* large harvest basket S 644.
berth *n.* birth M 679.
besawnt *n.* besant, a coin M 1218.
besely(e) *adv.* diligently, eagerly CR 147, 576.
besene, besyn *pp. adj.* dressed S 16; seen, considered M 54.
beshrew(e) *pr. 1 sg.* curse S 88, W 506.
besy *adj.* diligent K 56, W 406.
besyde *adv.* close by S 191; *prep.* in addition to M 1806.
besyn see **besene**.
besines, besynes(se) *n.* activity, endeavour CR 293; care, diligence S 166, M 985.
bet *conj.* see **but**.
betake *v.* commend, entrust (themselves) M 907.
bete *v.* beat K 205, CB 439; *imp.* M 1177 s.d.; **bete, bett, betyn** *pp.* M 863, CB 666, 684.
beteche *pr. 1 sg.* entrust M 465.
betyde *v.* happen S 193; *pr. subj.* M 1235; *pa. sg.* S 99.
betyll-browyd *adj.* with brows shaggy, prominent M 724.

betyme *adv.* immediately W 691.
betoknyth *pr. 3 sg.* symbolizes K 489.
betternesse *n.* bitterness M 604.
bettyr *adj.* bitter M 666; **beytterare** *comp.* M 997.
betwyx *prep.* between M 923.
bevteus, bewtews *adj.* beauteous M 949.
bewreke *v.* revenge M 1563.
by, bye, be *prep.* by means of K 48, S 2 etc.; near S 95, M 55; according to K 11, S 93, M 77, W 160, CB 288; during M 139; concerning M 1538.
by and by(e) *adv.* one by one, in succession M 1848; continually W 751; eventually CR 345.
bybyll, bybull *n.* Holy Bible S 159, 652.
bycchys, bycheys *n. pl.* bitches M 724, 927.
byddyng, beddyng *n.* command K 78, M 138, CB 797.
byd *v.* order, command M 1632; **bed, byd** *imp.* M 134, 1592; **bydyst** *pr. 2 sg.* S 522; **bad(de)** *pa. sg.* S 280, M 1518, CB 569, CR 660.
bide *v.* remain CR 547.
byġġyd *pp.* settled M 2023.
bylly *n.* belly M 1156.
byrd *n.* young woman M 356; **berdys** *pl.* M 51.
blabyr-lyppyd *adj.* heavy lipped M 927.
blasyd *pp.* burned M 745.
blasse *v.* shine, wave M 934.
ble *n.* countenance M 68.
bleryd *pp.* dimmed: ~ *is ower eye* we have been deceived M 985.
blynne v. refrain W 549.
blysch(e) *n.* bliss, happiness M 885, 1099.
blys(se) *v.* bless M 1517; *pr. 1 sg.* M 276; **blyssyt, blyssyd** *pr. 3 sg.* M 1931, 1932; **blyssyd** *pp. adj.* M 1933, etc.

blow(e) *v.* sound M 934, W 702; *imp.* W 707.

bobbyd *pp.* mocked, pummelled M 863.

bodely *adj.* bodily, natural K 534; *adv.* physically CR 657.

boy(e) *n.* servant M 1148; **boyes** *pl.* low-class persons K 312.

bome *pr. 1 sg.* buzz M 780.

bond *n.* slavery M 1838.

bonde *n.* bondman: ~ *nor fre* no one K 43, S 596; **bondys** *pl.* power M 732.

bone *n.* boon, request K 134, M 909; **bonys** *pl.* M 552.

boot(e), bot(e) *n.* remedy S 518, M 919; reward S 536, M 566.

bord, burde *n.* board, table M 630, CR 348.

bornyd *pp.* as *n.* what is burnished, shined M 443.

borons *n. pl.* barons M 50.

bosshop *n.* bishop M 2128; **busshopys** *pl.* S 418.

bost *pr. 1 sg.* boast W 586.

bost *n.* boast M 924 s.d.

bote see **boot(e)**.

bot(t) see **but**.

botell *n.* bundle S 85.

bounde *n.* reach K 333; **bovndys** *pl.* area M 1019.

bovnteest *super. adj.* kindest M 952.

bovntyowsnesse, bowntosnesse *n.* generosity M 209, 324.

bower, bowyr *n.* dwelling M 51, 363; womb (fig.) K 496; **bowrys** *pl.* palaces M 336.

bown *pp.* bound M 391.

bowth *v.* see **bey**.

brace, *v.* clasp, embrace CB 179.

brayd *n.* hurry M 1148.

brast see **brest**.

brede *n.* breadth CB 28.

brede *v.* breed M 457.

breellys *n. pl.* rascals M 927.

breke *v.* break S 171, CB 481, CR 395; *pr. subj.* M 1166.

bren *n.* eyebrows W 196.

brennyng *pr. p. adj.* burning W 281; **brent(t)** *pp.* S 258, M 1628.

brest *v.* burst, break K 384, M 1420; **brystyt** *pr. 3 sg.* M 822; **brast** *pa. pl.* M 969; **brostyn** *pp.* M 980.

brest(e), briste *n.* breast M 1224, CB 587, 780.

bright, brygth, bryth *adj.* bright M 2042, W 24; fair K 509, M 68; pure M 690, 2134; **brighter(e), bryter** *comp.* K 506, M 443; **brytest** *super.* M 958.

brygth *n.* brightness M 949.

bringe, bryng(e) *v.* bring, cause to bring K 416, S 209 etc.; ~ *forth* fetch K 266; ~ *yt abow3t* accomplish it S 498; ~ *to mynde* bring to attention W 296; **brynggytt** *pr. 3 sg.* M 1974; **browt(e), browth** *pp.* M 197, 279; ~ *ondyr* caught M 208.

brystchit see **brest**.

brochit *pa. sg.* broached CB 782.

brode *adv.* widely S 100.

bronde *n.* sword K 64.

brondes *n. pl.* torches W 114.

brostyn see **brest**.

brothyr *n.* brother M 79; **brether, brotheryn** *pl.* CR 507, M 1076.

brunt *n.* blow: *at a* ~ at a clap, suddenly S 569; sound of a blow CB 52 [ON *bruna* apparently confused with OF *bruit:* see OED].

brussid *pp.* bruised CB 666.

buke, bok(e) *n.* book M 178, 1181, CB 272.

burde see **bord**.

burthen *n.* burden W 53.

but(t), bet, bot *conj.* but, unless K 44, S 101 etc.; ~ *þat* except that M 695; ~ *if* unless M 421, W 363; ~ *yitt* yet, however K 94, CB 480; *adv.* only, merely M 810, S 176, W 305, CB 48; *prep.* except K 114.

cayserys *n. pl.* emperors M 936.

caytyff, caytyf(e) *n.* caitiff, low person S 632, M 191, CR 386; caytyfys, caytyves *pl.* K 317, M 58.

can, conne *pr. pl.* know K 556, M 529.

cann, kan *pr. 3 sg.* can, is able (to) W 68, CB 637.

cardyakyllys *n. poss.* of a cardiacle, heart disease M 1363.

care *n.* sorrow W 500, CB 498; fear CB 756.

carefull, carfulle *adj.* troubled, sorrowful M 1034, CR 4.

carid *pa. sg.* had concern CB 287.

case *n.* event, situation S 608, CB 452, CR 322; legal case W 641.

cast(e) *v.* arrange M 1367; cast away M 1421; *pr. subj.* devote W 239; ~ *no dought imp.* have no fear W 502.

cawt(h) *pp.* caught M 191, 195.

ceile *n.* happiness CB 72.

certeyn *adv.* certainly, surely K 326.

certeyn *n.* certainty K 371; *verrey* ~ proper form CB 607.

*certaynte, sertaynte *n.* certainty S 144, 229.

certify(e) *v.* affirm CR 661; *pr. 1 sg.* S 525; certifiede, certifyed *pp.* CB 47, CR 726.

certys *adv.* certainly M 1287.

chace, chas(e) *pa. sg.* chose CB 530, CR 294, 440; chose *pp. adj.* chosen W 16.

chalyngyd *pa. sg.* claimed M 1318.

chamlett *n.* camlet, rich fabric S 114.

chapetelet *n.* small head band W 16 s.d.; chapelyttes *pl.* W 164 s.d.

charge *pr. 1 sg.* oblige, bind K 116, M 1275; *pr. pl.* K 122.

*chelle *adj.* cold M 1613.

cher(e), chyr(e) *n.* mood, frame of mind K 467, S 131, M 48, CB 73, CR 145; cheres *pl.* CB 265.

cheueler *n.* wig W 1 s.d.; chevelers *pl.* W 164 s.d.

chevelered *pp. adj.* wearing a wig W 324 s.d.

chevere *pr. 1 sg.* shiver K 374.

chide *v.* abuse K 168.

chyff *adj.* chief M 5.

childer, chyldurn *n. pl.* children S 236, M 111, 851, CB 166.

chyr(e) see cher(e).

chongg *pr. pl.* change M 1617 s.d.; chonggyd *pa. sg.* M 1350.

choppe *v.* cut K 157; ~ *and chaunge pr. 1 sg.* barter and bargain W 639.

cypresse *n.* galingale, cypress root M 2046.

circumstaunce, cyrcumstance *n.* surrounding, condition M 359, CB 113; *colleccyon of* ~ state of affairs M 75.

cyte, cet(y)e, set(t)e *n.* city K 41, S 191, M 116, 473, CB 50; cetyys, sytyes *pl.* S 421, M 1983.

claret *n.* yellowish or light red wine M 477.

clary *n.* medicinal plant M 342; clary wynne mixture of wine, clarified honey and spices M 477.

cleyff *n.* cliff M 1740; cleffys *pl.* M 55.

cleymyd *pa. sg.* claimed M 1321.

cleyn(e), clene *adj.* spotless S 567, M 751, W 45, CB 32, CR 124; unmixed W 749.

clene *adv.* completely S 380.

clepe *imp.* call W 692; clepyd *pp.* M 713, W 136.

cler(e), cleyr(e) clyre *adj.* clear, pure K 506, M 46; plain M 255; perfect M 600; not counterfeit M 1920; morally pure CB 83, CR 597.

clernesse *n.* purity CR 427.

cleve *v.* cut K 540; clyvytt *pr. 3 sg.* M 1000.

clym v. climb CB 431; clymyth pr. 3 sg. climbs W 444.

close v. come to fulfilment M 539.

closett n. womb (fig.) K 398.

closse adv. secretly M 563 s.d.

cloth(e) n. shroud CB 816, CR 172.

clought n. clout, blow K 208.

clumme adj. silent W 521.

code n. cobbler's wax, pitch S 103.

cognycion, cognyssyon n. apprehension W 143; foreknowledge M 846.

coysyn, cosyn n. kinsman S 495, CR 312.

coleccyon see circumstaunce.

collusion n. conspiracy K 92.

colore, colour n. complexion M 516; colour(ry)s pl. disposition M 517; pretences W 379; rhetoric W 547.

coloured pp. perverted W 673.

comfert, comfurt(e), covmforth n. assurance K 521, M 481, W 205, CB 419; cheer M 456; courage W 704; relief S 335, CR 749; spiritual comfort S 262, CB 196, 856; covnfortys pl. M 1220.

comfortacyon, n. consolation M 792, 1901; see also take.

comfortatywys n. pl. comfortatives, comforting medicines M 338.

comfortt v. strengthen M 872; comfurth imp. CB 741; pp. CR 686.

comfurthlesse adj. without spiritual comfort CR 545.

comit see cumme.

comyt(e) pr. pl. entrust S 161; commyttyng pr. p. S 661; commyttyd pp. S 405.

commend n. care, protection CR 392.

commend pr. pl. entrust CR 765.

commendabyll adj. worthy of being trusted M 1266.

commyt v. perform CB 649.

comon adj. as n. ordinary, secular life W 443, 751.

comown adj. worldly, secular W 472.

compassyd pp. ordained, directed M 1467.

compatience n. compassion CR 270.

compyler n. author S 357.

compylyd pp. described M 806.

complayne, cumplayn v. express sorrow, elegize S 464, M 287, CB 59, CR 75; imp. CB 352; compleynist pr. 2 sg. reflex. CR 608.

compleyn n. complaint: to mak ∼ to lament CR 257.

complexion, conpleccyon n. temperament W 557, S 238; compleccions pl. W 343.

complyshe v. accomplish M 218.

comprehend(e) v. take counsel, plan together M 412, W 250; intend M 446; include M 708; pr. pl. W 715.

conceyve imp. understand K 107.

concepcyon n. imagination S 607.

concludytt pp. brought to confusion M 1564.

conctypotent adj. all powerful S 595.

condescende, condesend v. give way W 711; agree M 1600; pr. 1 sg. agree, take in hand S 171.

condicions, condycyons n. pl. manner of living W 626; situations M 950.

confyrmable adj. firm, constant S 484.

confoundys pr. 3 sg. overcomes S 547; confunddyd pp. defeated M 1579.

confusion, confusyon n. ruin, overthrow M 789, CB 341.

congruence n. comparison CR 221.

coniecture n. trickery S 631, W 354.

coniuracyon *n.* spell S 602.

conne see can.

connyngly *adv.* skilfully M 1397.

connownt *n.* agreed sum M 1802.

*conpunccion *n.* scrupulousness W 467.

conregent *adj.* ruling jointly, of one livery W 752 s.d. (poss. error for 'congruent'? See Eccles).

concyens, consyens *n.* conscience M 663, 1996, W 729.

consaue *v.* conceive CB 494.

consedere *imp.* accept M 518.

conseruacion *n.* preservation K 109.

conserve *imp.* protect M 1578.

consyngne *pr. pl.* attest M 719.

constryne *v.* control M 1118; constreyne *imp.* S 52; con-strayned, constraynid, con-streynyd *pp.* obliged S 220, CB 400, prevented CB 577, tortured CR 175.

contemplatyf(e) *adj.* meditative, spiritual M 680, 2002, W 417.

contynens *n.* modest behaviour M 77.

contynew *v.* continue S 616.

contynuance *n.* duration S 441.

contraly *adv.* contrarily M 940.

contrauersie *n.* opposition W 305.

contre *n.* interior country, away from the coast M 1212.

contrighte *adj.* contrite CB 252.

conuenyens *n.* appropriateness S 73; *be grett* ~ expeditiously M 1450.

conuenyent *adj.* suitable W 6.

conuersacion *n.* familiarity W 425; manner of life CR 307.

conuersaunt *adj.* familiar W 607.

conveye *v.* conduct K 433; con-vaide, conveid, conveyed *pp.* K 517, 232 s.d., M 563 s.d., CB 161.

copyr *n.* copper M 319.

coryous *adj.* sophisticated W 579; elegant W 609.

coroscant *adj.* gleaming M 953.

cors, covrs, curse *n.* course, way S 213, M 1438, 1495.

cost *n.* coast M 1212.

costodyer *n.* guard S 627.

couytys *n.* avarice S 531.

countenaunce *n.* appearance: *be* ~ with gestures W 687.

covrtes see curteys.

cowff *imp.* heave out (chest), clear the throat M 1224.

creacyon, creacyown *n.* creation M 67, 753.

creatur(e) *n.* creator M 1578, W 206.

creatur(e) *n.* a created being K 16, S 186, M 758, W 26, CB 36, CR 409.

credens *n.* belief M 1449, CR 727; *in* ~ on faith M 700.

cressyn *v.* increase M 1511.

crestyd *pp. adj.* made into a crest W 324 s.d.

crestyn, crysten *v.* christen M 1683, S 325.

Crestyn, Cristen *adj.* Christian M 1699, W 177.

crewelle *adj.* cruel CB 754.

crye *v.* make a loud noise S 470 s.d., M 963; *pr. 1 sg.* proclaim W 323, beseech M 261; *pr. 3 sg.* pray M 797; cryeng *pr. p.* making a loud noise S 432 s.d., W 550 s.d.

cronekyllyd *pp.* made a record of M 1329.

cumme *v.* come W 525; ~ *to* equal M 325; comyst *pr. 2 sg.* K 200; comit, com(m)yt, com(m)yth *pr. 3 sg.* K 248, S 119 s.d., M 1662; come, cam *pa. pl.* K 27, CR 86; cum *imp.* S 209, M 386; ~ *of* hurry up S 86; let's go M 379; ~ *on* make progress S 334; come *pr. subj. pl.* W 329; cummyng(e) *pr. p.* M 870, com(m)en, comyn, cum *pp.* K 19, S 129, CR 497; ~ *of* derived from M 1900.

cure *n.* care, S 77, CB 171; cure, healing M 793; charge, burden W 53; *take of* ~ taken responsibility for W 240.
cure *n.* cover M 294.
cure *v.* heal, assuage CR 6; *pr. 1 sg.* protect M 2127.
curyd *pp.* concealed M 1262.
curse see **cors**.
curteys, covrtes *adj.* courteous M 490, 1139.
curtesly *adv.* courteously CR 225.
customably *adv.* according to custom W 14.
custumme *n.* habitual usage W 520.

daysyys *n. poss.* daisy's: ~ *iee* marguerite M 515.
dalyaunce *n.* pleasantry K 133.
damage *n.* injury (the Passion) M 1347.
davnnys *pr. 3 sg.* dawns M 35.
debonarius *adj.* gracious M 444.
decend, desend *v.* descend M 1586; **decende, dyssend** *imp.* M 1369; *pr. pl.* M 1595; **descend** *pr. subj. tr.* send down M 1557; **descendit** *pa. sg.* descended CB 343; **dessendyd** *pp.* S 604.
declare *v.* explain K 487, W 102; *imp.* say K 444 s.d., *pr. pl.* describe S 396.
dectours *n. pl.* debtors M 650.
ded *n.* death M 1319.
ded *v.* see **do**.
ded(e) *adj.* dead K 171, M 773, CB 30.
dede *n.* deed, act M 633, W 218, CR 350; **dedes, dedys** *pl.* M 955, W 364, CB 251, CR 38.
dedenynglye *adv.* contemptuously CR 486 [Sc. *dedeign*; OF *desdeignier?* see OED 'dedeign', MED 'disdeinen'].
dedly *adj.* death-like CB 49, CR 5;

mortal S 320, W 545; deathly CR 600.
ded(d)yst see **do**.
dee see **dey(e)**.
deface *v.* disfigure W 174.
defawte, defawth *n.* lack M 1762, 1769.
defens *n.* defender M 713; defence (against) M 1357.
defilid, dyffylyd *pp.* desecrated CR 540, M 1033.
degre(e) *n.* social position K 119, S 362; quality M 262; *in eche* ~ in every way M 426.
dey(e), dy(e), dee *v.* die K 115, S 479, etc.: **diete** *pa. sg.* CR 95.
deylle, deyllys see **deuylle**.
deynty(y)s *n. pl.* luxuries M 335, 344.
deywl see **deuylle**.
delacion, delacyon *n.* deferment K 84; delay S 65.
delate *v.* delay S 497.
delecceon, dyleccyon *n.* beloved M 2045; love M 1323.
delectabyll, delectable *adj.* beloved S 253, W 255; desirable M 593; admirable M 955.
delectacion, delectacyon *n.* pleasure, joy W 366, S 68, M 69.
delectary *adj.* delectable M 751.
delevyr *pr. 1 sg.* give M 1692; **deliuer** *imp.* release CB 799; **deliuert** *pp.* CR 671.
delinge *n.* treatment CB 92.
delycyows *adj.* sensuously delightful M 335.
delycyte *n.* delight M 72; deliciousness M 2038.
demene *pr. subj.* treat M 1581.
dempte *pp.* judged M 662.
demure, demvr(e) *adj.* dignified M 1356; humble M 1902; simple CB 211.
departe *v.* part with M 102.
dent *n.* blow M 272.
dere *n.* injury S 192.
dere *v.* injure S 115.

derevorthy *adj.* precious M 1851.

derk, dyrke *n.* dark K 449, W 166.

deseyve *v.* deceive M 2010; **disceyvid, dyssayvyd** *pp.* K 83, S 487.

desepcyouns *n. pl.* disappointments M 458.

desevyr, desseuere *v.* separate M 302; discontinue CR 331.

desyer(e), desyyr *n.* desire S 43, M 648, 740, 1695.

desyyr *v.* desire M 424; **desyer desyre** *pr. 1 sg.* M 896, 2142; **desyerst** *pr. 2 sg.* M 1667; **desiries, desyrth** *pr. 3 sg.* M 215, CB 772, CR 578; **desyern, dysyore***pr.pl.*M721;**desyryng** *pr. p.* S 37; **desyred** *pp.* W 34.

despeyere *pr. pl.* despair W 467.

despight, dispight, dysspyte *n.* contempt K 144; outrage, injury M 366; *haue in* ~ hate W 338.

dessetres *n.* distress M 104.

dett(e) *n.* debt M 652, W 194.

deuylle, deylle, deywl, devyll(e) dewlle, dylfe, dylle, dyv(y)ll, dywll *n.* devil S 603, M 187, 380 s.d., 962 s.d., 1157, 1167, 1420, 1462, W 370, 508; **deuelles, develis, dewllys, dylf, dyllys** *pl.* K 224, M 563 s.d., 567 s.d., 1386, W 372; **deuelys, develys** *poss.* W 546, 700.

devere, devyr *n.* duty K 465, M 1180; **devyrs** *pl.* M 832.

deversarye *adj.* diverse M 754.

devyde *v.* oppose M 684; drive away M 787; **devydyst** *pr. 2 sg.* protect M 2033; **devydytt** *pr. 3 sg.* separates M 955; **devydyd** *pp.* arranged M 451.

devyn(e), divyne *adj.* divine K 537, M 708, W 31, CR 131.

devynyte, devenyte *n.* divinity S 239; divine nature M 712, CR 41; knowledge of God W 86.

devyr see **devere**.

devyse *v.* make use of S 494; plan S 501, M 421; **devysyd** *pp.* explained M 1052.

devyse *n.* plan M 413.

devodyd, devodyt see **dewoyde**.

devoure *v.* destroy K 264, S 418.

dew(e) *adj.* due M 34, W 434; *ewyn of* ~ just as deserved M 762.

dewchesse *n.* duchess M 515.

dewlle see **deuylle**.

dewoyde *v.* leave, exit M 691 s.d.; **devoydeth, devodyt(t)** *pr. 3 sg.* M 818 s.d., 1124 s.d., W 380 s.d.; **devoyd** *pr. pl.* M 1132 s.d.

dewresse *n.* duress M 281.

dewtee, dewty(e) *n.* duty CB 199, 847, CR 513.

dya galonga *n.* a drug of galingale M 339.

diete see **dey(e)**.

dyffylyd see **defilid**.

diffowled *pp.* stained W 130.

dyggide *pp. adj.* dug CB 364.

dight *pp.* prepared, meted out W 123; **dyth** brought M 1577.

dignite, dygnite *n.* honour M 1694; worth S 145, M 829.

dylfe, dylle see **deuylle**.

dyrke see **derk**.

disceyvid see **deseyve**.

discretly *adv.* with discerning W 145.

dyscry *v.* tell M 1004.

dyscus *v.* discriminate M 320; ponder M 892; examine M 1311; *pr. subj.* demonstrate M 1561.

disgysyng *n.* symbolic clothing W 150.

dysyore *v.* see **desyyr**.

dysypyll *n.* disciple M 1335 s.d.; **descyplys, dyscyplys, dyscypulys, dyssypyl(l)ys** *pl.* S 23, 305, M 704 s.d., 868 s.d., 871, 1323; **dyscyplys** *poss.* S 501 s.d.

dysmay *pr. 1 sg.* fear M 1035;
dyssemay *imp.* M 193; dis-
maid(e), dysmayede *pp.*
exceedingly afraid CB 93, 160,
CR 502.

disperbilit *pp.* dispersed CR 435.

displesaunce *n.* displeasure K
135.

dispose *imp.* prepare K 478;
disposeth, dysposyth *pr. 3 sg.*
arranges K 252, S 284; disposed
pp. adj. arranged K 471;
grounded W 222; inclined W
344.

disposicion *n.* arrangement W 29.

dyssayvyd *see* deseyve.

dyssend *see* decend.

dysses *n.* decease M 80.

dys(s)ese *n.* discomfort M 457,
1056.

dyssevyr *imp.* pick out M 27.

dysspyttyd *pa. pl.* scorned M 999.

dysstonddyng *n.* defence M 196.

dysstroccyon *n.* destruction M
1935.

distillinge *pr. p. adj.* falling in
drops, concentrated CB 264.

ditee *n.* song CR 795.

dyversyte, deversyte *n.* adversity
M 955, 1308.

dywll *see* deuylle.

do(o), don, donne *v.* do *aux. w.*
infin., periphrastic pres., past S 5,
M 410, W 149, CB 327; *verb*
substit., K 336, S 53, M 142, W
298, CB 467, CR 570; do, perform K 218, S 42, M 466;
ageynst me ~ work against me
K 63; *~ my cure* do my duty S
77; *~ delygens* make great effort
S 70, CR 54; *~ obeysaunce* obey
S 64; *~ reprobacyon* oppose S
46; *~ reuerence* revere, honour
CR 127; dos(e) *pr. 3 sg.* CB 730,
CR 542; dedyst *pa. 2 sg.* M 672;
ded, dyd *pa. sg.* S 101, K 307;
pa. pl. managed, dealt M 1325;
do, don(e), donne, down *pp.*

K 345, S 642, M 739, CB 218,
CR 33.

dobelet *n.* doublet, jacket M 502.

doblenesse *n.* duplicity W 726.

docctor, dowctor, dowtter *n.*
daughter M 99, 416, 877;
dovctors *pl.* M 68.

doctor *n.* teacher S 238; doctours
n. pl. K 562.

doctryne *n.* teaching K 403, W
383.

domenacyon, dominacion *n.*
authority M 31, 2031, W 31, 370.

dominion *n.* authority S 580.

domys *n. pl.* laws W 228.

domme *n.* judgment M 991.

don *see* down(e).

don(e), donne *see* do.

dongyon *see* dungeon.

do(o)le *n.* sorrow, grief CB 138,
CR 745.

doughtles, dowtles(e) *adv.* without doubt K 123, S 402, CR 448.

dovctors, dowctor *see* docctor.

dowes, dowys *n. pl.* doves K 416,
432, 436, s.d.

down(e), don *adv.* down K 243,
S 49, M 1663, W 16 s.d., CB 48,
CR 181.

dowt(h)(e), doth, dought *n.*
fear K 180, M 156, W 502; doubt
S 130, M 42, W 468; *put (—)*
owt of ~ make clear K 197.

dowtid *pa. pl.* doubted CR 426.

dowtyd *adj.* feared S 15.

dowtter *see* docctor.

drad, dred *pp. adj.* feared S 20,
M 247.

draw *v.* carry off M 187; approach
M 1451; drawethe *pr. 3 sg.*
comes to an end CB 859;
drayt approaches M 578; draw,
drawne, drewyn *pp.* disem-
bowelled M 236; pulled CB 674;
~ down felled M 831.

dred(e) *n.* fear K 258, M 694, W
432, CB 813, CR 441; awe,
authority M 1630.

dred(e) v. fear M 207; pr. 1 sg. K
159; imp. dread S 530, respect
W 88; dredys pr. 3 pl. W 632;
dredytt imp. fear M 1023.
dree, drye v. endure, suffer CB
259, M 1043.
dreffyn, drevyn pp. driven M
1954, CB 307, CR 477.
drench pr. subj. drown M 1746;
drynchyn pp. M 754.
dresse v. address, go M 561;
arrange W 698; pr. subj. pl. prepare M 961.
drewyn see draw.
droppid pa. sg. dropped, dripped
CR 162.
dulfulle adj. sorrowful CB 74.
dulfulnesse n. sorrow CR 546.
dumme adj. dumb W 523.
dungeon, dongyon n. prison K
449, S 474.
duresse n. pain M 284.
durst pr. 1 sg. dare K 134; pr. 2 sg.
CB 542.

ease v. make easy CB 608; easid
pp. CB 332, CR 560.
ebryson adj. pure, refined, referring to gold K 14 [cf. aurum
obryzum Job 28: 15].
eche, yche adj. each K 16, S 186,
M 35, W 238, CB 319.
eche, iche pro. each one M 1807,
W 692 s.d.
echon pro. each one K 466.
eclipped pp. eclipsed CB 356.
edyfey, edyfy(e) v. build S 172;
strengthen M 1850.
ee, ees see iee.
egall(e) adj. equal M 6, W 4.
eylytt pr. 3 sg. troubles M 1544.
eynd n. end M 544.
eke adv. also K 448, CB 207.
ekes pr. 3 sg. increases CB 138.
eleccyon n. choice S 235.
electe pp. selected S 310.
element n. the sky S 371.
elles, ellis, ellys, els adv. else K

79, S 395, M 199, W 506; not ~
nothing more W 80.
emange(s), emonges see amons.
emende see amend(e).
emme n. uncle M 1172.
empere, empyre n. empire M 8;
imperial majesty M 1297.
emprore, emprower, enperower
n. emperor M 252, 400, 933;
emperowers, emprorys pl. M
11; poss. M 208 s.d., M 248
s.d.
enabyte v. clothe M 683, see
abyte.
enbrace v. use illegally W 638.
enbrace, imbrace v. embrace K
442, CB 596.
enclyne see inclyne.
encomber v. hinder K 304.
encomberowns n. burden M
1531.
endeyn v. be disdainful, angry CB
730.
endyrecte n. an underhanded evil
(?) W 731, see note.
endued pa. sg. endowed W 382.
enhanse v. raise M 111; enhansyd, inhansyd pp. M 2022,
2055.
eny see ony.
enlumyned pp. enlightened K
460.
enmy n. enemy CB 341, CR 157;
enmyse pl. CB 172, CR 369.
enqueraunce n. inquiry K 376.
ensalue v. put salve upon CR 50.
ensuer, ensure pr. 1 sg. assure S
240, 624.
enteere, intere adj. whole K 28,
CR 635.
entent(e), intende n. intent K 17,
M 119; will S 140; with good ~
with good will M 670; see also
take.
entone v. entune, sing CR 632;
enton imp. CR 755.
equite(e), equyte n. justice and
mercy K 114, M 889, CB 131.

M

er, or *conj.* before K 563, M 1234, W 395; ~ *that* W 226; *prep.* M 503.

erbyr(e) *n.* garden, bower M 563 s.d., 568.

ere, are *adv.* before S 94, CR 321.

ere *n.* ear M 1778; erys *n. pl.* M 905.

erytage *n.* heritage M 1949.

erlys *n. pl.* earls M 50.

ermonye *n.* melody, song CR 755.

erth(e)ly *adj.* on earth, not divine K 73, W 146, CB 615, CR 275.

eschewe *imp.* avoid W 435.

euerychon(e), euerychoon *pro.* each one K 95, 295, M 986.

evidence *n.* experience CB 187.

evident *adj.* clear CR 191.

ewer, ewyr *adv.* always M 557, etc.; *pleon. with conj.* or before M 1234.

ewyrmore *adv.* for ever M 1240.

examynacion *n.* investigation W 371.

excellent *adj.* superior K 437; sophisticated W 87.

execration *n.* cursedness CR 239.

exile *v.* put aside K 497; exyled *pa. sg.* put away W 620.

expedient, expedyent *adj.* suitable W 705; speedy M 817.

experience, experyens *n.* tangible proof S 10, M 1846, W 63.

expyrede *pa. sg.* expired, died CB 223.

exposicion *n.* explanation W 26.

expownyng *pr. p.* elucidating K 436 s.d.

expres(se) *adv.* particularly S 346, M 82.

expres(se) *v.* declare M 167; read M 1184; relate CB 487, CR 276.

exseleyns *n.* excellence (form of address) M 1312.

exseptt *conj.* except M 1166.

exsortacyon *n.* urging M 201.

exsport *v.* put aside M 458.

extend *v.* stretch CR 476; extendit *pa. sg.* CB 179.

fabille *n.* fable, falsehood CR 723.

fader(e), fadyr *n.* father K 172, M 48 s.d.; God W 285, CB 301; faders *pl.* old men W 393; ancestors CB 405, CR 86; fadirs *poss.* Heavenly Father's S 360.

fay *n.* faith; *be my* ~ indeed W 556.

fayer(e), fayr(e), fayur *adj.* beautiful M 1161; W 129; light M 1892; pleasant W 477; pure W 242; honest W 719; pleasing to look at CB 541.

faile, fayl(l)e *v.* lack M 1433; become weak CB 269, CR 443; *pr. pl. subj.* fall short W 436; fayles *pr. 3 sg.* weakens CR 532.

fayn(e) *adj.* glad S 430, M 332; willing, desirous CB 727, CR 455; faynest *super.* most gladly CR 227.

fayn(e) *adv.* willingly K 422, M 354.

fayne *v.* rejoice S 469.

faynt *n.* faintness CB 31.

faith(e), feyth, fythe *n.* belief CB 216, W 127; *in trewe* ~ belief without question CR 561; *in (good)* ~ truly M 358, S 96; *be my* ~ indeed K 160, M 1720.

faytours *n. pl.* deceivers, robbers M 145.

fayur see fayer(e).

fakown *n.* falcon M 942.

fall(e) *v.* fall in estate W 582; fallith, fallyt *pr. 3 sg.* is fitting, happens W 11, M 1702; faulyth falls down S 182 s.d.; fallyn *pr. pl.* decline W 438; felle, fyll *pa. sg.* fell down CB 181; happened S 368; falle *pp.* come M 1827.

fallynges *n. pl.* failures W 200.

falt, fawte *n.* fault, sin CB 726, CR 290; fawtes *pl.* CR 277.

falter(e), faltyr *pr. 1 sg.* become weak M 280; *pr. pl.* K 388.

fantasticalle *adj.* imaginary CR 679.

fare *v.* get along M 1408; *pr. 1 sg.* travel M 931; *pr. pl.* behave CB 465; **faris** *pr. 3 sg.* happens CR 228.

fassion *n.* fashion, manner CB 858.

faulyth see **fall(e).**

fauorable *adj.* approving S 358.

fauoure, fawo(u)r *n.* favour M 638; mercy S 423; good will M 431; comfort M 483, W 209.

favarows, faworus *adj.* obliging M 673; pleasing M 942, 948.

fawte *see* **falt.**

febille *adj.* feeble CB 483, CR 300.

febylle *pr. pl.* grow feeble W 438.

feche, fet, fett *v.* fetch CB 362, CR 378; *imp.* M 1637; *pp.* M 563.

fectually *adv.* factually, earnestly M 643.

fed(e) *v.* feed M 721, CB 775; *refl.* W 459; **fedyth** *pr. 3 sg.* S 512; **fed** *pa. sg.* CB 406; **fedyng** *pr. p.* M 1510; **fed(e)** *pp.* M 1326, CR 348.

fe(e) *n.* payment K 198, M 132.

fegetyff *adj.* fugitive M 318.

feyne *v.* hesitate K 421.

feynt *adv.* cowardly K 342.

feyntnes(se) *n.* weakness M 786, W 437.

felachyp, falashep, felishipe *n.* companionship M 947, CR 58; company M 968.

feld *n.* battlefield K 62, M 931; country, rural area K 131.

fel(e) *v.* perceive M 522; **feyl(l)e** *pr. 1 sg.* K 387; experience W 462; feel CB 97, CR 317; suffer CR 5; **felit, felt(e)** *pa. sg.* understood W 63; experienced CB 505, CR 183.

felecyows *adj.* happy M 947.

felyng *n.* understanding W 95;

sense perception W 136; emotion W 154.

fell(e) *adj.* deadly, cruel M 280, CB 222, CR 76.

fell(e) *v.* knock down M 1464; **fellid** *pp.* knocked K 332.

felle *imp.* fill M 535; **fellyd** *pp.* filled M 1156.

felle *n.* skin CR 711.

fend(e), fynd *n.* fiend, the Devil W 294, CR 254; **fyndys** *poss.* M 1448.

ferdarmore *adv.* furthermore M 1997.

ferdelle *n.* bundle K 273.

fer(e), feere *n.* fear K 141, S 188, M 932, W 582, CB 457, CR 102.

fere *n.* companion: *in ∼,* in common M 1248.

fere *v.* fear K 80; **fer(e)** *pr. 1 sg* K 205, S 246, CB 445.

ferfulnesse *n.* fright W 374.

ferr(e), fer(e) *adv.* far K 207, M 585, 698; *∼ (and) nor nere* everywhere S 154, M 1921.

feruent *n.* lightning S 182 s.d.

fervenly *adv.* ardently M 2114.

fest *n.* ceremony K 1; feast (ironic) M 188.

fet, fett see **feche.**

fett *n.* fit, good one S 117.

fyer *n.* fire S 256; **fyrys** *poss.* M 967.

fyeryng *n.* torch S 432 s.d.

fyll see **fall(e).**

fyrye *adj.* fiery S 501 s.d.

fyrmament *n.* heavens M 1492, S 19.

fythe see **faith(e).**

flappys *n. pl.* whips M 188.

flaw *v.* flay M 191; **fleyyng** *pr. p.* M 188.

fle *v.* fly (through the air) W 567.

fle(e), fleen *v. tr.* avoid S 558; *v. intr.* flee K 71, W 91; *imp.* K 234; **fled** *pa. sg.: ∼ asondyr* dispersed M 968.

fles *n.* fleece M 1351.

flyt *v.* **waver** S 327.

flod(e) *n.* water M 1506; current W 491.

flokk(e) *n.* group K 156; followers CB 401, CR 434.

florychyd *pp.* adorned M 334.

fode *n.* young woman M 942; **fodys** *pl.* M 948.

foysonnes, foysonnys *pr. 3 sg.* supplies in plenty S (canc.) 11, 512.

folys *n. pl.* fools M 194.

folue *v.* follow K 427; **foluyth** *pr. 3 sg.* K 280 s.d., S (canc.) 14 s.d.; **foluyng** *pr. p. adj.* K 412 s.d.

fomen *n. pl.* enemies M 932.

fondenesse *n.* foolishness W 438.

fondlynges *n. pl.* children K 132.

fonnyd *adj.* foolish W 393.

foo *n.* foe K 44, S 54, M 15; **fo(o)n** *pl.* foes K 367, M 1288.

for *prep.* because of K 116, S 4, W 166, CB 31; in exchange for W 73; for the sake of K 262, S 54, W 230, CB 108; on behalf of K 227; for fear of M 141; about CB 391; as M 19; instead of W 221; ~ *to* to, in order to K 15, M 65, W 192, CB 76.

for(e) *conj.* for, because K 48, S 27, M 1761, W 20, CB 188, CR 146; ~ *that* M 682.

forasmoche ~ *as. conj.* because, to the degree that W 9.

fordoo *v.* remove CB 656.

forgon *pp.* lost M 1973.

forȝete, foryete *v.* forget W 449; *imp.* M 1748.

forȝewnesse *n.* forgiveness M 656.

forhongord *pp.* made very hungry M 1405.

forlorn *adj.* forsaken M 1422.

forme *n.* kind, version M 1469; manner W 749.

forse *pr. pl.* regard W 606; scruple W 739; **forsid** *pp.* forced CB 728.

forth(e), furth *adv.* forward K 151, M 1384; out CB 728; ahead CR 116; continuously M 1959; *bring* ~ *v.* produce K 266; **lede** ~ lead out K 280; *come* ~ *pr. pl.* advance K 462; ~ *dresse pr. pl.* serve M 961; *go* ~ *imp.* proceed K 156; *loke* ~ give attention M 1716; *put* ~ reach out S 208.

forthy, forpi *conj.* therefore CR 196, 451.

forwhy *conj.* because K 447.

founden *pp.* revealed W 28.

foundoure *n.* creator W 733.

fowl(l)e, foule *adj.* foul, dirty M 1083, W 157, CB 237, CR 236.

fray *n.* fight K 192; attack M 280; terror M 968; rage K 271.

fray *v.* rage K 39.

frangabyll *adj.* brittle M 320.

freale, freell *adj.* frail, sinful M 888, CR 453.

fre(e) *adj.* not under bondage S 596, M 971; excellent M 143, W 187; unpredestined W 290; without restraint W 300; generous CB 240; kind, pure CB 149; free of sin CB 433.

freelnesse *n.* frailty W 200.

freelte, frelty *n.* frailty, tendency to sin W 75, CR 450; **frealtes** *pl.* CR 436.

frely(e) *adv.* completely W 499; openly W 502; freely CB 643, CR 440.

fresly *adv.* eagerly M 931.

fressh(e), fresse, frysch *adj.* fresh, lusty M 942; newly dressed up W 511; eager W 648; **fresshest** *super.* most gaily dressed W 556,

frest *pro.* first M 739 s.d.

frest, fryst *adv.* initially M 971, 1272.

frett *v.* hurt M 1528.

fretth *n.* grief M 786.

fro *prep.* from K 3, S 18, M 2004,

CR 548; as a result of M 17; since W 18.

from(e) *prep.* from K 67, S 273 etc.; away from K 349, S 382 etc.; out of M 20, CB 126, CR 671; since CR 85.

froward *adj.* perverse K 47; hateful K 92; hostile S 135; disobedient M 45; magical(?) M 1326.

frowardly *adv.* perversely CB 657.

frowardnes *n.* recalcitrance S 74.

ful(l), fulle *adv.* completely, very K 267, S 51, M 46, W 45, CB 157, CR 611.

fute *n.* foot CB 685; **fet(e), fett** *pl.* M 556, CB 98, CR 474.

ğaf(e) see **ğif(e)**.

ğaynsay *v.* contradict S 65.

ğalonga see **dya ğalonga**.

ğame *n.* happiness M 346; pleasure W 40; sport W 603.

ğame *v.* play K 329.

ğan see **ğyn**.

ğarlement *n.* garment S 16.

ğarre *v.* make, cause CR 35.

ğe(e)re *n.* property K 278; (used satirically) S 98.

ğeyff see **ğif(e)**.

ğeyn(e) see **(a)ğeyn**.

ğenerall *adj.* whole S 157.

ğentille, ğentyll(e), jentyl(l) *adj.* kind, noble K 259, M 790, 1783, 1867, 1919, CB 604.

ğentilnes, ğentyllnesse, jentylnes(se) *n.* kindness K 525, nobility M. 105, 355, 1547.

ğentyl(l)man, jentylman *n.* man of rank S 93, 97; **jentylmanys** *poss.* S 90.

ğet(e), ğett, ğetyn *v.* receive K 208; catch K 333; obtain M 787; force M 370; ~ *owt* leave S 631; **ğit** *imp.* betake CB 547; *pr. subj.* win W 677; *pp.* obtained W 560.

ğif(e), ğyf(f)(e), ğeve, yeve *v.*

give, grant K 52, S 132, M 246, CB 794; *refl.* devote W 411; ~ *atendans, attenda(u)nce* listen carefully K 379, S 132, M 1306, CR 206; *pr. 1 sg.* S 80, M 24, CR 667; ~ *accordaunce* agree W 689; *pr. pl.* ~ *perfyth sentens* give considered agreement S 43; *imp.* ~ *affecyon* show good will S 168; **ğevytt, yevith, ğyf** *pr. 3 sg.* M 171, W 579; ~ *experyens* provides proof S 10; **ğaf(e), 3aff, yaff, yave** *pa. sg.* M 1343, 1510, W 410, CB 746; **ğevyng, yevyng,** *pr. p.* W 704; ~ *you charge* ordering you K 108; **ğifen, ğouyn, 3owyn, yovyn** *pp.* S 177, M 991, W 576, CR 206.

ğyddavns *n.* guidance M 1905.

ğyd, ğyd(d)e *n.* guide K 252, M 1710, W 319; rule M 1040.

ğyd(d)e, ğyddyn *v.* guide S 124, M 601; rule M 1981; **ğye** *imp.* M 1881; **ğydyng** *pr. p.* M 1688; **ğidid, ğydyd** *pp.* S 341, CB 634.

ğyn *pr. 1 sg. aux.* begin M 1880; **ğynneth, ğynnyt** *pr. 3 sg.* K 372, M 539; **ğan** *pa. sg.* K 430, M 1520; **ğun** *pa. pl.* K 495.

ğynne *n.* strategy, wile W 547.

***ğyntely** *adv.* elegantly W 16 s.d.

ğyntyll see **ğentille**.

ğyse *n.* custom W 516.

ğit see **ğet(e)**.

ğyve *conj.* if W 663.

ğlase *n.* glass M 969.

ğle *n.* joy M 1978; play, sport M 346.

ğlysteryng *adj.* glittering M 53.

ğood *n.* goods, property M 1295, W 502; a good one S 111.

ğoodly *n.* excellent one M 1295.

ğo(o), ğonne *v.* go K 292, M 992, 1011; *pr. pl.* M 924 s.d., 1234; **ğoo** walk K 380; **ğow** *pr. subj. 1 pl.* M 851; **ğoth** *imp. pl.* M

go(o), gonne (cont.)
847; 3ode pa. pl. M 1324;
go(o)n, 3ede pp. K 34, M 975.
go(o)stly, gostely adj. spiritual
K 390, M 721, CB 278, CR 744.
gost n. spirit M 809, W 282, CB
493; gostys poss. M 825.
gouyn see gif(e).
govele n. usury W 602.
gow see go(o)n.
gownyd pp. dressed W 724 s.d.
graciose, gracious, gracyus adj.
merciful K 249, S 266, M 274;
filled with grace M 1016; fortunate M 201; good, virtuous
M 838, CB 817, CR 36; en-
dowed with God's grace K 527.
gracioslye, gratioslye adv. with
God's grace CB 253, CR 659.
gramercy n. thanks CB 410.
grates n. pl. thanks W 190.
grave v. engrave M 1993.
gravid pp. buried CB 853.
gravnt n. due M 1804.
gravntyd pp. given M 2016.
grawos see grevos(e).
greyn adj. green CB 29.
grenne n. groin M 1171.
gret(e), grett adj. great, huge K
236, S 175, M 268, CB 164, CR
22; weighty W 448.
gretyt pa. sg. greeted M 2019.
greuance, greuauns n. grievance,
mishap S 261, 435, 481.
greve v. grieve, sorrow CB 704;
greveyng pr. p. M 141.
grevos(e), greuowse, grewos
adj. grievous M 861, CB 369;
deep M 852.
grocth v. grouch, grumble M 38
(poss. pr. 3 sg. grudge?).
grogly adj. rancorous M 549, see
note.
grom n. man M 489.
grome n. groom K 228.
gromys n. pl. clutches M 549.
gronddar n. founder M 326.
gronddys n. pl. the earth M 1021.

grone pr. pl. groan M 38.
grosse adj. coarse CB 775.
groundys pr. 3 sg. teaches S 545;
grounded pp. founded K 406,
M 2098.
growell n. gruel M 1156.
grudge pr. pl. complain K 70.
gubernacyon n. rule M 200.
gud(e) adj. good CB 14, CR 37.
gudly adv. Godly CR 307.
gun see gyn.

3a, 3e(e) interj. yea, yes indeed M
261, 365, CB 186, CR 655.
3af(f) see gif(e).
3eates n. pl. gates CR 498.
3ede see go.
3e pro. nom. ye M 105, CB 334;
3ou(e), 3ow(e) pro. obj. you
M 215, CB 803, 862, CR 558;
3our(e), 3ower poss. adj. M
130, CB 492, CR 556.
3eft n. gift M 262; gyftys, yiftes
pl. M 83, W 640.
3endyr see yonder.
3epe adj. prudent, wise CB 724.
3ere n. year S 107, M 1082; 3eres,
3erys pl. M 1566, CR 28.
3et, 3it(te) adv. yet M 637, 1928,
CR 231.
3ynge see yong(e).
3ode see go.
3ondyr see yondyr.
3onglinge n. child CR 29.
3owyn see gif(e).

ha, a interj. ha S 229, M 265, W
463.
hayle, heyl(l)(e) interj. hail K
429, M 250, 381, CR 666.
hayle adj. unharmed S 278.
haylsinge n. greeting, salutation
CB 744.
hayr n. heir W 159.
halid pp. pulled, torn CR 475.
halp pa. sg. helped M 1682.
hals n. neck M 745.

halse *v.* greet M 347, W 594; halsyd *pp.* M 2030 s.d, W 44.

hampord *pp.* hindered, maddened M 722.

han see haue.

hand(e), hond *n.* hand S 208, M 1799, CR 173; power K 246; protection K 386; *at thyn* ~ for thy direction M 1445; *in* ~ for consideration S 51; in agreement W 683; *out of* ~ immediately K 214.

handille *imp.* handle CB 441.

hape *n.* good fortune CB 628.

happe *pr. subj.* chance W 511.

happee *adj.* happy, fortunate CR 663.

harbarow *n.* harbour M 1398.

hard *adj.* painful S 184, W 434.

harde *adv.* cruelly CR 471.

hardy *adj.* fearless K 164, M 1465.

hardly *adv.* at all S 54.

harlott *n.* scoundrel K 193.

harneysed *pp. adj.* dressed K 352.

hart(e)ly, hertly *adv.* sincerely K 405, S 309, M 85, CB 576; CR 585; *adj.* unrestrained CR 653.

haue, have, han, a *v. aux.* K 22, S 258, M 633, W 18, CB 88, CR 217; *v.* have, possess K 6, S 267, M 82, W 19, CB 36, CR 422; receive K 33, S 12, M 92, W 95; *imp.* ~ *at* go to it W 615; haves(e), hast, has *pr. 2 sg.* K 146, S 300, M 484, W 321, CB 282, CR 439; hase, hat(t), hath(e) *pr. 3 sg.* K 237, S 141, M 183, W 13; haddist, had(d)yst *pa. 2 sg.* K 164, M 875; had(d), hadde *pa. sg. & pl.* K 1, S 105, M 1079, CB 87; *pa. subj.* CB 248.

haunt *v.* customarily wear W 609.

havns *v.* raise up M 2006.

hawdyens see audiens.

heare, her *n.* hair M 669, CB 100; heris *pl.* CB 266.

hed(e) *n.* heed K (canc.) 2, S 168, M 1046, W 457.

heder(e), hedyr, hidder *adv.* to this place K (canc.) 1, K 19, 308, CR 144; ~ *and thedyr* this way and that W 199.

hediows, hedyows *adj.* hideous M 1004, 1022, S 584.

heggys *n. pl.* hedges M 1198.

heghe, hey(e) see high(e).

heym see hem.

heynesse, highnes *n.* highness (form of address) M 1282, CR 730.

hele *n.* well being M 521, W 21.

helefulle *adj.* salutary W 89.

helyd *pp.* healed M 759.

hellys *n. pl.* hills M 1198.

hem, heym, hym *pro.* him K 37, M 852, W 664, CB 3, CR 25.

hem see thei.

hende *adj.* gracious W 45.

her see heare, she, thei, her(e).

her(e) *v.* hear, attend K 133, S 79, CR 199; *pr. 1 sg.* CB 55; heryst *pr. 2 sg.* M 435; here *imp.* K 406; hard(e), herd *pa. sg.* CB 51, 172, CR 32.

hereof *prep.* of this S 357.

hernest *adj.* serious M 1419.

herre *adv.* here M 252.

hert(e), hertt *n.* heart K 104, M 892, W 81, CB 542, CR 168.

hertoo *adv.* to this matter CR 727.

hestys *n. pl.* orders M 52, W 716 [prob. *hettys*].

hethe *n.* heath, flat land K 70.

heuynes(se), hevynes(e) *n.* sadness S 175, M 454, CB 326, CR 1.

heve *imp.* raise M 146.

hevee, hevy *adj.* sad M 1760, W 316, CB 225, CR 57; heavy W 53; hevyar *comp.* M 272.

hevilye, hevylee *adv.* sadly CB 352, CR 608.

hewen *n.* Heaven M 2032.

hy(e), high *v.* go quickly K 277, S 312, M 1391, CR 262; *imp.* K 209, S 196, M 790, CR 166.

high(e), hey(e), heghe, hye(e) *adj.* high K 119, M 107, CB 180; great M 157, W 61; **hyer** *comp.* more proudly S 550; **highest, h(e)yest** *super.* most noble M 3, 935, W 12.

hight *pr. 1 sg.* am called W 334; **hyth** *pp.* M 1821.

hinge *v.* hang CB 397; **hinges, hingeth,** *pr. 3 sg.* CB 71, 337; **hynge, hang** *pa. sg.* CB 176, CR 658; **hangyd** *pp.* M 236.

hird-man *n.* shepherd CR 434.

hyr(r)(e) see **she, thei.**

ho *pro.* see **who(o).**

hof *interj.* ha, ho M 491.

hold *n.* control M 371; *had in* ∼ kept in restraint M 150; **holddys** *pl.* prisons M 965.

hold(e) *v.* obey M 52; consider S 659; retain CB 265; hold CB 605; **hold(d)** *pr. 1 sg.* consider M 246; **holdest** *pr. 2 sg.* sustain W 317; **holdyth** *pr. 3 sg.* possesses M 126; *pr. pl.* consider K 125; have (bribes) W 723. **hold(e)** *imp.* claim M 1289: ∼ *vp* wait M 1228; *refl.* keep W 728; **hol(l)d** *pp.* considered M 935, W 585.

hol(e) *adj.* healthy S 320, M 677, W 187, CB 788.

holle, hoolye, holly *adv.* wholly M 572, 1988, CR 249.

holly *v.* hallow W 251.

hom see **who(o).**

home *pr. 1 sg.* hum M 1226.

homlye *adv.* familiarly CR 656.

hoolle, hole *adj.* whole K 29, S 52.

hop *pr. 1 sg.* hope CR 15.

hornpype *n.* a player of the hornpipe W 752 s.d.

hort *pa. pl.* hurt M 965.

hosyll, hossell *v.* administer the host to M 2080, 2086.

hossys *n. pl.* stockings M 502.

houkkyn *v.* to hook, prob. here to fornicate with M 1160.

hovrle *v.* hurl M 142.

how *interj.* ho S 85, M 511.

howbeit, howbeyt *conj.* although S 356, CB 482, CR 452.

howre, ower *n.* hour S 492, M 1657.

howse see **who.**

howshold *n.* followers M 403.

humble, humblye *adj.* humble CR 513; obedient K 251; *in* ∼ *vyse* humbled S 217.

humylnesse, vmbyl(l)nesse *n.* humility M 2071, 2089, CB 479.

hungor, hovngure *n.* hunger M 2033; the hungry M 1933.

hur(e) see **she.**

hurde *v.* hoard W 582.

iche see **ech(e).**

yche *n.* itch M 737, see note.

iee, iey, yee, eye, ee *n.* eye S 571, M 515, 1879, CR 267; **nye** with my S 396; **ees, eyen, yys** *pl.* K 447, M 640 s.d., CB 126.

ygnorans *n.* ignorance M 712.

ileȝant *adj.* elegant M 505.

ylk *adj.* each CB 844.

ille, yll *n.* harm S 193; evil S 243, M 845; **yllys** *pl.* evils S 231.

ille, ylle *adj.* evil K 324, W 550.

illumynows *adj.* enlightening M 623.

image, ymage *n.* semblance W 32; icon CB 796.

imbrace see **enbrace.**

in, inne, yn *prep.* in, into K 1, S 26, M 1 etc.; among W 253; ∼ *aspecial*, especially M 1137.

inclyn(e), enclyne *v.* submit, agree S 5, W 469; condescend K 400, CB 293.

indevre, induere, induour *v.* endure M 292, 309; remain M 652.

indignacion, indignation *n.* disdain W 693; wrath CB 733.

infectyfe *adj.* filled with disease CB 368.

infyrmyte *n.* state of sin M 759.

inflame *v.* cause to brighten CR 654; **inflamyd** *pa. sg.* caused fires S 257.

influens *n.* a flowing in of spiritual power S 6, M 2019.

inflventt *adj.* flowing M 1096.

informable *adj.* ready to accuse W 539.

inhansyd see **enhanse**.

innvmerabyll *adj.* impossible M 1100.

inoow, inowe *adv.* sufficiently K 270, W 368.

inow(e) *n.* enough W 416, 564.

inperall *adj.* imperial M 707.

inperator *n.* emperor M 1 s.d.

inperfightnesse *n.* imperfection W 697.

inperrowpent M 238, see textual and general notes.

inquyrans *n.* inquiry M 134.

insue *pr. subj.* follow S 350.

insufficiens *n.* inability W 193.

intellygens *n.* knowledge S 160.

intende *pr. 1 sg.* plan S 169; **intendit** *pa. pl.* CR 25.

intende, intent(e) *n.* will S 140; purpose M 466, CB 840, CR 100.

intere see **enteere**.

interlye, intyrely *adv.* finally CB 818; completely S 150.

interrupcion *n.* disobedience K 90.

intille *prep.* into CB 633.

intreyt *imp.* plead CB 592; **intraytid** *pp.* treated CR 485.

invard, inward(e) *adj.* inner K 533, M 1039, CB 171, CR 267.

invre *adj.* practised M 2101.

inwardly(e), inwertlee *adv.* within CB 147, CR 168, 359.

inwyttyssymus *adj.* most invincible M 285.

ipocryte *n.* hypocrite M 734; **ipocrytes** *pl.* W 471.

ir *n.* ire, anger M 599.

iryn *n.* iron M 317.

irke *v.* be troubled, pained CR 386; **yrkit** *pa. sg.* was unwilling, troubled CB 111.

ytt(e) *pro.* it M 226, 1401.

iwise, iwys, ywys *adv.* certainly, truly M 489, W 357, CB 506, CR 71.

javelle *n.* knave K 345.

jelopher *n.* gillyflower M 1363.

jentyl(l) see **gentille**.

joyen *pr. pl.* rejoice K 501.

joly *n.*: *la plu* ~ the most pleasant thing, experience W 511.

jolye *adj.* handsome W 566.

jorn(e)y, jurney *n.* journey K 250, S 84; (sexual pun) M 1153.

joroure *n.* juryman W 718; **jorours** *pl.* W 724 s.d.

jorourry *n.* bribing of jurors W 637.

jug(g)e *n.* judge M 231, CB 380; **juggys** *pl.* M 114.

jugge *pr. 1 sg. refl.* appeal M 308; **judge** *imp.* judge S 634; **juged** *pp.* doomed CR 487.

justyce *n.* judge M 1300.

iustyfye *v.* attest to S 397.

kan see **can**.

keyle *v.* cool CB 76.

keynd *adj.* kind M 1139.

kelle *n.* prostitute M 520 (actually a fishnet or a woman's cap; we know of no other use as here, clearly a 'loose woman').

ken *v.* know S 330.

kendnesse *n.* kindness M 1342.

kene *adj.* brave M 49.

kenred, kinred, kynred *n.* lineage M 204; relations W 576; descendants M 977.

kente *adj.* known CB 156.

kep(e) *v.* guard CB 814; maintain CB 150; preserve K 96, M 469; retain M 1328; *pr. subj.* guard M 1578; *imp.* guard S 627; observe S 316; preserve S 567, M 703,

kep(e) *(cont.)*
W 174, CR 382; **kepinge** *pr. p.*
retaining CB 717; **kep, kept(e),
keptt, kepit** *pp.* guarded S 650,
M 1889, W 312; held M 563 s.d.;
preserved W 242; retained CB
286.

kepe *n.* heed M 1727, see also **take**.

kepinge *n.* retention M 1830;
protection CB 849.

kertelys *n. pl.* outer skirts W 164
s.d.

kesse *v.* kiss M 1073.

kyd *pp.* recognized M 230.

kynd(e) *n.* nature M 94; human
nature K 399; manner W 297;
type CR 39; *ageyn* ～ contrary
to nature W 529.

kyn(ne) *n.* relation S 89; family
CB 654.

kithe *pr. pl.* demonstrate, ack-
nowledge CB 655.

knaue, knave *n.* commoner S 93;
scurvy boy M 1175; servant M
1716.

knav, knaw(e) see **know(e)**.

knett(e) *pr. 1 sg.* knit, bind M 58;
draw together W 196; *pp.* joined,
united M 77, W 231.

knyth *n.* knight S 119 s.d., M 348;
knythys, knyt(t)ys *pl.* S 62,
M 112, 373.

know(e), knav, knaw(e), knoo
v. learn, recognize K 201, S 90,
M 619, W 670; understand S
283, M 804, W 210, CB 5, CR
285; *pr. 1 sg.* K 403, S 569, M
876, W 563, CB 496, CR 71; *pr.
pl.* CB 514; **knawes** *pr. 3 sg.*
CR 613; **knewyst** *pa. 2 sg.* M
696; **knawen** *pp.* CB 653.

knowyng *n.* knowledge M 1273,
W 265; understanding W 93;
comprehension W 155.

knowlege *pr. 1 sg.* acquaint M 868.

labor *v.* labor M 1374; **laberyd,
laboryd** *pp.* brought M 1822;
occupied with S 563.

lace *v.* bind with laces W 578;
lasyd *pp.* W 16 s.d.

lad *n.* commoner M 43; **laddes** *pl.*
boys W 708.

ladee, lady(e) *n.* lady M 349, CB
203; Virgin Mary K 2, 464.

lay, lav(e) *n.* law K (canc.) 4, M
1856, 2065; **layes** *pl.* S 488.

lak, lakke *v. tr., pr. 1 sg.* lack K
59; *pr. pl.* find fault with W 165.

lam(m)(e) *n.* lamb CB 129, 206,
223.

land(e), lond(e) *n.* realm, country
K 248, S 147, M 1371, W 682;
earth M 1475; rental? M 1691;
shore M 1444; **londdys** *pl.*
realm M 1981.

langbaynnys *n. pl.* long bones,
wretches M 190.

langoure *n.* sorrow K 497.

large *adj.* lavish W 640.

largeys, lorges *interj.* largess: *a*
～ thanks for the gift K 153, M
547.

lase *n.* lace sash M 497.

lasyd see **lace**.

lat see **let**.

late *adv.* recently K (canc.) 17, S
431, M 917.

laudacion *n.* praise K 472.

laude, lavd, lawd *n.* praise S 662,
M 2029, W 323.

laude *v.* laud CR 750; **laudying**
pr. p. S 314.

lawe see **low**.

leche *n.* leech, healer M 461.

led *n.* lid M 1015.

ledar *n.* leader M 400.

led(e) *n.* lead, the metal M 272,
CB 225; lead weight used for
taking a sounding M 1440.

led(e) *v.* lead, direct, bring S 345,
M 1735, CB 777; *imp.* lead M
1591, W 472; *pr. subj.* S 551;
led(d) *pa. sg.* led W 420, CB 33;
pp. M 398.

lef(e), leffe see **leve**.

leffulle *adj.* lawful W 408.

legyown *n.* legion, military unit M 367.

ley, ly *v. tr.* place, put CB 549; *pr. 1 sg.* K 273; lay a bet M 1778; **lay, ley** *imp.* M 844, CB 809; ~ *on* beat K 348; ~ *on handys* bestow care M 778; **laid, layd(e)** *pp.* S 176, M 1012, CR 123.

lekeyng see **lykyng**.

lelly *n.* lily M 526.

lem *n.* limb M 13.

lemman *n.* lover M 1149.

lende *pr. subj.* give consent W 299.

lengar, lenger(e) see **long(e)**.

leng(t)he *n.* length; ~ *and brede* everywhere CB 28; *at* ~ finally S 438; ~ *of the yeres* long life W 36.

lepe *n.* basket S 644.

lere *v.* learn M 1471, W 303, CB 637; teach M 527.

les *n.* falsehood M 83.

lesyng, lesinge *n.* lie M 837, CR 680.

less(e) *adj.* little K 278, M 60; fewer CB 315; ~ *and more* lower and higher (classes) M 1202.

lesse *v.* lose CB 765; **lese** *pr. subj.* W 677.

lesson *n.* teaching W 100.

lest *n.* least S 343; lowest W 415.

lest *adj.* smallest W 50.

lest *conj.* lest K (canc.) 11, S 613.

letchour *n.* debaucher S 558.

letification *n.* joy K 26.

lett *n.* delay K 265, S 334, M 42.

let(t) *v. intr.* delay K 177; *imp.* K 176, S 334; **lettid** *pa. pl.* K 354.

let(t)(e), lat(e) *v. tr.* let, allow K 172, M 281, W 565, CB 298, CR 499; abandon W 51; cause to CB 377; *aux.* let K 261, S 477, M 48, CB 374, CR 719; *imp.* M 535, W 691.

letteryd *adj.* literate S 355.

lettyng *n.* delay S 84, M 1275.

leue *n.* permission CB 422.

leuer *adv.* rather S 618.

leve, lef, leuyn, leven, lyff, lyue *v.* live S 34, 148, 198, M 1997, CB 517, CR 7; **leffe** *pr. 1 sg.* M 766; **levith** *pr. 3 sg.* W 405; **levit** *pa. sg.* CB 16; **levinge, lyvinge, lyuynge** *pr. p.* S 15, CB 807, CR 130; **levid** *pp.* CR 236.

leve, lef(e), leue *v.* leave K 293, M 1707, W 409, CB 58, 200, CR 362; *imp.* M 595, W 470, CB 792; ~ *of* stop CB 466; *pr. pl.* S 649; **left** *pa. sg.* CB 49; *pp.* M 1049.

levynges *n. pl.* manner, way of life W 434.

lewdnesse *n.* ignorance M 1616.

lewyd *n.* unlearned person W 682.

lewyn *n.* lightning M 2042.

lybrary *n.* collected learning W 227.

lycens *n.* permission S 8, M 1548.

lycens *adj.* blameless S 659.

ly see **ley**.

lye *v.* tell a lie M 1436; *pr. 1 sg.* W 642; **lyyst** *pr. 2 sg.* M 1167; **lye** *pr. pl.* W 489.

lye, lyyn *v. intr.* lie, recline, exist K 296, M 597, CB 613, CR 160; **ly** *pr. 1 sg.* M 1409; *imp.* M 1791; **lyes(e), lyeth, lyth** *pr. 3 sg.* M 1884, CB 623, CR 65; **lay(e)** *pa. sg.* K 268, M 1757, CR 195; **lyinge** *pr. p.* CB 38.

lyfelod, lyfflod *n.* means of subsistence M 87, 99.

lyf(f), lyve *n.* life K 214, M 292, W 417, CR 129.

light *adj.* merry W 569; cheerful CR 637.

light, ly3t, lyth *n.* light S 255, M 689; guide W 22; **lyth(t)ys** *pl.* lights S 250, M 1609 s.d.

lightly *adv.* pleasantly CB 4; easily CR 280.

lik *v.* please CR 693; **liked** *pa. sg.* K (canc.) 12.

lik(e), lyk(e) *adj.* ~ *to* similar

like(e) (*cont.*)
to W 172, S 153; ~ *vnto* CB 281; *adv.* in the manner of K 196, CB 26; ~ *as* K 39; ~ *to* W 16 s.d.; *conj.* ~ *as* just as K 122, M 1028.

lykene *pr. 1 sg.* compare K 491; **likenyd** *pp.* K 11.

likinge, lykyng *n.* lust W 460, M 398; affection CB 574; wish M 647; **lykenges** *pl.* desires W 51.

lykyng, lekyng *adj.* pleasing M 617; filled with desire W 567.

lykly, lyke, lylly *adv.* likely S 394, M 1265, W 554.

lynes *n. pl.* lines of the play CB 55 s.d.

lynyd *pp.* lined S 114.

lynne *v.* cease M 558.

lyst *n.* pleasure M 340; *of my* ~ at my pleasure M 16.

lyst, list *pr. 1 sg.* wish S 429; *pr. 2 sg.* K 400; *pr. 3 sg. impers.* K 433, S 284; *pr. subj.* K 250, S 11, CB 1; *pr. pl.* CB 602.

lyth see **light**.

lythly *adv.* quickly M 1146.

lytynnyd *pp.* lightened, emptied M 975.

lyttural *adj.* of letters S 657.

lyue, lyve *v.* see **leve**; *n.* see **lif(e)**.

locucyon *n.* speech S 562.

lodesterre *n.* guiding star K 510.

lofe *v.* praise CR 751.

logge *n.* small house M 1577 s.d.

lok(e), luk(e) *v.* look S 352, CB 696; ~ *wele abought* take care K 206; *pr. 1 sg.* M 944; *imp.* take care K 105, S 56, M 742; look S 591, CB 89, 271; *pr. subj.* look S 94, M 1330, appear S 549; **lokyth** *pr. 3 sg.* looks S 112; **lokid, lukyd** *pa. sg.* CB 189, CR 366.

long *pr. 1 sg.* yearn S 432.

long(e) *adv.* a long time K 163, S 267, M 292, W 242, CB 16, CR 2; *as* ~ *as adv. rel.* S 267; **lengar, lenger(e), longar** *comp.* K 388, S 497, M 281; **lengest** *super.* M 309.

longith, longyth, longytt *pr. 3 sg.* belong K 118, 511, M 1185; **longe** *pr. pl.* W 686.

lordeyn, lurdeyn *n.* wretch M 1464, K 173; **lordeynnys** *pl.* M 189.

lore *n.* discipline S 110; learning W 418.

lore *pr. 1 sg.* frown W 326.

lorges see **largeys**.

losellys *n. pl.* rascals M 190.

lost see **lust**.

losty see **lusty**.

losyd, lost(e) *pp.* lost S 466, M 1469; CB 356; damned M 367; to no avail M 964.

loth(e) *adj.* displeased K 135; reluctant S 61, M 1436; pained CR 171.

louely *adv.* worthy of love W 43.

lought see **lowt(e)**.

love-day *n.* day to settle disputes W 698.

low, lowe, lawe *adj.* low S 362, K 119, M 247, CB 2.

lowe *n.* love M 352; **lowys** *pl.* M 1706.

lowlynes(se) *n.* meekness M 103, 796.

lowse *v.* loosen, untie CR 460.

lowt(e), lought *v.* make obeisance M 43; bow down W 503; reverence CR 751; **lowtt** *pr. pl.* bow down M 926.

lucens(e) *n.* brilliance M 770.

luk(e), lukyd see **lok(e)**.

lullay *n.* lullaby CB 719.

lurdeyn see **lordeyn**.

lure *n.* bait, device in falconry for recalling the hawk CR 471.

lust, lost *n.* fleshly desire, pleasure M 399, W 611; **lustes** *pl.* W 51.

lusty *adj.* pleasing M 505; **losty** lusty M 944.

mad(de) *adj.* mad, insane M 293, K 365.

mageste, magestye *n.* majesty S 426, M 2105.

magnifie, magnyfy *v.* extol K 468, M 174; **magnyfyed** *pp.* glorified M 808.

maile *n.* chain armour K 352.

may *n.* young girl M 416.

may(e) *aux. v. pr. sg., pl.* can, be able, K 148, S 199, M 137, W 78, CB 74, CR 42; **mayst, mast** *pr. 2 sg.* S 196, M 1220; **mown** *pr. pl.* M 392; **myght(e), my3t(e), mygth, myt(h)e** *pa. sg., pl.* S 403, M 1022, CB 36, CR 220.

mayntement *n.* the practice of maintenance W 706.

mayntenaunce, meyntenaunce *n.* unjust support (of retainers) W 671, 691: *hattes of* ~ hats for retainers W 724 s.d.

mayntyn *v.* support unjustly W 700; **meyntyn** sustain M 106.

makar, maker(e) *n.* creator S 594, M 632, CB 107, CR 95.

mak(e) *v.* perform, do K 289, S 29, M 134, W 371, CB 852, CR 62; cause, force K 71, S 320, M 28, CB 37, CR 260; create K 355; ~ *a fray* have a fight K 192; **makyst** *pr. 2 sg.* S 443; **makett, makyt(t) mase** *pr. 3 sg.* M 505, 1000, 1756, W 579; **mad(d)(e)** *pa. sg., pl.* K 32, S 118, M 147, W 268, CB 83, CR 92; *pp.* K 220, S 461, M 701, W 24, CR 229; established CR 672.

malewry *n.* misfortune W 667.

malycyows *adj.* malicious, full of evil M 1661.

malishosly *adv.* with evil intent CR 25.

malynacyon *n.* hostility: *make wyth* ~ be hostile M 128.

malyng *adj.* evil M 434.

malyngne *n.* evil M 720.

malmeseyn *n.* sweet wine of Monemvasia, Greece, M 476.

mament *n.* idol M 1553 s.d.; **mamentys, mawmentes** *pl.* K 243, M 1556 [OF Mahomet].

mancyon *n.* dwelling M 1461.

maner(e), manyr *n.* way K 92; kind (of) S 193, M 845, W 466; *in good* ~ willingly M 531.

manffulle *adj.* strong W 455.

manhed(e) *n.* human nature M 972, CR 96.

manyfold *adj.* multiple CB 87.

mankende, mankyn *n.* mankind K 480, W 543.

manly *adj.* courageous CB 125; *adv.* K 137.

marcy see **mercee.**

mare *adj., pro,* see **more;** *v.* see **marre.**

margaretton *n.* compound of pearls M 339.

margente *n.* margin CB 273.

marke *n.* amount of money, coin M 1739.

marke *imp.* notice CR 461.

marraner(e) *n.* mariner M 1867, 1919.

marre *v.* hurt M 39, CR 187; *pr. 1 sg.* perplex, join? W 346; **mare** *pr. pl.* harm CB 510; **marryd** *pp.* injured *M 192.

maruayle *v.* be astonished S 398; **maruayle, merveyll, mervelle** *pr. 1 sg.* wonder S 248, M 1325, CB 387; **mervellyt** *pa. sg. impers.* was astonished M 567.

mase see **mak(e).**

mas(s)age, masege *n.* message S 289, M 1270.

mat(t)er, matere *n.* business,

mat(t)er (*cont.*)
concern K 30, S 386, M 2136;
maters *pl.* S 410.
mavgre, mawgere *prep.* in spite
of K 94, 271.
mawt *n.* Maltese wine M 476.
meane, mene, meyn *n.* method
S 479; means M 1568, CB 255;
meanys *pl.* S 404.
mede *n.* reward M 267, W 217,
CB 778; bribery W 672.
medsyn *n.* medicine M 681.
meyne *n.* company W 735; meny
followers W 706; menyes *poss.*
company's W 729.
meyntyn see mayntyn.
mek(e)nes(se), *n.* humility S 547,
M 1607, CB 293, CR 234.
mekille, mykyl *adj.* much M 22,
CR 273; *pro.* S 109.
mekith *pr. 3 sg.* makes meek W
85; mekyd *pp.* brought low S 524.
mell *n.* trouble M 1003.
melleflueus, mellyfluos *adj.*
sweetly flowing M 794, 1446.
memoryall *n.* intention M 1134.
mencyon, mensyon *n.* memory
M 1342; mak(e) ~ recall to
mind S 524, M 1050.
mende see mynd(e).
mene *n.* middle singing voice W
618; see also meane.
mene *v.* mean, intend S 248; *pr. 1
sg.* K 453, M 434; menytt *pr. 3
sg.* M 1543; meyn *pr. pl.* CB 334.
meny *adj.* many S 403.
menyes see meyne.
menyver *n.* white fur, prob. stoat
W 16 s.d.
mensyon see mencyon.
menstralle *n.* minstrel, musician
W 692 s.d.; menstralles, menstrellys, *pl.* K 565, W 701.
mentyll *n.* mantel, cape M 1604;
mantelys *n. pl.* W 164 s.d.
merakyll *n.* miracle M 1550.
merciabille *adj.* capable of mercy
CB 758.

mercury *n.* the metal mercury M
318.
mery *adj.* enthusiastic, merry K
348, M 295, W 492; joyful W
494; pleasant CR 632.
meroure, merrour *n.* appearance
M 319; model, reflection W 31;
merrorys *pl.* excellencies M 73.
merveyll see maruayle.
mervelously *adj.* miraculously S
601.
mesteryys *n. pl.* mysteries M
2040.
mesuer, mesure *n.* moderation
M 1581, CR 329; measure,
standard M 296.
mesur(e) *imp.* moderate CB 264,
CR 405; mesured *pp.* measured
CB 370.
met(e) *n.* food M 1403, W 473,
CB 143.
mete *adj.* fitting CB 686.
mete *v.* meet K 495, S 281, M
1109, CR 552; mett *pp.* M 793
s.d.
meve see moue.
mevynges *n. pl.* actions, deeds W
226.
mich, mych(e) see moch(e).
myght *n.* mite K 142.
mygth, my3t, myth *v.* see may.
myght, mygth, myt(e) *n.* might,
power K 108, S 285, M 1006,
CB 46; myghthtys, mytys *pl.*
M 110, 632; faculties of the soul
W 177.
my3ty, myth(t)y, myty *adj.*
mighty K 62, S 263, M 12, 257,
1457.
mykyl see mekille.
mynd(e), mende *n.* the cognitive
faculty W 183; disposition W 42,
CB 583; inclination W 199;
intention K 47, S 66, M 648,
CB 556; memory W 197, CB
197, CR 42; remembrance W
189; thought S 76, W 381;
understanding W 210, CR 450;

have ~ reflect W 185; remember W 208.

mynde *v.* call to mind CB 14; **myndes** *pr. 3 sg.* CR 537; **myndinge** *pr. p.* remembering CB 226, CR 170.

mynystyr *v.* serve M 2091; **mynystryyd** *pp.* M 2066.

mynystyrs *n. pl.* attendants M 1487.

mynystracyon *n.* charge M 329.

mynstrelly *n.* music M 1141.

mynnate *n.* instant CB 518.

myrable *adj.* marvellous S 254, W 41.

mys *n.* sin W 363.

mys *adj.* amiss W 403.

***mysbelef** *n.* heresy M 1469.

myschanse, myschaunce *n.* misfortune K 76, M 39.

myschef, mysheff *n.* misfortune K 79, S 524, M 1655.

myschevose *adj.* calamitous CB 652.

myscreauntys *n. pl.* unbelievers S 391.

mysfare *v.* go wrong W 496.

mys(se) *v. tr.* overlook M 1491; fail CR 400; *intr.* be lacking W 248; fail CR 227; **myste** *pp.* avoided S 287.

myt(h)e see **may**.

myth(t)y, myty see **my3ty**.

moch(e), mych(e) *adj.* many, much S 490, M 20, W 632.

moch(e), mich, mych(e) *adv.* much S 262, M 504, W 414, CB 132, CR 730.

mode *n.* disposition M 1909.

moderation *n.* restraint CB 600.

moder(e) *n.* mother K 8, CB 110, CR 481; **moders, modyrs** *poss.* K 496, CB 487, CR 30; *pl.* CB 164.

moderlye *adv.* with the feelings of a mother CR 530.

mold *n.* earth M 1811, CB 549.

mollyfyed *pp.* softened CR 527.

mon(e) *n.* lament CB 201; **monys** *pl.* moans M 1020.

mone *n.* moon M 316.

monycyon *n.* warning S 635.

monyment, monument, monvment *n.* sepulchre M 894, 1011 CR 98.

mo(o) *pro.* more M 192.

mor(e), mare *adj.* more, greater K 266, S 415, M 337, W 97, CR 229; *adv.* more K 335, S 338, M 351, W 414, CB 192, CR 229; *pro.* K (canc.) 10, S 107, M 1825, W 646, CB 143; ~ *or lesse* great or small CB 315; *lesse and* ~ low class and high M 60, W 740; **maste** *adj.* greatest CR 87.

moryd *pp.* increased M 1099.

morowe *n.* morning K 168, CB 55 s.d.

mort *adj.* dead M 455.

mortal(l)(e) *adj.* deadly K 298, S 509, M 199; **mortel** CB 36.

mosed *pp.* deceived W 348.

moteryng *n.* muttering M 128.

motyon *n.* direction S 418.

mot(t)(e), mut *pr. 2, 3 sg., pl.* may K 523, M 107; must K 319, S 642, M 1228; *so* ~ *I the* so may I thrive M 1731.

moue, meve *v.* affect M 1134, CR 668; move CB 3; express S 508; *imp.* urge S 478; **movyth** *pr. 3 sg.* speaks of S 561; **movyd** *pp.* urged S 419.

mowe *v.* grimace K 296.

mownt *n.* mountain CB 28.

mowrn(e) *v.* mourn, lament CB 270; CR 709; *imp.* CB 451.

murtherid *pp.* murdered CB 729.

mvske *n.* musk, medicine M 1362.

naylle *v.* fasten with nails CB 402;

nailet, nailit, naylit *pp.* CB 673, CR 11, 471.

name *n.* reputation K 364, W 602; **namys** *poss.* M 2043.

namid, namyd *pa. sg.* named, called CR 296; *pp.* S 218.

natur(e) *n.* human nature M 1888, W 110, CB 346; life S 554; physical condition K 7; creative force CB 785; **naturs** *poss.* CB 44.

navta *n.* sailor M 1716 s.d. [*Lat.*].

ne *correl, conj.* nor S 119, M 337, W 64, CB 102, CR 82; *neg. part.* not K 148.

necesse *adj.* necessary W 442.

necligence, neclygens *n.* sins by omission M 703, CR 203; negligence S 71.

ned(d)es, nedes, nedys *adv.* necessarily K 468, M 524, CB 241, CR 211.

nede *n.* distress M 1631; necessity M 1487; want W 458; *at my* ∼ in distress S 81; *is* ∼ is necessary W 504.

nede *v.* be obliged S 553; **nedith** *pr. 3 sg. impers.* is necessary W 148.

nede *adv.* of necessity S 553, CB 255.

nedfull *adv.* necessary M 287.

nemyows, nymyos *adj.* beyond measure M 857, 1112 [L. *nimium*].

ner *prep.* close to CB 128.

ner(e) *conj.* nor S 517, M 1365.

ner(e), nerr *adv.* almost K 365, M 293; close M 482, CB 442, CR 122; *hold* ∼ come near M 1863; *full* ∼ here M 1110; **nerre** *comp.* closer CB 391.

nether(e) *adj.* lower W 145.

neuer, neuyr, nevyr *adv.* at no time K 147, S 94, M 76, 545, W 68, CB 19, CR 15; not at all M 336, CB 160; ∼ *so* no matter how W 679.

nevyn *pr. pl.* say M 315.

new(e) *adv.* recently M 494; afresh W 433.

newe *n. on the* ∼ novel K 338.

next *adj.* nearest CR 263; *adv.* M 1487; *prep.* S 413.

ny *adv.* near M 230.

nye see **iee**.

ny3t, nyth *n.* night S 133, M 139.

nyse *adj.* foolish W 476.

nysete *n.* triviality W 651.

no *interj.* no indeed M 1419, W 399.

nobley *n.* nobility W 4.

nocent *adj.* harmful S 321.

noght(e), nought, nowth(e) *n.* nothing M 591, 1476, W 201, CB 392, CR 92.

no3t, nought, nowt *adv.* not K 233, W 107; **ryth** ∼ not at all M 193.

noyose *adj.* vexatious, troublesome CB 650.

noyttment *n.* ointment M 640 s.d.

nominate *pp.* named S 414.

non(e), noon *pro.* none, no one K 59, S 139, M 6, W 658, CB 229, CR 58; *adj.* no, not any S 89, M 785, W 676, CB 255; ∼ *nay* it cannot be denied K 37, W 152; *adv.* no, not, not at all S 561, M 984, CB 778.

none *n.* noon M 979.

nortur *n.* breeding M 529.

note *imp.* note, remark CR 461.

nother, nothire, nowther *correl. conj.* neither S 60, 116, CB 814, CR 522.

nothinge, nothyng *adv.* in no wise M 1925; not at all CB 686, CR 82.

notycyon *n.* written words S 12.

notyfy *v.* announce S 22.

nowmbere *v.* count CB 302.

o see **one**.

obbey, abey *v.* obey M 928, 1569; *pr. 1 sg.* M 426; *pr. pl.* M 2015; **obeyyn** *pr. pl.* M 2017; **obbeyed, obeyit, obeyyd** *pp.* K 519, M 31, 149.

obedyentt *n.* obedience M 1805.

obeisaunce, obeysavns, obes-

syawnse *n.* respect M 765; obedience M 34, W 81.

oblacion, oblation *n.* offering K 424, CB 630, CR 429.

oble *n.* offering M 2018 s.d.

obscuryd *pp.* overshadowed M 714.

obserua(u)nce *n.* ceremony K 418; attention, care CR 513.

obserue *v.* obey K 101; *imp.* S 316.

obtayne, obteyne, optayn *v.* succeed S 324, 638, M 182, 1090; **opteynyd** *pp.* S 462.

obusyouns *n. pl.* deceptions M 457.

occedentt, occydent *n.* west S 18, M 1495.

odyr, othyr, tother *adj.* other M 415; *pro.* M 81, 743 s.d.

of *adv.* off M 146, CB 466, CR 163.

of, off *prep.* about, concerning K 31, S 155, W 25, CB 1, CR 215; by M 15; by reason of K 7, S 37, M 259; ∼ *reason* logically W 113; belonging to, of K 2, S 421, M 1015, W 703, CB 56, CR 237; by means of S 203, W 638; characteristic of K 451, S 38; for K 297, S 266, M 1040, CR 248; from K 280 s.d., S 31, M 126.

ofer, offre *v.* offer M 1142, K (canc.) 18; **offred** *pa. sg.* CR 79; **offrid** *pp.* K 464.

ofer *prep.* see **ouer.**

offend(e) *v.* transgress, sin against S 139, W 710; displease W 297; *pr. pl.* W 436; *imp.* S 187; **offendyng** *pr. p.* giving offence S 397; **offendyd** *pp.* sinned against M 633.

office, offyse *n.* religious service M 1225; position M 1303, CR 589.

oft *adv.* often S 561, W 221, CR 446.

onbynd *v.* relieve, release M 96; *imp.* M 801.

onclypysyd *adj.* uneclipsed M 1349.

oncuryd *pp.* uncovered M 769.

ondyr(e), vnder *prep.* under S 9, M 160, 862, CB 604; within M 266.

ondyrneth *prep.* underneath M 357 s.d.

ondowtyd *pp.* undoubted S 463.

on(e), an *prep.* on, upon K 70, S 404, M 264, 1684, W 381, CB 28, CR 33; in K 178, S 307, M 301, CB 15, CR 67; of CB 530; ∼ *slepe* asleep CB 719; *adv.* *com(e)* ∼ advance K 548, M 1536, CB 829; *daunce* ∼ continue dancing W 734; *ley* ∼ strike blows vigorously K 348, place M 778; *think* ∼ think about M 1753.

on(e), o(o)n, o *indef. pro.* one K 171, S 94, M 653, W 558, CR 259; *adj.* S 477, M 44, W 277, CB 286.

ones, on(y)s *adv.* once W 520, CB 422, CR 445; *at* ∼ immediately K 548, M 52, CB 756; *at* ∼ all together M 547.

ony, eny *adj.* any K 86, S 74, M 36, W 351, CB 729, CR 693; *pro.* K 213, S 574, M 26.

onymentys *n. pl.* ointments M 668.

onored, onoryd *pp.* honoured M 933, 2021.

onpossybyll *adj.* impossible M 913.

onquarte *adj.* weak M 779.

ons see **on(e)s.**

onshaply *adj.* badly formed M 1158.

onstabyll, vnstabille *adj.* changeable M 588, CR 303.

onto, vnto *prep.* for M 132; into, to K 526, S 175, M 386, W 202, CB 148; toward S 311; *lik* ∼ like CB 281; *likenyd* ∼ compared with K 11.

ontru *adj.* untrue M 1255.

opynly, oppenlye *adv.* in the open M 2018 s.d., in view of all CR 246.

oppres(s)e *v.* be overwhelmed (*pass.* in meaning) M 2110; *imp.* cast down CB 756.

optayn, opteyn see **obtayne**.

or, are *conj.* or K 44, S 40, M 1308.

oratorye *n.* prayer K 459.

ordeyn(e) *v.* direct S 429; arrange CR 118; **ordeigned** *pa. sg.* destined W 475; **ordeyned, ordeynnyd** *pp.* prepared M 574; destined W 191, 243.

ordenaunce, ordynowns *n.* plan K 249; arrangement M 579.

ordere *imp.* regulate, control CB 811.

ordynatly *adv.* in order, properly W 138.

ordire, ordor *n.* arrangement K 476, M 313; command CR 440.

orebyll *adj.* horrifying M 962 s.d.

oryent *adj.* radiant, brilliant M 441.

os(e) see **as**.

oth(e) *n.* oath S 60, M 1914; *wythowt* ~ by natural right M 1949.

othyr see **odyr**.

otys *n.* oats S 85.

ouer *adj.* higher W 300.

ouer, ofer, owere, owyr *prep.* over S 427, M 1854, 1870; *adv. gon* ~ to another place, area M 1142; over (the sea) M 1730.

ouerawe *adv.* everywhere CB 653.

ough *see* **owe**.

ought *adv.* see **out(e)**.

ouir, oures see **we**.

out(e), owt(e), ought, ow3t(e) *adv.* out K 232, M 1280, CB 371; away K 196, CB 533, CR 423; displaced W 524; ~ *of* away from K 359, S 532, M 288, CR 94; from under K 189;

from within CB 37; ~ *of hand* without hesitation K 214; ~ *of mesure* immoderately CR 329; ~ *sought* brought to bear CR 91; *tell* ~ tell directly S 451; *interj.* alas K 381, S 433, M 963.

outhere *conj.* or K 506.

out-wrynge *pr. 1 sg.* squeeze out W 619.

owe, ough *pr. 1 sg.* ought, should W 100; owe W 190; *pr. pl.* W 212; **owth** *pr. pl.* M 808; **owttyst** *pa. 2 sg.* M 674; **owt, aught** *pa. sg.* M 653, CB 440.

ower see **howre**.

ower(e), owerys see **we**.

pacyfycal *adj.* peaceful M 1592.

pagent *n.* scene S 167.

pay *n.* satisfaction K 215, M 1602; liking M 960; money payment M 1799.

paynfully *adv.* inflicting pain CB 92.

pakke *n.* pack K 275; *Wattys* ~ *n.* paunch M 1154, see note.

paleys, palesse *n.* palace M 1353, CB 22.

parde *interj.* by God M 521.

parelle, perelle *n.* peril M 1915, W 312; **perellys** *pl.* M 1751.

parisch *pr. pl.* perish W 410.

partie, party(e) *n.* people K 244; *on eche* ~ in every particular M 215; *for oure* ~ with regard to each of us K 466; **parties, party(y)s** *pl.* regions S 412, M 34; divisions W 135.

pase *n.* pace: *on* ~ frequently CB 509; see also **apaas**.

passaunt *adj.* in vogue W 610.

passe *v.* depart K 261; go M 1370, CR 196; *hens* ~ die M 109; cross M 1370; **pas(se)** *pr. pl.* die CB 166; **passis, passyt** *pr. 3 sg.* surpasses M 1944, CB 134; **passis** *pr. pl.* pass CB 277; **passid, passit, past(e)**

pp. passed, past M 1340, CB 744, CR 28.

passible *adj.* possible W 97.

passion(e), passyon *n.* suffering M 861, CB 185, CR 339.

passyve *adj.* suffering, redeeming CR 96.

paternyte *n.* fatherly rule M 903.

pawsacion *n.* pause W 463.

pawse *v.* pause CB 260.

pece, peas(e), pes *n.* peace K 493, S 269, M 93; silence K 305, CB 819; *hold my* ~ keep silent K (canc.) 13.

peck *n.* peck measure S 85.

peyn(n)ys *n. pl.* pains M 96, 519.

peneawnt *adj.* wide and loose M 496.

pense *n. pl.* pence M 653.

pepell, pepille, pepyll, pepul(l)e *n.* people S 20, M 18, 36, CB 50, 277; **pepullys** *pl.* people (coll.) S 646.

pepur *n.* pepper M 342.

perambulacyon *n.* walk S 67.

perauenter, perauentur *adv.* by chance S 617, CR 465.

perce, perse *v.* pierce K 99, M 219; **percytt** *pr. 3 sg.* M 994.

perceyvable *adj.* discernible W 595.

pere *n.* peer, equal CB 82.

perfight, parfight, perfyth *adj.* perfect K 446, S 348, M 611, W 56, CR 322, 425; complete S 292; believing S 325.

perfightly, perfitlye *adv.* perfectly W 233, CR 33, 269.

perfightnesse, perfitnese, perfythnes(se) *n.* perfection M 581, 586, 603, W 377, CR 428.

perhenuall *adj.* everlasting M 637.

perlys *n. pl.* pearls W 1 s.d.

perplexite(e) *n.* distress M 519; confusion CR 720.

perplyxcyon *n.* distress M 1985.

perse see **perce.**

perseuer *v.* be steadfast S 521.

persue, porsue *v.* pursue S 32; follow M 610.

perswade *v.* change M 1976.

perteynyng *pr. p.* pertaining M 315, W 592.

pertely *adv.* openly M 206.

perturbacyon *n.* worry M 1531.

peruerse *v.* pervert W 379.

peruert *pr. sub. intr.* be led astray W 292; *pr. 1 sg.* lead astray W 362.

pes see **pece.**

pesabyl, peseable *adj.* peaceful M 25; quiet K 52.

pese *n.* cup, small portion M 535 [OF *piece*], see note.

pesyn, see **poyson.**

pete, pyte *n.* pity K 116, S 222, M 239.

peticion, *n.* entreaty M 848; **petycyons** *pl.* requests S 44.

phy *v.* trust M 1068 [AF *fier*].

phylyssoverys *n. pl.* philosophers M 164.

physnomy *n.* physical appearance S 93.

pycche *v.* cover with pitch M 738.

pyn *n.* pine tree M 1360.

pynne *n.* peg: *on a mery* ~ in a happy mood W 492.

pynsynesse *n.* anxiety M 606.

pyrles *adj.* peerless M 358.

pystyll, pystull *n.* epistle, letter M 1267, 1313; **epystolys** *pl.* S 38.

pyteose, pytous, peteose *adj.* deserving of pity CB 158, 322, CR 13, 88; full of pity S 6, CR 247.

piteosly(e), peteosly *adv.* arousing pity CB 233, CR 12, 474.

pitture, picture *n.* representation K 14, W 350.

place *n.* acting area K 25, S 210 s.d., M 563 s.d.; dwelling place W 132; position W 327.

play *n.* drama CB 55 s.d.
playn, pleyn *adj.* clear, S 513, CR 458: *adv.* clearly M 880.
playnly, plenly *adv.* clearly, simply M 1406, W 62, CR 295.
plase *n.* *in euery* ~ everywhere M 429.
plate *n.* plate armour K 352.
plece see **plese.**
pley *v.* perform a play K 49; *pr. subj.* act K 197; **played, playyd** *pp.* performed a play M 2132, CB 55 s.d.
pleyyng *n.* dalliance M 504.
pleyn *adj.* full M 1692.
plenerly *adv.* fully W 404.
plente(e) *n.* plenty M 471, CR 759; *in full* ~ to the last drop CB 681.
plenteose *adj.* plentiful CB 372.
plenteosly, plentuosly *adv.* in full measure CB 298, CR 478.
plesaunce, pleseawns, plesowans, plesawnt *n.* pleasure M 90, 648, 1639; enthusiasm S 66.
plesa(u)nt, plesavnt, plesawnt *adj.* pleasing K 59, S 82, W 132, CR 407.
plesauntly, pleseavnttly *adv.* pleasingly M 242; with good will M 1539.
plese *v.* please K 279, M 459; *impers.* be (your) will S 365; *pr. 1 sg.* please K 422; **plese, plece** *pr. subj. impers.* M 167, 646; **ples(e)yng** *pr. p. impers.* M 1299, 1490; **ple(a)sid** *pa. sg.* pleased W 413, CR 308; **plesett, plesid, plesit** *pa. sg. impers.* M 1513, CB 429, CR 306; **ple(a)syd** *pp.* pleased S 108, M 45, W 468.
ples(e)yng *n.* pleasure, will M 1505, 1645.
plight *pr. 1 sg.* pledge K 339.
plungid *pp.* pierced CB 462.
poynt(t) *n.* instant CR 468; *a* ~ about, likely (*to*) M 1408; **poyntys** *pl.* essentials M 105.

poyson, pesyn *n.* evil K 455; poison CB 533; **poyson(ne)s** *pl.* evils S (canc.) 9, 510.
ponderite *pa. sg.* bore CB 217.
ponysch *v.* punish M 1985.
porchas(s)e, purchase *v.* acquire K 505, M 22; relieve M 1375; **porchasyd** *pp.* gained M 689.
porposyd see **purpose.**
portature *n.* supporter M 306.
porvyawns, porvyowns, purviaunce *n.* arrangements M 577; hospitality M 582; foresight K 48.
posses *v.* win a place S 557.
poste *n.* position, power M 1558.
postulacyon *n.* *make* ~ request S 44.
potenciall, potencyall *adj.* powerful S 360; mighty M 9.
potestacyon *n.* power, authority S 177.
potyt see **put(t).**
pouer, poure, powr(e) *n.* power S 2, 232, 416, 580; **pourys** *pl.* S 322.
pouert *n.* poverty W 667.
prayyn *v.* pray, ask M 1752; **prey, prye** *pr. 1 sg.* K 541, M 1571; **prayyt, preyyt** M 253, 215; *pr. 3 sg.* commands; **prayyng** *pr. p.* praying M 711.
praysinge, preysyng *n.* eulogy, elegy K 483, CB 794.
praty *adj.* pretty M 495.
pratyly *adv.* cunningly M 1160.
precept, preseptt *n.* order S 57, M 899; **preceptes, preceptys** *pl.* K 379, S 316.
precharsse, prechours *n. pl.* preachers M 29, W 488.
precios(e), precy(o)us, precyvs *adj.* priceless M 1018, 1907, CR 479; valuable CB 363; expensive, splendid W 454; most highly esteemed S 585; esteemed (ironic) M 1175.
preciosnesse *n.* value *W 33.
predycacyon *n.* preaching S 306.

pregedyse *n.* injury, prejudice M 234.

preyse *n.* praise M 2029.

preysseabyll *adj.* worthy of praise M 551.

prensses *n. pl.* princes M 521.

preor *n.* prayer M 1560; **preors** *pl.* M 1137.

***preparate** *v.* prepare S 137.

prerogatife, prerogatyve *n.* right CB 588; property W 49.

presedent *n.* ruler M 237.

present *adj.* as *n.* the one present, here M 250.

preseptt see **precept.**

presporyte, prosperyte *n.* prosperity M 22, 957, W 37.

presse *n.* distress CB 318.

pretend(e) *v.* intend M 1076; claim M 1558; venture 1963.

prevaylyd *pp.* become strong S 465.

prevely *adv.* secretly M 206.

pryd(e) *n.* pride S 446, M 1556, W 529.

prye see **prayyn.**

prykkyd *adj.* attired M 358.

prymatt *adj.* principal M 306.

pryme *n.* beginning M 1660.

prynt *imp.* express M 459; **pryntyd** *pp.* imprinted M 992 s.d.

pryse *n.* prize M 417; choice M 1708.

prysse *n.* price M 569.

privyde *pr. 1 sg.* provide M 956.

proces(se), prosses *n.* play, drama K 49, S 14; design S 575, M 1479.

procession, processyon *n.* entertainment K 484 s.d., S 157; *go* ~ go in procession K 470.

profite *pr. subj.* benefit W 457.

profyth, prophet(t) *n.* prophet (Christ) M 581, 750.

profred *pp.* given CR 80.

progressyon *n.* journey S 134.

promission *n.* promise CB 407.

promyssary *n.* procurator, officer M 237.

promtyt *pp.* prompted M 602.

proper *adj.* own S 579.

prophetabyll, prophytabyll *adj.* beneficial S 126, 482, M 1268.

propyrly *adv.* by nature W 9.

propyrte *n.* attribute W 1.

prosses see **proces(se).**

proteccyon, protexcyon *n.* guardian M 1048; care: *do* ~ act diligently S. 42.

proue *n.* proof CR 191.

prove, preve *v.* demonstrate M 866, W 378; discover CR 599; *pr. 1 sg.* demonstrate W 642; **prevyng** *pr. p.* W 541; **provid, provyd** *pp.* tested K 147; demonstrated S 510, M 1484.

provysye *v.* prophesy K 537.

provostycacyon *n.* power of the provost M 163.

pure, puer(e), pvere *adj.* untouched K 398, S 3, M 679, CR 472; unadulterated M 316; uncorrupted W 219.

purfyled *pp.* bordered W 16 s.d.

purge *v.* cleanse W 305; **purgyth** *pr. 3 sg.* S 322.

purificacion, purification *n.* ritual purification K 31, CB 629.

purpos(e) *pr. 1 sg.* am resolved K 203, W 384; *pr. pl.* K 29; **porposyd, purposed, purposid, purposyd** *pp.* K 469, 561, S 370, M 1065.

pursewe, pursue *v.* pursue, follow S 170, W 387; **pursuyd** *pp.* K 235.

purveye *v.* make ready K 430.

put(t), pot *v.* subject S 395, M 239; *pr. 1 sg.* place, put M 572; **put, pott** *imp.* S 295, M 1556; **putyth, potyt** *pr. 3 sg.* S 323; causes M 606; **potyt** *imp.* take M 458; ~ *down* suppress S 49; ~ *forth* extend S 208; ~ *of* remove M 902 s.d.; ~ *owt* remove K 197, get rid of CB 533.

quat see **what(t)**.
quell(e) *v.* kill M 1168; destroy W 542.
quene, quvene, quewne *n.* queen S 3, M 1358, 1938 s.d.
quenys *n. pl.* queans, whores K 305.
quessyon, whestion *n.* question M 662, CR 445.
quest(e) *n.* jury of inquiry W 643; **questes** *pl.* W 638.
quyet *n.* quiet M 775.
quyte, qwyt, whit *v.* repay M 1882, CB 850; *pr. subj.* acquit, conduct K 196; *imp.* K 131.
quod *pa. sg.* said W 518; **quod-a** *pa. sg.* said he S 442.
qwat(t) see **what(t)**.
qwy see **why**.

rage *n.* wild frenzy K 238; furious speed M 1331.
rage *v.* act wildly S 574; **ragid** *pa. sg.* was angry CR 82.
raygne, rayn(e), reyn(e), reyngne, ryngne *v.* reign, rule S 143, 517, 639, M 180, 285, 881, 887, 1088; *pr. 1 sg.* S 427, M 229; **rayneth** *pr. 3 sg.* S 490; **regnyng, reynand, reynyng, renynge** *pr. p.* M 889, 1455, CR 625; flourishing W 679; **regnyd** *pa. sg.* reigned CB 659.
rayse *imp.* erase CB 473.
raysed see **reisest**.
rampaunt *adj.* rising, foreleg elevated W 692 s.d.
rappys *n. pl.* blows M 1177.
ravyne *n.* violence W 727.
ravyssyt *pr. 3 sg.* transports M 447; **rauysshid** *pa. sg.* seized S 374.
rawnson *n.* ransom CR 494.
reasone *v.* discuss CB 422.
rebellers *n. pl.* rebels K 71.
rebellyous *n.* rebellious persons S 39.

rebon *n.* answer M 1465 [OF *rebondir*].
rechases W 722, see note.
reconsyle *v.* reconcile, restore CB 256; **reconcyle** *imp.* CR 397; **reconsiled** *pa. sg.* CB 253.
record(e) *v.* attest CB 35, CR 24; **record** *pr. 1 sg.* recall CR 219.
recownte *v.* tell, relate CR 332.
recummend *pr. 1 sg.* commit, entrust M 706, 2112; *imp.* command M 264; **recummend(e)** *pr. pl.* M 710; **recommendyng** *pr. p.* W 324; **recummendytt** *pp.* M 1314.
recummendacyon *n.* praise M. 951.
recumpens *n.* atonement M 701.
recure *v.* heal S 187; thrive M 311; recover M 655; obtain W 217; cure, save CR 335; **recuryth** *pr. 3 sg.* takes possession again W 654.
recurse *n.* return journey S 586.
red(e) *adj.* red M 153, W 692 s.d., CB 29.
redarguacyon *n.* opposition S 47.
redde *imp.* rid K 214.
reddure *n.* harshness, severity M 1579, W 76.
rede *n.* advice M 540; adviser M 1792.
rede *v.* read S 11; *pr. subj.* CB 3; *pr. 1 sg.* counsel M 233, W 469.
redeym, redemyn *v.* redeem M 888, CB 295.
redemptoure *n.* redeemer K 499.
redy, rydy *adv.* ready K 274, S 122, M 1388; direct W 644; promptly M 136.
redres(se) *v. reflex.* turn attention to S 13; *imp.* restore again M 282.
reducyd *pa. sg.* led back W 313.
redulent *adj.* fragrant M 2011.
reflexite *n.* shining M 441.
reformeth, reformyth *pr. 3 sg.* forms anew W 120, 127.

reformyng *n.* substitution W 337.

refrayn(e), refreyn(ne) *v.* hold back, restrain S 301; abstain M 1116, CB 365; *refl.* M 526, CB 60; *pr. pl.* hold back CB 798; **refreynyd** *pp.* CB 403.

refuse *v.* reject, betray CB 531; refuse CR 245.

regalye *n.* royal divinity K 242.

regalyte *n.* royal authority S 36.

regard *v.* judge CB 411.

regensy *n.* reign M 212.

regent *n.* regent, ruler K 125, M 117.

regent, regyon *n.* region, province S 129, M 220, 2085; **regeouns** *pl.* M 12.

rehers(s)e *v.* repeat, relate S 399, M 172; *pr. 1 sg.* S 565; *pr. pl.* M 1474; *imp.* M 1656; **rehersyd** *pp.* recounted M 241, pronounced M 1559.

reynand, reyn(e), reynne see **raygne.**

reynd see **rende.**

reyn(n)e *n.* reign M 164, 1329.

reynnys *n.* linen of Rennes M 496.

reioyce, rejoye *v.* rejoice S 139, CR 455; delight M 583; *pr. 1 sg.* M 110; **reioysyth** *pr. 3 sg.* brings joy to M 202; ~ *of* feel joy in M 259; **reyoyet** *pa. sg.* filled with joy CB 742; **reioysyng** *pr. p.* M 704 s.d.

reioyse *n.* joy W 613.

reioysseyng *n.* joy M 559.

reyse, rese, ryse *v. intr.* rise, arise M 878, W 202; *imp.* K 233; **reysyth** *pr. 3 sg.* W 231; **ros** *pa. sg.* M 1338; **resen(e), resyn(e), resun** *pp.* M 981, CR 137, 149, 193, 670.

reisest *v. tr. pr. 2 sg.* lift up W 318; **raysed** *pa. sg.* caused to rise CR 129.

reythfull *adj.* rightful M 1571.

reytyus *adj.* righteous M 212.

relacion, relacyon *n.* report M 2047, W 422.

releace *n.* deliverance CB 136.

relent(e) *v.* return S 259; soften CB 145; *pp.* softened CB 153.

reles(s)e *v.* release M 1773; remit, forgive CR 446.

releve, releff, relyff *v.* reward M 41; relieve M 1602; **relevyst** *pr. 2 sg.* rescue M 1945; **relevyd** *pa. sg.* M 755; **relevid, relevyd** *pp.* M 1099; nourished M 1583; rescued CR 338.

remayn *v.* continue M 173; remain CR 2; *pr. subj.* M 40.

rem(e) *n.* realm S 307, M 114, W 162.

rememb(e)rance, remembe- ravns, rememberowns *n.* memory K 1, M 1965, CB 193, CR 165, 511; *pot in* ~ intend M 572.

remission *n.* forgiveness of sins CB 242.

remoue, remove *v.* remove W 68, CB 575; affect, stir W 596; **remeve** *pr. 1 sg.* remove M 900.

rende *v.* tear W 533; *pr. 1 sg.* K 383; **reynd** pluck M 1083; **rendyt** *pr. 3 sg.* burst M 271; **rente** *pp.* ripped CB 146.

render *pr. 1 sg.* return CR 643.

renewe *v. tr.* regenerate W 386; bring back CB 565; *pr. pl.* bring back CB 417; *v. intr.* be restored W 668; **renuyd** *pp.* CB 165.

ren(ne), ron(n)(e) *v.* run K 190, M 374, CB 298, 728, CR 181; go quickly M 872 s.d.; **rynnys** *pr. 3 sg.* CB 472; **rennyt** *pr. 3 sg.* spreads M 585; **rynnes** *pr. pl.* CB 644; **ran** *pa. sg.* ran CB 178, CR 341.

renogat *n.* renegade M 238.

renovn *n.* renown M 130.

repeyere *v.* have recourse W 71.

repelle *v.* repel K 455; attack M 283.

repente *v.* sorrow CB 611.

replycacyon, repplycacion *n.* reply, argument W 447, M 127.

replye *v.* complain M 674.

report *imp. reflex.* corroborate CR 680; *pr. pl.* bring in the verdict W 730; **reporte** *pr. 1. sg. refl.* give an account CB 711; **reportith** *pr. 3 pl.* describe W 603.

repreffe *n.* disgrace M 40.

reprehende *v.* rebuke W 714.

represente *pr. 1 sg.* declare W 84.

reprobacyon *n.* objection S 46, M 161.

reprouable *adj.* blameworthy W 537.

requere, require, reqwire *v.* demand CB 811; *pr. 1 sg.* request CB 235; beg CB 551.

rere *imp.* rear: ~ *vp* raise M 1877.

resayuyth see **reseyue**.

resaruyd *pp.* held back CB 289, CR 302.

rese see **reyse**.

reseyue, reseyve *v.* receive S 379, M 2026; **resayuyth** *pr. 3 sg.* S 56 s.d. **reseyve, resaue** *imp.* M 225, CB 442; **receyuyng** *pr. p.* S 319; **reseyvyd, reseyvyt** *pp.* M 2095, M 2108 s.d.

resen(e) see **reyse**.

resydent *adj.* present M 954; *to be* ~ remain M 467.

resort *n.* followers W 692.

resort(e), resortt *v.* return M 453; proceed M 1450; reappear CB 350; turn CB 569; *pr. pl.* return CB 834; **resortid** *pa. pl.* returned K 93.

reso(u)n, reason, *n.* reason M 660, W 298, CB 288; rational faculty W 141; *as (good)* ~ *is* as would be according to reason M 300; *by* ~ in accord with reason W 10; *of* ~ justly W 113; *have* ~ be right W 445; *with* ~ by reason M 451.

rest(e), rist *n.* tranquillity S 148, M 65, W 742, CB 515, CR 261; rest CR 522.

rest(e), restyn, rist(e) *v.* rest K 411, W 380; remain M 568, CB 779, CR 4; **restyng** *pr. p.* W 132; **restyd** *pa. sg.* remained M 1350; **restyt(t)** *pr. 3 sg.* remains M 1978; *pp.* was fixed M 313.

restoratyf(f) *n.* cordial M 486; something capable of restoring M 651.

restor(e) *v.* restore K 514, CB 348; re-establish W 239; atone for M 1664; *pr. 1 sg.* restore S 296.

restryne *v.* restrain M 290.

retenaunce, retynawns *n.* retinue M 362, W 686.

retorn *imp.* come back CB 245.

reuelle *n.* revel, merry-making W 505.

revart, reverte *v.* return S 501; remain M 782.

reve see **ryve**.

revyue, revyve *v.* revive M 1896, CB 461.

rewe, rue *v.* regret K 343, S 614, M 1414.

rewle, rule *n.* musical rule M 1229.

rewle, rewlyn *v.* rule M 181, 1689.

ryal(l), ryalle *adj.* royal M 10, 336, W 585.

ryally *adv.* royally M 229.

ryalte *n.* splendour M 65.

rydy see **redy**.

right(e), ryte, ryth *n.* justice K 109, W 668; prerogative M 130; law CB 44; *of* ~ by law, justly CB 251.

right(t), ryght, ryth *adv.* very K 153, S 290, W 201, CB 88; directly, immediately M 1591; justly CB 338; exactly W 628; rightfully W 121.

rygorously *adv.* cruelly K 323.

rygorus *adj.* severe S 424.

rigo(u)re, rigur, rygore n. severity K 494, M 1582; cruelty CB 103, CR 34.

rynnes, rynnys see ren(ne).

rythewys adj. righteous M 889.

rythfull adj. just M 990; legal M 991.

rythwysnesse n. righteousness M 587.

ryve, reve v. separate, deface K 232, W 175; rofe pa. sg. split M 970.

roch n. rock M 1784.

rody adj. ruddy M 959.

rokke n. distaff K 159; rokkes n. pl. K 224.

ron, ron(n)e see ren(ne).

rood, ro(o)de, rud(e) n. the Cross K 539, CB 128, CR 163.

rore v. roar S 470 s.d.; pr. 1 sg. W 325; roryng pr. p. S 432 s.d.

rote n. root M 1083.

rottyt pp. rotted M 915.

rought, rowte n. packed crowd K 178; number K 194; group M 374.

rought v. make a riot W 505.

row v. row (a boat): ~ ageyn the flode live differently from others W 491.

rownd adj. round M 1218.

rownd v. whisper M 495.

rud(e) see rood.

rue see rewe.

ruth(e) n. pity M 274, W 316, CB 153.

sacryed pp. ordained M 2065.

sad(d) adj. serious M 297, CB 211, CR 23; sorrowful CB 712, CR 673.

sadly adv. steadfastly M 614.

saffe adj. safe M 1434.

say(e), sey(e), seyn v. say K 213, S 108 etc.; tell M 414; pr. 1 sg. command K 209, M 1223; pr. pl. how ~ ye what is your opinion S 386, CR 725; imp. tell S 393, M 1695; sais, seith, seyth pr.

3 sg. says K 127, CB 434 s.d., W 478; sey(e)ng, seyyng pr. p. K 516 s.d., M 304 s.d., W 16 s.d.; seid, seyd pa. sg. M 757; mentioned W 237; pp. K 155, 474.

sayle see seyle.

sakor pr. 1 sg. consecrate M 2067.

salue, salve n. salve (salvation) M 594, 1952.

sanctificatt pp. sanctified M 1554.

sapyencyall adj. wise S 80.

sauacyon, savacyon n. salvation M 1456, 1670.

saue, save prep. except M 162; ~ that conj. CB 209.

saule see sowle.

sauour v. taste, experiment W 87.

save, saue, sawen v. save, preserve K 8, M 852, CB 285, CR 420; pr. subj. give salvation (to) M 1862; protect M 845; savydyst, sauyd, savyd pa. 2 sg. M 1582, 1946, W 311; savyd, savyt pp. M 690, 854.

sawe n. reiterated intention S 385; report CR 647.

scant, scantly adv. scarcely CB 120, CR 47.

scho see she.

scyens n. knowledge S 657.

scolys n. pl. doctrines W 86.

scornyd, skoernyd pp. taunted, mocked M 863, CR 486.

scowrges n. pl. whips CB 305, CR 492.

seas see sesse.

seche see seke.

seduet pp. led astray M 716.

se(e) n. sea S 502, M 1782.

see n. dwelling place W 132.

se(e), sen(e), seyn v. experience M 638, W 59; know K (canc.) 7; perceive M 507; provide for M 723; see K 316, CB 17; behold M 844; ~ þat see (to it) that M 33, W 298; sestt, syest, seest pr. 2 sg. S 106, M 1541, CR 269; seynge pr. p. CR 338; save, se,

se(e) (*cont.*)
sey, sye *pa. sg.* S 104, 396, M 1487, 1908; **saughe** *pa. pl.* CR 707; **seyn, syn** *pp.* K 447, M 1106.
segnyte *pa. sg.* signed, indicated CB 723.
seyld *adv.* seldom M 929.
seyle, sayle *v.* sail M 1427; *pr. subj.* M 1426.
seyll *n.* occasion M 1411.
sek(e), seche, sekyn *v.* seek M 613, 793, CR 262; purge M 1361; *pr. 1 sg.* M 1070, CR 605; *pr. pl.* CR 134; **sekes, sekest** *pr. 2 sg.* M 1058, CR 603; **sought, sowȝt(e), sowth** *pa. sg.* tried to obtain W 18; *pp.* sought K 199, S 428, M 307, W 21, CR 91; chosen M 1929.
seke *adj.* ill M 763, CR 600.
seker(e), sekyr *adj.* certain M 217, W 368, 534.
sekyrnesse *n.* certainty W 60.
sell(e) *n.* cell M 2054, 2072 s.d.
sembled *pp.* assembled M 403.
seme *v. intr.* appear M 503, W 52; *tr. pr. pl.* think W 608; *it* **semeth** *pr. 3 sg.* it appears W 480; *me* ~ *impers.* it appears to me W 445, 554.
semely *n.* assembly S (canc.) 3.
sem(e)ly, semle *adj.* attractive M 51, 1249; **semelyare** *comp.* M 554; **semlyest** *super.* *M 563.
sen see **syn**.
sen(e), senne see **see**.
sensyble *adj.* capable of feeling W 96.
sensualite *n.* sensuality W 135.
sentens(e) *n.* meaning S 367, M 1452; opinion S 43; command S 277; judgment M 199; problem M 657; substance M 1672.
senture *n.* centre M 312.
sepoltur, sepulture *n.* sepulchre M 844, CR 217.

sere *adj.* various CR 489.
sere *n.* sir W 397; **serys, syrrys** *pl.* S 259, M 242.
serjauntys *n. pl.* sergeants-at-law M 1249.
sermon *n.* speech M 1159.
serve *v.* do the will of M 766; **serue** *pr. 1 sg.* serve W 630; **serva** *pr. pl.* treat (beat) M 739 s.d.
servyse *n.* divine office M 1150.
sesar *n.* caesar, ruler M 1252.
sese *v.* put in possession, endow M 1957; *pr. 1 sg.* M 1687.
sesse *v.* cease S 205; M 563; **seas** *pr. 1 sg.* K 331; *pr. 2 sg.* K (canc.) 14.
sete *n.* seat M 19; see also **cyte**.
seth *conj.* see **syth**.
seth *n.* atonement W 122.
set(t) *v.* set M 368; fear S 116; *pa. sg.* placed CB 72, CR 261; ~ *of imp.* embark M 1742; ~ *vp land* M 1740; *pp.* seated K 267; established K 493; endowed M 359; fixed W 229; ~ *bye* esteemed W 600; ~ *with* endowed W 219; see also **syt**.
set(t)e see **cyte**.
sew(e), sue *v.* follow K (canc.) 21, S 63, W 431; result W 369; seek W 665; *pr. 1 sg.* M 532.
sewynne *adj.* seven M 2043.
sewte *n.* appeal, suit S 428.
shal, shall(e), sal, schal(le), shulle, xal(l) *pr. sg.* shall K 222, 424, S 132, M 180, 2078, CB 513, CR 435; wish W 586; must M 1272; wishes S 233; *elliptic* shall be W 109; **shalt** *pr. 2 sg.* K 151; **sho(v)ld, sholld, shuld(e), shulld, suld, xold, xuld** *pa. sg. and pl.* K 46, S 175, M 174, 366, 915, 1628, 1963, W 702, CR 209; **sholddyst, xulddys** *pa. 2 sg.* M 1163, 2064.
shaper *n.* creator S 502.

shap(p)e *n.* outward appearance W 20; form, body CB 626.

sharme *pr. pl.* scream K 142.

sharpnes *n.* severity K 494.

she(e), sho, sche, scho *pro.* she K 8, M 419, CB 155, 159, CR 52; **her, hir, hyr, hyrre, hur(e)** *obj.* M 377, 378, 380, CB 162, CR 528; *poss. adj.* K 540, M 424.

shene *adj.* bright S 250.

shenshippe *n.* shameful conduct W 634.

shent *pp.* injured K 127, S 394.

shepman *n.* sailor M 1863; **shepmen** *pl.* M 1438 s.d.

sheppyng *n.* shipping M 1392.

shett, shytt *pp.* shut S 628, 646.

shew(e), shewyn *v.* show K (canc.) 10, M 898, 1092; make known to K 155, * M 1452, CR 696; demonstrate, prove K 244, M 105, W 377; present a drama K 31, * S 9; **schewes, shewyth** *pr. 3 sg.* demonstrates S 544; makes known to CR 194; **schew(e), shew(e)** *imp.* demonstrate K 54, M 1291, W 726; make known CB 148, CR 567; *pr. pl.* demonstrate M 105; **shewit, schewed, shewed, shewet** *pa. sg.* demonstrated M 2037, CB 131, CR 428; showed CR 195; **shewid** *pa. pl.* showed in a play K 25; **shewed(e), shewet, shewid, shewyd, shuyd** *pp.* showed in a play K 552, S 166; showed W 746, CR 677; demonstrated K 504, M 86, 2040, CR 322.

shewyng *n.* dream M 1620.

shortly *adv.* briefly S 48.

showyr *n.* pain, attack M 822; **shourys** *pl.* S 237.

shrank *pa. sg.* drew back CB 626.

shrewede *adj.* wicked, mischievous W 550 s.d.

shrowdys *n. pl.* lines of ship rigging M 1719.

shuyd see **shew(e)**.

sich, sych, soch, such(e), swych(e) *adj.* such, of that kind K 71, S 410, 507, M 39, W 305, CB 34, CR 749; *non* ~ no similar S 152; *adv.* K 312, S 91, W 441, CB 103, CR 32; *pro.* K 120, S 42, 104, M 40.

syde *n.* side: *on* ~ *adv.* aside W 565; *n. pl.* **sydys** M 1757.

syde *adj.* long W 16 s.d.

sight(e), sygth, syȝt, syte, syth(e) *n.* view, vision K 111, M 2132, CR 266; appearance K 402, S 104, CB 323, CR 213; perception W 118; power of vision S 223, 296, CB 40, 45; something seen W 573, CB 395, CR 13; **syȝhtys** *n. pl.* perception S 568.

signyfie *v.* symbolize W 149.

sygnis, synys *n. pl.* symbols M 992 s.d.; indications M 2020.

syyn *v.* sigh M 1972; **syhe, syth** *pr. 1 sg.* M 499, 788; **syest** *pr. 2 sg.* M 1061; **sighid** *pa. sg.* CB 175.

syyng *n.* sighing M 63.

sympylnes *n.* lack of rhetorical decoration S 659.

syn, sen *conj.* since K 369, M 830, CR 518; *adv.* M 1320.

syn see **see**.

synamom *n.* cinnamon M 343.

synamvyr *n.* cinnabar, red sulphide of mercury used for purging M 1361.

singulere, syngler(e) *adj.* needless W 452; unique K 500; exclusive W 574.

synys see **sygnis**.

synke, synkyn *v.* sink M 746, CB 142.

synows *n. pl.* sinews CB 674.

synseryte *n.* purity M 517.

sypres *n.* cloth of gold from Cyprus W 1 s.d.

sypresse *n.* sweet cyperus, galingale M 1977 [L. *cyperus cyperos*].

syrybbe *n.* sibyl? and scribe M 33, see note.

syse *n.* size CB 274.

systynovns *n.* sustenance M 2007.

systyr, suster *n.* sister M 463, CR 645.

syt, sett *v. intr.* sit S 411 s.d., M 48; **sit(t), syt** *imp.* M 630; **sytth** *pr. 3 sg.* M 1486; **settyng** *pr. p.* M 728; **satt** *pa. sg.* ~ *vpon* divided M 1498; **set** *pp.* M 414.

syth, seth *conj.* since S 501, M 624, W 107, 680.

syth see **syyn**.

syth(e) *n.* time K 402, M 613; *in* ~ quickly M 1649.

sithen *conj.* since K 91, CB 703.

sytyes see **cyte**.

skore *imp.* cut, whip M 737.

skorn *n.* mockery, joke M 1418.

skowte *n.* guide M 375; **skowtys** *pl.* scouts, term of contempt K 313.

skrybe *n.* scribe M 114.

slake *v.* diminish K 494, CR 556.

sle(e), slo(o), sloon *v.* slay K 189, 239, 295, CB 69, 347, CR 93; *imp.* K 44, CB 53; *pr. pl.* CB 766; **sloes** *pr. 3 sg.* destroys CB 73; **slaw, sleyn, sloon** *pp.* K 361, M 189, CB 488.

sleight *n.* trickery W 725; **sleightes** *pl.* tricks W 674.

slevys *n. pl.* sleeves M 496.

slewth, slowth *n.* sloth M 350, CR 203.

slewthfulle *adj.* slothful CR 230.

slugyshnes *n.* sloth S 531.

smarte *v.* hurt CB 503.

smyte, smyth *v.* strike K 204, M 733; **smet(t)** *pa. sg.* S 372; *pp.* M 519.

soch see **sich**.

socor, socour(e), sokor(e), sokower *n.* help S 519, K 523, M 481, 763, 824, 1962.

soferaynte *n.* authority S 416.

sofere *v.* endure M 1022.

soferons *n.* sufferance M 864.

soiettys *n. pl.* subjects M 500.

solas, *v.* entertain K 55, M 573.

sole, *n.* sole, bottom of foot CB 685.

soleyne, solem, solenne, solom *adj.* ceremonious, solemn K 1, M 1535, 1603, W 577.

solemnyte *n.* ceremony M 1147.

solytary *adj.* unique M 749.

somyr *n.* summer M 501.

sond *n.* message M 214; intention M 1503.

sond(e), son(n)d *n.* land S 502, 594, M 1439.

sound *adj.* healthy CB 788.

sounde *n.* sound S 252.

sonder see **sunder**.

son(e), soone *adv.* at once K 208, S 418, M 1528, CB 8, CR 660; shortly K 267, M 396; **sonest** *super.* most easily M 425.

sonnd see **sond(e)**.

so(o) *adv.* so, very K 148, S 82, M 51, W 49, CB 2, CR 13; *conj.* thus K 391, S 544, M 14, W 376, CR 228; ~ *that* in order that K 395, W 367.

soppys *n. pl.* bread M 536.

sor(e) *adj.* grievous M 1756.

sor(e) *adv.* greatly K 516, S 222, M 279, CB 123, CR 175.

sor(e) *n.* wound, sin CR 479; sorrow CR 379.

sory *adj.* sorrowful CB 88.

soroyng *pr. p.* sorrowing M 290.

sosteynne, susteyn *v.* support M 1115; aid M 1655.

sote *adj.* sweet K 13, M 1071.

soth, sowth *adj.* true M 1261, 1929.

soth(e), sowth, suth(e) *n.* truth M 100, 930, W 750, CB 500, CR 201.

sotyl, subtyle *adj.* tricky S 479, 620.

sottys *n. pl.* fools M 203.

souerayn, soverreyn, sofreyn

adj. supreme, highest M 517, 556, 1261.

souereynly, *adv.* supremely, above all W 254; above everyone W 259.

soueren, souereyne, sofer(e)yn *n.* ruler M 7, 136, 929, 1297, W 69, 261; **souereignes, sovere(y)ns, sufferens** *pl.* gentlemen K 551; rulers M 409, 500, 2131; superiors W 588; **soferens** *poss.* ruler's M 1290.

sow *v.* scatter seed M 1082.

sowke *v.* suck K 270; **sowket, sowkid, sowkit** *pa. sg.* CB 625, 780, 788.

sowle, saul *n.* soul M 364, CB 296, CR 562; **sowl(l)ys** *pl.* M 1115, 1940; *poss.* M 286.

sowters *n. poss.* shoemaker's S 103.

sowth see **soth(e).**

sowth *n.* soot, smoke M 743 s.d.

sowthfastnesse *n.* truthfulness M 2068.

space *n.* space of time M 1378, CB 605; area, place W 719, CB 90.

spare *v.* spare K 97, S 59, M 235; hold back M 139; refrain CB 501; save W 584; *pr. 1 sg.* spare M 239; hold back W 508; *imp.* avoid S 559; spare CB 754, 763; *pr. pl.* save W 736; *pr. subj.* spare W 614; **sparith** *pr. 3 sg.* shuns W 76; **sparid** *pa. sg.* spared K 356, CB 439; **sparid** *pp.* CB 286.

sparkyllys *n. pl.* flames M 353.

spece, speche *n.* speech M 1072, S 507, W 275.

speceows *adj.* pleasing M 628.

specifie, specyfie, specyfye *v.* tell fully K 245, S 468, W 65; **specify, specefy** *pr. 1 sg.* relate M 664; mention explicitly W 407.

specyallte *n. of* ~ in a special manner M 1267.

spectakille, spektacle *n.* sight CB 101, 322.

speculation *n.* spectacle CR 309.

sped(e) *n.* success S 159, W 636; good M 692.

sped(e) *v. tr.* hasten S 84, M 1277; *pr. subj.* help M 1809, W 508; *v. intr.* evyll mut he ~ may he not thrive S 625.

spek(e) *v.* speak K 227, CB 374, CR 398; tell S 356, W 40, CR 542; *pr. 1 sg.* talk S 432; *pr. 2 sg.* tell M 1470; *imp.* speak M 1541, CB 468; declare S 270; talk M 438; **spoke, spokene, spokyn** *pp.* declared W 64; spoken S 412 s.d., CB 385.

spelles *pr. 3 sg.* understands W 275.

spend(e) *v.* expend CB 429, CR 478; use S 411; *pr. 1 sg.* spend W 646; *pr. pl.* W 736; **spente** *pa. sg.* CR 664; **spent** *pp.* M 487.

spendyng *n.* ability to pay M 1732.

speryt, spryte *n.* spirit M 602, 716; *pl.* **spiritus malyngny** bad angels M 428; **spirites, spretes, sprytys** bodily spirits, spiritual being K 501, M 202, CR 682.

spille, spyll(e) *v.* destroy S 611, W 526; suffer damnation S 505, W 215; waste W 292; *pr. pl.* shed K 175; destroy W 713; **spilt** *pp.* shed CB 641.

spye *v.* observe suddenly M 2044 s.d.

spynys *n. pl.* thorns M 2023.

splendavnt *adj.* bright M 516.

spore *n.* sharp point S 184.

spornyd *pa. pl.* kicked M 998.

sport(t)ys *n. pl.* pleasures M 459, 508.

sprede *v.* extend M 205; lie down M 1763; spread W 453; **spredyng** *pr. p.* extending M 1833.

spretes see **speryt.**

spryng *n.* leaping group W 747.

springe *n.* source CR 649; **springes** *pl.* wells CB 371.

spryng(e), springe *v.* leap K 481; arise from S 613, M 204, flow CR 756; *pr. pl.* grow M 1085, W 92; **sprong(e)** *pa. sg.* grew M 2011, W 124.

stabyll *imp.* make stable S 568.

stabyl(l)grom *n.* stable boy S 119 s.d., 120.

stacyon *n.* episode in the play S 155; **stacyons, stacyounys** *pl.* holy places M 1848; stations of the Cross M 1910.

staff *n.* distaff K 334.

stande, stond(e) *v.* stand K 388, M 1842, S 286; ~ *in grace* stand in favour K 375, M 638; endure S 597, M 1789; *pr. 1 sg.* ~ *in dred* fear M 265; *pr. pl.* prevail W 678; ~ *in ony necessyte* need M 333; *imp.* stand M 147, CB 442, CR 68; **standes, standith, stond(yt)** *pr. 3 sg.* stands S 504, M 1724, W 289; *how ~ with you* how are things with you? CR 639; exists M 6; originates W 220; **stood, stude** *pa. sg.* CB 176, CR 368; **stondyng** *pr. p.*: ~ *in dystresse* being troubled M 1039; ~ *in hevynesse* grieving M 1041.

starke *adj.* completely CB 40; stiff CB 86.

start(e) stertt *v.* escape S 178, M 222; spring out CB 126.

starte *n.* short time CR 551.

sted(e) *n.* place S 324, K 360, M 542.

stedfastnesse *n.* faithfulness, constancy CR 425.

stey *v.* ascend M 1077; **steyyd** *pa. sg.* M 1341.

stekytt *pr. 3 sg.* sticks M 1256.

stele, stylle *n.* steel K 106, M 1636.

ster *v.* stir M 1668.

stere *v.* direct W 527.

steryng *n.* urging W 153; **sterynges** *pl.* W 304.

sterrid *pp. adj.* starred K 397.

sterrys *n. pl.* stars M 1492, W 29.

stertt see **start(e)**.

stevyn *n.* voice M 1009.

stewys *n. pl.* houses of prostitution W 749.

stylle *n.* story, manner of events M 1825.

stynte *v.* stop CR 374; **styntyth** *pr. 3 sg.* stops (at) S 555.

styntt *n.* covenant M 1805.

stodyes, stodyys *n. pl.* meditations M 488; studies W 470.

stokke *n.* block K 154; lineage M 1173; vertical beam of a cross CB 402.

stollyn *pa. pl.* took by stealth M 1263; *pp.* taken by stealth M 1322.

stomachyr *n.* vest, waistcoat M 501.

store *n.* value, benefit M 1238.

stounde, stownde *n.* time M 1220; time of trial S 249; place S 151; **stovnddys** *pl.* times M 1018.

stowth *adj.* strong M 373.

strayte, straytt *adv.* directly M 2092; at once CR 116.

straytlee, streightly *adv.* tightly CB 674; frugally W 584.

streight, streyte *adj.* strict K 122, W 729.

streynes *n. pl.* streaks CB 678.

streytnes *n.* severity M 97.

stremyt *pa. sg.* streamed CB 26.

strenth *v.* strengthen M 258; **strengtheth** *pr. 3 sg.* W 55; **strenthyng** *pr. p.* M 255.

stritchid, stritchit *pp.* stretched CB 274, CR 475.

stryffe *v.* strive M 1996; **stryve** *pr. 1 sg.* W 661.

stryk(e) *imp.* lower the sails M 1395; **strikyn, strykyn** *pp.* struck down S 460, CR 434.

stryppys *n. pl.* stripes, blows M
1176.

stryttwaye *adv.* directly M 427.

strond *n.* shore M 1724.

stunt *pr. subj.* cease S 568.

sturdynesse *n.* stubbornness W
693.

subdewe, subdue, subdwe *v.*
destroy S 39, 578; overcome CB
342; subduyd *pp.* overcome S
181, CR 157.

subiectary *n.* subject, slave M
752.

subjugal *adj.* subordinate M 7.

substans, substaunce, substawns *n.* property W 80; *of* ~
sumptuous M 574; *in* ~ truly,
essentially M 463.

succede *v.* follow S 67.

sudare *n.* winding sheet M 1049.

sue see sew(e).

sueke *n.* illness (deceiver?) M
1576.

suernes *n.* certainty S 31.

suffer(e), suffyre, suffre *v.* allow
S 26, M 204, CB 606; endure,
undergo K 75, S 268, M 861, CB
105, CR 432; *imp.* allow CB 640;
sufferd(e), sufferyd, suffert(e)
pa. sg. suffered S 4, CB 499, CR
151; endured CB 736, CR 766;
allowed CR 242; *pp.* endured
CB 282; sufferyng *pr. p.*
enduring S 237.

suffysith, suffysyth *pr. 3 sg.*
satisfies, is sufficient (for) W 147,
465.

suld see shal(l)(e).

sumtym(e) *adv.* once M 295, W
425, CB 746.

sumwhat *adv.* to some extent CR
426; *pro.* something S 92, CB 5.

sundre, sonder *adv.* apart CB
675; *in* ~ asunder CB 358, CR
395.

supernall *adj.* heavenly S 422.

supplexion *n.* superior knowledge
S 359.

supplycacyon *n.* plea: *make* ~
plead M 332.

sure, suer(e) *adj.* certain, safe
K 97, S 125, M 2103, W 264,
CB 119, CR 218; suerly(e) *adv.*
surely S 622; securely K 352;
assuredly W 50.

surerender *n.* return of property
belonging to another CB 301.

suspiration(e) *n.* sighing, lament
CB 64, 509.

sustynavns, sustinons, sus-
tyno(v)ns *n.* sustenance M
1583, 1769, 1902, CR 650.

sute *n.* suit of clothing, livery W
324 s.d.

suters *n. pl.* suitors CB 770.

suth(e) *n.* see soth(e).

suthlye *adv.* truly CR 202.

swame *n.* scale S 298.

sward, swerd(e) *n.* sword K
104, 540, M 144; swerddys,
swerdes *pl.* K 283, M 219.

swauer *v.* fall S 447.

swertt *adj.* black M 780.

swet *n.* sweat CR 340.

swete *pr. 1 sg.* sweat CB 31; swet
pa. sg. CR 335.

swet(e), sweth *adj.* beloved K
412, M 526, 1221, W 70, CB 489,
CR 113; pleasant K 270, S 375,
M 613, W 92, CB 245, CR 559;
precious K 490; swetter *comp.*
sweeter M 94; swetist *super.*
most beloved CB 545.

swetyng *adj.* dear M 565.

swych(e) see sich.

swown *n.* faint CB 459; *falles in* ~
faints CB 455 s.d.

swown *pr. pl.* swoon CB 509;
swownyd *pa. sg.* CB 155.

tabernacle, tabyrnakyll, tapyrnakyll *n.* box for the Host W
167; the body as a holy container
K 496, M 1352, 1941.

tayve *n.* lit. a struggle, here ex-
haustion by struggle containing

tayve (*cont.*)
the idea of decay? CB 38 [ON
tava, see OED 'tave'].

tak(e) *v.* take K 135, S 129, M
1520, W 640, CB 435, CR 308;
understand K (canc.) 11; ∼
avysement, awysement consider M
254, (*imp.*) 812; ∼ *entent* heed
W 228; ∼ *good hert* be courageous K 206; ∼ *the way* proceed
K 151, S 242; *pr. 1 sg.* ∼ *no
kepe* pay no attention M 1727;
pr. subj. overtake K 361; *imp.*
take K 173, S 51; receive from
K 509; experience CB 475; ∼
comfortacyon be comforted M
792; ∼ *them in hand* accept them
S 51; ∼ *hed* pay attention K
(canc.) 2, S 168, M 120; takith,
takyt, *pr. 3 sg.* takes S 146, M
256 s.d.; receives W 483; ∼ *to
spowse* takes as spouse W 57;
tokest *pa. 2 sg.* took M 1127;
toke, tuk *pa. sg.* K 191, S 572,
M 1046; takyng *pr. p.* deriving
W 111; takid, takyn, take *pp.*
S 141, M 978, W 240, CB 122,
CR 143.

tapire *n.* candle K 486; tapers *pl.*
K 462.

tasppysstere *n.* barmaid M 495.

tawth *pa. sg.* prophesied M 1259;
techyd *pp.* taught M 1382.

tell *v.* tell, announce K 469, S 189,
M 179, W 62, CB 354, CR 32;
count W 583; *imp.* S 189; tellys,
tellyt, tellyth *pr. 3 sg.* S 352,
M 868 s.d.; *trobyll* ∼ spreads
harmful stories M 123; telles
pr. pl. W 270; told *pa. sg.* CB 113,
CR 501; *pp.* M 938; expressed
in words W 64.

temtyd *pp.* tempted M 603.

ten *adj.* ten K (canc.) 20, M 534
(see note).

tende *pr. subj.* listen to W 355.

tendre *imp.* regard W 461.

tendreshippe *n.* regard W 631.

tene *n.* anger K 162; injury
M 1563.

tene *v.* torment M 438.

tenor *n.* tenor voice W 617.

testify, testyfy *v.* witness CR 133,
710.

teterre *v.* tear to pieces CB 305;
totorn *pp.* CR 154.

thay, þay, thaime, thair, tham,
þam, thair, they see thei.

þan(ne), þan, then, þen *adv.*
then K 32, M 1518, W 139, CB
632, CR 214; *conj.* than K 492, S
592, M 157, W 33, CB 131, CR
222.

thar *pr. pl.* need M 1437 [OE
þearf].

thar(e), ther(e), þer, thore *adv.*
at, in, to that place K 42, S 194,
M 405, W 107, 329, CB 628,
CR 99; in that respect W 413.

that(t), þat, *adj.* that M 32, W 72,
CB 36, CR 100; *conj.* that K 22,
M 5, W 59, CB 16, CR 9; in order
that K 229, S 193, M 92, W 296;
but ∼ except CB 464; *yf* ∼ if
M 333, CR 617; *whan* ∼ when
W 750; *where* ∼ wherever W 46;
pro. dem. that S 564, M 855,
W 82, CB 106, CR 201; *pro.
rel.* who, that K 63, S 35, M
124, W 3, CB 1, CR 93; that
which W 504, CR 705.

the *v.* thrive M 1731.

thedyr, thether(e), þethyr *adv.*
thither, to that place S 196, M
1036, W 199.

thef(f)e *n.* thief M 731, CB
173.

thei, they, thay, þay, þey *pro.
pl.* they K 38, S 21, M 129, W
46, CB 165, CR 285; thair,
their(e), ther(e), þer, hir,
her *poss.* K 35, S 25, M 1510, W
438, CB 13, CR 35; thaime,
tham, þam, them, þem, hem
obj. K 44, S 26, M 40, 1518, W
68, CB 268, CR 626, cf. he.

þeyn, þen, thyn, þyn, þin *pro.
*poss. before vowel, 'h' M 21, 903,
905, 1551, CR 267.
þer *adv. rel.* where M 621, W
667.
þerat *adv.* at that place M 967,
CB 1 title.
therby, þerby *adv.* by that means
S 116, M 677, CR 157.
therd, thrid(e) *adj.* third M 809,
CB 519, CR 505.
ther(e)inne, therin, þerin *adv.
rel.* in that, in that place S 102,
M 1082, W 308, CB 38; in that
fact, condition W 302.
therfor(e), þerfor(e) *adv.* for that
reason K 84, S 352, M 233, W
13, CB 136, CR 111.
therknesse *n.* darkness M 689.
thyn *adj.* meagre M 1732.
thynk(e), thinke *v.* consider,
think K 254, S 95; thynk(e),
think(e) *pr. 1 sg.* M 369, CB
213; thynġk *pr. 1 sg.* M 1527;
thynkys *pr. 2 sg.* M 591;
thynkyt *pr. 3 sg.* M 553;
thynkynġ *pr. p.* W 195;
thought, thowȝte, thowt *pa.
sg.* K 46, S 455, CR 447;
thowth *pa. pl.* M 1320.
thynketh, thynkyt(t), think,
thinkes *pr. 3 sg. impers.* it seems,
appears K 336, M 1731, 1880,
CB 55, CR 611; thought, thowt
pa. sg. S 252, CB 384.
thyrlite *pp.* pierced CB 268.
this, þis, thys(se) *adj.* this K 1,
S 7, M 59, W 189, CB 3, CR 1;
pro. K 37, S 287, M 97, W 38,
CB 19, CR 97; thes(e), þes(e)
adj. pl. K 17, S 50, M 83, W 149,
CB 98, CR 27; thes(e), þes(e)
pro. pl. S 534, M 160, W 402
CB 266.
tholit *pp.* endured, suffered CB
276.
thondyr, thondore *n.* thunder
M 691 s.d, 970.

tho(o), þo, *þos *adj. pl.* those K
87, M 27; *pro. pl.* K 69, S 46, M
536, W 163.
thore see thar(e).
thorow, throwe, thurgh *prep.*
through, throughout K 537, S
18, M 149, W 311.
thorowoute, thurgh(e)out *prep.*
throughout K 85, 285, S 68.
thorsty, thrustye *adj.* thirsty M
1933, CB 210.
thowgh, thow(ȝ)e *conj.* though
S 268, 447, M 544.
thowgth, thoȝt, thowth *n.*
thought, mind K 356, M 633, W
236; anxiety S 470, CB 498.
thraldam, *n.* enslavement M 1007.
thrall(e) *adj.* enslaved M 971, CB
108.
threst, thryst, thrust(e) *n.*
thirst M 492, 1613, CB 215.
thretys, *n. pl.* threats S 23, W 712.
thrid(e) see therd.
thries, thryys, thris *adv.* thrice
M 2055, W 646, CR 363.
thrift *n.* prosperity W 644.
thryste *v.* thrust S 286; thrust *pp.*
forced CB 306.
thryve *pr. subj.* succeed W 662.
thronge *pp.* pierced CB 672.
throwe see thorow.
thrustid(e), thrustyd *pp.* thirsted
K 516, CB 214, 220.
thu, þu, thow(e), þow *pro.* thou
K 216, S 549, M 177, 795, W
311.
thurst see threst.
tyde *n.* time K 378, M 273, W 317.
tidiose *adj.* late, tardy CR 212.
tight *adv.* without moving W 742.
tyl, tyll(e), tell *prep.* until K 168,
S 106; *conj.* S 499, M 570, W 380.
tille, tylle *prep.* to K 173, M 1858,
W 52, CB 2, CR 12; *w. inf.* CB
428, CR 125.
tym(m)es, tymys *n. pl.* times
CR 448; occasions M 533, W 401,
CB 154.

tyn *n.* tin M 320.

titelle, tytelle, tytyll *n.* title K 109, 126, M 603.

tobrake *pa. pl.* broke apart CB 307.

tobrost *pp.* completely broken M 966.

tochyd see towche.

toddys *n. pl.* toads M 1199.

tondyre *n.* tinder, wood M 915.

tong, tunge *n.* tongue S 562, M 278, CB 320; tonggys *pl.* languages M 1343.

ton(ne) *n.* tun, vessel K 515, CB 783.

to(o) *adv.* too S 529, M 1004, W 482, CB 335, CR 212.

to(o) *prep.* to, toward K 2, S 18, M 816, W 4, CB 45, CR 29; according to M 308; in order to K 28, S 9, M 88, W 19, CB 37, CR 50; *for* ~ in order to K 18, M 65.

to(o) *adj.* two K 88, M 560.

too *n.* toe CB 310.

tord *n.* turd S 101; tordys *pl.* S 98.

torent *pp.* completely torn K 76.

tormentry(e), turmentry *n.* torture K 297, M 1002, CB 330.

totorn see teterre.

toukkyng *n.* touch M 969.

towch *v.* touch CB 180, CR 245; towche *imp.* M 1074, CR 620; towcheyd *pa. sg.* M 969; tochyd *pa. pl.* tempted, tried M 983; towchid *pp.* touched CR 473.

towellys *n. pl.* linen cloths M 911 s.d.

towyr(e) *n.* tower, castle M 360, 764; towyrs *pl.* dwellings of Heaven M 1077.

trace *n.* a dance W 746; traces *pl.* (fig.) course of action W 717.

translat *v.* interpret S 357.

treasone, treson *n.* betrayal M 1322, CB 423.

treator *n.* traitor S 620.

trebyll(e) *n.* treble voice M 1227, W 619.

tre(e) *n.* tree, the Cross M 1938, CB 258, CR 12; wood CR 252.

treyte *n.* treatise CB 3.

treytory *n.* treason S 400.

tremyll *v.* tremble M 1553 s.d.; tremyl, trymble *pr. 1 sg.* S 188, M 555; tremelith *pr. 3 sg.* K 382.

trespace, trespas, trispesse *n.* crime S 25, M 731; sin CB 727, CR 280.

tretyth *pr. 3 sg.* relates S 564.

trevbelacyon, tribulacion, trybulacyon *n.* affliction M 818, 1533, W 427.

trew(e), true, trw(e) *adj.* absolute M 581; accurate, truthful S 399, M 855, CR 705; faithful M 143; honest W 736; *in* ~ (as *n.*) in the True (God) W 385; *adv.* truly S 614.

trewly, truly, trwly *adv.* accurately M 662; faithfully K 113; genuinely S 379, W 409.

triacle *n.* treacle, a medical restorative K 451.

try *adj.* tried, excellent W 641.

trobelows *adj.* afflicted M 1610.

trobyll *n.* disturbance M 123.

troblyth *pr. 3 sg.* disturbs S 453; trobelyd *pa. sg.* disquieted M 1621; trobyllyd, trovblid, trowblit, *pp.* disturbed CB 359, CR 610; injured M 269; interfered with CB 355.

trompys *n. pl.* trumpets W 702.

tronys *n. pl.* thrones M 554.

trossyd *pp.* bound M 910 s.d.

trost *n.* trust, confidence M 634.

trott(e) *pr. 1 sg.* hurry M 438; jump M 555.

trouth(e), trewth, trowth(e), trwth *n.* belief M 307; loyalty K (canc.) 24; truth M 231, S (canc.) 6, S 468, W 676, CB 496, CR 424; *by (be) thy (my)*

~ in good faith K 145, S 110, M 408, W 493.

trov, trow(e) *pr. 1 sg.* believe, think S 17, M 1326, CB 58, CR 105; *pr. pl.* believe W 621.

trumpes *pr. 3 sg.* blows a trumpet W 692 s.d.

trussid *pp.* packed K 278.

trust *v.* trust K 169; **trust(e)**, **trost** *pr. 1 sg.* believe S 647, M 697, CB 351, CR 200; hope CB 860; *imp.* trust M 1750; believe CR 555; **trustyd** *to pa. sg.* relied upon S 454; **trosted** *pp.* K 163.

turne *v.* change S 389; *pr. pl.* S 174; **turnyth** *pr. 3 sg.* turns W 281; **tvrne, torne** *imp.* change M 1615; turn M 1617; **turnyd(e)** *pa. sg.* changed, turned M 995, CR 132; **turnyd** *pp.* turned S 456, CB 29.

vmbyl(l)nesse see **humylnesse**.

vncurteslye *adv.* discourteously CB 655.

vnderstondyng *n.* reason W 180; **vnderstondynges** *pl.* perceptions W 514.

vndyr(e)stond, ondyrstond *v.* understand M 166, 804; *pr. 1 sg.* M 1606.

vndowȝtyd *adv.* undoubtedly S 469.

vnfayned *adj.* undisguised S 655.

vngude *adj.* evil, terrible CB 675.

vnyuersall, vnyversal *adv.* everywhere S 20, M 4.

vnkunnynge *n.* ignorance W 580.

vnlefully *adv.* unlawfully S 552.

vnnaturallye *adv.* not according to human nature CB 537.

vnpaciente *adj.* impatient CR 82.

vnthryfty *adj.* sinful S 557.

vntyll(e) *prep.* until S 338, CB 57.

vnware *adj.* unaware CR 364.

vpon, opon *prep.* on K 66, S 15, M 17, W 1 s.d., CB 6, CR 10; for K 322; about S 164; at CR 366; upon M 1498, CR 253.

vprisinge, vprysyng *n.* resurrection M 1834, CR 209.

vpryght *adv.* erect S 286.

vpward *prep.* up CB 388.

vsage *n.* practice, custom K 32.

vsande *adj.* practised W 681.

vsaunce *n.* habitual use W 655.

vse *n.* custom M 834.

vse *v.* employ W 434; *pr. 1 sg.* consume M 344; ~ *for to were* wear S 113; ~ *joroury* bribe W 637; *imp.* spend S 552; use W 442; *on me* ~ *thou* treat me CR 588; **vsed, vsyd** *pp.* employed S 304, W 409; practised W 684.

vttermest *n.* limits K (canc.) 9.

vagabundes *n. pl.* wanderers, strangers CB 653.

vayn, veyn(e), wayn *adj.* worthless M 595, W 195; *adv.* without purpose K 443, CR 256.

vayn *n.* vein CR 343; **vaynes** *pl.* CB 674.

valentynys *n. pl.* lovers M 564.

vary *v.* change S 462.

variaunce, veryawns, waryovns, weryawns *n.* change M 2004; dispute K (canc.) 19, M 2097; divergence from truth K 395, M 767, 1903; opposition M 36; *without* ~ forever M 92.

varyacyon, waryacyon *n.* change S 328; *make* ~ oppose M 1814; **varyacyounys** *pl.* dissensions M 923.

verament *adv.* truly S 336.

vereabyll, veryabyll *adj.* inconstant, variable M 590, 1925.

verely, veryly(e), werely *adv.* truly S 75, M 172, W 98, 151, 546, CB 213, 299.

vergyn(ne), vyrgyn *n.* the Virgin Mary K 398, S 3, M 679, 1895, CR 124; **wergynnys** *pl.* virgins, young girls K 546, M 2022.

veritabille *adj.* capable of proof CR 201.

very, ver(r)ay, verrey(e) *adj.* true K 76, S 12, M 846, W 30, CB 414, CR 221; actual CR 414, 424.

vernage *n.* white Italian wine M 479.

verray, verrey(e) *adv.* very CB 168, 823, CR 16.

vertu(e), vertv *n.* goodness K 429, M 419, W 382; power, strength S 311, M 1387; **vertues, vertuys** *pl.* virtues M 685, W 288.

veruens *n.* fervour M 1093.

vesyte *v.* visit M 1128.

vesture *n.* clothing CB 413.

vexacyon, wexacyon, *n.* anger M 340, 2033.

viage, vyage, wyage *n.* voyage K 226, S 129, 141.

vycys, wycys *n. pl.* vices S 540, M 1083.

vyolacyon *n.* violent handling S 179.

vyctore, wytory *n.* victory M 1448, 2012.

violatt *adj.* profane, impure M 1556.

violence, violens, vyolens *n.* violence K 298, M 1661, 1317; harm W 108.

vyse see **wyse.**

vysered *pp. adj.* with masks W 724 s.d.

vysers *n. pl.* masks W 752 s.d.

vysytacyon *n.* manifestation S 266.

voce, voyce, woys, woyce *n.* voice S 253, M 920 s.d., 1004 s.d., CB 55 s.d.

volunte, wolunte *n.* wish M 3, 12.

voluptuosyte *n.* sensual desire S 446.

vow(e), wow *n.* vow S 104, M 1400, W 372.

wacchyd *pp.* watched M 1258.

waite, wayte *v.* attend, remain CB 195, CR 115; watch K 186; **waytyng** *pr. p.* attending K 522; **waytid** *pp.* kept watch CR 207.

way(e), wey *n.* way, path K 34, S 87, M 1029, W 509, CB 375, CR 116; road M 401; means M 369.

wayn see **vayn.**

wake *v.* awaken W 223; stay awake W 433.

wald see **will(e).**

wall *v.* go on a pilgrimage M 1847 [OE *weallian*].

waltyr *pr. 1 sg.* roll, toss M 819.

wan *n.* waning, decline, woe W 346.

wanyng *pr. p.* decreasing M 140.

wanne, whan(ne) *rel. conj.* when K 38, M 931, 934.

wantyng *pr. p.* lacking S 223, M 194; **wantyth** *pr. 3 sg.* S 220.

war see **be.**

warant *pr. 1 sg.* guarantee S 118.

warantyse *n.* certainty S 216.

wardere *n.* staff of office W 692 s.d.

wardly see **war(l)dly.**

ware *adj.* wary S 401.

ware *imp.* beware M 492; see also **be.**

warycyon see **varyacyon.**

waryawns, waryovns see **variaunce.**

war(l)dly, word(e)ly *adj.* worldly M 98, W 33; secular CR 293.

warne *pr. 1 sg.* warn K 84, M 141; threaten K 175.

wastyd *pp.* been weakened W 437.

wavys, wawys *n. pl.* waves M 819, 1200.

wax see **wex.**

wax, wex *n.* candle wax K 487.

weche see **w(h)ych(e).**

wede *n.* clothes S 501 s.d., W 454.

wedys *n. pl.* weeds M 1083, W 91.

we(e) *pro.* we K 10, S 43, M
92, W 75, CB 41, CR 62; **ouir,
our(e), ower(e), owr(e), owur**
poss. adj. our K 2, S 28, M 103,
W 70, CB 76, CR 64; **oures,
owerys,** *poss. pro.* M 299, CR
192; **us,** vs. *pro. obj.* K 22, S 4,
M 48, W 231, CB 2, CR 103.
week *n.* wick K 487.
weelle, weile see **well(e).**
wey see **way(e).**
weyyd *pp.* weighed M 990.
weyys *n. pl.* methods M 817.
weylyng *pr. p.* wailing M 840.
weylle see **well(e).**
weke *n.* week W 751.
wele *n.* riches M 1611.
wel(e)fare, wylfare *n.* well-being
K 485, M 1105, W 625.
well(e), weile, weylle, wyll *adv.*
elegantly S 114; properly S 434,
CB 47; satisfactorily K 131, S
629, M 1634, W 222, CB 390,
CR 43; thoroughly K 201, M
635, M 47, CB 279, CR 71; *os*
~ *os* the same as CR 72.
welth(e) *n.* well-being K 58, M 23.
wende *v.* go K 518, M 1738, W
531; **went** *pa. sg., pl.* K (canc.)
18, S 100; *pp.* M 820.
wene *v.* expect W 57; *pr. 1 sg.* K
381; think S 102; *pr. pl.* M 520,
W 750; believe M 493; **wenyd,
went(t)** *pa. sg.* thought K 164,
S 96, M 1079.
wery *adj.* weary K 502.
weryauns, weryawns see **variaunce.**
weryfyyt *pr. 3 sg.* confirms M 178;
verefied, verryfyed *pp.* made
true, certain CB 43, CR 728.
werke, werkyn *v.* carry out K
354, M 380; **werkyn** *pr. pl.* M
152; **werkytt** *pa. sg.* accom-
plished M 976.
wesdom *n.* wisdom M 1213.
wesh *v.* wash CR 242; **weshid** *pa.
sg.* CB 99.

wessell *n.* ship M 1788.
westment *n.* vestment, ceremonial
attire M 1183.
wete *v.* know, learn M 1816, W 1;
wat, wott *pr. 1 sg.* K 404, CR
143, M 1034; **wot(ty)st** *pr. 2 sg.*
M 434, 1216; **wote** *pr. 3 sg.* W
560; **wete** *imp.* M 1565; **wist,
wyst** *pa. sg.* K 38, S 92, M 1059,
CB 84.
wether see **w(h)ether.**
wethyr *n.* weather M 1776.
wett see **wytt.**
wex *v.* grow, become CB 97; **wax**
pr. 1 sg. M 779; **waxeth,
waxit, wex** *pr. 3 sg.* K 342, M
455, CB 225.
wexacyon see **vexacyon.**
wexyd *pp.* vexed, disturbed M
1576.
wha see **who(o).**
whanhope *n.* despair M 694.
whantite *n.* quantity CB 621.
what(t), whate, quat, qwat(t)
adj. whatever, what K 73, S 142,
M 155, W 66, CR 319; *adv.* how,
to what degree CR 61; *interj.*
what, look K 345, S 87, M 1149;
interrog. pro. K 441, S 189, M
273, W 73, CB 334, CR 399.
whattso *pro.* whatever M 302.
whattsomewer *pro.* whatever M
1235.
whech(e) see **w(h)ych(e).**
wheyl *conj.* while M 766.
whele *n.* wheel M 312.
whens(e) *adv.*: of ~ from where
M 1425, 1725.
wher see **be.**
wheras, wheros *adv. rel.* where S
274, M 1012, CR 113.
wherefor, wherfor(e) *adv. rel.*
therefore K 21, S 145, M 691,
W 323, CB 349; CR 57; *interrog.
adv.* why S 376, CB 464, CR 298.
wherethorow *adv. rel.* because of
which M 922.
whereto *adv. rel.* to which W 344.

wherin *adv. rel.* where CB 371, CR 586.

w(h)erynesse *n.* weariness, fatigue M 996, 1494.

wherof *adv. rel.* because of which S 430, by means of which W 194.

wherso *adv. rel.* wherever M 610.

whersoeuer, whersoeuyr *adv. rel.* wherever K 320, M 370.

wherwith *adv. rel.* with which CR 445.

whestion see **quessyon**.

w(h)ether, wethyr *conj.* whether M 984, 1308.

whether, whider(e) *interrog. adv.* whither, to what place S 202, CB 751, CR 571.

w(h)ych(e), wich(e), whech, weche *pro.* which, who K 12, S 4, M 181, W 134, CB 30, CR 10; *þe* ∼ who M 314, CR 210.

w(h)y(e) *interrog. adv.* why S 87, M 410, W 108, CB 401, CR 67; *cause* ∼ the reason for that M 1793, W 432; *interj.* M 1402; as *n.* CB 354.

whight *adj.* white W 16 s.d.; **whyte, white** *adj.* as *n.* white clothes M 1623; white part of soul W 155.

whik *adj.* alive CB 814.

whiklye *adv.* quickly CB 444.

whyle, while *n.* period of time M 1369, CB 752.

whypyng *pr. p.* wiping M 640 s.d.; **wipet, wyped** *pa. sg.* CB 100, 266.

whyppe *interj.* quick W 517.

whyrre *interj.* cry used in driving sheep W 552.

whit see **quyte**.

whytly see **wygth**.

who(o), wha, wo, ho *rel. pro.* who S 158, M 940, W 50; whoever W 57, CB 637; *interrog.* K 305, M 325, CB 150, CR 6; **w(h)os, whoys, howse** *poss. adj.* whose K 3, S 5, M 1316, CR

128; **w(h)om, whan, hom** *obj.* whom S 467, M 287, 1953, W 264, 338, CB 43, CR 134.

whorshep see **worshep(e)**.

whoso *pro.* whoever S 352, M 150.

wy see **w(h)y(e)**.

wyage see **viage**.

wycys see **vycys**.

wyde *adv.* far W 549.

wight(e) *n.* man, person K 263, CR 764.

wygth, whytly, wythly *adv.* quickly M 227, 270, 376.

wyhyllys *n. pl.* tricks M 377, see note.

wikkit, wykkyt(t) *adj.* noxious M 341; evil M 1051; wicked CB 224, CR 178.

wikkitnese, wyckydnes(se) *n.* sin, sinfulness S 534, M 1967, W 378; wickedness CB 309.

wild, wyld(e) *adj.* savage K 366, CR 27; wild M 140; amazing M 986; insane W 616.

wyld(d)yng *n.* **wielding,** power M 59.

wyle see **w(h)yle**.

wylfullnese *n.* stubbornness CR 178.

wyly *adj.* crafty W 341.

wyly *n.* crafty one W 604.

will(e), wyll(e), wyl, wol(l)(e), well, wul(be) *pr. sg. and pl. aux.* will K 276, S 228, 418, M 267, W 395, CB 465, CR 395; desire to S 121, M 1038, W 511, CB 800; intend to K 76, S 226, M 298, 510, W 361, CB 767; wish K 61, S 187, M 646, W 711; CB 560; **wylt** *pr. 2 sg.* M 619; **wal(l)d, wold(e)** *pa. sg. and pl.* K 134, S 95, M 354, W 40, CB 174, CR 53; **woldest, woldyst** *pa. 2 sg.* K 145, S 189, M 1149.

wille, wyll(e) *n.* faculty of choice W 180; desire K 86, S 272, M 512, W 215, CB 702, CR 465;

fre ～ free choice W 290; **wyllys** *pl.* wishes S 58.

wynde *n.* spirit, rage K 45.

wynd(e) go, wander S 202, M 545.

wyn(e), wynne *n.* wine M 46, W 473; **wynys** *n. pl.* M 471.

wynne *v.* entice M 377; *pr. 1 sg.* W 548; **wynnand** *pr. p.* getting wealth W 677; **wonne** *pp.* overcome M 986.

wyre *n.* dispute M 1027.

wys *pr. pl.* guide, direct M 895; **wysse** *pr. subj.* M 2116.

wise, wyse, vyse *n.* manner, way S 217, M 264, CB 160, CR 701; *in* (*on*) *this* ～ in this way K 175, S 630, M 301, CB 15, CR 404; *in al* ～ in every way M 665; *in no* ～ in no way W 116.

wyse *adj.* clever M 470.

wysely *adv.* with understanding S 591.

wist, wyst see **wete.**

withalle, with-awe *adv.* in every respect CR 437; thereby CB 4.

with(e), wyth *prep.* against K 168, M 38, W 339; in the company of K 272, S 97, W 23, CB 12; by S 646, M 1258; by means of S 14, M 39.

wythholdyng *pr. p.* restraining S 512.

wythly see **wygth.**

withouten, wythowt(t)yn *prep.* without S 272, M 42, 696, W 191.

wythstand *v.* oppose S 285.

withstandinge *adv.*: *not* ～ in spite of CR 427.

wytystsaff *pr. 2 sg.* vouchsafe M 624.

wytory see **vyctore.**

wytt, wett *n.* intelligence M 1213, 1944.

wittes, wyttys *n. pl.* senses, mind K 365, S 80, M 1701, W 137, 479.

wytty, wetty *adj.* intelligent M 470, 1250.

wyttnesse, wetnesse *n.* witness S (canc.) 12, M 1500.

wyve *pr. 1 sg.* marry W 663.

wnderfull see **w(o)nderfull.**

wo see **we(e), who(o).**

wo(o) *n.* woe K 370, M 631, CB 13; **woys** *n. pl.* M 205 (voice?).

wo *adj.* woeful K 366, CB 203.

wobegon *adj.* overwhelmed with woe CR 409.

wode *n.* woods W 741.

wodman *n.* insane man K 39.

woyce, woys see **voce.**

woydyt *pr. 3 sg.* leaves M 1617 s.d.

woys see **wo(o).**

wol, wolle see **will(e).**

wold *n.* forest M 401.

wold(e) see **will(e).**

wolunte see **volunte.**

wom see **who(o).**

wommanned *n.* womanhood M 1747.

wond *v.* refuse, hesitate M 1608.

wonddyd, wowndit *pp.* wounded M 605, CB 78.

wonddyn *pp.* wound, wrapped M 23.

wonder, wondyr(e) *adv.* extremely S 250, M 941, W 616.

w(o)nderfull, wondyrfull, wundyrfull *adj.* astonishing S 254; extraordinary W 752 s.d.; miraculous S 368, 608, M 976.

wonderoslye *adv.* miraculously CB 34.

wondes see **wound(e).**

wont *pp. adj.* accustomed M 571, CR 473.

wood(e) *adj.* mad, insane K 282, M 1610, W 489.

woord, wurd *n.* word S (canc.) 2, M 190; see also **world(e).**

word(e)ly see **war(l)dly.**

wore see **be.**

world(e), word *n.* world K 8, S 2, M 4, 140, W 442; **worddys, worldes** *poss.* M 1611, W 578.

worshep(e), worship(e), worchep, whoreshep n. honour K
10, M 211, W 578; devotion K
550; worshepys, worshippys
n. pl. honours W 513, 514.
worshepfull, wyrshypfull, wur-
shypfull adj. honourable S 7,
361, M 1693.
worship(pe), worchep v. give
devotion, honour to K 28, S 422,
M 1813; worshep pr. 1 sg. M
1671; worshippe pr. pl. K 547;
worsheppyd pp. M 2032.
worthely adv. with reverence CB
12.
worthy n. outstanding one M 1294.
worthy, wurthy adj. deserving M
155, CB 392; honourable W 69;
outstanding M 326; worthwhile
M 87, S 141; worthyest super.
most honoured M 19; most
valuable M 305.
worthynes(se), wurthynes n.
honour, respect S 37, M 1519,
W 186.
wos see who(o).
woso pro. whoever M 57.
wote, wotst, wott see wete.
wo(u)nder n. surprise CB 111,
359; wounders, wondyrs n.
pl. marvels M 1254, CB 46.
wow see vow(e).
wrake n. destruction K 370; harm
M 380; damnation M 1826.
wrake v. tear, rip CB 308.
wrangfully adv. wrongfully CR
487.
wrecchednesse, writchitnesse
n. misery M 676, CB 226.
wrech(e) n. harm M 121, W 695;
pain M 1363.
wrech(e), wreth n. wretch, low
person W 66, CB 249, CR 410;
wrecchesse n. pl. M 925.
wreke pp. revenged *M 736.

wringe v. wring, suffer pain CB
721, CR 250; wryng pr. 1 sg.
twist, suffer M 1409; wrynge
pr. subj. squeeze, torture W 614.
wri(t)chit adj. wretched, CB 840,
CR 569.
writchitlye adv. miserably, basely
CR 413.
wryth v. write M 1365.
wroking n. effect, wreaking K 366
[poss. metathesis of working].
wrought, wrow3t(e), wro(w)th
pp. performed K 351, CR 41;
brought K 370; created S 503,
M 979, W 20.
wulbe see will(e).
wurd see woord.

xal(l), xold, xuld see shal(l).

ya, ye(e), 3a, 3e(e) interj. yea, to
be sure K 335, S 117, M 879, W
487, CB 274, CR 262.
yaff, yave see gif(e).
yeelyd n. eye lid M 1237.
yeld(e) v. repay W 194; surrender
CB 294; pr. 1 sg. yield M 783;
yeldyng pr. p. repaying W
391.
yen, yone art. yon, that K 486, M
732.
yeve see gif(e).
yiftes see 3eft.
yond adv. yonder, in the distance
M 1435.
yondyr, 3endyr adv. yonder, over
there M 1443, 1784, CR 104;
farther off M 1346.
yone see yen.
yong(e), ynge, 3ynge adj. young
K 157, 416, M 503, 1242.
yougthe n. youth W 18.

zenzybyr n. ginger M 343 [OF
gengibre].

PROPER NAMES

ONLY those proper names are listed which might cause the reader some difficulty because of their obscurity, or because of their possible confusion with the same or similar names, or because the spelling idiosyncrasies of the scribes might disguise an otherwise well-known name.

Abacuk Habakkuk M 1583.

Abyron Hebron M 159.

Abram, Abrahame Abraham M 977, CR 85.

Alapye Aleppo (Syria) M 158.

Anania, Ananias, An(n)anie Ananias S 211.

Anna, Anna Prophetissa daughter of Phanuel, prophetess K 471.

Anna, Annas Annas, high priest S 30.

Anna, Anne, Seynt Anne mother of Virgin Mary K 2.

Aramathye, Baramathye Arimathea, Judea, birthplace of Joseph of Arimathea M 1260, CB 10.

Assye Asia M 158.

Baramathye see Aramathye.

Bariona, Bar-Jona surname of Simon Peter CR 295.

Bedlem, Bethle(e)m Bethlehem K 285, M 159.

Belfagour Belphagor, a devil M 725.

Berzaby Beersheba M 159.

Beteny Bethany M 62.

Candelmes Candlemas day, February 2, in commemoration of the presentation of the infant Christ in the temple and the purification of the Virgin Mary K 1 s.d.

Cesar, Sesar Tiberius Ceasar S 180, M 232.

Chana, Cana, Judea, place of first miracle CR 132.

Cyrus, Syrus Cyrus, father of Lazarus M 55.

Cleophe Mary Cleophas, one of three Marys at Christ's tomb CB 612, CR 52.

Coppyn, Sentt M 1151, see note.

Corioste, Coryossyte the sin of Pride as Idle Interest M 550,511.

Couetyce, Coueytyse personification of avarice S 495, M 329.

Damask(e), Dammask Damascus S 134.

Dragon Dagon, the Philistine deity M 1244.

Gallys Galicia, Spain M 478.

Gyldyr Guelderland, province of Holland M 478.

Golyas Goliath M 1243.

Grobbe common name for a lout M 1716.

Groine area of Coruña, Spain M 478.

3af Jaffa, Israel M 1798.

Hawkyn, Hawkin, server of parody mass M 1143.

Holborn Holborn, borough of London W 721.

Isaye Isaiah M 697.

Jacob Jacob, son of Isaac and Rebekah CR 22.

Jacobee, Jacobye Mary Jacobee, mother of James the apostle CB 612, CR 104.

Joseph(e) Joseph of Arimathea M 1260, CB 77; Saint Joseph, husband of Virgin Mary K 7; son of Jacob and Rachel CR 23, 37.

Jubyter Jupiter, the planet M 320.
Jude, Judea Judea K 351, M 170, CB 35.
Judeon Gideon, great military leader (Judges 6: 11) M 1351.
Kyrchon girl's name mentioned by server at parody mass M 1161.
Liba Libya, North Africa S 32, see note.
Luxsurya Lechery M 469 s.d.
Mahond, Mahound(e) Muhammad K 127, M 143.
Marcury, Mercury(e) Mercury, messenger of Belial S 496.
Marcyll(e) Marseilles, land visited by Mary Magdalen M 938.
Mercuryus Mercury, the planet M 318.
Maryon Marion, girl's name mentioned by server at parody mass M 1161.
Maris Mars, the planet M 317.
Martha Martha of Bethany M 72, W 413.
Martys Mars, the god M 257.
Mavdleyn castle of Magdalen M 59.
Morell name mentioned by server at parody mass; sometimes black or fat horse M 1155, see note.
Nichodeyme, Nichodemus Nicodemus, disciple who brought ointment for Christ's body CB 12.
Pasche Easter CR 1 s.d.
Ragnell name of demon M 1200, see note.
Roffyn name of demon M 1200, see note.

Sale Saul, S *passim.*
Salomon Solomon W 168.
Sapyens Christ as Wisdom M 709, 886.
Satan, Saternas Satan M 359.
Satyllye Antalya, on the southern coast of Turkey M 1437.
Symeon, Semyon Simeon, son of Judah, promised by God he would not die before he had seen the Christ (Luke 3: 25–32) K 394, CB 500.
Symon Simon the Pharisee (Luke 7: 36–50) CR 232.
Symond, Symont Leprus Simon the Leper but confused by the M poet with Simon the Pharisee (for the different Simon the Leper episodes see Matthew 26: 6–16 and Mark 14: 3–11) M 614, 641, see note to ll. 572 ff.
Symovnd Simon, the gardener for whom Mary Magdalen mistakes Christ (not named in John 20: 15) M 1079.
Syrus see Cyrus.
Solamee Mary Salome, one of the Marys at the tomb (speaker's name) CB 142.
Tyr Tyre, Lebanon M 158.
Torkye Turkey M 1435.
Watkyn comic soldier of Herod K 145.
Wattys *pakke* M 1154 (dimin. of Walter), see note.
Wyan Guienne, province of France M 479.
Zebedeus, Zebedee, father of James and John CB 161.